Apologise Later

The
Biography of **Later**

ROBERT NEWTON

by Mark Penrose

First published November 2013 using print on demand from Lulu

The Olchon Press

Revised Edition March 2016

ISBN: 978-1-291-63872-1

Produced at simonthescribe

simonthescribe

'Helter-skelter, hang sorrow, care kill'd a cat, up-tails all and a louse to the hangman'.

Ben Jonson

"Whenever I dither about making a decision, I hear Bob's celestial tones boom out... 'Do it first Billy... apologise later!'"

Billy Milton quoting Robert Newton. 1929.

For my Mother who started the whole thing...

Acknowledgements

An author is a re-teller of tales, encouraged by an audience, spurred on by friends. This book is the product of many hands, each vital in its different way. My thanks go to Nicholas Newton, Robert's son, to Dan Budnik, Robert's brother-in-law and Dominick Penrose of Killiow. To the Morrab Library, Penzance, the BFI, London, The Imperial War Museum, London, The National Portrait Gallery, London. The Penlee Gallery, Penzance. To Patrizia of Lundy, Jill Garnier, Angie Chambers and to Lucy. To James Whittaker for research on Algernon Newton's war record. To the lady who phoned up about the hat. To Joseph Gallagher, Simon Mitchell and so many more good, kind people.

To my wife Lorraine who has lived for so long with that third person in our lives.

And to Bobby Newton himself, for showing us all how to live joyously and cut bibles.

Contents

List of Illustrations

Introduction

NEWTON, Robert: b. Shaftesbury, Dorset, 1 June, 1905; s. of Algernon Newton, A.R.A., and his wife Marjorie Balfour (Ryder); e. Newbury Grammar School and in Switzerland; ... Recreations : Fishing and shooting. Address : The Old Cottage, Whitwell, Herts. Telephone No: Whitwell 81: or c/o Connie's Ltd., 92 Regent Street, London, W.1.

Who's Who in the Theatre; 1947.

Robert Newton's life was recorded in the fish-eyed camera lens and the seedling tabloid press. Each produced only warped images that blurred together the real and fiction and created a new, ready-bottled unreality.

The truth was a man boozy and destructive, subtle and passionate. He was neither a hero nor a coward. He was an exile and a patriot, a thunderously boisterous and quietly private man. He was full of laughter.

He was a rebel, and always his own man. His off-screen exploits were more extraordinary than those he acted. Survivor of the most bitterly cruelty of wartime services, urbane and penniless, he was a beach-bum who loved Rolls Royces. Impeccably dressed and falling-down drunk; ever homeless, he was the eternal strolling player. He was a rebel, an iconoclast; he had no time for intellectualising or Bloomsburyite gloominess. He was the man who would tell you, and the rest of the crowd, loudly, with his mouth full, that the emperor was naked.

Married four times he had three children; he loved passionately and tempestuously, he cheated as a husband and failed as a loving father. He abducted a son from a dying wife and didn't set eyes on his only daughter for the first sixteen years of her life. Throughout he battled with and gloried in the curse of alcohol. Newton made friends for life, possessed instantly the heart of everyone he met, enchanted them and infected them with his laughter and left them reeling in his wake. Fifty years after his death, the mention of his name brings out a twinkling grin and growling 'Long John Silver' line. He suffered joy and success and guilt and desperation. His end came early and he died thunderous and unrepentant.

I first came across Newton in Quebec. I was sheltering in a monochrome, run-down cinema, from the dreary, interminable city sleet. The film was 'Treasure Island'. Even though Newton's rich, growling West Country accent was mulatto'd into a scallion's Frenchification the thing was a joy. Returning home I saw the film again and enjoyed it again. I made a habit of indulging in a medicinal dose of 'Treasure Island' regularly, and always felt much better for it. And then, over a Sunday dinner table, my Mother said "Oh, yes, Robert Newton, we used to see him, up to Zennor, during the war... he lived up there." And then my neighbour, a gentle man, turned out to have been his Rolls Royce chauffeur in London once…

So I started looking for the man. I put a piece in the newspapers asking for information. There were some great replies, great yarns. Weeks after the flurry had died down there was a tentative call from a dear old lady from Falmouth. Apparently Bob used to drink at the Chain Locker pub there, and when he was filming 'Treasure Island' he hung his hat up above the bar. Next day I called up the pub; nothing doing. Fifty years had passed and the place had changed hands a dozen times. "You could try phoning Dick at the bowls club." "Hello...is Dick there?" "Dick who?" " I don't know... just Dick....". "Dick! Phone call for you..." Yes, Dick knew about the hat, but he had no idea what happened to it. "How don't you call Harry... he might know.." Harry didn't but... So the chain of calls went on and on. "Hello, my name is Penrose... and I am calling about Robert Newton's hat, and...." Silence from the end. "Yes, I know it.... the bugger's hanging up above my head!"

The Wink, Lamorna. The man on the phone was the son of the old landlord of the Chain Locker. When his father had quit the place his son, who was running his own pub, picked up a few bits and pieces.

That weekend I went down. "There it is...", he said. Not the pirates tricorn I had dreamed of, just a rather nicely made straw boater; yellowed with smoke.

A hundred years, and a bit of Bobby Newton had done a full circle; his hat had returned to the valley where he had grown up.

Mark Penrose 2013

1. Dawn in the Bohemian Valley

"He was never an actor, he was always like that, a little devil...!" The man laughs; laughter in his voice and in his eyes. Gladness at the richness of the memory. Lamorna, Cornwall, June 2005, a hundred years after Newton's birth.

.....

The County of Cornwall has always come with a romantic baggage, a misty-eyed delusion of Eden. Comes with a mirage of the picturesque and the picaresque, of sleepy villages, cream teas and slow-drawling straw-chewing locals, the vestiges of smuggling and bodice ripping piracy. The least 'English' of the counties and blessed with a mild, almost Mediterranean climate, Cornwall has always been a magnet for the industrialist and outcast, the tourist, the artist and the beachcomber.

Now in the twenty-first century the county still draws in those who come looking for their own Avalon. It witnesses phlegmatically the annual migratory transit of city-rich adolescents who seek the sun and the instant surf lifestyle. It draws in the second-homers, haggard after the Friday night motorway race, who look for the concept of community and for the Swallows and Amazons that their childhood lacked. They trail in their slipstream the ideal of superstore gentrification and dream over their Chenin blanc to create a wholemeal, organic, peat-free lifestyle. Think to walk on the heathery summer cliffs and on the pastel sunset beaches, and to give up the city life and...

But the Sunday-supplement philosophy is a mocker and the reality is a summer that is a brief transient, one that arrives on the swallows' wings and departs with their last shrill cry. The real Cornwall is a hard place, bleak and brutal, scoured out and spat from the ocean, devoured by it again in an unending cycle. A land of wind and storm, wrack and mundic damp and the all-pervading reek of the salt sea; a land man-altered and man-made, despoiled and poisoned; a wild place, filled up with ghosts and wraiths. It is a land born of a primitive people who worried a living out of the unyielding soil, clawed into its guts to tear out its treasure and toiled on the terrible black-hearted ocean. A place of ragged Celts whose parents were hardship and desperation and whose children were creativity and dynamism. A place where the romance of smuggling was a tawdry crime committed by a people driven by need and the grasping at the hem of Wesley's god as a superstitious touching of wood.

Perhaps in the soft green folds of Somerset and Dorset the sleepy paradise is to be found, but never here. Yet the lies persist, and the deception is perpetuated by the time-share pimps and the traders of dreams. It persists now in the wide-awake, 24/7, twenty-first century, when Tesco and McDonalds make the portcullis gate of every town. Draws in a new generation of dreamers. The artists have always come, jaded professionals, tawdry copyists, students, amateurs, the genius and the lunatic. Potters, sculptors, writers, all seeking to escape, seeking to find, looking to define the quicksilver quality of the people and the land, the sky and the sea. They become the next stage in the gaudy, noisy, Mardi gras procession of progress.

In 1936 Robert Newton described the place of his childhood, Cornwall. He spoke with a tired, longing regret of a 'forgotten people and language', and the 'last of the real Cornish'. He talked of a race, a land and a community that he had grown up amongst and had 'passed away in his lifetime'. Perhaps he understood that he was part of the unstoppable metamorphosis, and that his presence there and that of his family signalled and, in its way, precipitated the demise of that world.

It was in 1913 that Algernon Newton, Robert's father, a gentleman artist, brought his family to Cornwall and the valley of Lamorna.

.....

Algernon's Grandfather, Henry Charles Newton, was descended from a prosperous Nottingham family. Apprenticed as a painter and grainer he was a keen amateur artist, frequently visiting Cornwall and the Lamorna valley. Crucially, and in the great Victorian spirit of innovation, he was also an enthusiastic amateur chemist.

In the July of 1828, at the age of twenty three he married. Four years later he formed a business partnership with his childhood friend William Winsor. Combining their passions for art and science the two men opened a workshop in Kentish Town and began developing new paints.

Whilst Henry Newton supervised his watercolour laboratory, Winsor concentrated on the oil side of the business. Together they set out to revolutionise paint technology. Their invention of the metal paint tube was inspired, and the impact of it cannot be underestimated; it simply changed everything. It freed art from the chore of grinding and blending and mixing; suddenly painting was easy, anyone could do it, and do it anywhere. Winsor and Newton then did the same thing with watercolours, inventing water-soluble colour pans; delivering pigment at a touch of a wet brush, they were another instant success.

Consolidating their business, Winsor and Newton took a financial gamble and opened a shop, with a home above for the growing Newton family; Number 38 Rathbone Place, Fitzrovia, was right at the heart of London's fashionable artists' district and came just at the right time. Suddenly they found themselves supplying the great William Turner. Even Queen Victoria joined the queue. Business boomed and the enterprise sprawled left and right into numbers 37 and 39 and the Newton family shifted to a prestigious residence in Gloucester Place.

In 1879 William Winsor died childless and his half-share of the business was absorbed by Henry Newton for the sum of £71,000.

Henry's first child was a son, Arthur Henry; another son was soon produced but died in infancy. The passing years saw Arthur, as the only male heir, groomed to take on the family business and after college studies and training in art he became a director. Travelling with his father on a painting holiday to Cornwall, Arthur met

Georgiana Tregonning Nicholls, the young woman who was to become his wife.

Georgiana was the daughter of an old Cornish family that originated from the Manor of Treglistian. Infatuated, Arthur fell at her feet, and haunted the Nicholls' home, a solid four-square residence near the village of Bodriggy, from which it took its name.

The land around Bodriggy was a warren of industrial devastation. Ten miles east of the teeming mines of St Just, it lay within sight of the red stained ocean. Tin was king in Cornwall and Bodriggy's Wheal Alfred mine complex was a rich working which brought the Nicholls family, as majority share-holders, a princely income. The gathering pace of the industrial revolution saw demand for metals soar and despite boom and bust cycles, prices maintained staggering levels throughout the early 1800s. The discovery of surface tin and copper ores in Malaysia and Australia, however, sounded the death-knell of the labour intensive Cornish mining industry. Crashing prices and the inevitable depression of the Cornish economy were reflected in the fortunes of the Nicholls family and by the end of the century their interest in mining had ended.

The union of the Newton and Nicholls family was nevertheless considered sound; London business boomed as Cornish faltered and the lack of dowry was no impediment to the marriage.

Arthur and Georgiana's union was a happy one and plentifully blessed with children. Algernon Cecil, the youngest of four sons and three daughters, was born in February 1880.

A serious and sensitive child, Algernon led a pampered life in a loving and very much matriarchal society. His entry at the age of nine into a boarding school shattered his comfortable world and abruptly ended his childhood. It was a society he hated; brutality was commonplace and part of the 'character-forming' process. A small and studious boy, Algernon was homesick and bewildered. He liked neither the masters, the lessons nor the sports. As a reaction to the bullying, he became a fanatic for physical fitness. He learned to box and exercised daily with Indian clubs, a practice that he continued throughout his life. The result was an imposing figure of over six feet.

A difficult five years passed before, at the age of fourteen, he was rescued by an adoring mother who at last melted to his pleas.

Private coaching at home led to a spell of cramming, then entry into Clare College, Cambridge in 1899. College life however suited Algernon no better than his school and he left after a year. With three older brothers to take on directorships of the family business Algernon found himself free to follow his own will. Uncertain of his direction but with his mother's approval he decided to carry on the family tradition of art and enrolled at Frank Calderon's School of Animal Painting in London.

In the spring of 1903, at the age of twenty-three, and following a cautious courtship and a long engagement, Algernon married. Marjorie Einelia Balfour Rider was a handsome and spirited girl, but, as the daughter of a Southampton stoker she was far from the Newton family's ideal of gentility.

The honeymoon period was nevertheless a happy one and the year saw the arrival of their first child, a boy they named Nigel Ramsay. The year also saw one of Algernon's paintings hung, prestigiously, 'on the line' at the Royal Academy. For the family it seemed an opportunity for celebration, but typically Algernon interpreted the accolade in terms of his own artistic typecasting and shortcomings; enviously he looked at the radical art that was emerging from the continent and saw in it his own ingrained and stultified middle-class mentality. Restlessly, he shifted his studies, moving on from Calderon's to the Slade and then quickly to the London School of Art in Kensington.

By 1905 the family was living in rented accommodation in the pretty hamlet of Cann just outside Shaftesbury and it was here on 1st June, a Thursday, that a second boy, Robert Guy, was born.

Two years later Algernon had finished his formal studies and the family, now increased by the addition of their first daughter, Pauline, had moved to Eton. By July the family was back in Hampstead. There Marjorie produced their fourth child, another daughter, who they named Joy.

By now Algernon had come to focus obsessively on his art; he was angry and disillusioned with his lack of progress and the hectic realities of family life only made things worse. Vaguely he began to notice that his marriage was drifting into crisis.

Looking to satisfy Marjorie's restlessness and to find some new inspiration, he took his family to the artists' utopia of Glion, in Switzerland. This move however brought neither satisfaction nor success and the family returned home. Algernon swore that he had finished with art. In desperation he wrote to his Uncle Reginald, who had emigrated some years previously to British Columbia and was now a successful stock-man and farmer, and suggested joining him.

With growing trepidation Algernon and his family crossed the frigid winter Atlantic and the interminable whiteness of the Canadian landscape. The family welcomed them warmly, but as the weeks passed in what was still very much a frontier land, the extremes of climate, the hardships and uncertainties of farming and colonial life seemed much less attractive than the comforts of home. The stay was brief; the family returned to England in the spring of 1910 and took rented accommodation in Northchurch in the Chilterns. The English summer came as an endless heatwave. Chastened, perhaps refreshed, Algernon quietly returned to his paints.

Throughout his adult life Algernon kept a meticulous record book of his work. There were few recorded periods of the domestic tranquillity that he found so necessary for his work to develop yet after the Canadian debacle his time in the Chilterns was a rare happy period. Here he produced a number of works, mostly in gouache, with which he was grumblingly satisfied.

The family's next move, to Cornwall and Lamorna, was to be seminal for both him and each member of his family.

By now Algernon and Marjorie found that the infatuation of their youthful love was spent and they had developed into very different personalities. Perhaps the Newton family had been right; Marjorie was an unsuitable partner. Algernon, aged thirty-one, had become a distant, solitary figure, serious beyond his years. Reserved both with family and strangers, he found small-talk and socialising difficult. He wanted only to be left to concentrate on his work and was frequently angered by the demands of his rowdy and chaotic family. Increasingly withdrawn, he found it difficult to show the love he had for his children and was seen by them as mean with his affection, his time and his money.

Once Algernon had looked to his wife for support; now he turned to the community of artists.

Whilst her husband retreated to his art, and to his old London haunts, Marjorie bloomed into a vivacious, irrepressible and dynamic woman. Temperamentally his exact opposite, volatile, she loved company and filled the family home with friends, laughter, music and literature. Fully playing the role of the fashionable bohemian she, unlike her abstemious husband, smoked and drank. Adoring her children, she spoiled and lavished love on them to compensate for their father's distracted manner.

This was a significant period for the children. They had grown up as itinerants; Cornwall and the valley of Lamorna was to be a 'home' at last.

In the years before the Great War, Lamorna, like St Ives and Newlyn, had become home to a distinctive artists' community. A lush, river-carved fold three miles west of Penzance and lying within the ancient Hundred of Penwith, the valley had its own unique presence. It was a little Eden, hollowed out of the wind-blasted uplands. The people of the valley were a race rooted in the mediaeval and the past that had encompassed the lives of fathers and grandfathers lived in the present; feudal Lords ruled the land and the people on it and the Christian church sat uneasily, palimpsest upon an ingrained and more ancient tyranny.

Subdivided by a tumbling, boulder-strewn stream, the valley's Eastern bank was controlled by the powerful St. Levan family of St Michael's Mount, the West by the Paynters of Boskenna Manor. The Paynters were an old Cornish family and their estate dominated the land. A personal fiefdom and private kingdom, it was also a hard-worked business. The century's turn was inexorably bringing changes even this far West. The certainties of the past were shaken and the wealth and prestige of the gentry were no longer guaranteed. However new faces were appearing, the holidaying English rich, tourists, curious visitors and of course the artists. The Paynter family quickly grew aware of the potential that these exotic migrants brought.

Though only a mile or so from Newlyn the Lamorna artists owed nothing to their neighbours. The platinum white light on the sparkling granite sea-cliffs and in the mouth of the valley was blindingly bright. For Alfred Munnings, one of the valley's artists "such scenery was entirely new... Nothing like this coast exists quite anywhere." Astounded, the Lamorna artists captured the blinding colours with raw pigment straight from the tube.

The works of the French impressionist had had a startling effect on a whole section of British artists. Overnight they had abandoned the standard depictions of stiff-backed maidens, fluffy kittens and the high-society. Many began painting outdoors, discarding the lessons of their masters, the dim studios and the muted tones, discovering a bright new world dangerous with realism. With strong contrasts and primary colours they produced pieces that sparkled with a childlike spontaneity and simplicity and shocked both the traditionalists and the public. Snatching up the new, ferruled, square-ended brush they adopted the continental technique of working bold strokes. Now a dab and a broad stroke could represent a face or a figure. The critics were outraged. Works that today represent the essence of traditional respectability were scorned and ridiculed. Norman Garstin's 'The Rain it Raineth', a piece replicated the world over on biscuit tins and chocolate boxes, was in its day rejected by the Royal Academy for being too shockingly 'French'. Penzance Town Council was acutely embarrassed to inherit it and, fearing that its depiction of the town's rain-lashed promenade might tarnish its reputation as the 'New Riviera', banished it to the cellars for decades. (Ironically this same concern was voiced in recent years; on loan to a German exhibition, it was stipulated that the piece was buttressed by two 'sunny' depictions of the town.)

The bustling fishing towns of Newlyn and St Ives had seen their first tide of artists in the late 1800s, now they were being re-discovered. Samuel 'Lamorna' Birch was amongst the first of the new wave to arrive in valley. Others soon followed, some of them students of Stanhope Forbes' school in Newlyn, described then as the most significant body of painters now in England. Harold and Laura Knight arrived in 1908. Alfred Munnings soon after. Augustus John, one of the most controversial artists of the time, became a frequent visitor. Suddenly there was a demand for houses and studios and the Paynters gladly opened up land for building.

Enabled by wealth, Algernon had clung to the tail of the changing art world, shifting home with impatient and excitable regularity. Now, bowing to Marjorie's need for a permanent home for their children and a structured approach to their education, the Newtons planned to move to Lamorna in the Spring of 1913.

They were to have a house built for them. Algernon had met Colonel Paynter's land-agent Gilbert Evans the previous summer and had surveyed a long rambling piece of land bordering the stream. With a price agreed, plans had been quickly drawn up.

There was much talk amongst the Cornish locals in Jory's pub, The Wink, the 'who', the 'why' and the 'when'. Land and structure to cost a thousand pound all told, they murmured, only a little less than Gascoigne Heath's 'Menwinnion' up at the top of the hill.

The house was named 'Bodriggy' after the family home of Algernon's mother nine miles away on the north coast. Susie Mitchell, a Lamorna girl, remembered the building, "… every day I walked down the valley to work, at a set time, returning every evening' ... 'I was courted by Mr. Mitchell who was employed there, so twice a day, whenever I was due to pass down the road, there would be Mr. Mitchell working on the side of the house nearest the road, so we could pass the time of day together. This practice continued over the whole of the building of the house, so one end of the house was built and perfect long before the end nearest the stream….". Like the other village girls, Susie was a frequent sitter for the resident artists, sitting stiff and posed, paid three pence an hour for doing nothing!

Both decidedly grand and quaintly cottage-like, Bodriggy was set below the roadway and punctured by romantically small paned windows that looked up and down the valley. The Newtons arrived at Penzance by rail, coming down on the ten o'clock from Paddington, travelling on the line that was later to carry the famous

'Cornish Riviera'. Tired and cold they were carried up from the bustling station by Lamorna villager Samson Hoskin in his wagonette. Laden down with baggage they crossed slowly over Newlyn bridge and up Chywoone Hill, then on across the rich fields before dropping down into the cool green valley.

The voices of four children, foreign and loud sounded suddenly in the new house. Out in the gardens amongst the old watching trees, down by the winding stream, looking and touching, they did the timeless, classless things. Algernon standing in his purpose built upstairs studio, lit his pipe and looked up through the north facing roof lights at the fast passing clouds and admitted a twinge of satisfaction. For Marjorie there was much to be organised, curtains and crocks to be unpacked, water to be drawn from the well in the woods, firewood stacked. But that was for later, now they stood and smelled the air. Moist, tainted, different; not clay, not plant, but thin and sharp, fast and hissing, the iron stink of granite stone. But over everything the salt of the sea.

The neighbours called in, the other artists, the Knights, the Birches, the Procters, Gascoigne Heath, old friends met the previous summer, the other English folk. All were welcomed in. They brought flowers and little gifts, assessed and were assessed in a second, those who will be friends, who will be close on first name terms, and who will be called "Mr." and "Mrs." Then the family walked down through the trees, through the long evening shadows and the pools of clear light, between the stream and the little meadows. Past the warmth of the pub, past the Temperance Hotel. The locals, curious and reserved, touch their hats and nodded greetings. And then the sea; the silver dark-darting, endless-toiling mercury sea. And that was the reason for the place, the why. Curled and worked, fearful, frightful, the fast spume white bright, made their pulses race, made their hearts pound.

It was the year 1913. Robert was seven years old, brother Nigel nine, his sisters three and four.

For them the valley and their new world will soon change forever but for now there is the day school, the little stone room that lay just over the bottom garden hedge, that doubled up as a Sunday school, village hall and bible-bashing mission. The children walked in, hand in hand, on their first nervous worrisome day, stood to be stared at. The girls were sent to the infants' class with the village teacher, the boys to the upper class with the headmistress, Miss Nichols. Forty-odd children attend in all, the sons and daughters of the farmers and fishermen and quarrymen who fretted their days away learning their letters and to add and take away a little. For most the future was certain and they would go out when they reached eleven or twelve, to be farmers or fishermen or quarrymen. But for now it was straight backs and slates, silence and dragging minutes and hours.

The day-by-day politics of childhood were done, the contacts tentatively made, in the school room, outside by the little shop that sold sweets, lamp oil, stamps and tobacco. The new order was made, friendships bonded, fights fast done, tears spilled. Inevitably Bobby was in the thick of it. The new boy, taller than the habitually stocky Cornish, well built, strong and a fast runner, he stood up for the honour of his brother and sisters. And he was a natural leader from the very first, boisterous and loud. For what else was a newcomer, an English kid, a 'Sowsnek', to do. He must either gain his peers comradeship or their fear or go under, and what better way than to out-do them in their outrages! They said a generation later… "Bobby Newton, he was no actor, never was, he was always like that… a little Heller!" So the little gang of four, in their muddy, crumpled, posh kids clothes, all over the valley, smoking stolen cigarettes, scrumping apples; hellers!

All too quickly Marjorie's little tribe became too much for the school to contain. The children were politely removed and a domestic governess was engaged, the Birches helping to bear the cost by sending their two daughters up to Bodriggy to attend the makeshift classes.

Like those in Newlyn and St Ives, the gaggle of artists made strange neighbours for the Lamorna locals; "a godless, though profitable nuisance" they grumbled "who brought a lot of money into the place but also frivolity and rebellion…". Duty, responsibility, community and church were the pillars that the Cornish saw as upholding decent society. Repression, secrecy, drudgery and narrow-mindedness were its strait jackets, yet for most in the valley ignorance and naivety were seen as bliss. The old fishermen shook their heads at the wonder of the English newcomers; "...the artists are like fish, we never know what brings them in. Or drives them away..." For them the painters were exotic migrants who didn't 'know the rules' and who transgressed the laws and the understandings that had been built up unwritten through generations.

The Lamorna artists formed a society both close and loose and within it Algernon found himself to be a stylistic individual. He found inspiration in the colours, the air, the epigrammatic and the intangible metaphysical. Yet there was another, more fundamental, human dimension. A next generation artist, Peter Lanyon, summed it up. For him, as for the Lamorna artists, coming to Cornwall was a tremendous relief. "There was safety in numbers, and a surprising tolerance from the local people. They say artists came... for the light. That's all balls: they came for the comradeship".

But this was the end of an era for the valley. Progress was coming, fast on silent wheels, through wires and with the printed word. This was the century of Change and Revolution. Agriculture was changing, fishing, the very demographics of society. A new road in Newlyn had paved over the tide-washed flat and conjoined into one the two disparate communities of 'Town' and Street-an-Nowen; already the artists there were fretting at the destruction of the simple old ways and places. In Lamorna valley new studios were being built, new faces appearing. Tourists from Penzance and beyond come across the cliff path, littering their way from Mousehole in the fair weather to see the 'mad artists'. And even now war overhung them all.

But that was tomorrow, far away, and today life was rich, and there was contentment in the valley. The locals toiled and growled and laughed, the English folk daubed and peered. All mixed down in the 'Wink'. So the valley rang with innocent laughter and music; carts and traps came and went and the artists put on their concerts, plays and garden parties, cricket matches, musical evenings and exhibitions...

So it was into this half-caste, half-real world that Robert Guy was raised. In Cornwall, in the valley; for Cann and the dove-fat fields of

Somerset were only a vague memory. His grandmother's Cornish blood flowed in his veins now. This place was real and his companions were the local boys whose homes he cheekily invaded. To sit harking to the yarns of the claw-handed old fishermen, to listen, to hear the last of the vanishing generation, the tales of Lyonesse and sea monsters and wrecking, of storm and tempest. Of the fast French luggers in the moonless dark that outstripped the Revenue men's cutters, of the dark skinned Spanish murderers, of the little people and the spirits, of the yesterday Gods that the parson forbade and of the great ragged stones up on the moors, of the evil places hag ridden black with bane. Of the sea, the great thick fathomless murdering ocean. Like blood upon the hands of every Cornish man, thick in his heart. And yet to also live amongst the artists, the blithe Bohemians, who lived close amongst the real world but were never part of it; who neither toiled nor sowed; beings of another planet.

Declaring Lamorna the only warm place north of the pyramids in winter, Augustus John was a frequent visitor. All the artists, complete with families, were summoned to attend John's frequent 'beanos'; "terrifying affairs", Laura Knight recalled, "we feared to shorten our lives!". His party tricks and feats of strength outshone even those of Munnings. "John would perform all manner of amazing tricks, opening bottles of wine, tenderly, without a corkscrew, flicking from a great distance pats of butter into people's mouths, dancing on the point of his hand-made shoes upon the rickety table and other astonishing feats until dawn. Then, while the others collapsed into exhausted sleep, he would go out in search of his wife Dorelia, and do little studies of her in various poses on the rocks...". John made a deep impression on young Bobby, and despite the disparity of their ages they became close friends, remaining so throughout their lives, meeting whenever their wandering lifestyles allowed.

Whilst Algernon, self-contained and solitary, struggled with his vision, Marjorie exposed her children to everything that was new and exciting. The house was filled up with drawings and plays, people and pets. Of all the artists of the valley, Laura Knight figured most significantly in Bobby's life. A beloved member of the artist community, she was equally well regarded by the locals. Bounding with the energy of six she was single minded in her art. Lively and charming, her presence in the valley was like the arrival of summer. Bobby, like all the children in the valley, 'sat' endlessly for the artists, especially Laura Knight. Of Pauline and Joy, Knight remembered "…a lovely pair of long legged colts, full of mischief…". But perhaps it was young Bobby, irrepressible and tireless like herself that she felt to be the child, the son, she never had. There is a painting by her, still in the valley today, of a small boy, golden with sun, standing brave astride a plashing wave. "Bob" is its title, the upturned face cheeky with big dark eyes. Knight considered it one of her finest works.

In these disparate worlds that rubbed along, Bobby Newton found his world. By day he played the ragamuffin, out in the gales to see in the winter's crop of shipwreck, down at the dangerous mill, fishing with the local boys off the rocks. Up in the quarries, down in the harbour larking in the punts and boats, swimming in the deep rock-pools under the sun blistered cliffs. Weekends and the long summer evenings brought the chance to mix with the artists, to join their expeditions, to daub paints, to sit in their studios and watch, touch and experiment. In that different world, women, artists models, 'from up the line', the locals whispered, posed naked. These were indeed professional models, brought down from London, for no local woman would ever 'undress'. In this extraordinary company Bobby listened to the talk of free love and narcotics, wine and travel and exotic foods, all the things that were never known or spoken of in the cottages.

Newton grew up with a foot in each camp; he was the product of both local Cornish and English artists. Like the artists, he was aware, even in his childhood, of the special nature of the land he was in, and of the people there. An observer from the outside, he saw what those close inside did not see, saw the fantastic and extraordinary in what was mistaken for normal and mundane.

Soon 'Bodriggy' was full and overflowing. Already too small to cope with the children's governess and the regular stream of family visitors it now had to find room for both the succession of

Algernon's paying students and another artist, Charles Walter Simpson.

Growing too old and rebellious for a governess, Bobby had been enrolled at the little school in Trewarveneth Street in Newlyn, travelling daily over and down the steep hill. The school was packed with 120 children, 67 to a class; most had to stand. His headmistress was Elaine Harvey. She remembered that though no scholar, 'Bobby' was a lively and happy boy. At a time when schools were generally unpopular and Cornwall was only just creeping out of the shadow of judgement that declared the county as 'having the worst record of attendance of any county in England', the little school was well liked both by parents and children. Built on a steep lane, high railings surround the playground; mothers passed buns through the bars 'like feeding time at the zoo'.

Algernon's protracted visits to London, where he lodged with Dod Procter's mother, had long become a regular feature of family life and in his absence and in a society where there were no gods, no rules, no old, hand-me-down morals, everything was up for discussion, examination and rejection; parties and social events were frequent and all the artists would gather, including sometimes those from Newlyn. Every Saturday evening they would crowd into the Birch house where Marjorie, beautiful and exuberant, would play the piano and sing. Drinking carried on late into the night and the raucous laughter, ringing irreverent in the still darkness, woke the early-to-bed Methodists.

For the chosen, Boskenna Manor was always the favourite gathering place. Betty Paynter, the daughter of the house, born in 1907, was a headstrong girl and a striking beauty. Even at an early age she too knew the valley was special. "I remember as a child seeing Aleister Crowley holding a ritual in the woods, we weren't supposed to be there, not even as secret spectators.... a real orgy fit for the News of the World!" In her book, '*Penzance to Land's End*', she recounts, 'Lawrence of Arabia would roar up and down the drive on his motor cycle, and he was quite mad about my Mother; Einstein would come over from Sennen when I was a small child and explain his complicated theories to me, D. H. Lawrence himself, on founding his own vision of Utopia, would come here from Zennor, Augustus

John was a regular visitor. We had marvellous parties, it was not the thing to invite the trade… but artists were always welcome."

The artists might have been welcome but, for the county's old families, it was the start of a slippery slope; the Paynter family were gaining a dangerous reputation for being 'fast'!

Guglielmo Marconi, the pioneer of the wireless transmitter, was experimenting at this time nearby on the Lizard peninsula. A frequent visitor to Boskenna, armed with science and garlicky romance, he moored his steam yacht *Elettra* in the cove and pursued his seduction of Betty. Looking to dazzle with magic, he set up his radio transmitter in the schoolroom, to the wonderment of the locals. The demonstration was a big success but the courting was not. Bob, the yarn goes, was once chosen to row the great man out to *Elettra* at the end of an evening's entertainment. Marconi's legacy to Boskenna was a font of memories and a foul-mouthed parrot...

Growing up quickly Bob began to show that he had inherited his mother's traits and developed a character that was independent, headstrong, sometimes angry and frustrated, often wild and uncontrolled: by now he had followed Nigel and transferred to the Newlyn Board School at the top of Chywoone Hill. Marjorie, Pauline and Joy ran the house and family whilst Algernon, a distant figure, existed only on the periphery of all their lives. He was now becoming 'known' and demand for his paintings was growing. More concerned with his art than with family life, his absences from the valley began to stretch from days to weeks.

A great tradition in the valley and the social highlight of the season was the Knights' midsummer party. Held in the woods beside their studio, everyone, artist and local was invited. Centrepiece of the gathering was the grand pagan bonfire and this was the passion and responsibility of a fringe member of the Lamorna group, William H Davies. An extraordinary and remarkable figure, Davies exemplifies well the sort of social anomaly that was drawn to the valley. Known as the 'Super Tramp' he was a frequent visiting migrant. A Cornish ex-patriot, a global wanderer, a poet and a writer, a beggar and a gentleman, he had survived starvation, royal acclaim and social exclusion. Scorning habitation he slept in the woods by the Knights' studio. Fire was his passion; he knew that fire meant the difference between survival and death, and the mid-summer bonfire was always his star moment. One year however the carefully prepared kindling failed to fully catch. Bobby was amongst the watching crowd. Suddenly impatient, he kicked out, viciously, collapsing the delicate structure and extinguishing the sacred flame. A gasp went through the gathered crowd. Davis was outraged, "That lad will live to be a sorrow to his mother... don't you think I'm ever going to forgive that Bobby Newton for the mischief he has done!"

The looming inevitability of war shook the idyll of Lamorna. Many of the artists left the valley; the Knights reluctantly moved back north in 1913.

Alfred Munnings, an extraordinary figure, even amongst the artists, carried with himself the seeds of his own tragedy. After two years of bitterly unhappy marriage, his wife, Florence, a student of Forbes, now committed suicide in the valley. A spirited and lovely girl, her horrible death was a shattering shock to everyone. It was like an omen.

Filled with pacifist ideals Algernon was not deceived by the war-jargon that had been doled out so relentlessly from pulpit and the press and had the courage to speak out against war. In the spring Colonel Paynter had addressed the assembled village and barked out the old lies, dispensed patriotism and ale and called on the young men to take up the king's shilling. Many raised their hands, many left the valley; few would return.

Lieutenant Colonel William Edward Bolitho, the commander of the Royal 1st Devonshire Yeomanry, a Hussar regiment, was another local oligarch. With a hunting lodge at nearby Trevelloe, he too saw the Cornish men as his own and looked to the Lamorna men to join his regiment. "You'll all be back by Christmas, lads!" his recruiting sergeant yelled.

As the weeks passed and the death toll on the Western Front rose, the moral pressure on those who had not already joined up became unbearable. The young men from the valley, the familiar faces, vanished one by one. The names of those who had gone into the services were told with pride and sorrow and those who remained chewed on their consciences. It was inevitable that Algernon would be swept up in the madness and at last gave way to coercion. With bitter misgivings he signed his name and on September 3rd 1914 was inducted into the Territorial Force at Exeter as private 2405. He was 34.

Without surprise and yet with a sense of resigned irony he found himself assigned to Bolitho's Yeomanry. Booted and clad in regulation drab he faced weeks of gruelling physical training, route marches and square bashing with stoicism; under a physical regime and in a society that was very different to that which he knew in Lamorna he felt lost and alone.

By February however he was pulled out of the ranks; with his education and demeanour he was deemed worthy of elevation and officer training and was given a commission. In the first egalitarian war officers were being swept away as swiftly as the men.

Swapping army for navy, a rarity in wartime, Algernon was commissioned into the Royal Naval Volunteer Reserve with the rank of Sub-Lieutenant. Quickly he was attached to Churchill's newly formed Royal Naval Division, a pool formed by the many thousands of men surplus to immediately available posts on ships of war.

Initially he was posted to the Brigade depot at Crystal Palace, London, but in July and after a further period of training, he was transferred to the Training Staff at Blandford in Dorset, as an Assistant Musketry Officer.

The use of small arms were a vital part of service training, certainly in the Navy where landing parties were often called upon.

Sometimes office bound, sometimes out on the windy rifle ranges on Blandford Downs, Algernon's duties were neither glamorous or comfortable, but whilst he saw his time as wasted, or worse, that he was training men to kill, he knew that he must do his duty like everyone else.

His letters home were self-censored and terse.

Marjorie's in return only spoke of loneliness, a struggle to put food on the table and four children that needed the structure and discipline only he could provide. The Cornish newspapers seemed to conspire to disseminate gloom; articles spoke of labour shortages at the tin mines, 'fowls stolen' at St Just, the Board of Trade threatening to cut tobacco imports by a third and the scandal of the English 'Non-Conscription Fellowship' that had made 'statements likely to prejudice recruiting'.

All of the valley was talking about the trial, the leading figures of the movement were facing the charge of High Treason and the gallows, and yet the young men of Penwith, fired with zeal, were eager to get to the Front.

On May 16th the first batch of attested eighteen year olds left Penzance station by the 4.30 train. Thirty men, or boys, to become the next set of bald statistics... perhaps as the waited on the platform they read through that days issue of *The Cornishman* newspaper and the latest official casualty list; 63 officers and 1248 men... and spliced around those figures were the notices of death; the sons and brothers and fathers that had gone before, and the pathetic gratitude of the mothers.

And yet, inevitably, amongst all the woe there was the story of the first cuckoo of the spring, heard outside Penzance, wedding rings for £4/10 and dentures for £2/2, 'Grasshopper Ointment' to cure almost any woe and steamship passages to the sunshine of South Africa...

Algernon was never robust in health; the damp chills and winds of autumn struck and he was admitted to hospital in the October suffering from a chest infection. Within three weeks he was discharged as fit for service and attached to the 7th Reserve Battalion but by March the condition returned and he was re-admitted to hospital, now with pneumonia, a potentially fatal condition.

Unknown to him his old comrades from the Yeomanry faced their own devils far away. Seeking a back door into Europe and a way to break the deadlock on the Western Front, British eyes had turned to the Dardanelles. In April 1915 a hastily assembled force made from the scrapings of the Empire had been thrown ashore at Gallipoli. The Australians and New Zealanders clung to a strip of land they called Anzac Cove; the British on Cape Hellas. The landings were a shambles and the campaign that followed floundered from one disaster to another. The death rate was atrocious, as bad as that in European mainland. Within days all impetus was lost and opposing forces burrowed into the ground; it was everything that the generals didn't want.

Inevitably more men were thrown into the carnage; the Yeomanry tumbled bravely ashore just as the winter was setting in. At first they has the 'soft job' of digging trenches; within the month they were front line troops.

No position was safe from the big guns and the snipers; corpses rotted and littered the ground between the opposing trenches. On Manchester Ridge the Yeomanry manned their machine guns and suffered the same deaths that they paid the Turks. In the heat of the day and the chill of the night the conditions were appalling; there was little clean water to drink and basic hygiene was impossible. Inevitably fever and dysentry became rife and as many of the Yeomanry died of disease as from combat.

It was not until December that the British admitted that the game was up; what was left of the Yeomanry was evacuated along with the rest. The campaign was supposed to have been the breakthrough. In 259 day nothing had been achieved; a quarter of a million men had died.

By April Algernon had struggled through his own personal battle and back from the brink. Deemed well enough to be discharged both from hospital he was also discharged from the Navy. With very mixed feelings he knew that his service days were over.

Marjorie rushed north to carry him home; gaunt and weak he was a changed man, shocked and silent, a man she hardly recognised. It fell to her to break the news of the death of Algernon's beloved mother; it was another blow, another severing from the old life. Over the weeks Marjorie nursed her husband back to some semblance of physical health, though the damps and mists of a Cornish winter did little to help. Today he would have been labeled with PTSD, post-traumatic stress disorder; panic lurked in the corners of his room, depression, a silent ghost, hid everywhere.

The children were brought in slowly, to meet the man they had already half forgotten.

Slowly contact was made with the artists of the valley and tight little family of friends there, yet nothing seemed as it was. Algernon was aware that his life in Cornwall was ended. The horrors of war were too real, even there; no one was immune from the spectre of death. Laughter seemed irrelevant or perhaps irreverent and 'art' that turned its attention to anything but pain seemed the same. Yet the play went on, the hollow pretence that one day everything would be back to how it was. But they all knew that it was a lie.

Emblematic of that ended era and life, Bobby, now eleven, was enrolled into St Petroc's, a boarding school in Bude, in the North of the county.

Clinging to the cliffs the school had been founded just four years previously, and already had a reputation for discipline. Nigel, forever a castaway within the family, quiet and studious like his father, had joined just a year previously. In May, firmly under Marjorie's control, Bobby was installed.

Sensing a new freedom Bobby threw himself into school life; tall and robust, he was instantly popular and was drawn into both the football and cricket first XI. Significantly, however, he was already showing signs of asthma, a condition that was to plague him throughout his life.

Lamorna was much changed however. Alone with Marjorie in Lamorna, Algernon found that everything had changed. In the absence of any visible enemy, paranoia had invaded; such was the fear of spies that outdoor sketching and painting without a permit was deemed a criminal offence. Food shortages had hit hard, meat was a luxury, potatoes scarce. Simple things like matches were hard to find, whisky was almost unobtainable. Socialising had now become infrequent, parties and celebration rare. A sombre mood filled the air. The happy old days were over and though insulated from the grimmest realities of war, the valley had fallen silent and the gladness of the light faded. Demand for artworks had dropped dramatically and prices failed to keep up with the spiralling cost of living. Few had time for art when there was a war to be done and times were hard for artists with no alternative income.

Only too aware of this Laura Knight was showing her new works at the Leicester Gallery in London. An army colonel viewing one of her works, a group of women in beach scene painted in Lamorna, exclaimed "Who is that girl? I must have her to train, she's exactly what I have always been looking for, is she really like that, are her insteps really so flexible!" Knight assured him that the likeness was accurate. The Colonel was ecstatic; he "would make her the Example of Physical Perfection for the whole world". The woman was Marjorie Newton. Knight knew that Marjorie desperately needed an occupation and she promised to send the Colonel details. But it was not to be. That evening she collapsed with the dreaded 'war-flu'. For weeks she teetered on the brink of oblivion; when she had recovered the moment was lost and the opportunity gone forever.

Algernon, still recovering, found little will to resume his art. His trips to London became more frequent but his diary notes showed that he produced little work, certainly nothing remarkable.

In 1918 Bobby turned thirteen and he was taken out of St Petroc's. Nigel had come home nine months previously. For very different reasons it was a crushing blow for both boys; it was not what either Algernon or Marjorie wanted, but the reality was that the family could no longer afford school fees. A troublesome teenager, he was bored and frustrated by schools and by a war that promised to drag on for ever. Family life limped on, making a brave pretence of pre-war normality, but even the children could see the fractures opening up. The joy of life, once so tangible, was drowned in their fathers silent suffering. That year summer never came, only relentless dreary winds and rains that destroyed harvests across the land.

In the Autumn Arthur Newton, Algernon's brother, travelled down to Cornwall and came to stay at 'Bodriggy'. Laura Knight recalled the day when the war ended. "The morning of November 11th 1918 was one borrowed from summer. There was not a cloud in the sky; everything was peaceful. The great doors of the studio stood wide open, sunlight streamed along the floor, Harold paced restlessly up and down. I tried to occupy my mind with trifles. We dared not hope. At eleven o'clock we heard a vessel hooting in Penzance. Algernon Newton's house lay a little lower in the valley. "They might not have heard." I went to tell them; the door was opened by Arthur Newton. He stood for second listening to the sirens that were then in full blast. Suddenly he broke down, he had lost both his sons…. It was impossible to realise that the awful weight of misery was lifted. The Armistice had actually come….".

Then something came to change Bob's life. A friend of the Knight's had come to the valley to visit and to have his portrait painted by Alfred Mungings. Barry Jackson, a millionaire industrialist, was an amateur artist and a generous patron of the arts. More importantly he was the founder of the new and already famous Birmingham Repertory Theatre. Knight had met Jackson in Penzance in 1912; Jackson had been attending an outdoor production of 'Othello' there, "A strange affair" he recalled, "made inaudible by the countless rooks settling for the night".

All of the Newtons' children were close to the Knights but, sensing intuitively a very special quality in Bobby, they urged that he especially was introduced to Jackson. Laura Knight used her influence and intelligence to answer the question of what was to be done with the boy. She saw that he was too much of an independent to simply take up the brush like his father and that he was nothing of a scholar, understood that Bobby would need to find his own way, to make his mark himself. Perhaps Jackson also saw some special quality in him. Conversation turned inevitably to his theatre and it was tentatively suggested that after he had finished his schooling Bobby might like to travel up to Birmingham and see how the stage worked. Marjorie was delighted and enthusiastic, Algernon sceptical. But the die was cast.

In the January of 1918 a show of works by Picasso and Matisse opened in Paris. They were a sensation. A contemporary critic called their works 'the prodrome of the Great Terror'. For some it was 'the end of the world', but for Algernon it signalled a beginning, a new way forward in his art.

Unknown to Bobby and his sisters, though vaguely suspected, another beginning was being made, and an end. Algernon and Marjorie could now both see that their marriage was effectively over.

Perhaps their relationship was another victim of war, but Algernon now found life in the city more attractive than the endless chaos of Bodriggy. And Algernon and Marjorie were now two very different people from the couple that had courted and wed. Yet only Algernon saw that the rift between them had become unbridgeable. Slowly, through a period of protracted separations, he had effected a parting. He wanted it to be a gentle separation, not an acrimonious one, the tears and red eyes dressed in public as a part of the Bohemian 'experiment' with relationships. Marjorie, perhaps less of a Bohemian than she affected to be, failed to see the end coming. Unknown to her, Algernon had long harboured a dark secret; his 'painting trips' to London, where he lodged with the Procters, had been part of a passionate and protracted liaison.

In the happy pre-war days, sketching and painting had been a fashionable distraction for young ladies, and Lamorna had been constantly full of genteel visitors. The home of every artist had overflowed with students, pilgrims and hangers on. Like everyone else, Dod Procter and her husband Ernest had found their own home invaded. Amongst the visitors was Dod's cousin, Emily Richards. Emily, or Janetta as she preferred to be called, was another keen amateur painter and she had been suitably introduced to the circle of artists. The meeting between herself and Algernon was profound, the attraction immediate. Janetta was in love and Algernon found his soul-mate. Now, unable to lead a dual life, and finding that his relationship with Marjorie was impossible, Algernon had at last revealed his secret. He had stayed with the family until the children were old enough to be considered adults, now he only wanted to be with Janetta. He wanted the undivided attention of a woman who understood and shared his passion, and to find an ordered environment where he could work undisturbed. He wanted to return to London society and the Chelsea Arts Club. In the valley they said, archly, that Algernon "liked the high life....". The news spread quickly along the valley and shocked everyone. Only the Procters knew more than they cared to admit.

Betrayed and unable to face a society with whom she had been so intimate, Marjorie knew her time in Cornwall was over. Bodriggy was rented out to Charles Simpson and she and her restless little tribe moved north to Berkshire and a rented house in the little town of Theale.

Algernon, the villain of the tragedy, despite the fulfilment he found with Janetta, struggled to come to terms with the loss of his children, especially Joy, with whom he had an especially close bond.

Without a husband and a father for her children Marjorie sought to re-create some sense of family and normality, yet her children had outgrown her. Like Bobby, both Pauline and Joy were headstrong and brash; only Nigel took after his father. Quiet and restrained, often scandalised by his siblings behaviour, he had long ago drifted away from the little gang. Ever acquiescent, the eternal black sheep, it was decided that he would follow the family tradition and turn his hand to art. The girls looked, as girls look, to the glamour of ballet. Bobby, still of school age, was always the problem. Desperate and finding herself unable to cope, Marjorie enrolled him as a weekly boarder to the famous St Bartholomew's Grammar School, in nearby Newbury.

Catering for about a hundred and fifty boys, St Bartholomew's had a long distinguished history. The headmaster was Edward Sherwood Smith, a man of vision and passion, and under him many boys gained entry to Oxford and Cambridge. His best efforts however were not enough to trammel the wild nature of young Bobby Newton. Though intelligent and spirited, he was also ill-disciplined and disruptive. Constantly in trouble, he received endless reprimands, punishments and warnings.

Before the end of the first term Sherwood Smith wrote to Marjorie asking to meet her. The letter suggested that the meeting would not be a happy one. "Unfortunately, Mrs Newton, although we are all very fond of Bobby, we just cannot keep him here, he's too disruptive..." Marjorie sobbed and sniffed. "...if I could make a suggestion, you might think of finding Bobby a job on stage as an actor!"

The scene was set and Bobby Newton defined.

.....

Long years and a lifetime later Bob would fondly recall his idyll childhood in Lamorna and how, when the family had disintegrated, he had dreamed of running away to sea, of joining the navy. It was every schoolboys fantasy, but it was also a semiotic that would shape his future. Throughout his life he would always search for, but never find, the security of home and the family he had lost.

But that was the future; for now there was the excitement and glamour of the theatre.

2. Oil Paint and Grease Paint

In the aftermath of the Great War, Britain lingered in stasis. The years of conflict had seen a voracious appetite for the matériels of destruction but the peace brought only starvation. The men returned from the trenches to the remnants of their old lives and the women, briefly liberated, returned to the servitude of their kitchens.

For Bobby the transition from a cosseted school and family environment to city life was stark and sudden. In early March he travelled north. He smelled Birmingham before he saw it; a great throbbing coal-blacked mill, it lay in the twilight shadow of its own wasteful filth. The faces of the people were markedly different from those of Cornwall. Pale and silent, hard, pinched with an unseen cold, the scars of war cut into the faces of the dour proletariat. Kenneth Tynan damned it 'the ugliest town in Europe; that cemetery without walls'.

On the throbbing streets motor carriages and tramcars mixed with the horse-wagons, choking the air and making an underworld darkness of the days light. There seemed no place here for beauty, no time for Bohemian affectations and scant time for art. This was the hub of Philistine industrialism. Beyond the city centre the drab suburbs sprawled across the mired and blackened landscape. The pale faces of half-starved children, ragged and gaunt, stared up from the gutters. This was a factory, making money of muck, making day night, making possessions the new gods.

The British people had faced manumission uneasily; the war had torn away the last bindings of Victorian morality but now they willingly become slaves to the machines. Gone was the stultifying respectability of the Puritan Sabbath; the people were learning to dance to the frenzy of Negro Jazz. The sun was setting on the ponderous Victorian industrial structure and the major impact of change hit the old centres of production. Coal, steel, shipbuilding, textiles, the lifeblood trades of the economy, fell into a steep decline. But with the death of the old came new opportunities. They came in electricity, in radios, in the minds of the people but mostly with the motor car. The motor car changed everything. It created a whole new self-sustaining industry, creating jobs and wealth. It opened the country up to a new generation of mobile people looking for things to want. And it was all happening in the North.

Bobby Newton was fifteen. He had shed no tears at the railway station. He was a determined young man now, confident, tall, well built, well dressed, handsome. He had shouted his farewells to sisters whilst mother kissed and wept; sat restless through the long, hot crowded journey, and tried to mask his apprehension. At Birmingham's throbbing station he was met by Maud Gill, one of the theatre's associate stage managers, and taken to his digs; there he was introduced to Colin Keith-Johnston, another theatre new-boy.

Early the next day, grand with the title, 'acting assistant stage manager' Bobby met theatre. He walked for the first time upon the 'sacred boards', sniffed up the rank, lardy smell of greasepaint, breathed in the very reek of theatre itself. Stark and small he stood before the footlights' unblinking eyes. The place was a tangle of rope and cloth, a labyrinth of corridors; hectic with shouts and clutter and faces it was very much like a ship, yet somehow it felt like home. Theatre. He mulled over the word. Theatre, that woke only at the stirring of dusk to conjure up a vision for the eyes of the few, before the vision was no more. Made laughter and tears. Enraged and silenced.

This was a whole new world for Bobby Newton, a stab in the dark. And in a whirl of confusion the title 'acting assistant' became 'dogsbody', tea boy, sweeper, runner and fetcher, painter, and stage-hand. Faces shout at him, orders, to do this and that in the arcane code-talk of theatre. And suddenly Barry Jackson was no longer a friend of a friend. Now, even if everyone else was 'Ducky' and 'Darling', he was 'Mister Jackson', to be doffed to and 'sir'd.

During his first week, just as a performance was about to go on, Bobby was astonished to see a man in the wings trying to set some muslin curtains on fire with a match. "If it catches alight... the place will be burnt down while the audience is here!" Bobby yelped. "I know...I know..." replied Maud Gill, "..but these people have to do their duty in the interest of safety."

The next day, during rehearsals, he was sent out to investigate a strange noise; the same diligent fire officer was testing the concrete stairway with a blowtorch. Not to be caught the second time Bobby casually reported back. "It's all right... it's only the fire officer burning down the theatre!" The cool irony was not lost on the company; within days fire really did hit the theatre.

Just before midnight the stage curtains somehow caught alight. Thankfully the innovative sprinkler system that Jackson had insisted on installing dealt with the blaze. Just turned into bed after the evening's performance, the company were roused out in a desperate race to help clear up the mess. By four in the morning the situation was under control but the water from the sprinklers had done considerable damage to the offices which were on the lowest floor. Worse was the condition of the electrical and lighting system both of which were thoroughly soaked and were to give trouble perpetually in the weeks after. That night, with the stage slippery and the lighting decidedly dangerous, the pinchbeck magic was done and the show went on.

For the first time Bobby found himself treated as a man and not as a child by a pandering mother. As the weeks passed and the theatre became an exciting home, the all-too-frequent letters from Theale made him glad he was away. His mother's affections had become cloying and he saw that he had become the substitute for Algernon. Suddenly the memory of Cornwall and the valley had fallen away, too small a place, too incestuously claustrophobic. Now at last he could be himself, anonymous if he wanted, lost in the great multitudes.

He had no idea if he would settle to this new, unreal life, the life of an actor, where his future would hang upon newspaper reviews and the clapping of hands. And Repertory. Rep' - a bastard offspring that was impossible to define. A quintessentially English thing, a thing not conventional, not copyist, a progenitor rather, a seed-bed for new ideas and new faces. They said. A workshop that put out the old favourites but would rather toy with the new, present the stage in new ways, dismiss limits and, like the Lamorna artists, aggressively shrug off the rules. 'Rep" might have been a state of mind, yet even within its own ranks, it was not a term always appreciated. Often it was considered to be an unflattering second class in a world where London's West End theatres were the standard and the goal.

During the war years the populace had sought escapism and theatre had prospered. Jackson's little kingdom had evolved rapidly. Writing, acting, producing and designing, the stage had long been his passion. Heir to a booming dairy empire and dubbed the 'Butter King', he had the time and the wealth to dabble in grandiose amateur theatricals. Soon he found that his artistic creativity had outgrown the rooms and public halls he could rent and that his little band of friends, the Pilgrim Players, needed a permanent home.

The transition from amateur to professional was fraught but the process of having his own theatre built was a mark of Jackson's passion. Personal fortune and the backing of influential donors smoothed the way, demanded and bought grace and favour, but if he had influence in the city, it was certainly a city that already had its full quota of theatres and music halls.

The city's *Theatre Royal*, founded in 1774, had seen appearances by the greats of the day. The *Prince of Wales* had opened in 1856 as a music hall and the Alexandria (1901) worked with popular melodrama and pantomime. 1913, the same year as the Rep's opening, had seen the launch of the *Bordesley Palace* and *Aston Theatre Royal*, both of which dispensed standard kitchen-sink melodrama to the sprawling new suburbanites. In addition to these, five music halls produced the unvarying diet of bawdy variety twice nightly. Somehow Jackson's theatre had to work outside the sphere of these other operations. It had to be different and fresh and, despite both the government's hated entertainment tax and competition from the glitzy cinemas that seemed to be springing up everywhere, show a profit. The clamouring masses, as ever, packed into the music halls, but a new and troublesome intelligentsia had emerged. This group was looking for something beyond slapstick burlesque and sticky nostalgia and it was these people that Jackson set his sights on.

Jackson's new theatre had been built in Station Street. Trammelled by existing buildings it had been shoehorned into an awkward plot. Whilst it was sited conveniently close to rail and tram stations it sat somewhat uncomfortably amidst a decaying and rather squalid quasi-industrial environment. The roadway outside and immediate environs were irredeemably dull and grit and smoke billowed across from the sidings. The building's deliberately stark exterior added little beauty to the area. The first purpose built repertory theatre in the country it was a rather dull pearl set into the city's midden. Austere and sober it was, however, built as a home for art and culture, the literate and the liberal and not as another bear-pit for the rabble. In the closed world of theatre, and especially Rep', reputations came and went, yet from the outset Jackson's theatre stood head and shoulders above the rest and set the standard.

Before the first brick had been laid Jackson and his architect had visited the new theatres of Europe, especially in Germany, and much attention had been given to design. In a time when theatre had changed little since the nineteenth century and comforts for artistes were few, his new Rep, whilst nodding to conformity with a rather starchy façade of classical columns, gloried in its ten bespoke changing rooms. There were five for men, five for women, each heated and ventilated and each decadent with both a toilet and a hand basin. Function now overrode traditional appearance. Décor in the public areas was deliberately minimalist. Designed not to distract from the events on stage, subtle browns were used and natural stone and wood. There was no place here for gilt cherubs and the traditional overburden of blowy baroque strumpetry. Although smaller than many venues, Jackson's design brief stipulated that 'no seat was further than 70 feet from the stage'. The stage itself was small by the standards of the time, measuring 42ft by 28ft and had presented designer problems from the outset. As Bobby was soon to find out the layout was aptly described as 'a cigar box, a long narrow auditorium... because of the steep rake, you presented yourself night after night to a wall of faces, you weren't projecting yourself into or across a void, you found yourself invited, forced even, to interact with the audience; it was intimate, 450 seats, but not pint size'. Musical accompaniment was provided by a discreet and compact quartet and piano.

The theatre had opened with a self-effacing fanfare and civic flourish in the rainy Birmingham spring of 1913. Allying itself firmly to the arts the foyer became a gallery, hosting one man shows that lasted eight weeks. During the war many artists, constrained by censorship had turned their interests from landscape to interiors, especially ballet, circus and theatre and Laura Knight made intimate studies of the Rep's stage, rehearsals and life behind the sets.

In the style of the new German art-houses a strict code was dictated to the audience; actors would not take curtain-calls, entrance 'rounds' were discouraged and late-comers were barred from entering during a scene.

From the opening night box-office prices were fixed competitively; balcony seats were 2/4, Stalls 4/6, and private boxes at £1.3.0. Always an innovator and certainly a philanthropist, if a naive one, Jackson wanted to 'educate his public' of both manual workers and new intellectuals. A hard-headed business man and a cautious risk taker he had the comfortable buffer of wealth to support his passions. More importantly he also had an eye for talent both in new writers and in actors. He had no time for fools and he quickly saw something beyond the every-day in the tall boy that Laura Knight had summoned up and who now awkwardly cluttered up his stage. The boy was certainly good looking, but Jackson also saw in him a special quality. The way he used his hands, his natural predilection for display, some flash of the extra ordinary. Perhaps. Only time would tell.

Extraordinary too in those still conventional times, Jackson himself stood out. Tall, blue eyed and enigmatic, a chain-smoker, notorious amongst those in the know as one of theatre worlds extensive 'pansy fraternity', he kept a permanent suite in the city's Queens Hotel where he lived and dined with his lifelong partner. Likened to an old married couple, they were two nevertheless very traditional gentlemen, scrupulously polite in their tweeds or black ties. Every

Christmas Jackson tipped the hotel staff exactly one pound; to be shared equally amongst them all.

The mainstay of Rep' at this time was the works of George Bernard Shaw. A hairy and punctilious Irish fireball, he understood the influence Rep' was having even in London's unassailable West End. A frequent visitor to Jacksons theatre, he declared it "a place where all genuine artists have found themselves happily at home". By 'artist' Shaw however meant 'author'.

The post-war world had seen theatre grow up. Jackson's theatre rejected the tradition where it was the histrionic waving and perorating of famous players that led. Now it was all about plot structure being interpreted by skilled players. On the opening night the Daily Telegraph immediately understood the egalitarian ethos of Jackson's theatre, 'The company is a constellation of small stars, too many of our London companies are more apt to resemble a comet, one large star followed by a trail of little ones... here there is no tendency towards precocity and highbrowism'.

Not all reviews were so kind. Jackson was passionate that his theatre should have a broad range of plays and he decreed that each work should be put on only for a limited time, repeated at intervals throughout the season if demand was great enough, but never, in the familiar West End pattern, flogged to death. Brushing aside initial press rebuffs he had brought before the Birmingham intelligentsia the emotionally gruelling works of Chekhov, Ibsen and Strindberg, a choleric collective aptly known as the 'North Sea Depression' who joyously brought bored, syphilitic misogynists to the English stage. Single-handedly he also resurrected, to tumultuous applause, forgotten classic Restoration, Elizabethan and Jacobean plays. Shakespeare was of course ever popular, representing the Plimsoll line to which all other works had to measure and always filling the house.

Jackson knew that audiences would always turn to a cosy old favourite, but his stage maintained a swashing policy. It was, however, a policy that audiences did not always appreciate. The theatre business was a precarious one, the Gaiety in Manchester had just foundered. In Jackson's empire utter flops and drastically curtailed runs were horribly common. Boos and hisses would rattle across the stage and actors often faced chillingly empty houses and shaking heads that made for the exits halfway through acts. But controversy and outrage made good press that in turn brought new feet through the doors.

To Newton's delight the action was never confined behind the footlights and he saw that players would 'walk on' down the gangway or stand up suddenly amongst the audience or shout out from the balconies. Controversy was rarely avoided, courted more like, but plays were nevertheless always chosen on their merit rather than their money-making potential. Merit however was, then as now, gauged by popularity and Jackson understood the aesthetic of publicity and pushing boundaries of public morality...

It was during one of Henry Fielding's London productions in 1737 that a member of the audience, who happened to be the Prime Minister, became so incensed by what he saw and heard that he clambered onto the stage and punched one of the actors... the next day censorship came to the stage in the form of the Lord Chamberlain and the Licensing Act.

Cautiously skirting these legal constraints, the Rep's 1916 season saw a near riot when the latest production, The Tinkers Wedding, was portrayed in the press as 'representing the Catholic priesthood in an untrue and unfavourable light'. On the opening night shouts from the balcony drowned the players' voices; knives, bottles and lumps of plaster followed, raining down on the stage. The police were called as scuffles broke out. It was the stuff of the next morning's banner headlines; another of Jackson's glorious publicity 'experiments'.

Now approaching sixteen, an age when his Lamorna school friends had been at work for four years or so, Bob was at last earning a living. Like all new boys he had at first been a useless liability, however his Lamorna pedigree and his father's artistic talent was accepted as genetic and, tongue in cheek, he was put to daubing backdrop scenery, the 'flats', for his shilling a week and keep.

This was nevertheless his first step towards the stage, this was his apprenticeship; not in a drama 'school' or RADA, but in life and by observing the professionals. More importantly this was also his new home and these people were his new family.

Newton never spoke of how he had been affected by his parents' separation and the dissolution of the only real home he had ever known. Perhaps he vaguely understood why his father had to break away and make a new life, but the parting had been unexpected and it had hit hard, shattering the joyous rough and tumble, half-wild world of the valley and left in him an emotional hole that was never to be filled. The weekly letters from his mother, needful and teary, showed that she had failed to move on to a new life. Too often the dream of returning to Lamorna cropped up. Always used to plenty and never a careful manager of the family budget she was finding it a struggle to keep a roof over her head. Bob's letters back were carelessly dashed off and infrequent.

Quickly the things of the past became strangers and the theatre people became his new family. Loyalty to the theatre was fierce; Martha Jordan had joined the staff in 1914 as an usher and went on through the years to become an institution. Tirelessly she worked in every department, mothering everyone, even Jackson himself, dispensing tea and buns, sympathy and encouragement to the succession of new faces. Here was everything Bobby sought, a close and interdependent group, full of little clans and sub-friendships, a carefully constructed hierarchy where Jackson was the father and he could be comfortable as one of the boisterous children.

By this time Bob and Colin Keith-Johnston had moved on, more than once, from their original digs. Exuberant and unruly, they tested their landladies patience beyond the limit. The final straw for one landlady came when Bobby, cold and 'tired', had settled down next to the lounge fire late one night. Rocking back and forth he vaguely noticed a bell ringing insistently somewhere, but omitted to notice that his hand was resting on the spring of the old-fashioned bell by the fireside. The landlady and her husband clambered out of bed, searched the house, only to find Bobby ringing peal after peal. It was 2 am. By default Colin Keith-Johnson was evicted along with Bob and it fell, inevitably, to Maud Gill to take them both into her own home.

Very much the old-fashioned theatrical mother, she took them happily under her wing; at least she had no longer to walk home late at night unescorted. Bob brought laughter and life into her home, along with a mountain of books, golf clubs and old motorcycles, and she loved every minute.

Joyously immersed in his new family Bob was nevertheless pleased to receive a letter from his father. Algernon desperately missed his children and now, settled into his own new life, sought to re-establish a relationship. Bob could not find it in his heart to judge his father and Algernon was invited to visit and to stay. An attendance at a performance at the Rep' was, of course, de rigeur; afterwards conversation fell to a critique of a 'sunset' reproduced on stage. Algernon was in his element and suggested various methods of producing a more realist effect; late into the night the scheme had become elaborated to such an extent that it had taken over the theoretical 'show' and had to be unwillingly abandoned.

Quickly Bobby became an established character at the theatre. "One night" Maud Gill remembered, "Bache Matthews, the company's business manager, was proudly showing some Whistler etchings he had bought recently, to the members of the company. Bob displayed great interest until, sensing the moment, he exclaimed "Have you the picture of the old girl among them? You know, 'Old age must come... Take your Holidays early'!" 'Whistlers Mother' was, at the time, being used as a poster campaign by the Government to get people to buy Savings Certificates, so that the State did not have to provide a pension. The spontaneity of humour and irony was not lost on the business manager or the others.

As with the artists in Lamorna, backstage chat covered everything. Politics was a subject that had however, so far, failed to ignite Bob's interest; conversation had turned to past Premiers and Bonar Law was mentioned; "Who's this Mr. Bona Fide, anyway...?" growled Bob.

Bob had joined the rep during its tenth season, the acting 'company' consisting of eight men and five women. Jackson was always there, always with his cigarette, the enabler, in the wings, on the stage. Urbane and charming, his authority was never questioned. His lieutenants were A E Filmer and H K Ayliff. Both old-school perfectionists and master-craftsmen they were utterly devoted to their art. Ayliff, always 'Mister Ayliff', was a skeletal figure with a suitably sepulchral voice that never praised. Bobby Newton soon fell under his gaze and quickly learned to watch for the terrifying warning signal for the unwary and the inept. Ayliff sat at rehearsals with legs crossed at the knee and when displeased would swing the leg and foot like a pendulum of doom. All recognised the signal and trembled. Under this terrifying eye and after just a few months of looking on safely from the wings it was decided that Bobby was fit to face his first appearance on stage.

The dress rehearsal was less than satisfactory... 'Bad dress... good show' the cast chirped, spinning out the old adage. Suitably daubed with the ubiquitous and smelly number 5 and 9 standard greasepaint and with his pale cheeks dabbed with carmine, he walked onto the stage on 27th November 1920. As part of the build-up to the hectic Christmas season Shakespeare's *Henry IV, parts 1* and *2* were being put on. It was a Saturday night, the theatres traditional first night. Dry mouthed and sweating, Bobby had no doubt about the importance of the occasion, held under the eagle eyes of the local newspaper critics. His was simple, a silent, walk-on part, but it was a make or break moment. Stiffened with a quick nip, he walked out and carried his part well enough.

The two plays ran for just two weeks each, with a three week break between them, long enough for the actors to work up their roles, but in Rep' style, not so long as to tire audiences. Newton, like all the players rehearsed and rehearsed again under a dozen watching and unforgiving eyes. Between the excitement of performances there were lines to learn for the next production as well as the day to day business of stage management.

His first Christmas away from home took in the traditional pantomime season; now, at last he was 'noticed' by the press. The Birmingham Post approvingly noted his appearance as 'the stupendously ugly supplanter' in *The King of the Peacocks*.

Satisfied with Bobby's progress, Jackson nodded a grudging approval and he was given another part on March 19th of the following year. This time he had a few words to spit out. Appearing on stage alongside Jackson himself, his was a minor but visible role in a working of Shaw's piratical adventure *Captain Brassbound's Conversion*. Very much an evocation of Stevenson's *Treasure Island* the play saw 'depytations', mutinies and much similar piratical baggage. Act three, and Newton's big moment, was set '...back in the missionary's house on a torrid forenoon'. Bob walked on as 'an American Petty Officer', suitably uniformed and with the line "Captain Kearney's cawmpliments to Lady Waynflete; and may he come in?". The production ran for a full two weeks, with 'matinees on Saturdays at 2.30'; reviews were mixed but the run saw sixteen flawless performances for Newton.

On April 4th, and with growing confidence, he appeared again, now in a production of *Witch*, a dark and cadaverous tragedy played out in front of surreal monochrome sets. As ever, public reaction defied logic and the play proved outrageously popular, seeing a run of 41 performances. Running on from '*Witch*' and into a sweltering summer, Newton appeared on stage again in a repeat of the successful *Henry IV* productions. The play ran for a week before *The Second Part of Henri the Fourth* followed on 23rd and ran for six weeks. Rushing to cope with costume changes Newton appeared three times on stage in this cast-heavy production; first as Humphrey of Gloucester, later as Peto an 'Irregular Humorist' and finally as Shadow, a 'Country Soldier'. In both works Jackson struggled with a large cast and a small stage area; skilfully splitting and subdividing the stage, opening and closing curtains, he created stages within the stage to represent the various outdoor and tavern scenes.

A striking hybrid of respectable Victorian and the Bohemian, Jackson was a strict disciplinarian and kept a paternal eye on the youngest members of his little family. The regular correspondence that passed between him, Marjorie and Laura Knight regarding 'Bobby's' progress and behaviour indicated that his efforts were more than satisfactory. In the March of 1920, just before the 'Henry IV' run, Knight had written from her studio in London to Jackson, "My dear Barry, many thanks for your letter, I am so glad Bob is doing all right, I think he is very keen about the job, his letters home are very enthusiastic, Mrs Newton has got your letter and is very pleased and grateful to you…"

If Marjorie found pleasure in her favourite's progress she also missed him terribly. Quietly she mourned the break-up of everything that had made her life and turned to God and the bottle. Algernon's departure had spelled the end of the dream life in Lamorna, now the passing years saw the emotional diaspora of her children; once the vibrant mainstay of the family, she now found herself redundant. For Bobby the transition from childhood into adult life had coincided with the cessation of a homesickness that had always been problematical. With a new maturity he realised, and accepted, that he no longer had a 'home' to return to.

In the August of 1921 Britain wilted under a heatwave. Working under the eyes of his 'landlady', Maud Gill, Bob's talents were by now considered developed enough to allow him to drop the word 'acting' from his job title and assume the full grace and, as he was now finding, more importantly the wage, of 'Assistant Stage Manager'. On stage his presence was increasingly seen more to the fore and his parts, now speaking parts, were developing beyond the typical beginners 'spit and a cough' to 'small but meaningful'.

The task of stage management was one of the most arduous in the theatre, especially in one that turned out an average of nineteen new works each year. As such Gill was granted two assistants. The tally of tasks she and her assistants shouldered included 'the calling of the players to rehearsal, co-ordinating the setting and removal of both scenery and lighting, obtaining furniture and props for each play, controlling the 'wardrobe', keeping records and making up the prompt books for every play'. Further to these undertakings 'plots' had to be written up for each production, detailed lists of the requirements for each department within the theatre pertaining to each new production. On stage and roaring out his lines, Bob often found his thoughts bogged down in the logistical implications of the next production. Traditionally stage managers or assistants didn't act on the stage they created, however Maud Gill certainly did. Jackson saw that no one in the theatre was denied the opportunity to perform and as such Bob was fully accepted as fledged and 'in the company' from the 8th season, 1919-20.

By now the nocturnal routine and the hectic upside-down timetable of theatre life seemed normal to Newton. The combination of rehearsal in the mornings starting at ten, study in the afternoons and performing in the evenings and in matinees was exhausting but never dull. Weekday after-show carousals were, by sheer necessity, relatively restrained; lines had to be learnt in the first week and woe betide the sinner who was still 'on the book'. Full dress rehearsals invariably took place the day before opening, firing the backstage with a palpable buzz. As the following evening darkened, rumours from the box office about ticket sales circulated back-stage. The house doors opened at six thirty, an hour before curtain-up. Management and cast took turns to man the foyer, to meet, greet and press the flesh. Here the latest art works on display were discussed, the previous performances debated and comments noted. The orchestra assembled in front of the stage, tuned up and ran through their scores, and the bustle in the dressing rooms reached fever-pitch. Back-stage shouts and laughter threatened to drown out the sound of the gong that announced 'one minute' before the curtain went up. Then, a pregnant silence settled across the audience, the lights dimmed, the second gong sounded and ... curtain-up!

"Visiting the theatre leads to fornication, intemperance and every kind of impurity..." St John Chrysostom had famously observed some centuries previously. With his easy good looks and a twinkle in his eye, Bobby Newton had become a popular member of the troupe and he saw that there was indeed a delicious truth in the statement. With Colin Kieth-Johnston he made the perfect double-act. One night the pair, along with Maud Gill, were travelling home on the last tram. There were only two vacant seats, Gill took one, Bobby the other, and Colin sat on top of him. At the next stop a pretty girl got into the tram; dutifully Colin got up, "Do take my seat, madam...!"

Like his mother, Bob was instinctively gregarious. He needed friends and the friends he made, both male and female, became friends for life. In a profession ably staffed with closet homosexuals his ardent and developing interest in the female members of staff was soon noted. Tall, handsome, always well dressed and filled with bohemian affectations, his advances were rarely scorned. Final night after-show parties were well fuelled with alcohol and the younger cast members spilled out rowdily onto the streets and into the bars and the dance halls...

For Bob the memory of the family and the Lamorna years melted into the past, subsumed by the vibrancy of his new environment. Only the weekly letter from his mother in Theale reminded him of his former life. The past came racing back to meet him now however; news that the Lamorna house had been sold came as a sad blow. The last link with his childhood had been broken for ever. Marjorie was distraught. The event had been inevitable though, and the children understood that a reconciliation between Algernon and Marjorie and a return to the old life was inconceivable, no matter what their mother thought. Joy had heard the news first from her father, and to her at least, it had come as no surprise. Struggling to provide for both his children and Janetta, and following a poor public reaction to his first one-man exhibition, Algernon had been reduced to the indignity of touting his paintings on street corners.

Newton's second Christmas season at the Rep' began with a part in a working of James Barrie's *Quality Street* on 3rd September. The piece proved popular and ran for 42 outings. Now a stage regular, he next walked on in the Moliere classic *The Would-be Gentleman* on 8th October. Convinced of the work's value Jackson put out a vigorous reinterpretation of an eighteenth century translation that included an original musical score and a pretty ballet scene. Ever contrary, the good burghers of Birmingham, however did not take to the work, and an end was called after a disappointing 21 outings.

Newton had to wait until the end of the month to walk out onto the stage again; then he appeared in a production of 'Las Pastores', *The Two Shepherds*, a typically cast-heavy, two act, comedy work by the romantically labelled Gregorio Martinez Sierra. Well produced and critically well reviewed this play also stumbled at the first hurdle; ticket sales remained stubbornly poor and the production closed after only 14 performances.

Coinciding with the launch of the Reps' own in-house magazine 'The Gong', the first week of December saw the bulk of the company, including Newton, 'on tour'. Very much like excited children they travelled north to the glittering fleshpots of Manchester and the Prince's Theatre where *Therese Raquin*, *Getting Married*, *The Importance of Being Earnest*, and another Martinez Sierra work, a three act comedy entitled *The Romantic Young Lady* ('Sueno de una Noche de Agosto') were staged. The company was well versed in these pieces, each having been put on previously at home, and public reaction was good. For the next twenty weeks they tramped across the land, then shifting to Dublin via Glasgow. In the absence of the full home company, two operettas, *Don Pasquale* and *Cosi Fan Tutti*, occupied the Birmingham stage and Jackson.

Laura Knight was a frequent visitor to the Rep'. Each appearance was a priceless opportunity to sketch and her rapid pencil drawings now showed Bobby backstage as a dapper young man. Handsome in evening dress, cigarette in hand, he smiled confidently, surrounded by his colleagues. A large oil portrait by her, executed at this time, showed him to be an elegant figure. Seated with a coat draped over his arm, serious, with striking eyes, his hands, beautiful and expressive. Ever Newton's mentor and go-between with his mother, Knight watched his progress with a justifiable pride. Passing on letters, cakes and gossip from the family was part of the familiar routine. She relayed the news that his sisters were both doing well and that at last Nigel was settling to his studies at St Johns Wood School of Art. The finalising of the legal separation between his parents was matter-of-course but it was with trepidation that she announced that Algernon had, as everyone expected, married his quiet and demure Janetta...

The new year saw the company split once again. Jackson made the bold decision to send out a group on a protracted five month tour of the main towns in England as well as a few in Scotland and Ireland. Newton was bitterly disappointed to find that he was selected to remain with the 'home' company, even one that was to be augmented by a number of temporary cast members that included the celebrated Cedric Hardwicke, and misunderstood the very real compliment Jackson was paying him. He was soon to find, however, that remaining in Birmingham gave him a greater stage presence. The spring of 1922 saw him take the prestigious central role of 'The Father' in the Scarlatti-Lucas play *The Shepherdess and the*

Chimney Sweep. Opening on March 18th the work was well received, Bob's acting was roundly applauded and the work declared a critical success with a full 28 performances.

His next stage appearance was another brush with Shakespeare. May 27th saw the opening night of a grand production of *Romeo and Juliet.* The cast was headed by Jackson himself; Bob's part was small but central, Balthasar, the servant to Romeo. The production was well received and throughout its two-week run reviews were good. The Rep's eleventh season, 1922-23, commenced on September 2nd and Newton appeared in *The Admirable Crichton*, another play by James Barrie. Well attended, the play ran on for 47 outings.

During this period Newton's unquestionable talents were rapidly evolving. Having overcome the jittering stage-fright that cursed so many and mastered the knack of effortlessly remembering his lines, he was developing both a recognisable presence and a tangible passion for the stage. Not only was he now seen more often on stage but he was being given key parts. Walking on as Fabian in *Twelfth Night* he took a leading part in the Rep's exhausting five week Shakespeare tercentenary celebration. The programme saw productions of the notoriously unlucky *Macbeth*, (always tremulously referred to within the superstition-racked theatre world as 'The Scottish Play'), *The Tempest* and *The Merry Wives of Windsor*, each performance being accompanied by lectures, debates and addresses by the good and great.

The Rep's next production was another of Jackson's publicity coups. Eden Phillipots' *The Secret Woman*, a salacious tragedy larded with illicit affairs, murder, incest and suicide, had been banned by an enraged censor when it had first appeared. With his considerable influence, Jackson had now managed to get the play licensed. In a career first, and showing Jackson's confidence in his abilities, Newton took the central role, that of Jesse Reverse. The work opened on October 14th and for each of the 14 showings, the people of Birmingham flooded in, greedy for anything that smacked of Sex. With the public came the critics. The press became aware of a handsome young face; suddenly Bob was getting good notices.

November 25th saw newspaper headlines around the world blaring out the news of Howard Carter's golden discoveries in Luxor; for Bobby it was another exciting evening on stage. Working with Colin Keith-Johnston he took the role of 'Dodger, Servant to the Earl of Lincoln', in the Thomas Decker comedy *The Shoemakers Holiday*. An enduringly popular comedy first published in 1600, the piece ran to 14 outings.

At the onset of the Christmas season Newton got his second shot at being part of a touring troupe. The chosen programme was eclectic and included *The Interlude of Youth*, *The Mock Doctor* and scenes from *Twelfth Night*. The first appearance was at the Abbey Hotel Assembly Rooms in Kenilworth on 12th December, they then went on to play to audiences in the major towns of the Midlands. By 23rd of December, Tom Bawcock's Eve, the little flock was again gathered back at Birmingham where Newton appeared in a production of *The Admirable Crichton*. After a short break and a quick visit to his mother in Theale, he appeared again on Boxing Day for the opening of *Christmas Party*. A matinee only work, written especially for children by Barry Jackson, the piece got off to a decidedly rocky start. The script was hurriedly revised, the work found both its feet and a wildly appreciative audience and ran to a remarkable and exhausting 164 performances.

The new year brought Newton a part in a short play by H E Holm, *High Tea* which ran for two weeks; February another in St John Hankin's *The Return of the Prodigal*. Well received, the earlier production was chosen to be included into the Rep's next tour which was being carefully arranged for the spring. Newton was by now one of the leading players and was named as part of the touring group along with four other men and six women, his role comprising of both actor and stage manager. The tour promised to be an exhausting one, twenty full weeks, and covering Milne's *The Romantic Age* and Wilde's evergreen *The Importance of being Earnest* and *Everybody's Husband*.

The chosen numbers were briefly tried out on the citizens of Birmingham, then, on February 19th, despite the seemingly endless string of crises that were rocking the country, a national strike that had been barely averted and competition from the booming cinemas, the concert party set out in high spirits. With the repercussions of war entrenched in the public mind, the distraction of entertainment was still in high demand and the tour was a resounding success; Newton's work, both as manager and player, found ringing approval with the older members of the company and his future seemed assured.

Fully aware that his budding star was now becoming known both within the theatre world and to the public, it came as no surprise to Jackson that his Cornish apprentice was now being head-hunted. The offer came from the well-known actor/manager Percy Hutchison. With the assurance of an immediate engagement as juvenile lead, a selection of parts and a tidy wage, the offer was tempting, but the clincher was the promise of an imminent South African tour. Newton fretted and chewed over his options. Leaving the Rep and the new family that had adopted him seemed unthinkable, but he also knew that the offer represented a big career break, a step toward the West End and an escape from the intellectual claustrophobia of the industrial north. Turning away a prestigious overseas trip would simply be folly.

By mid-tour he had decided that the offer was one that he could not refuse and wrote to Jackson informing him of his decision. His departure from the company was quick and he quit before the tour's July finish. There was some grumbling amongst the older players, some jealousy, but his departure was not altogether unexpected. Certainly Jackson was not surprised that Newton had been snapped up and understood that any young actor with ambition would do the same.

Filled with excitement Newton packed up his traps and said his goodbyes with all the sentimentality of a seventeen year-old. He had been with the Birmingham Rep' for three years during which time he understudied and acted in over forty plays, both in the city and on tour. The experience and knowledge he had gained under the demanding gaze of Jackson and Ayliff was priceless; the breathless pace of weekly and fortnightly performances had taught him the self-discipline he needed to pursue a career.

Travelling south to the vaunted lights of London, Bobby reviewed his prospects. Earlier in the year 'Stage' magazine had carried an article on the joys of touring South Africa; 'One of the plums of theatrical touring' it had crowed, '...with its wonderful voyage out and its strange scenery and its glorious climate'. Very much at the heart of the Empire, a carefree absentee from the genteel suburbs of the Mother Country, South Africa was both affluent and homesick. Hungry for all things that smacked of 'the old country' it was a popular and profitable destination for English touring companies.

At the ripe age of forty eight Percy Hutchison was well known within the trade and his gaudily titled 'Powerful London Company' an established and headlining fixture on the touring circuit. Now winding up a successful summer season at the imposing eleven-hundred seater Queens Theatre in Shaftesbury Avenue, the prospects for the tour were good. With some trepidation, but stiffened with a stop at the lobby bar, Bobby met his new colleagues. Company manager and leading man, Percy Hutchison was a hardened professional who had seen many tours. His leading lady was the famous Elsie Strannnack and his troupe saw support from nothing less than a genuine peer of the realm, the eccentric and slightly antique, Lord Lyveden. The summer season had been good and finding himself with an undeniable stage hit on his hands, Hutchison planned the coming South African tour around the same production, *Bulldog Drummond*.

Worked up from a 1920 novel by Herman 'Sapper' McNiele (another Cornish man) the play had been a blockbuster from the outset, packing in the crowds at Wyndhams Theatre in 1921 for a non-stop 430 performances. Pre-dating Fleming's 'James Bond' character, the plot was a thumping, old-fashioned adventure yarn. Centring on a muscle-bound and muscle-brained aristocratic hero and a glamorous and swooning heroine, both serviced by an obsequious and very much 'lower class' valet/cook, it was a blatant, if unsubtle, Zeitgeist of the long dead pre-war world. Action packed, larded with an irony that was largely lost on audiences, and heavy with a pastiche of obsolete aristocratic characteristics, Drummond's suave and insolent persona embodied all of the old but irrevocably lost British values.

Its appeal to a nostalgic and snobbishly xenophobic post-war generation was, as box-office takings showed, unfailing.

The cast was putting out its last London dates to packed houses and simultaneously preparing to hit the road. Bobby, once again the new-boy amongst a crew of old hands, had to learn his parts quickly. Hutchison had worked the South African circuit a dozen years before; now managing a formidable eighteen strong company as well as costumes, props and staff, he had his hands full to close down the town run and seamlessly transfer to the docks at Southampton and aboard the newly built, lavender hulled, four stack, RMS *'Windsor Castle'*.

With clockwork precision the ship pulled out into the Solent late on Wednesday afternoon, packed with 870 passengers. Leaving the English shores and travelling south through seas that turned from grey to blue, Newton experienced the unashamed luxury that came as standard aboard the Castle Line's largest ship. There was a brief stopover at the sunny and exotic Madeira, then *Windsor Castle* continued south and across the equator. Then, like all of the first-timers, Bob faced the liquid pleasures of the initiation ceremonies that marked his maiden crossing of 'The Line'.

As the voyage drew to a close Hutchison, never averse to publicity, arranged for rehearsals to be run through on the deck. In front of an impromptu audience Bob appeared alongside his fellow actors, trotting out his lines and fashionably tricked out in plus-fours and trilby hat, cigarette case in hand and with his hair slicked back.

The stunning view of Table Bay and the famous mountain lit by a chilly late June sunshine marked their arrival in Africa. There was little time spared for sightseeing however, the timetable was hectic and Hutchison struggled to shepherd his open-mouthed crew through customs and into the melting pot of Cape Town. The plan was to open the season in Johannesburg, cover Pretoria and the Rand, move on to Durban and then wind up the tour during the lucrative Christmas and New Year season back in Cape Town.

With a pro's touch Hutchison made sure the troupe's arrival was covered by the local press. The 'Argus' photographed and interviewed a 'thoroughly fit' Hutchison, a man with 'a splendid air of vitality' who 'seemed the very apotheosis of Sapper's romantic hero'. 'It's a clean, virile play...' said Hutchison, 'with plenty of thrilling incident. There is a fight in it which is one of the most realistic ever staged. After playing it at several London theatres I was a mass of bruises'. Then the showman's touch gave the press the sort of yarn it loved. 'We practised the fight on deck one morning. Two ladies saw it and hurried away to tell the Captain that Mister Percy Hutchison was flinging a man about the deck in a horrible fashion...'.

Bundled onto a sleeper train the company crossed the seemingly endless grasslands of Africa, stopping only briefly in Bloemfontein before rattling on again to Johannesburg. The journey seemed endless; chilled and cramped, everyone quickly wearied of the dreary succession of anonymous dust-red farm towns and the black faces that peered in from the outside. All too quickly the foreign landscape shed its romantic gloss; blurred and anonymous through smeary windows and tired eyes, the exotic became simply mundane.

Saturday evening saw first night nerves behind the scenes at Johannesburg's magnificent 2000 seat His Majesty's Theatre; runners were dispatched to assess the size of the queues. The theatre had only just emerged from a protracted closure at the end of the war and now cinema was a threat. Lon Chaney's *Hunchback of Notre Dame* was showing at the city's Bijou Cinema; a smash hit, it had just recently come across from London where it had packed in the crowds for over a hundred showings. Worries however were quickly dispelled. The news from the box office was more than satisfactory; the pre-publicity had worked its magic and the white folk of Johannesburg were queuing up.

Bulldog Drummond didn't disappoint the audiences and the same faces fell as greedily on the following week's offering. After a quick warm-up one-acter, entitled *Elegant Edward, Nightie Night* was a saucy little three-act bedroom farce that sent queues around the corner. The London press had branded the work 'One Big Yell' and the perspiring faces that looked up to the stage every evening agreed.

For actors more used to an English climate the action-packed routine was exhausting; Hutchison was a driver and a perfectionist and working at an altitude of 3,500ft above sea-level in high humidity, the pace of work was breathless in more ways than one.

The Johannesburg season rounded off with another two-part programme. Opening with *Her Dear Friend*, a witty little one act comedy, it quickly moved onto the main event, *The Luck of the Navy*, one of Hutchison's own works that he had successfully toured across Canada. A 'bright, breezy, jolly and rollicking play' it was all done in full navy fig and 'as played before H.M. the Queen'. Thoroughly patriotic, it was a flag waving smorgasbord that the audience loved. The evening was suitably rounded off with Hutchison reciting a poem, 'The Passing of the King', which produced wet eyes and a thunderous applause.

Buoyed by good press notices, houses were often sold out in advance; with seat prices ranging from two shillings to seven and six, a financial and popular success seemed in the bag and the cast found themselves to be instant celebrities. Nightly they availed themselves of the after-show hospitality laid on by ever-generous hosts. Eternally sentimental, the colonials were hungry for the latest news and gossip from home and parties wound on through the perfumed nights and into the dawn...

After an exhausting eight week run that took in Pretoria and the outlying venues, the last performances were put on and the harassed technical crew were sent ahead to prepare the stage in Durban. The cast said their farewells and followed behind, staggering into Durban's Theatre Royal and gearing up to repeat the whole routine. Here at least they were working at a lower altitude and were able to relax in the warm airs that came off the deep-blue Indian Ocean. The prospect of sea bathing was a richly anticipated bonus, yet it was not to be; a complication in bookings and dates threw their calendar into turmoil. Opening on the eighth of October the company worked the stage at Durban for just five nights instead of the announced eight, dropped the matinee, then hurriedly boarded a steamer, south to Capetown.

There, the cast were once again thrown into the deep end and in front of a clamouring audience. But by now they had honed their act to perfection. The pace was exhausting, but night after night, through the frenetic run-up to the Christmas holidays and then into the new year, they stepped out into the lights and worked their magic.

As the tour wound down to a close everyone was satisfied that it had been a sell-out success. Too quickly the ecstatic last night came and went. The final curtain-calls were done and done again, then the thunderous applause died away and the theatre lay silent. The closing night party went on into the dawn.

The end of the tour meant the disbanding of the company. For Newton, as with the rest of the cast, the hurry of saying goodbyes and the excitement of seeing home and family was mixed with thoughts of an uncertain future.

3. A Winter of Discontent

After six months under the unblinking African skies, the lights of London that had once seemed so rich, now appeared to Bob as rather feeble. The lucrative frenzy of the Christmas season had ended and Hutchison's tour had wrapped. Embarked on the same Castle Line steamer, the company had headed back home, both excited and reluctant, north through the tropics and towards a chilly and drab winter England.

Marjorie had desperately missed her favourite and Bob found the reunion trying. Tanned and grand with wealth, he was laden with gifts and full of tales and Marjorie saw that her son had grown into manhood. Certainly he had changed but he found that his mother had changed too. She looked older, the girlish outdoor freshness of her Cornish life faded. Smoking heavily and drinking too much too often, her ready laughter now smacked of eccentricity. It was not lost on Bobby that his mother, always the bohemian, was suffering from a sense of shame over her divorce from Algernon. In Lamorna it was she who had fully played the nonconformist, Algernon the stuffy conservative; the separation had cost Algernon the children he loved, but he had successfully moved on, found a new direction and was prospering; Marjorie, tearful in her cups, only clung to a dream and sobbed the old doctrine that marriage was for life.

Newton knew that his future lay in London's West End. Going back to Birmingham and the Rep' was unthinkable, but he knew too that finding work in the capital was going to be very different from the cosy predictability of his former life. Blown up with the excitement of the British Empire Exhibition, the 'twenties had spawned the birth of the roaring 'celebrity' business; cross-Channel swimmers, American movie actors and fiction writers were all being gilded up as 'stars'. To get a foot in the door and West End auditions, Bob knew he would now need the leverage of an agent, or as they were snidely called in the trade, 'flesh-peddlers'. Solidly grounded in Rep' and with a prestigious foreign tour under his belt he was quickly taken on by 'Connie's', one of the leading London theatrical agencies.

Run out of a Regent Street office by Constance Chapman, the agency represented many of the big stage names. Connie may have been the public face of the outfit but it was Alfred Vere-Barker, however, a pretentious social climber, who financed and ran the company. The archetypal 'Mr Ten-Per-Center, he was a man that Bob would come to know intimately in the coming years. Photographed, aggrandised and biographised Bobby Newton now became, for the standard 10%, a 'face', a 'name'.

London had managed to stay largely detached from the economic agues that gripped the post-war years. Affluent and free of the almost endemic gloom, it had remained the vibrant heart of the fracturing Empire and the centre of the world and the new generation of city rich, the Bright Young Things, had taken the West End, the clubs and theatres as their own. Broken by their own war, the Sabatarian finger-waggers found themselves powerless in a society of bobs, snobs, boyishness and blatant bisexuality. This was a time of emancipation, of birth control and sexual liberation, of divorce and adultery, drink, drugs and dance crazy clubs.

Dance and jazz had become everything and choreographed the frenetic life of the 'moderns'. Spilling out from the honky-tonks of the American deep south, hot jazz filled up the night air and was damned from pulpits across the land. In the capital Ciro's was *the* place to go, to dine and drink and to watch the sensational cabarets. And always there was the Ritz, or the Café de Paris, the Criterion or Oddenino's. Or the Piccadilly Hotel where Jack Hylton's band played into the dawn. Even the Savoy had two floors of dancing. Soho's Kit-Cat Club nightly brought on the hottest new acts direct from the States. Stumbling out of a blacked-out war, London was witnessing an explosion of intoxication and sex.

The responsibility of cheap London digs clashed with Newton's reckless attitude to money; perhaps he had inherited that trait from his mother, but certainly it was to be a theme that was to run through his life. The soaring cost of living bit into his pocket and a long, hungry winter broke into spring before he at last auditioned successfully. He was billed to appear at the Shaftesbury Theatre alongside some of the leading players of the day and *A Perfect Fit* had a good script and promised a successful run. Returning gladly to the hectic clutter of the stage, Bob fell back easily into the routine of rehearsals.

Just three years before the sensation of the talking picture and riding on the back of huge popularity, the international movie industry had developed fast. Still in its infancy, film however owed as much to paintings and popular engravings as to literature. Even in films with a strong narrative drive such as D. W. Griffith's 1915 *Birth of a Nation* the effect was that of a moving painting. In the pre-war years British film production had grown steadily if not spectacularly. By 1914 a quarter of the films shown in Britain were home produced, yet by the mid-1920s the industry was well on the way to extinction. The root of the problem lay not in exhibition but in production. Cinemas were thriving; between 1910 and 1925 the number had doubled from 1,600 to 3,873, by the mid '30s the figure had risen to four and a half thousand; British audiences were hungry for anything on celluloid, but it was American film that filled the gaping vacuum. The reality was that the war had taken its toll on the British industry and it was a role the Americans were only too happy to exploit. Rich with war-loan repayments, Hollywood had boomed and by the mid-1920s US film export to Europe had increased fivefold. Before the war American productions had taken only half of the UK market; by 1926 they had grabbed almost total control.

Though film was seen by many theatre traditionalists as a scourge to the acting profession, the medium was also perceived by many as a threat to British identity itself. Ironically this was an identity which now seemed defined by the very act of cinema-going. In response the government instituted the British National Film League, promoting the home-grown industry with 'British Film Weeks' to the groans of audience thirsty for gangster movies and flickering six-gun westerns. Newton, a film-fan like everyone else, and a professional actor, had neither the inclination nor the affluence to reject film work. One of Percy Hutchison's troupe, Kate Carew, had just appeared on screen in *Sinister Street*; now, in the midst of stage rehearsals, a hurried call from Connie's saw Bob face his film début.

Very much a film industry leader Oswald Stoll, a music-hall impresario and true-blue, teetotal, patriot, had created a studio set-up out of an old aircraft factory in Cricklewood, north-west London, and had quickly become the UK's largest film producer. Stoll was a hard-nosed businessman but his studio also represented a one-man fight-back against the unending wave of Hollywood imports and American culture. Knowing quality when he saw it and ignoring the unkind tag of 'A Stoll film is a dull film', he harvested his inspiration and scripts from the literary classics of the day. In 1921 he had bought the film rights to Conan Doyle's hugely successful creation Sherlock Holmes, and shot a series of perfectly watchable films. Now, with a 'gaslight' studio set-up standing idle, his eyes had turned to the Baroness Orczy's new version of the Victorian 'penny dreadful', her famous 'Old Man in the Corner' tales.

In Stoll's studio Newton found a working environment that was an introduction to the art of chaos. Quickly he un-learned all the skills so patiently instilled by Barry Jackson; no silence greeted his walk-on here. The crazy stop-start jumble of 'shooting' was accompanied by an incessant and deafening uproar. Hammering and sawing spilled over from adjacent sets and competed with the roar of generators. The director yelled at the cameramen through a megaphone, the cameramen yelled at the lighting men, lighting men yelled at the dolly. Everyone yelled at the actors... "Dim the overheads!", "Slower on the dolly...!" "Action!"

The film was *The Tremarn Case*, the penultimate of a dozen of Orczy's works, revolving around the literal and definitive armchair detective, played by Rolf Leslie. A cinema 'short', running for just thirty minutes, it was the standard low grade, two-reeler, to-be-talked-through 'filler' before the big feature. Shot at 16 frames-per-second the picture was made up of 1900ft of stilted, flickering and grainy stills, but under the direction of Hugh Cruise, a Cornish man, Newton carried his rehearsal well and looked good on film. With his face thickly slapped over with a bright yellow paste for the benefit of the monochrome film-stock, he appeared as the suave young heir Philip Le Cheminant. His screen time was tragically brief however; the victim of character assassination, he received a stiletto through the neck and all too soon became a handsome corpse. Everyone quoted the old adage that the camera did not lie, but Newton now found that it could and did; that was the whole point of it.

With the novel delight of seeing his own name bright on the cinema screen, Bob walked out on the opening night of *A Perfect Fit* on April 24th 1924. Headed by Ernest Milton and Isabella Jeans, the play was launched with an ostentatious blaze of publicity and fanfare and the signs were good. The audience, however, did not see the joke; praise from the critics was faint and door numbers dropped away. The work folded after a disappointing twenty performances and Newton returned to the round of auditions.

On the third of June, just after his nineteenth birthday, he arrived at a landmark in his career. Though his part was small, not even warranting a mention in the cast-list, he was engaged at the Theatre Royal, Drury Lane, to appear in *London Life*. 'A play in Three Acts and Nine Scenes' it was the work of the prolific and hugely successful team of Arnold Bennett and Edward Knoblock and looked to be a spectacular hit.

Seating over two thousand and grandly refurbished at a cost of £150,000 just a couple of seasons before, the Theatre Royal was the capital's largest venue and justifiably called 'the greatest theatre in the world'. Suitably it was also the most haunted. Grand with the most advanced stage and lighting equipment in Europe the theatre had a reputation for the extravagant and grandiose. Produced and directed by Basil Dean, one of the big movers and shakers of the day, the show was launched with the customary pomp. The cast included popular stage names and the plot circled around an affluent city solicitor taking on both family and politics. The production was expensive, with nine enormous sets, including an inn courtyard, the terrace of the House of Commons, the office of the Secretary of State for the Colonies and 'the gardens of a grand house'. On the opening night the audience was duly impressed by a full size ship 'leaving harbour' on stage. Bob's roles included a male and a female character connected with the House of Commons, a waiter and a policeman. In all the stage staggered under the weight of eighty supernumeraries, and yet this work failed utterly too and was savaged by the critics. Set back in 1913, it all seemed distinctly passé; "A too thin slice of ham in an otherwise too thick sandwich" they wailed. "It should have been in the little Ambassadors Theatre" another critic grumbled. The work ran from June 3rd to July 5th, only 39 performances, before giving up the stage to the ghosts.

Theatre management now found a prematurely empty arena on their hands and in a panic hurriedly screened a movie, *The Thief of Baghdad*. The film starred heart-throb Douglas Fairbanks and the theatre was packed for two months, screening the film 112 times. Here, in the heart of theatre, was the shape of things to come. In an irony that Newton richly appreciated, *London Life* was to be acclaimed, retrospectively, as one of the theatres 'great productions'...

These flops were not all bad news for Bob however; he had had his name put out into the public domain and had made two valuable contacts. Both Ernest Milton and Henry Ainley would come to his aid later in life.

Banking on a long run, Newton had squandered his wages and now faced a Christmas broke and out of work. A visit to Theale and family was a mixed pleasure; Pauline and Joy were flourishing but Marjorie was coping badly. Her drinking and smoking were affecting her health and now she was turning to crank religion. Money was a constant problem.

By this time Algernon had moved into Chelsea and the heart of London's artist society. In his youngest son Algernon saw a handsome and confident young man; in his turn Bobby found his father, once distracted and distant, now happy and vibrant. And none of the children could find it in their hearts to dislike Janetta. Devoted to their father, neat and demure, she had her own strong presence and sharp sense of humour. With her support Algernon was painting the silent canals and haunted, empty city streets; his talent was at last being recognised and his works were selling for good prices.

Bobby's year ended with a short, stop-gap engagement. Appearing at the Barnes Theatre 'For three weeks only', he took bottom footing on the programme as 'Peter, Ivanov's Manservant' in Chekhov, cast heavy, four act, *Ivanov*. Good, if slightly gloomy Christmas entertainment, the work ran from Boxing Day until January 15th.

A dreary spring brought Newton another big career boost - a season with a UK touring company.

Far from being a second-best, touring gave actors both valuable public exposure and a regular income. Spring and autumn tours neatly filled the gaps in the west-end seasons, and more than 150 companies worked the cities and outlying towns.

White Cargo had been *the* play to see in the capital. A roaring success, it had run for nine months and an astounding 821 performances at the London Playhouse and a staggering fourteen months in New York. Still pulling in the punters it was now the turn of the provinces to taste the sizzling, sexed-up trials and lascivious temptations of 'white men in the steamy tropics' of West Afrika. The tour opened on February 23rd at the New Theatre in Cambridge, 'Six nights and a matinee'.

Risen quickly from the sidelines and unnamed parts, Newton had now landed the high-profile lead role of 'Langford', 'the man who came out' into the fleshpots. Playing opposite the exotic 'Tondelayo', the 'coloured sexual temptress', he began gathering ecstatic reviews. The tour was a relentless hit; it ran breathlessly through the summer and the cast was hounded back and forth across the anonymous industrial landscapes well into the autumn; only then did the play eventually fold, simply from sheer exhaustion.

Back in the reassuring sophistication of the West End, the enthusiastic endorsements Bob had received on tour quickly resulted in another engagement; cast in the role of Sussex villager George Bristow in *The Ring O' Bells* he employed a suitably rusticated accent in a comedy that gently mocked English village life. The play opened at the Comedy Theatre on November 24th 1925; if newspaper reviews were good the work however was essentially out of step with public taste and the play closed after only a short run.

Throughout the dreary winter of 1925/6 conversation seemed to revolve endlessly about the rain and the politics of poverty; the economy looked to be sliding back onto the rocks and the prospect of a general strike loomed once again. The air of uncertainty was crippling for theatre business, even in the capital. Rumours and threats of theatre closures were rife and too many new faces were auditioning. Now patronage seemed to count more than talent and the plum jobs seemed to be quietly earmarked even before auditions. As ever, Newton's cavalier attitude with money equated to a shaky financial position. Out of work, exhausted by the drab English landscape and with his South African tan paled to a pasty white, he was itching to travel again. Heartily sick of the endemic 'British gloom', his thoughts now turned to the vaguely remembered wilderness of Canada. Algernon's works were now selling well and, carrying a burden of guilt, he was able and only too willing to finance his son's yearning to travel.

On the third of January 1931 Bobby waved his farewells to his tearful mother. Like so many others he had taken in his share of American movies and his mind was filled with the romance of the west. All things 'American' were in vogue and the lure of adventure and the mercurial promise of fortune made theatre's four pounds a week, 'bed and board', a dull alternative.

Travelling across to Liverpool Newton boarded the vast White Star liner *RMS Baltic*, sister ship to *Titanic*. The Atlantic crossing to New York was rough but there was plenty of young company. All the races of Europe seemed to be heading to the 'Promised Land'. Armed with a letter of introduction and an invitation, Bob headed for the Newton ranch in British Columbia. There he found that his 'fame' had been ably transmitted across the Atlantic by his adoring mother and the family treated him like royalty. Employment for soft-skinned actors was lacking in this hard land, yet Newton took his place as a dollar-a-day ranch hand with all the energy of youth.

June 1st, 1926, his twenty-first birthday, saw him with a pistol at his hip and astride a horse. Under the blazing sun and deep in the wilderness, he was working for a native Canadian. Far from the effeminate comforts of civilisation he was herding sheep, camping and living rough in the mountains. Autumn saw plenty of work and good pay, cutting timber and working the grain harvest.

With an artist's eye Newton perceived the unapproachable beauty of the land, yet it was the close, rough-house comradeship of the bunk room that he thrived on. He lived, like all of the disparate rag-tag of wanderers that were his companions, for the Saturday night drinks and the Saturday night girls. English newspapers and letters from home reminded him of a different, distant, world; told of a General Strike come and gone and an economy that was being slowly pulled out of recession.

As the days shortened into winter and the ground was hardened with frost, the excitement and glamour of London life and the stage began to beckon. The prospect of a frigid Canadian winter seemed suddenly unappealing; his head was full of ideas and stories and it was time to head home.

Gladly back in the millrace of the capital he took his father's advice and a little of his money and found digs in Bywater Street in Chelsea. The area was yet to see gentrification and the drab Pooteresque rows housed a cabal of disreputable artists and literati who were busy reshaping society. The house quickly filled up. Inevitably Pauline and Joy joined him. By now both had gravitated to the bright city lights and, following their brother's lead, were dabbling on the fringes of the stage. All too quickly strangers and hangers-on, family and spongers came to visit and stayed. Littering the kitchen, hallways and bedrooms there were people everywhere. Chaos ruled. Empty bottles and full ash-trays, Aspirin and nameless bodies, all rubbed for space; late-night fry-ups, gramophone music too loud in the half-light of the dawn...

In Newton's short absence theatre had moved on. The plays that he knew were suddenly yesterday's news. Now the talk was all about John Barrymore's new working of *Hamlet*, Noel Coward's *Fallen Angels* and the American phenomenon, Tallulah Bankhead. Bob tried for a part in *Hamlet*, unsuccessfully, but the audition did, however, bring him into contact with John Barrymore, a man notorious for his drinking and womanising and his dandy dress style. An immediate friendship sprang up between the two and overnight

Bob found that Barrymore's sister, Ethel, had joined the list of those crashing-out in his Bywater Street house.

Impatient for success and filled up with his overblown yarns of the 'wilds of Canada', Bob auditioned for Nancy Price and her prestigious 'Peoples National Theatre' and was hired as part of an upcoming regional tour. An illustrious cast had been assembled and the tour had the promise of success, hitting the big provincial cities with a variety of popular plays.

The first show went out at Birmingham's Prince of Wales theatre and was something of a homecoming landmark for Newton; on October 4th, 1926, he walked on as Richard, the Duke of Cleveden, in *The Duchess Decides*. Throughout the Christmas and New Year holidays the theatre was packed. The pace was relentless and box-office takings good. By May the cast had settled in at the New Theatre, Oxford for a production of *The Secret Woman*. Having carried the lead role at the Birmingham Rep' Newton was familiar with the work and once again took the lead part of Jesse Redvers. Forever packing up and moving on the company worked the usual 'six nights only, matinee on Sat at 2.00' throughout the spring. The letters from home always seemed to trail behind the tour's progress; now the big news was that Pauline had managed to land a bit-part in Noel Coward's glitzy new production, *Home Chat...*

The year passed by hectically and Price's company prepared to return to 'town' for the popular winter season. Newton however declined the flattering offer to stay with the troupe; instead he chose to transfer to another tour. It was not such a strange decision to make. In something of a career coup he now stepped into the role of 'lover' to the new stage sensation, Gladys Cooper.

One of the most glamorous women in theatre, Cooper had previously taken the lease of London's seven-hundred seat Playhouse Theatre and staged Somerset Maughan's smash-hit *The Letter*. The play had run with enormous success for six months; now the work was preparing to be thrown out to the sticks and Newton had been offered a plum role. In a double bill that concluded with *The Drums of Oude*, *The Letter*, like *White Cargo*, was deliciously sordid and melodramatic in the extreme. Opening with the heroine unloading a revolver into her lover the work dragged its audience through a steaming mire of infidelity, sex, murder and a 'Chinese mistress'. Framed with this classic formula, the work was a runaway success in the provinces; delighting audiences nightly, the tour was a sell-out through the Christmas holidays. By February the troupe had moved on to Manchester's Princes Theatre; 'A Personal Visit of Gladys Cooper', 'six nights only' the programme shrilled...

After an exhausting fifteen months, during which time his name had been frequently linked with good reviews, Newton was now in the position of being offered work within the West End. He was now recognised both within theatre circles and to a wide audience and his career was flourishing. His sister Pauline, however, was not. Despite high expectations and a good cast, Coward's *Home Chat* had crashed utterly on the first night, Coward himself had been booed and hissed off the stage...

Before returning to London, and remembering his roots, Newton fulfilled a debt of gratitude; revisiting the Birmingham Rep' he made a quick appearance in *Polar Post*. Now he was the 'star' guest artiste...

By the spring of 1928 he was again on tour; this time in a production of *Henry VIII*. Amongst the eclectic cast was Wilfred Lawson, a talented if dangerous actor. Five years older than Bob he had been out on tour for so long that he had lost count of the number of parts he had played. After some weeks the production trundled into Glasgow, and the Alhambra Theatre, one of the most notoriously difficult venues for English actors. The yarn went that the first few performances struggled through well enough, but after the Saturday matinee, Bob and Lawson had slipped out for a few drinks. They arrived back at the theatre, worse for wear, late for the half-hour call, and with only ten minutes to spare. The curtain was held while they were poured into their costumes and the tough Glasgow audience, sensing trouble, became restless.

There was a brief backstage panic and Bob was shoved onto the stage as Prologue with: "I come no more to make you laugh." The flourish at the end caused a titter from the audience; sensing trouble Bob ploughed on: "Things now, That bear a weighty and serious brow, Sad, high, and working, full of state and woe... Such noble scenes as drawn the eye to flow, We now present..." An over-long pause ensued before he desperately picked up the next line. By the time he had reached "Only they that come to hear a merry bawdy play... will be deceived", the audience realised that something was up; suddenly someone shouted "He's dished!". Quick as a flash, back came Bob's response. "If you think I'm pissed, wait until you see the Duke of Buckingham!" Perfectly on cue, out came Lawson, obviously slaughtered and with his tights pulled up over his head; "Good morrow and well met" he slurred. "How have ye done since last we met in France?" The house collapsed in roars of laughter. So the legend was born; taken, corrupted and recycled. Now the truth is forgotten, was it Bob and Lawson who did it or some other pair? No one will ever know...

Back in London's West End, and after a long spell of rehearsals, Newton next stepped out at the grandiose 1200 seater Lyric Theatre. The Lyric's previous productions had each seen long and lucrative runs; *The Gold Diggers* and *The Garden of Eden* had seen respectively, 180 and 232 performances. Significantly, the success of both works pivoted around appearances by a charismatic crowd puller, the controversial and sensational Tallulah Bankhead. The theatre's next production, this time sans Bankhead, was *My Ladies Mill*. Written by Eden and Adelaide Phillpots, it was a dark 'West country' comedy, centring on a misogynist's battles to raise his grandsons in a similar vein and the women who drag both love and a happy ending into the plot. The work opened in July, and Newton took the role of Jacko Baker, the 'artful seducer' and one of the grandsons. Reviews were gratifyingly good and the weekly dramatic newspaper, *The Stage*, praised Newton as 'a promising young player' and applauded him for his authentic accent.

By August the work folded. Newton however was asked to remain at the Lyric to prepare for the next production. He had been cast in the role of Paul Guisard in the sizzling sex-comedy *Her Cardboard Lover*. A French bedroom farce adapted by P G Wodehouse, it starred and was directed by Leslie Howard. It was, however, the omnipresent Tallulah Bankhead who promised to draw the crowds.

Three years older than Newton, Bankhead was an American phenomenon who carried all before her. Dazzling, bitchy and beautiful, her name was a by-word for the outspoken and outrageous. *Time* magazine had her number, 'Bankhead can quote readily and at impressive length from Shakespeare, the Bible and the public lavatory wall...'. On stage she *was* the stage and to the delight of audiences she eclipsed, out shouted and overpowered even the leading man. Off stage she was equally outrageous. She had swept into London in 1923 to become an overnight success. A sensation for being a sensation, the daughter of an Alabama congressman, unmistakably beautiful, she was both aristocratic and arrogant. As pure as the driven slush she was wildly promiscuous; her father had warned her about men, but had failed to mention women. With a precocious taste for champagne and cocaine and she loved to shock. 'Hello...' she would say, introducing herself at parties, 'I'm a lesbian. What do you do?' The meeting between her and Newton was portentous and Newton revelled in it. Her previous role in *Fallen Angels* saw her as one of two Mayfair golf widows who entertain an old flame and after revealing a catalogue of indiscretions drunkenly fantasise about having their dull husbands 'killed on the golf course'. To twenties audiences still haunted by hand-me-down mores it was all too deliciously horrifying. The moralists were outraged, denounced the work utterly and queued for 28 hours to see it. Winston Churchill saw it no less than five times...

After a brief working up in Leeds the play hit the West End. Newton melded with the theatrical wonder seamlessly; both took anarchic views on society and the sexual attraction was mutual. 'Everybody knows that Tallulah is one of those girls who could lure a Scotch elder into any indiscretion...' the papers said. Bob needed no luring. For neither of them did the dullard conventions of morality apply. Deeply flawed yet intelligent and big hearted, Bankhead's affections were liberal. After-show carousing was de rigger and both she and Newton fell to with a will.

Her Cardboard Lover opened to packed houses. Adroitly 'skating with maximum deliberation over the largest quantity of the thinnest ice possible' the plot cut as close to the bone as it dared, portraying another steaming tangle of sex, immorality, jealousy and betrayal.

'Down go the lights and up goes the curtain, and in a few minutes Tallulah, in a sheath of ebony velvet, shoulder-strapped with diamanté, insinuates herself on stage. The famous husky voice with the break in it is there, the swift, lithe movements of the body and the rapid and disarming changes from hair tossing and tearing to chuckling, wheedling tenderness. As a vivid, irrational, emotional Frenchwoman she carries the vein of unrestrained farce without a moment's departure for subtlety. Beautiful? Oh, quite! Feline? Yes, with the broad, languorous movements of a blue Persian kitten whose claws are never far concealed. She can scream, too, not unlike the wail of a cat in the night...'.

Newton's role was that of the jealous ex' who tangles with a newly moralised gigolo. On stage Bankhead and Newton instantly formed a slick double-act, both playing blatantly to the gallery and hamming up their parts. Clad, just, in her flimsy pyjamas Bankhead was as ever followed by her coterie of wealthy groupies. Her costumes created waves in the fashion world that lapped out over the London suburbs. 'Tantalised by the ferments of my followers, some of the London reviews said that their frenzy was due to the fact that I was forever undressing on stage, or smouldering in sheer negligées...' Bankhead said, 'The charge was as false as a smuggler's tax-return. In only two plays: *The Garden of Eden* and *Her Cardboard Lover* did I bounce about in anything approaching the buff, the better to agitate the leading man...'. Suitably agitated, Newton was himself setting sartorial standards out on the streets. Douglas Byng, a fellow actor, saw that Newton was not just 'with it', but way ahead of it; "He was the first young man in London to be seen dressed in a fawn corduroy suit, pink shirt, bright green tie and Tyrolean hat... he looked like he had stepped out of an Italian painting…".

Of course Bob tumbled into Bankhead's bed; it was almost obligatory. "I'm not promiscuous.." she argued "...promiscuity implies that attraction is not necessary. I lay my eyes on a man and have an affair with him the next hour. But the attraction is serious...!" Glur Taylor, another of Bob's many girlfriends, was invited around to Bankhead's Mayfair flat. Bob answered the door; once inside she heard a voice from upstairs. "Come on up, and bring another glass with you". Tallulah was in the bath...

Buoyed by rave reviews the play ran remorselessly. For both the cast and the gang of hangers-on that usually included Pauline and Joy, the transition between stage and party became seamless. Booze, cigarettes and cocaine littered the tables and sideboards. "I'm sick and tired of Tallulah's parties..." one friend complained "every morning they run out of cocaine and it's me who's sent down to Limehouse to get some more!" The parties wound through the velvet summer nights and the boaty set was drafted in. Off the Chelsea embankment Bob, centre-stage, was riding the crest of a wave and loving every minute. The first pale light of dawn was often saluted by the sight of him diving overboard with a bottle of champagne in each hand. Of course drink always broke the ice, tore down any reserve; surrounded by a coterie of friends and lovers, solitude and silence were banished and Bob's life, filled with voices, music and laughter, was complete. Deliriously hung-over, back-stage became a stage itself. Ever the rule-breaker he had always urinated where and when he pleased, doorways, hand-basins, out of windows. Now during productions he would climb up into the 'flies' above the stage and laughing uproariously, piddle over the actors below...

Testing the censors' patience to the limit *Her Cardboard Lover* ran for six months and packed in 173 performances. Audiences were wild for it. Throughout Newton consistently received rave notices, judged as showing both a 'genuine liveliness' and 'a refreshing quietness'. Inevitably, however, it was Bankhead, in 'the brief intervals during which she was clothed and in her right mind' that stole the show, the notices and the plaudits.

The show was folded, with reluctance, and Newton moved on to fill a sudden vacancy, taking the part of aristocrat Errol Kerr in *Clara Gibbings* at the seven hundred seater Vaudeville theatre. A lightweight three-act drama, the work was never going to be a block-buster, and was merely a vehicle for aspiring burlesque and music-hall performer Violet Lorraine.

In the new year, 1929, Newton was back his old dressing room at the Lyric. With the nagging thought of Barry Jackson glumly reviewing his progress he was delighted to have landed a part in a serious production. In *Byron* he took two very different roles, first as John Murray, a dour and quarrelsome Scot and then, in total contrast, as the quintessential fop, the Prince Regent. The critics didn't approve however; the Times said "It's all pitched so high that one almost ceases to expect any truth in it..." Newton carried his characters with both enthusiasm and skill and the critics found it in themselves to nod a grudging approval; "...but there are instances of truth now and then... in Mr Robert Newton's sketch of John Murray".

Eternally in love with women, Bobby was always to be found with a beautiful girl on his arm. Passionately and almost perpetually besotted he was forever 'engaged' to one stunning face or another. One evening and amid the swirl of another impromptu pub-crawl, Bob ran into Augustus John. Late into the night John brought the conversation around to a 'friend' of his in Romney Marsh who had fallen on hard times. The friend was Petronella Walton, 'Peta'; the hard times were the shame of an illegitimate child. Turfed out by her parents she was alone and living on the bread-line. Perhaps, he suggested, Bobby could call around one evening, just to cheer her up...

Some days later, filled up with philanthropic goodness, Bob and his latest girlfriend headed out to Romney Marsh. The meeting between him and Peta was a fateful one; instantly Bob was in love.

He and his 'fiancée' had arrived late in the evening and had found Peta nursing her three year old baby girl beside the fire. Still deeply affected by his own parent's separation and fundamentally seeking a family, the attraction was irresistible. The romance was a purely sentimental one, but it was rapid. Bob was besotted with the concept of actually 'being in love'. He dreamed of giving his name to the beautiful little girl and creating a home for her.

Marjorie had been through it all before but she heard about this love-story too late and she knew that this time it was fatal. Bob had listened to Peta's story and was deeply moved by it. "Oh well, we've got to do something about this..." he had said, "come up to London and marry me". It was the end of one engagement and the beginning of another.

Marjorie's tears and pleading did no good. The marriage was simple. A church wedding was, of course, out of the question and a quick ceremony at a registry office had to suffice. On a chilly January morning, squeezed between performances, Petronella Margaret Millicent married Robert Guy. All of the *Byron* cast turned up, rice was thrown, the kisses done. Pauline and Joy were already favourite aunts with Peta's little girl. Marjorie sobbed. Who could be good enough for her favourite?

That was Bob's side of the story, Peta's never came out, was never 'spoken of' in the family. For both, however, the romance was a mutually expedient one; Bob had found an instant substitute family, and Peta had found a way out of a desperate situation. She and her little girl, Jane, were moved into Number 14, Bywater Street. It was not quite the grandiose mansion she had been led to expect, just a dowdy, run-down place in a dowdy run-down district. But Bob saw none of this; suffused with romantic happiness he slipped into the role of the loving, domesticated husband and ideal father to his new family, and turned back to work.

Byron ran for three months. Then, riding on the acclaim he had gathered for his role in *Her Cardboard Lover*, Newton auditioned and successfully landed another plum role. The work was a musical revue, Noel Coward's classic, *Bitter Sweet*.

As Bernard Shaw's world was swallowed by the bored yawn of history, Coward's had emerged. Meteorically risen from his stumbling learning days and some crashing failures, he had flowered into an overnight sensation and an unstoppable success. Suave and clipped, the new face of theatre, he had become a cultural icon to the industry's well-stocked homosexual enclave. Coward had seen and approved Newton's acting in *Byron* but they were, however, already 'acquainted'. Coward had appeared briefly at the Birmingham Rep' in 1918 in *Scandal*, and a year later in a minor part in a minor and rather forgettable burlesque comedy piece appropriately entitled *The Knight of the Burning Pestle*. Coward had already acquired a reputation for being priggish and the meeting between the two men had been less than cordial. Coward, ever the disciplinarian professional, found it difficult to disguise his distaste for Newton's boyish attitude.

Nursing an ambition to act the plays he so brilliantly penned, Coward was, however only too aware of his lack of stage credentials. His reaction was a slowly developing neurotic avoidance of the great actors of the day and Bob's over-large personality, boisterous and demonstrative, still sat ill alongside his own reserved yet domineering style. Nevertheless Coward was only too aware of Newton's charismatic stage presence, and, more importantly, the value of his name on a billing.

This was a big break for Bobby and Billy Milton, another of Connie's stable and an old, sexually ambidextrous, friend, decided to throw a party to celebrate it. Milton had also been given a small part in the production so the celebration was a double one; the Thespian arriviste crashed into his Kensington home bottles in hand. Peta, already disenchanted with her husband's drunken antics, attended reluctantly; bouts of morning sickness meant that partying no longer came high on her list of priorities...

After protracted rehearsals in London's Scala Theatre, Coward's players took a deep breath and prepared for the opening night in Manchester. First nights were always nervous; Coward had a catalogue of failures behind him and he understood only too well that theatre was a cut- throat business. Now his play was competing with the first British-made talking film, Hitchcock's *Blackmail*...

Few cinemas were equipped for sound and Hitchcock's film had achieved only a limited distribution, yet everyone knew that it signalled a massive change in the industry. Chaplin had initially dismissed 'talkies' as a fad, but the public thought otherwise and were voting with their feet; within the year almost every cinema in the country was to be upgraded for the sound revolution. The joke was that as theatre and cinema bickered away, Logie Baird, unnoticed by them both, proudly showed off his new invention, a little flickering box he called 'television'; 'It is ridiculous to claim that television is yet 'entertainment" the press said '...it is even more foolish to deny the enormous effect it will have on entertainment in the future, it will not do away with films, but...'.

In Manchester the curtain drew back to reveal a glittering stage filled with the gay chatter of high society; the plot was revealed, choreographed by a delirious swirl of musical scores; Dolly Chamberlain, a well-bred English girl, deserts her stuffy fiancé,

Bob's 'Hugh Devon', and elopes with her penniless Johnny-Foreigner music teacher. The audience were stunned. Nothing had ever been seen like this before.

The next day the newspaper critics carped, of course, but the ecstatic roar from the first-night audience had already dictated that *Bitter Sweet* was nothing less than a sensation. Overnight Coward became the doyenne of society and the three week 'try-out' in Manchester a 'riotous sell-out'. The antithesis of Coward's hallmark cynicism, *Bitter Sweet* was an unashamed celebration of a richer, more glamorous and forgotten world. A fairy-tale romance filled with swirling waltzes, lavish costumes and luxurious sets, it was the perfect panacea for a world sliding into a slump. Finding themselves out-flanked by public opinion, the newspaper reviews now became almost incoherent with praise.

Riding the crest of a wave, the London season opened at His Majesty's Theatre. Braving the throng of autograph hunters, Prince George and Lady Mountbatten attended, trailing the good and the great in their wake. Tickets had sold out, even at 24 shillings for a stall seat, and a lively black-market had sprung up. Excitement was at fever pitch as the curtains rose for the first night, Thursday, July 18th.

As ever the first night was something of an anti-climax; the audience of London sophisticates played it fashionably cool. Ever the tail-end of the dog, the London press, with whom Coward had developed a decidedly bad attitude, gauged the public mood wrongly. Haughtily they gave the show only eight weeks to run. Then the audiences began to thaw and the play bloomed into a runaway success. Theatre audiences had not seen its like for years; a spectacle of melody and colour, it swept all before it. Spiced with homosexual overtones and complete with a happy ending it was hailed 'the theatrical event of the summer'. Audiences gave every minute of the two and a half hour performance a rapturous thumbs-up and the songs and melodies became an overnight sensation, hummed and whistled everywhere across the country.

Riding on the thunder of applause the play ran and ran to packed houses, throughout the long hot summer, into the Christmas holidays and on, inexorably, into the next spring. As the weeks and months passed, the casts initial exhilaration faded into exhaustion; the nightly routine became merely mechanical and inevitably, boredom set in.

Sidelined, with his character almost lost amongst the huge cast, Bob found himself pasting on his moustache and side burns and simply going through the motions each night. For a man used to taking the lead role, his lines were risible; during the second act 'Hugh' didn't appear at all; only at the end is he addressed by his ex-fiancé... "I treated him abominably you know..." she said, "he was dreadfully upset, weren't you Hugh?" All Bob had to work with was a strangled "Yes, indeed, I was..."

Manfully Bob stuck it out; he was at the heart of the theatre world and he was gathering satisfactory press reviews and the golden spattering of fame. Certainly his weekly wage made up in part for the lack of a prestige part; at this time a working man's house cost about £240 and his pre-tax £40 weekly salary was more than substantial...

Bob might have been comfortable in his topsy-turvy nocturnal routine, but his home life with Peta had quickly became problematical; the Bywater Street house, witnessing only a series of dislocated and drunken meetings, was not the 'home' she looked for. Compared to the swirling, multi-coloured, millrace of the theatre, Bob had soon become bored with the role of the stay-at-home family-man. With a fortune in cash in his pocket and the world at his feet he realised his mother was right; the marriage was a big mistake.

Neglected and rejected Peta found herself sidelined; heavily pregnant, waddling histrionically and with a small child to care for, she was tired, angry and usually asleep by the time Bob staggered home. Bitter rows and accusations too often marred their rare meetings.

For Bob all the fun had quickly gone out of the thing. Despite his dreams and his good intentions he was never cut out to be the obedient pipe-and-slippers husband. His sole contribution to domestic bliss had been a hungry, disreputable and very much second-hand Great Dane. With the 'family' thus increased Peta had the long, lonely evenings to reconsider the wisdom of her choice of husband. Noisy drunken homecomings with a gaggle of hangers-on were standard; not returning at all a welcome relief. Inevitably rumours and gossip filtered back, all of the gleefully recounted second-hand tales trailing through their relationship. Tales of the drunken nights and the other women. Of the night when he had swept into the Café de Paris, and throwing his opera cloak to the attendant, had waded down the grand staircase stark naked before anyone could stop him. Women had gasped as the waiters dashed out to wrap a tablecloth around him. Fighting and swearing, swathed like a Roman emperor, he had been carried out and bundled into a taxi ...

Domestic spats might have been part of the rich tapestry of life for Bob but at work he had also received his quota of warnings. Coward, 'gracious, socially, as a royal bastard', was not impressed by 'his' actor's antics. Bob had been dismissed, twice, but had, on both occasions, been reluctantly reinstated.

Billy Milton shared Newton's dressing room, and they inevitably became drinking partners. After one Saturday afternoon matinee Bob had taken Milton to visit 'his pal' Augustus John in his Mallard Street studio. A bottle of whisky had been all too quickly dispatched and Milton had suggested a hearty meal to sober them both up for the evening's performance; Newton declined, and made straight for the theatre bar.

The third dismissal came quick on the heels of the 'final' reinstatement. Called from his dressing room to the offices, Bob, fearing the worst headed up via the bar. Knocking back a double whisky he turned to find a startled Charles B, 'Cocky', Cochran, the shows producer and his boss. Finding himself in a corner, Bob, half drunk and glowing, took the initiative. "Mr Cochran, I wish to speak to you". Cochran stepped back "Mr Newton, I have nothing whatsoever to say to you, do you understand, nothing!" "But you must have my side of the story." Newton pleaded. "Well…what is it? said Cochran, already losing the battle. "The reason I am intoxicated tonight is that you have given me such a piffling part when I am so talented... it's driving me mad, give me something where I can show my ability and I will remain sober!" Cochran paused for a long moment. "Mr Newton, listen to me very, very carefully, Mr Coward is planning to take his new play *Private Lives* to New York, I want you to follow the company there and you will be engaged as Mr Coward's understudy. I will make all the necessary arrangements." There was another long pause. "Goodbye, Mr Newton". Cochran headed for the door; Newton turned back to the bar...

Running at the Phoenix Theatre simultaneously with *Bitter Sweet*, *Private Lives* was set to be another Coward smash hit. Laurence Olivier appeared alongside Coward himself. Audiences were wildly appreciative and the theatre had been full every night since the opening, yet Bob felt distinctly uneasy. Somehow he felt that Coward's world and the artistic direction he took was not his own. He had grown a taste for the fiery passion of the stage and loathed the prospect of another of Coward's bland, 'Amiable Evening' shows. The protracted run of the saccharine *Bitter Sweet* had grated on him; now he faced another almost certainly lengthy bout of the same. He knew however that an American trip was not one he could afford to refuse, neither financially or career wise; and there would be other compensations...

Anticipation now only made the boredom worse. After almost seven hundred performances, *Bitter Sweet* was getting bloody dull. The promise of the foreign engagement however succeeded where Peta's nagging had failed and Newton bluffed his way through the remaining weeks and managed to keep his nose clean.

With the knowledge of a marriage firmly crashed on the rocks, Peta went into labour and on the ninth of November Bobby found himself to be a father to a little girl. For him the event came as a startling revelation. Filled up with a new wonder the baby was named Sally. Bob was ecstatic, Peta was besieged with visitors and flowers and the occasion degenerated into yet another party. Spirits became exuberant and everyone was called in to attend; cast, friends, neighbours, even the dustman pushing his cart down the street had a glass thrust into his hand and was dragged in. "I've just had twin boys...!" Newton crowed. Suddenly all was forgiven. Everything would be different now he declared. The new baby was laid in the basket with the Great Dane and the party went on into the night.

Inevitably a glitzy showbiz christening was thrown; Tallulah Bankhead was duly signed up as the child's Godmother and arrived at the church with a string of Cartier pearls as a gift for the baby.

With 697 performances itching under the cast's skin, the London season at last wrapped. Over a million people had seen the show; throughout stall seats had been priced at 24/- and Coward had grossed a cool £250,000. A whole new cast was engaged and *Bitter Sweet* was dispatched out on tour to the culture-hungry provincials who in their turn gobbled it up.

Coward had been proved right; he had judged the mood of the country with stunning acuity and had given his audience exactly what they wanted. *Bitter Sweet* had been a dazzlingly pretty and desperately needed distraction from the reality of a country that was burning itself out. Society was changing, everything was changing; the new death duties had destroyed the last vestiges of the old order and for those who managed to cling on, a succession of stock market slumps and agricultural crises meant near bankruptcy. Shaken by the first faraway implications of the Wall Street crash and with a government and economy rooted in a past of traditionalist values, Britain was sinking fast - again. Both Coward and Newton could see that it was a good time to leave and the prospect of work in the New Jerusalem of America was thrilling. Peta had taken the news without surprise or tears; the baby was kissed and a score of promises were made in the throes of a score of farewell parties.

The winter crossing took seven days, an all too short week of the opulent variety of luxury that Cunard's RMS *Aquitania* was well equipped to supply. A lavish floating hotel, a 'Savoy' away from home, she boasted five-star restaurants, plush bars, glittering ballrooms and every type of open-handed decadence that Newton was only too well inclined to enjoy.

As the ship nudged into the Hudson River and into the shadows of the iconic Liberty statue, Newton stepped open-mouthed into a world of neon modernity. The Chrysler building, the beacon for the new mass-modern world, towered above all, stamping 'Deco' on the cityscape and the minds of New Yorkers. After the gas-lit smogs of Victorian London, the crisp glare of the Manhattan spring was nothing less than dazzling. Bewildered and enchanted he headed for 44th street and the Algonquin Hotel. One of the great old-fashioned hotels, its wood panelled public rooms had long been the favoured watering hole for the elite of the witty literati. That afternoon he ventured out into the improbable brick and concrete canyons, the die-straight streets and avenues. Everything was in motion and nothing stood still. Crossing the road was a dangerous adventure. Times Square, the very hub of Broadway, reeked an overwhelming glamour that took his breath away. The evening drew into night and the lights flicked on, illuminating the huge blown-up photographs of the stars, spelling out their names in electric bulbs.

Soon after his arrival, Newton was summoned to Coward's plush hotel suite. And he knew what was coming. A little, private, seduction dinner for two had been arranged. It was the same with every new boy. Olivier had already been through this initiation some months before and his career was never going to look back. Doors opened effortlessly now for the callow, giggling new-boy. Smiles welcomed him into the cream of society. Recognition, plaudits, praise. Knighthood, at the appointed time. Newton knew the plot and he came prepared. He arrived with his latest conquest, a drunken floozy, on his arm, her cheap laughter and cheap perfume filling the immaculate apartment....

The next morning down on Broadway and the Times Square Theatre, catching up with Olivier and meeting the assembled cast was not the pleasure Newton had anticipated. Despite the sell-out houses in London and a New York season that was as good as in the bag, overnight Coward had decided that he was 'fatigued' with his stage role. Turning to Bob he coldly informed him that he was turning his own role over to an American actor, Otto Kruger; Newton's role, as the lead's understudy, had been scrapped and he was instead going to take Olivier's part. Oliver was also leaving and Newton immediately understood why; he was deadly bored by an outside role within what was virtually a duet.

Unlike *Bitter Sweet* the new play was an unashamed vehicle for Cowards acting talents and his contradictory feelings for his female lead, Gertrude Lawrence. A suave and cynical tale of sexual rebellion and inversion it was very different from his previous cast-heavy production. A minimalist, two-handed work of bickering one-liners and cutting ripostes it left the other players to flounder as good-looking puppets and little else. The news came as a blow to Newton, but he knew he had little alternative other than to accept. As Olivier had found, the dangling carrot of a £50 weekly pay-cheque was simply too alluring to refuse; in New York that wage would guarantee easy living; 35c would buy a substantial breakfast, a dollar a four-course steak dinner in one of the finest hotels. A room in a swanky hotel came in at $5 a week. Newton clearly saw that fifty pounds would buy a lot of pleasure.

The show opened on January 27th 1931, in the newly built Phoenix Theatre and to a New York high-society that was, with an all too common irony, greedy for anything English. A collage of artful bickerage, *Private Lives* was a technical masterpiece. The script, rich with explicit sexual rebellion, toyed remorselessly with convention. "I'm glad I'm normal" cries Victor. "What an odd thing to be glad about. Why?" Amanda bites back. "Well, *aren't* you?" he asks. "I'm not sure I'm normal..." she answers. Riddled with a dialect of youth that ruthlessly mocked the older generation, the work was a stunning amalgam of a changing society and its creator's contradictory personality. Ignorant of old-world affectations and snobbery, the first-night audience roared approval and the next morning's paper reviews trumpeted another Coward success; 'An admirable piece of fluff' the critics trilled. The *New York Times* dubbed Newton's 'Victor Prynne' glowingly as "personable". Getting into his stride Newton threw himself both into his work and 'the wicked city'...

In the October of 1929 the American stock market had collapsed; $30 billion dollars worth of stock had been converted into so much worthless paper and the whole world precipitated towards depression. Anticipating the crash that was to come New York was revelling in a last-minute orgy of pleasure and America experienced the same moral emancipation that Newton had experienced in London. It was the birth of America's turbulent era, an era of crisis and sexual liberation, drink and drugs.

Dance clubs choreographed a society discovering the joys of divorce and adultery. In fashionable Harlem, at the movies and in the front-row at the Fifty-Fifty club's wild cabarets, Newton immersed himself in a world of pleasure. A prestige guest he took his rightful place in the Lambs Club, the sacred gathering ground for actors. Like the city itself, New York people were fast. Hard-drinking and hard-living, far removed from the 'genteel' patrons of London's West End, prohibition had washed the city with crime and liquor. Forbidden fruit as ever tasting the sweetest, lethal bathtub gin had become the new fire-water, speakeasies and shabby dives the new social hit. Newton's infrequent letters home to his wife told of a land of too many opportunities. A handsome young Englishman abroad, he was showered with the attention he craved. Ever the bohemian, marital fidelity lay outside of his remit...

Since the hotel suite incident, Newton's relationship with Coward had been, to say the least, strained. Now Bob found himself perpetually cold-shouldered; he was definitely not one of the 'little darlings'. Coward was nevertheless satisfied with Newton's stage work. Both men played it stand-offish, but their personal lives were however to meet head-on once again. Coward had received a tearful letter from Peta; Bob was not sending her any money and she was struggling to pay the rent and feed her children. The meeting was short and clipped. Coward took the paternalistic role, imperiously reprimanding Newton for failing his family. Newton, backing away, headed for the bar, apologising and swearing reform.

Outside, in the real world, storm clouds gathered. The deepening depression, seeded by the Black Tuesday crash, had cast a shadow across the land. The American brand of rampant capitalism had failed and Bob's arrival in the Promised Land had coincided with the worst global depression of the century. The cocktail parties of the Roaring Twenties now woke to the hangover of the Hungry Thirties. It was a paradigmatic case of boom and bust. Suddenly every conversation was punctuated with apocryphal tales of stock-market ticker-tape machines running out of control, brokers hurling themselves from high windows and life-savings going up in smoke. As ever, hardship had started at the bottom of society, hitting hardest and first those least able to deal with it. Seemingly overnight ragged gangs of the unemployed and unemployable, men, women and children, black and white alike, were to be seen shambling from town to town. All looked for the jobs and the charity that did not exist. Four and a half million men became wordless statistics. Even within the affluent heart of Manhattan, 'Hoovervilles', slum shacks, were growing up between the islands of wealth; cardboard shanties sprung up under the bridges and in the vacant lots. Brash self-reliance perished on the long shuffle up the breadline; everywhere there was a sense of panic, fear, dislocation and despair. Haunted looking beggars skulked around the playground flagstones of Times Square, shivering men lined up outside the church soup-kitchens and waited for hours for a cup of watery broth and a hunk of bread. Death crept behind the weak and the diseased, felled them where they lay, left them to be swept up with the morning's trash.

As ever, immense wealth and grinding poverty sat close together. Suicide was common and egalitarian, bodies littered alleys, drunk or drugged or dead. No one looked; all had their own cares and their own plan of survival. Thin drab faces and useless idleness stood in queues. Poverty, theft, vice and back-street abortions were never meant to be part of the clean, white, Art Deco future. The perfumed rich, nightly entering the bright-lit theatre, turned blind eyes to the outstretched begging hands yet the grim reality hit even here. Wealth was going underground and taste in entertainment was retrenching, turning away from Coward's vision of self-indulgent, champagne sipping, English aristocracy. By the late summer half of Broadway's theatres were closed. Those that stayed open played to almost empty houses. Inevitably Coward's play failed too, and closed on May 9th.

Out of work, Newton fell victim to the American actors union 'Equity' and its 'foreigners' rule that dictated a six-month lay-off period between engagements. Suddenly he found himself both penniless and friendless. Seeking work within an industry that was in crisis seemed hopeless; going home was a bland option and one he could not afford. Decamping from his plush hotel he took digs in the Hell's Kitchen district in the Lower East Side. Crowded with poor Irish and Italians, it was the vaunted social 'melting pot'; now it only crystallised its victims into disparate and isolated cells. Ironically it was just a block away from the jaded glitz of Broadway and the theatres.

Trading on his good looks and his accent, Newton took whatever jobs he could find. For a while he was waiter-cum-barman, table wiper and doorman at the Café Anglais; it was a dream job, but all too quickly he was fired for blatantly sampling the customers drinks. The reality of poverty was not exactly new to Bob, but here, far from home and family, he quickly sweated out the deception of New York glamour. His next job, as a floor waiter at the Hotel Chelsea on 23rd street, didn't last long either; drunken nakedness and room-service didn't mix, even in New York...

Then, inevitably, he hit lucky. He bumped into an old friend, Lewis Milestone, the famed director of *All Quiet on the Western Front*. Milestone had been a frequent backstage visitor during the run of *Private Lives*; now, commiserating over a drink, Milestone confessed that he was no better off than Newton and that like so many, he was heading west for Hollywood and the gold rush of the talkies.

Hollywood was now leading the world film industry and it was an industry that was changing fast. The silent stars were past their sell-by date and were toppling every time they opened their mouths; Hollywood was searching for a new class of actor, one that could both act *and* talk. For a long time studio scouts had been stalking the Broadway stages. During his time in *Private Lives* Olivier had cannily made a number of screen tests and catching the eye of RKO he had gathered some lucrative contracts and headed west. Milestone was in the same financial fix as Newton; on his beam-ends and without the train fare, he was going to drive cross-country and offered Newton a lift. Newton jumped at the chance.

The journey was long, hot and sobering, choked up with dry throats and red dirt-roads. A land that had once harvested prosperity from foreign wars and political isolation now lay as a wilderness. Foreclosure, eviction and misery seemed the only crop. The Depression spread like a plague, a Black Death moving across the land; thousands of jobless and destitute tramped and hitched, always looking for jobs, always moving on to nowhere. Most were adult males, but as the year went on, whole families hit the road, packed into rusting jalopies stuffed with their every possession. Some saw it as a divine retribution of course, snatched up their bibles and howled for repentance. Perhaps they were right. Now another nemesis hit the land, a Biblical plague, laying the misery of the broken-backed dollar even to the substance of the rich earth. Once so rich in its yield, the very soil of the land now failed. The age old grasslands, ploughed up by the new prairie settlers, collapsed. Smitten by drought, the fragile loam was plucked up and blown in choking clouds onto the streets of the cities. The great plains of Missouri and Kansas, the whole of the vast prairie, the very heartland of rural America, was becoming an arid desert. A harvest of ruined homesteaders packed up and quit. These were the despised dust-bowl migrants that filled route 66 with the stench of poverty; and all were heading for California.

Throughout the long days Newton and Milestone watched each others backs, pistols in their belts. At night they slept uneasily in shifts. Then the air was suddenly filled with the scent of orange blossom and the San Fernando Valley opened out around them. The road climbed up and over the wilderness of the Santa Anna Pass. Then the deep blue Pacific lay before them, the cool breeze cancelling out the burnt up lands. A sign read 'City Limits' and the horizon opened out into a sprawl of civilisation; this was Los Angeles, the beautiful, the 'cesspool of vice'. And on the city's northern edge was their destination, Hollywood.

Part industry, part technology, part chimeric style and a bogus quality of mind, Hollywood was in reality a negation of all these things that boiled down to a hunger for money and power. Somehow the place looked raw and unfinished, as though it was hurriedly run up. Some of it was unbridled luxury, some a repulsive sore. On the fringes of the city amongst the barren burnt-out wastes, the roadsides served as parking lots. Between lay a litter of cheap and awful clapboard bungalows, glaring advertising signs, petrol pumps and the freaky architecture of junk-food restaurants. Yet in the heart of it all, under the glorious sunshine, there was a picture-postcard town, ringed with mountains and ocean, basking in the all-pervasive air of a perpetual vacation.

Cynics had been able to make a few dents in the illusion of the beautiful Hollywood, but the tricksters had smothered the truth. Now the two sun-parched men were persuaded that the touter of glamour was itself glamorous. Back in the twenties, Congress had sat in rapt attention as the lifestyle of the Hollywood elite was elucidated and damned... "Hollywood is a colony of these people where debauchery, riotous living, drunkenness, ribaldry, dissipation and free-love seem to be conspicuous. Many of these 'stars' ... do not know what to do with their wealth...!". Talk of second-rate actors raking in three thousand dollars a week seemed a fantastic dream, drunkenness, ribaldry and dissipation a very attractive option.

The two men stood in their ragged shirts, with empty pockets and empty bellies, suddenly in a fantasy land where the in-crowd whooped it up in an atmosphere of staggering luxury, and immaculate, chrome laden cruisers, sleek and very fast, raced along the asphalt, and vanished into bright white villas. Above the side walks towering billboards bore tanned and smiling faces that peddled lifestyles and families, possessions and desires, pills for health and cures for the ailments that did not exist. Peddled the dream of wealth.

There were no buses. Only cars. No one walked.

Homeless and hungry Bob desperately needed a break and turned to the two Hollywood contacts he knew, Tallulah Bankhead and John Barrymore, yet even they could offer little more than vague promises. Along with Milestone, Bob trailed in the wake of all the other hungry faces, out towards the sprawling electric city of studios.

With a name and a reputation Milestone got them both through the screen of security. There the reality of both the studios and studio life was an education. A crazy muddle of day and night, of truth and illusion, where all the languages of the world made a Babylon, the place was a dream factory that fed unashamedly off the collapse of the real world outside. Milestone shrugged; Hollywood had never allowed itself to be shackled by mundane reality. Busby Berkeley had produced musicals of wild excess; when Tom Mix finally stopped cleaning up the Old West, Roy Rogers had taken over, and when Shakespeare appeared on celluloid it was 'A Midsummer Night's Dream' and not 'King Lear' that was subjected to movie magic. And it was a magic that revolved about the dream of Getting and Spending. This was the seedling vision of a post-depression age, an age of greed and mass consumption. The mass flowed through film; somehow it was all both terribly exciting and terribly familiar.

Using all of his influence, Milestone managed to land Newton a month's employment as a bit-part actor. Still in its formative years, Hollywood's 'professional extras' did not yet exist. If a director wanted background bodies someone just went out and found somebody, anybody; there was always a gaggle of onlookers and starstruck loafers outside the studio gates and it was never difficult. Now these casual idlers had become hungry and wanted to be paid. 50c an hour became the going rate, and it attracted in every bum, itinerant and would-be star, clogging up the streets outside the studios. Gradually the 'bull-pen' system had sprung up, a rough house holding tank where the hopefuls assembled each morning.

By the mid-twenties the studios saw the system creaking under its own weight and found it impossible to filter out the genuine talent from the waster. By the thirties a rudimentary 'filing' system had been set up and the Central Casting Corporation was born. Eighteen thousand names were quickly scratched onto the books and the established actors suddenly found themselves part of the most overcrowded industry in the world. The day-rate hopefuls were now subdivided into four categories. First were the elite, the $10 a day 'Dress extras' who could rustle up their own specialist costumes. Next came the 'General extras', the presentable behind-the-star crowd of 'fine, but not too good looking' nameless faces. Further down the pecking order came the swilling mass of 'crowd extras', each subdivided into a rigid ethnic group, that, if lucky enough to be hired, were mercilessly herded like cattle from set to set. Finally there were the 'shit-kickers' the specialist cowboy extras that hung out in lofty isolation at 'Gower Gulch' off Sunset Boulevard.

Doing its best to deter the faint hearted, the filter system started at Central Casting's front door where a big banner was nailed up... 'Don't try to become an actor. For every one we employ we turn away a thousand'.

Newton found the work arduous and dumb. It began at six in the morning and often went on well into the night, for no extra money. Working under the studio lights was swelteringly hot, the waiting endless and boring, the canteen grub lousy and the pay just enough for cheap digs and cigarettes. Ready to throw it all in, Newton now had a typical stroke of luck that others would have killed for.

Actor/manager Richard Bennett was looking for a handsome leading–man for a touring stage production; Bob auditioned, pulled every stage trick he had ever learned out of the bag and was hired. It was a plum job and the pay was good. Even better he found that he would play opposite Bennett's glamorous daughters, Constance and Joan. With admirable prescience Bennett could see stardom and fortune writ large across his daughters' flawless profiles and he was carefully grooming them for the screen. Jealously guarding them from predators, he was simultaneously and cautiously exposing them to the world. The rehearsals went well, perhaps too well, and there was a palpable frisson on stage. Almost too late Bennett saw the seduction happening; he was directing it on his own stage and he was paying the lousy Brit' for doing it.

Not everyone in Hollywood approved of the British; 'Loud mouthed, arrogant, clannish and all too inclined to regard the whole business of film-making as a kind of schoolboy prank' the Yanks muttered. Bennett, a committed alcoholic and at the best of times irrascible, certainly didn't like them. Living up to his reputation, he could stomach no more and with a mouth full of obscene rage he fired Newton on the spot. "Why!" roared back Bob, "Because... your accent..." Bennett screamed, "is too God-damn English!".

Of course the collision was inevitable. Mixing Bobby with two pretty girls was always going to be fatal. The seedling romance was over but their paths were to cross again. Newton turned back to the beachcombing existence and rejoined the lines of jobless and homeless.

Actors, along with every other trade under the sun, were arriving in California daily and in droves and Newton knew that his Broadway credentials were devaluing rapidly. His days were spent jostling with scores of others, cadging smokes, looking for jobs that did not exist, the nights spent with the same faces. Bonded in desperation, the hungry brotherhood slept rough in a shallow cave on Santa Monica beach.

Trailed in with the itinerants, the spectre of depression now began to affect even the movie industry. Fearful of the damning Sodom and Gomorrah finger of judgement, the unbridled hedonism of the early days was being reined in and covered up, and the industry began to turn in on itself. Suddenly reactionary, reeling from the threats of anti-vice committees, churches and Bible-waving women's movements, the screens were being sanitized. There was to be no more immorality, no more smooching kisses and no more oversexed 'foreigners'; forty million Americans were going to be 'saved' by the moral clauses that were hastily slapped onto the contracts of remaining stars. Private detectives, snoops and tale-tellers began to terrorise the screen community. A covert list of blackened names was created, 'stars' were dumped, careers were axed overnight and film suddenly found itself crippled.

As the months passed and the recession bit deeper the penniless masses found that even the escapism of film was a luxury they could not afford. Crazy special offers and inducements were touted in an effort to boost ticket sales; two-for-one ticket deals, double features and free hair-do's for women were offered, but attendances halved. The Hollywood boom time was over. Only the vice continued. Prospered quietly. Squalor and broken dreams living alongside wealth and extravagance.

In a crazy upside-down world Bob was a frequent visitor to Tallulah Bankhead's apartment; Tallulah was 'in-town' filming *Thunder Below* (Her 'second worst ever' film) for Paramount. She hated film, but a $6,000-a-week fee somehow persuaded. Another of her coterie of regular visitors was Marlene Dietrich; Bob was in his element. Sucked seamlessly into the social glitterati, Bob received a printed invitation to a swanky party at Barrymore's mansion. All of his worldly possessions were crammed in a duffel bag, yet down at the bottom, creased and grubby, was an evening suit and black tie...

Braving the good-hearted derision and jeers of his threadbare companions he sponged his glad-rags off the best he could and set out. The message he left with was crystal clear however; if he wanted to come back he had better not do so empty handed. The party was an unashamedly glittering affair, the food was rich and the champagne flowed; Bob made the most of the luxury, yet he remembered his comrades. The duffel bag was loaded with bottles and choice goodies and at the close of the evening he set off home on foot. A crashing short cut through the brush saw him tumble out onto the road, pinned down in the headlight of a car. The occupants were fellow party goers who swept Bob up and deposited him, bag and all, no questions asked, at Santa Monica beach...

Living rough in the sun might have been acceptable as long as the booze and fags and the good fellowship held out but Newton saw that the Hollywood film game was up. A chance meeting with a young Canadian who had experience of ranching and was now headed north, made Bob finally realise that it was time to quit and he decided to tag along. Hitching, jumping freight-cars together, bumming up the coast, through the endless autumn of golden grasslands and up into the towering dark forests of Oregon, they could see that the effects of the depression were all-embracing. Winter was coming to the land; there were no jobs and Government work camps for single men seemed the only alternative to starvation. Shovelling snow for a few cents a day and a belly-full of rough food wasn't a living and the two men turned inland to the Thompson Plateau of the Rocky Mountains.

Originally a fur trading post, it was now the meat trading capital of the region. There Bob introduced himself to a ruddy-faced ranch owner, Lachlan McLeod, whose family had emigrated to Canada from Lewis, in the Outer Hebrides. Unsurprisingly McLeod was less than fulsome in his welcome; unlike the young Canadian, Bob didn't look like a cow-hand, and worse, sounded English. "How do you earn your bread?" McLeod growled. "I'm an actor." replied Bob. "An actor, y' say... well this is a man's job and ye don't look much like a man to me!" Exasperated and desperate Bob uttered a rounded Cornish oath. McLeod grabbed him by the throat and threatening to throw him off his land, demanding to know what language Bob had used. "Cornish", gasped Bob. This appealed to McLeod's Celtic notion of clansmanship and, suddenly, he was all smiles. Bob was offered a months trial, rock-bottom pay, and all the meat he could eat.

Bob settled in at once. The life was rough and dangerous, but he was happy. Once again he had found a home and friends. Weekdays were filled with backbreaking labour amid the hard beauty of the land and, as ever, the Friday and Saturday nights saw him on the town. Grub and drink, a chance to leer at the flyblown floozies and squander recklessly and gloriously every dollar he had. Christmas came and passed and the snow fell and obliterated the land. Yesterday's news came up late and yellowed and was read out in the dark evenings. Torn magazines and month old newspapers; Capone, jailed for tax evasion, Brit' girl Amy Johnson's lone flight to Australia, Bella Lugosi's 'Dracula' and Karloff's 'Frankenstein' showing in the big city cinemas. Coward's new stage hit. And the film of *Private Lives*. Letters from home, from girlfriends and mothers and wives.

As winter melted into spring Newton knew that he had to return to England, to the half forgotten woman who was his 'wife', to his child, to his mother and sisters and to the stage. He said his farewells and headed east. Somehow he got to driving a taxi and then someone booked a fare all the way to New York. The fare and the tip were just enough to pay the passage home to England. Before boarding the boat, Bob phoned the taxi company, told them where he had parked the cab, wished them good luck and promised to send the fare later...

4. The Shilling Theatre; His Own Rep'

Once again Bob stepped back onto English soil; it was the late spring of 1932. The same cold grey coast had emerged, fog-horn nebulous, muffled in the soft rain. Then at the dockside, in the confusion and crush, amidst the rich polyglot of English tongue, where the faces of strangers seemed somehow familiar, he knew that he was home.

Pauline and Joy were there to meet him, the 'kid' sisters he had left now both married women. Handsome and dressed to kill, they were dangerously vivacious. Bundled into a taxi, a flask of brandy and smothering kisses were his welcome home.

London had not changed. So little had changed. Except that there were more cars and more faces, and everything was rich and fat and bright and everyone was rushing and busy. There were big new shops, and big new buildings. Radios and Fascists. Warm English beer and English cigarettes, and war in China and bread that was sold already sliced. PG tea, Heinz soups and Mars Bars. The age of big ideas and mass consumption had swept in from America and covered up the old monochrome past. Now there were bright futures to strive towards and dull todays to escape from; London was a mass of overlapping cultures, spattered with red, where individuals had to tread carefully.

His mother laughed and cried in turns as he told his tales, recounted everything a dozen times; New York and California, Hollywood, the prairies. He was home, back in the place and amongst the people he had longed for, yet somehow the comforts felt too hot and too close, the rooms too tight. Air stale. He ate and drank too much. And he slept. Slept and slept, in soft, white laundered sheets, with the gentle sigh of English rain, on the roofs and on the neat suburban lawns and on the tarmaced pavements.

And then he remembered and was told. And somehow Peta was gone out of his life, and the baby, his daughter. The house in Chelsea was gone, shut up, the lease surrendered. The bits and pieces, all that was left of his marriage, thrown into boxes. He thought back to the sheaves of papers he had signed in New York, the solicitors gabbled babble, Coward's petulant nagging. The pages of crabbed print he had not bothered to read. The separation was done, final and absolute. He was to have no contact with his daughter, until she was sixteen and an adult. Absolutely; banned by writ. The news was shattering and he mourned into his whisky, dramatically and briefly; sentimental for the thing that never was.

But if his marriage had collapsed his career now promised to flourish; London was once again booming and Connie's agency was quickly on the phone. Almost too soon, dates and times and auditions were fixed. His America sojourn and Coward's plays had done his reputation no harm; Connie's had varnished up his successes and his Hollywood adventures and the theatre people wanted him back.

In early March, broke, lean and hungry, he secured his first contract. But not the stage work he expected; Connie's had booked him for another film role, a bit part in a sixty minute talkie 'short' entitled *Reunion*.

Commissioned at the gleaming new Shepperton studios, and a blatant vehicle for the talents of Stewart Rome, it was the first production for Sound City Film, a spin-off from the MGM combine. A virile, 'rugged man' pin-up star, whose allure lay in his looks rather than his limited acting skill, Rome had enjoyed a prolific movie output. Battling to escape the albatross appellation of Septimus Ryott, his first appearance in film was back in 1913; now he was proving to be one of the rare survivors of the transition to sound.

Set in sixty acres of parkland, the atmosphere that greeted Newton at Shepperton was utterly different from the carnival chaos of Stoll's silent stage. The advent of sound had seen an explosion in the growth of the film industry. If Hollywood was the industry's leader in terms of sheer production, it was an undeniable fact that intellectual and artistic leadership came from Europe. Relatively few films may have been made in Britain, and perhaps no great ones, but the country was the fertile seeding ground for cinematic quality.

Created just two years previously, Shepperton was plush, prestigious and fully geared-up for sound recording. Expecting bedlam Newton found instead a clinical and deadly silence. "Talkies, squeakies, moanies, squakies... just give them ten years to develop and you're going to see the greatest artistic medium the world has ever known." D W Griffith had crowed a decade before; now he was being proved right.

In order to survive, the film industry had been forced to move on; by the late 'twenties audiences had grown bored of silent flickering images and had begun to drift away. Suddenly radio was the new threat. Cheap and cheerful it was in almost every home and the lazy choice on a rainy night. The advent of the talkies catapulted the whole industry forward and films began to tell complicated stories with plot and depth. Perhaps predictably, the screen critics, who had spent years perfecting the art of sneering at silent film, suddenly reversed their positions; paeans of praise were being poured out over the 'beautiful art' that was dying...

Like Chaplin, the die-hards clung on to the past, but Newton could see the future; it was here, now, and he was part of it.

Film had grown up and, as Olivier had found in his New York run of *Private Lives*, it was to the stage that the film executives were turning. Theatre teetered on what seemed the brink of oblivion and actors began to cast eyes at the film dollar; most met rejection and the problem lay in their past. Grounded on tradition too many had a deep-rooted and artificial 'stage style'; orotund and declamatory their voices fell flat at the feet of film. Amongst the new generation of actors, Newton was young enough and clever enough to adapt.

The new technology of sound recording was however fraught with difficulties; ironically it demanded utter studio silence. This meant the development of a new form of stage lighting that did not give out a bedevilling low-frequency buzz. The new lights may have been silent but they threw out a terrific heat. Film stock had also advanced and shooting was done at 24 frame-per-second; this demanded three times the light of the old 16 frame-per-second process. Compounding the difficulties for actors, this combination meant that make-up had to be plastered on even more thickly to compensate for the flood of light that washed out shapes and features. On set, actors drooped visibly under the withering heat.

The search for silence also saw the camera locked into a tiny soundproof box; this seriously restricted its movement and so the actors had to perform around it. From watching Rome, Newton learned that instead of projecting out into an audience, it was the camera compartment and the microphone that had to be played to and a temporary immobility acted into the script for every spoken word.

"Quiet please, quiet... quiet!" The red light went on, silence stalked the sound-proofed studio like a monster and everybody but the terrified actors froze. Under the blazing lights conditions were hellish, mistakes and re-takes were frequent and the days dragged on endlessly. Film stock cost 2½d a foot, and up to 14,000 feet of film could be shot in a single day; hundreds of yards would be scrapped if the shadow of the microphone boom scythed across the set or a player fluffed his lines. Costs rocketed, the logistical difficulties were a nightmare and the eternal bug-bear was maintaining sound quality.

Reunion was an all-male, moral piece with a thirty-strong cast. An ironic little British character study, it saw Rome as 'a most likely to succeed type' giving a speech to his old chums about self-sufficiency and optimism in the face of worldwide depression. Unable to finance his trip to the gold paved streets of London, he is obliged to hock everything he owns. His gradual regaining of self-respect makes the focus of the drama.

Manipulated and directed by Ivar Campbell, Newton played out an unnamed background role and found the whole experience fascinating.

In the few years since *The Tremarn Case* British film-making had copied the American model and turned pro. The introduction of sound had changed the film-making process fundamentally. It had moved away from simplistic pictorial entertainment and towards that most central element of realism, character. Film-makers were beginning to use the same plot-structures as novelists and films had become sequential biographical narratives not just pictures that moved. For a stage actor used to the logical sequence of continuity, the stop and start process of film-making was, however, a nightmare. He could never act his part through from the beginning to the end except in his imagination. Hurled from moment to moment, the actor's time was dictated by floorspace, technical detail and the director's whim. All was held hostage to sound and continuity.

Yet for the public the talkies were the new wonder and, as they flocked to the cinemas, theatre faced oblivion. The music halls were worst hit. Outside London nearly all the provincial theatres closed their doors. It was only in the big cities that the mass of stage survived, destined, too often it seemed, to be patronised by the middle-brow middle-class, American tourists and parties of fidgeting schoolchildren.

British film-making may have grown up but it was still far from attaining the glamour of Hollywood. The Warner Brothers' toe-tappers were now the vogue, and glitzy musicals like *42nd Street* and *Footlight Parade* (1933) swept all before them. Home-grown film, still leaden paced and with relatively poor production values, struggled eternally against the British public's underlying puritanism. Neither had the British film actors yet been fully metamorphosed into 'stars' and the industry lacked the magic ingredient of 'marquee names'.

The process had started however; film producers were beginning to invest in their actors, putting them under contract and under the public gaze. Fan magazines were proliferating and popularity polls and talent competitions were all part of the creation of myth. British 'stars' lives were written up in the daily rags and in glossy books; they popped out of blazing billboards and smiled toothily from postcards. Advertising stepped in and the process of mutual promotion was begun. But somehow the idea of a 'British Film Star' was always an oxymoron and British film still lay somewhere between a fairground novelty and a new form of science.

The industry was nevertheless booming and millions were flooding into picture houses every week. Silent film was dead but the talkies had emerged from the still-warm corpse and were suddenly everywhere. By 1929 Hollywood was turning them out faster than British cinemas could convert to screen them. The American depression had devastated lives but it had also spawned an explosion of new art forms. Film meant escape and that, like Coward's *Bitter Sweet'*, came in the *Gold Diggers of 1933*, a soaring musical fantasy where hope meant survival in the face of seeming disaster. It came in laughter with Laurel and Hardy and the Marx Brothers and it came in horror, Lugosi's *Dracula'* in 1930, Karloff's *Frankenstein* in '31, *The Mummy* in '32 and the startling *King Kong* in '33.

Fascinated by the potential of film Newton was, like many actors, still dismissive of it as an art form. Film made the player a mere automaton, a slave to the director's eternal and maddening 'take' and 'take again'. He was a puppet to the script and the director, the sound and lighting engineers, and each had the puppet-masters say in every step and posture. In contrast theatre was untrammelled and spontaneous, where ad-lib and bluster and audience reaction were all part of the organic magic. Pocketing his pay cheque, Newton had very mixed feelings.

A call from Ivor Novello, an old family friend from the Rep' days, took Newton back to the more familiar and reassuring environment of theatre. Another of the new breed of 'stars' of the Coward mould, Novello was a supreme all-rounder; both stage and screen actor, a matinee idol, playwright and composer, he was dubbed 'the handsomest man in England'. The product of a puritanical Welsh background he was for millions of women the charming gay to vainly swoon for. The epitome of jazz age metrosexuality, offering an intriguing melange of drugs, inversion and utter respectability to the mass-market, his public persona had been laundered into middle-class whiteness by a domineering mother.

Like Coward, Novello was a driven and compulsive perfectionist, but where Coward's bitchily satirical works were a sour gall, his were brimming with glossy smiles and sunny good humour. His musical scores were on everyone's lips and across the country and across the empire 'Keep the Home Fires Burning' had become an unashamed retro patriotic anthem. Everybody's friend, he had toiled doggedly up the success ladder and graduating through minor successes and a few failures he had at last come into his own. Charming and generous, the eternal philanthropist, he happily contracted Newton into his new play.

Coincidentally Novello had been in America at the same time as Newton, but they had moved in very different worlds; as Bob had sweated up his dollar-a-day, Novello had basked in the fragrant Malibu world of Hollywood's good and great. Just returned to England and a hero's welcome he had two new plays tucked under his arm. The first was, *Party*, an overt piece of meta-theatre, in which he had pencilled in a bit-part for Pauline Newton. In the second, a bubbling, three-act comedy entitled *I Lived with You*, he had crafted a central lead role exclusively, and of course, around himself. It was a blatant piece of self-praise, and now he was gathering a constellation of satellite luminaries to reflect his brilliance.

Rehearsals were comprehensive and rigorous, the sets expensive. The winnowing process was thorough and those players who did not 'quite please' were quietly dismissed. The prospect of a successful run was almost certain; more gorgeous than his leading lady, Novello's presence alone equated to seats being sold out for weeks ahead. With professional precision, the play opened to a packed house at the Prince of Wales' Theatre on the 23rd March.

Newton walked on as 'Mort'. Another *Bitter Sweet* character, a social under-dog, 'Mort' was once again the dismissed boyfriend, the dullard fall-guy languishing in the glitter of Novello's showmanship. As in *Bitter Sweet* Newton's stage time was brief and his lines were sparse, eleven in the beginning of the first act and another six at the end. It was few enough for an actor who had become used to the status of leading man, but Newton was glad to be back in theatre, back in the incestuous little world he knew and loved, back with money in his pocket. In his own irrepressible and individual way he made the most of his lines.

The work was a familiar format comedy of misunderstandings. Laughter was splashed with a dash of bitterness, mixed and centred around Novello's camped-up character of an eccentric and penniless Russian prince who lodges with an equally eccentric Fulham household. A vodka cocktail, fizzing with saucy wit and romance, the work was an instant hit. The opening night saw Novello take a two-minute standing ovation. Even the curmudgeon critics were forced against their will to like it; "Novello's comedy was liberally sprinkled with quips that provoked that immediate ripple of laughter in the audience which indicates that they are without doubt enjoying themselves..." They called the casting "brilliant"; it was indeed Novello's 'best play to date' and seemed set to run on relentlessly through the summer nights.

The production did not go without a hitch, however. The usual run of colds and coughs hit the cast and as the days passed, freak summer heat sent temperatures inside the theatre soaring. Then, weeks into the run, and inevitably grown bored with the unchallenging secondary role, Newton committed *the* unforgivable sin; he appeared on-stage not only drunk but obviously drunk. Novello was outraged. A bundle of contradictions shot through with religious hypocrisy, he loathed and despised drunkenness. It was an act of betrayal that he could not, and did not forgive. His charm was more than skin deep but when angered, his eyes would narrow to pin-points of icebound fury whilst his ever-smiling mouth gave vent to a stream of shocking profanity. Guilty as charged, Newton took it on the chin.

As the weeks passed the heatwave brought the city to a near stand-still. The quality headed out to the sticks and the theatre season came to a premature close. Novello's play folded after a disappointing 120 outings, but the provincial tour was planned and was already over-booked. Expectations amongst the cast were high but Newton's services, however, were suddenly, but not unexpectedly, 'no longer required'. Never one to hold a grudge, Bob tried to patch things up at the traditional close-of-run party; he greeted Novello with good humour and an outstretched hand. Novello turned away coldly; "Don't *ever* expect me to shake hands with you", he hissed.

It was the end of another beautiful friendship.

Bob's part in Novello's play was nevertheless a publicity boost and another job soon came. Once again he was contracted by Nancy Price and her 'Peoples Theatre' for a production of the eternally popular *The Secret Woman*.

This was Newton's third stab at the piece. Banned in 1913 (although filmed in 1918, much diluted) and having caused a stir in parliament because it dared to touch on the murky subject of adultery, the author had bravely stood his ground and refused to bowdlerise his work. Now, in a cosmopolitan society where incest and murder were the standard comestible, the play, which had never actually been performed in the West End, still came with satisfying frisson of the risqué despite being deemed 'no more poisonous than a pint of cider...'. Staged at the five hundred seater Duchess Theatre in the West End, Nancy Price directed and appeared on stage as Anne Redvers; Newton took his old leading part as Jesse.

The 'Peoples Theatre' was a remarkable phenomenon; run 'for the people and owned by the people', each subscriber would be offered discounted seats and free admission to poetry readings, concerts and debates. Like Barry Jackson, Price refused to simply present the popular works and in the search for diversity turned to Shakespeare, Yates, Ibsen and Chekhov. Something of a red-tinged eccentric, she was a woman of unusual tastes and uncertain temper, content to operate out of a drab flat in Bloomsbury that she shared with a cantankerous and vilely incontinent parrot.

The Secret Woman opened to queues, a packed house and seats that were block-booked for weeks ahead. The critics approved, applause coming from the *Daily Sketch* who described the play as 'one of the finest pieces of acting to be seen in London just now'. Another critic judged the performance as 'unattached to un-commercial 'highbrow' values: a pretty piece of acting...'

London lay withering under the seemingly endless heat and in the late hours the velvet darkness seemed always to be filled up with the crackling radio dirge of Gourlay's *Brother can you spare a Dime*. Milking dollars from depression, the song raised up the ghost of a melancholic yesterday that seemed never to be shaken off.

Despite successes, more and more theatres were playing shortened runs or simply closing down. The theatre industry was in crisis and cinema was thriving in the wreckage. The talkies were here to stay. In 1929 only a handful had been produced, now, in 1932 alone, over a hundred and twenty had been shot in the UK. Hollywood, smelling gold, raced to make the technology its own. For the western masses, cinema had become part of the routine. Every week twenty million Britons, sixty per cent of them women, packed into the glamorous Art Deco palaces. Small provincial towns like Scunthorpe could offer the choice of nine 'flea-pits', the cities, dozens.

Central to the new age of film was the culture of the 'screen star'; mass-produced cultural icons, they were salesmen and saleswomen for everything from cars to cigarettes. Brilliant, artificial constructs, they were mimicked and adored by the millions. People would queue for hours to see the new 'picture', and when not at the flicks, they could dream of their idols with the cards they pulled out of their cigarette packs.

In November Newton joined the back of a cinema queue. He paid his shilling and sat down to watch the release of the latest picture, Reunion and as the people around him clapped and laughed and cheered, he enjoyed the surreal experience of watching himself perform.

Newton was now living in a rented place in Cheney Walk and, taking his father's advice, was rubbing shoulders with the capital's good and great. In the shiny new post-war world the class barriers had been pruned to mirror the forest of neat suburban hedges and the gentry now slummed it with the fashionably shabby-chic, the actors, writers and the penniless artists of Chelsea and Fitzrovia. With an appetite for nocturnal pleasures, Bobby, like many, gibed under the constraints of the pub opening hours that had been instituted to control the thirsty war-time munition workers. Tapping into this unfocused and potentially lucrative pool, David Tennant, a Cambridge graduate and husband of the actress Hermione Baddeley, had set up a private club in Soho's deliciously titled 'square mile of vice'.

The Gargoyle Club, he announced, was to be 'a chic night-club for dancing, but also an *avant garde* place... where people can express themselves freely in whatever manner they please.' The Gargoyle faced competition however, Ivor Novello's Fifty-Fifty Club, catering pretty much for the theatre 'Us' crowd, lay nearby. But with its walls adorned with ultra-chic mirrored tiles and paintings by Matisse and its rooftop garden overlooking the Kingdom of Theatreland, the Gargoyle soon became the alternative venue for society's peacocks. A place where rules were made to be broken and every passion catered for, and the club both encouraged and indulged. Here Noel Coward and Tallulah Bankhead could mix with the likes of Virginia Wolfe, T.S. Eliot, H.G. Wells and Randolph Churchill. Augustus John was an opening-night member alongside the patchwork of literati and twilight nobility.

Initially envisaged as a meeting-place for the rich, the famous and the well-connected, the more Dionysian factor of the worthy 'artistic poor' was, however, soon beating at the door. It was Newton's time to sign his name, with Augustus John his sponsor.

The Gargoyle had three floors and two faces. By day it passed as a relatively sober luncheon club, patronised by minor aristocracy and the wealthier Whitehall set. At night it transformed into a cosmopolitan arena, a theatre of sexual, social and intellectual challenge, of bravura display and emotional piracy where lofty minds stooped to dine on wayward beauty.

Imbued with Barry Jackson's ethic of art over commerce, and with an eye to Nancy Price's left-wing brand of stage politics, Newton had his own ideas about what made good entertainment; what the pubic wanted and what it needed. Reacting to the increasing dominance of cinema, frustrated by the endless succession of dumb, fall-guy parts and stung by Novello's icy rebuff, he longed for artistic independence. He wanted to prove his worth both as an actor and a manager and now looked to turn the dream of running his own theatre into a reality.

He had discussed it endlessly with anyone who would listen. Kicking the idea about with his mother, who was now practically living with Bob in Cheney walk, and his sisters, he found that all three were wildly enthusiastic. The how and the where, the pounds and shillings were abstract, mythological figures that were endlessly pulled from the smoky air, penned onto napkins and poured out of empty wallets.

In the provinces the theatre habit may have become an anachronism but in London it was still a richly anticipated pleasure for many of the gentry. Evening dress was de rigeur and the bonus was shuffling off for a late supper in a swanky club. With over forty theatres operating within a few miles of each other Bob knew that the competition would be stiff and that the core issue would be box-office pricing. Not everybody could afford a theatre ticket, or evening dress, and cinema was now a cheap, easy alternative. A visit to a glitzy 'Alhambra' or 'Alcazar' cinema cost as little as a shilling but a stall seat in any of the London theatres cost over twelve times as much. Even a decade before at the Birmingham Rep, the cheapest seats cost half a crown. Mainstream theatre, Newton argued, had effectively become an unaffordable luxury for most working people.

His plan was to run a big venue and to put on two performances every evening of the week, one at 6.30pm and another at 9.00pm; there were to be no boxes, no booking, and no segregation. Every seat would be priced at just a shilling, the same as a cheap cinema ticket.

The all too easy process of finding premises that were both vacant, suitably capacious and close to the heart of London should have rung warning bells about the state of the industry. The Palace Grand Theatre, Fulham, was once the home of musical comedy. A massive and crumbling baroque pile with a ghastly gingerbread interior, its architecture nodded heavily towards a pseudo Louis XIV style. Overloaded with gilded cherubs and caryatids, mirrors and marble, it belonged to a long gone age. Built in 1897 it was certainly vast, and it had probably never been full. Covering an area of twelve thousand square feet it had an enormous eighty foot by forty foot stage. More importantly, in economic terms, it had a huge pit and an expansive gallery and seated over two thousand. South-west of the city, near Putney Bridge, Fulham was a smut-grey and decidedly unredeemed district, a teeming ghetto far from the gloss of the West End; it had, however, a huge potential audience.

Suddenly finding their castle in the air a massive brick and stucco reality Marjorie, Pauline and Joy unleashed a charm offensive. Relentlessly they called in favours from old contacts, lovers and swanky friends. In an act of pure showmanship, Pauline and Joy, now also paid up Gargoyle 'belles de nuit', set up as 'pavement artists'. Both were now married, Pauline to Basil Murray, an aristocratic rake, and Joy, to 'Pung', Igor Vinogradoff, a similar type. Blithely they chose the hallowed flagstones outside the Ritz Hotel as their pitch; it was the regular watering-hole of both their husbands. Nor were the insouciant members of the Gargoyle Club spared the onslaught...

Amused and curious as to what exactly would come of the idea, the well-heeled opened their wallets; funds trickled in and a list of tentative backers was bullied into line. A meeting was arranged with the owners of the site, London District Council, and an outline business plan was presented. The council came back with a favourable decision but with a stinging caveat; for health and safety reasons they insisted that audience capacity should be capped at one thousand, less than half of the building's capacity. Worse, they dictated that the backers would have to stump up the estimated three thousand pounds needed to put the building into some sort of repair. The decision was a blow, appeals were made, but the council would not budge. At a gathering of the conspirators, the numbers were recalculated. Late into the night it was decided that the project was still viable.

Hands were shaken over a lease agreement, a management committee was assembled and the eminent and affluent who had laughingly nodded their support suddenly found themselves on the 'committee'. The declared lessees were 'Robert and Joy Newton', the Chairman the 'Earl of Carlisle'. The Committee itself was an eclectic mix, most were society names, all swept in from the very heart of London high society; Viscount Castlerosse, Lady Georgina Mure, Baroness Ravensdale, Lady Ankraet Jackson, Marjorie Newton, Count John McCormack, Henry Ainley and Margaret Bannerman, William Hutter, Robert Boothby MP, and Augustus John.

This cosmopolitan mix was very much to Newton's taste and style. Viscount Castlerosse, an Irish peer was the director of the Evening Standard, Baroness Ravesdale was the daughter of Lord Curzon and wife of Oswald Mosely. Henry Ainley and Margaret Bannerman were prolific film actors and household names. Robert Boothby was a genius whose morality was as catholic as his politics. John McCormack was another Irish-American, a world-renowned tenor and concert performer. The named supporting 'Artistes' were Margaret Bannerman, Roy Emerton, Edwin Ellis, Manna Karina, Ben Weldon, Joy Vinogradoff (Newton), Bennett O'Loghlen, Geoffrey Wilkinson, Gabrielle Casartelli and Eric Maturin, all household names who encompassed a wide experience in film and stage.

The chaos of getting the theatre actually up and running seemed, for Bob, very much like being back in Birmingham only twelve years earlier; sweeping, painting and effectively living rough seemed strangely familiar. But now he was also handling endless meetings, hiring theatre staff and players, setting up a bar, contracting an orchestra, organising rehearsals and all the time drowning in a vortex of bureaucracy. The telephone never seemed to stop, "Putney 2248...". No one got much sleep in the days running up to the opening. Something of the old Lamorna spirit had swept in with Augustus John however, and the old family had gathered back together. Algernon had been imperiously summoned and obediently appeared.

In the autumn of the previous year Algernon had staged his first solo exhibition, his striking studies of sun-soaked stucco walls put on display at the prestigious Leicester galleries; now a can of gloss and a brace of haggled brushes were thrust at him and he found himself daubing the sets and scenery cloths that John had designed. At first there was a difficult reserve between himself and Marjorie; Algernon saw clearly that his decision to leave Marjorie had been the right one, and that a life with her would have become an impossibility, yet there was little time for social niceties. Marjorie was everywhere and everything, acting book-keeper, secretary and accountant; she answered the telephones, interviewed and hired staff and had a say in the choice of planned productions. Pauline and Joy, still both fund-raising, threw themselves into the event unstintingly. Between the spates of frantic work, frequent calls to the King's Arms, conveniently just next door, were obligatory. Christmas was almost forgotten, lost in the boozy, frantic, blur. Of brother Nigel there was no sign. He was over in Dublin, they said, struggling with his oils.

The grand venture was named the 'Shilling Theatre', (Interestingly in 1912 the theatre had often been used as a cinema; then it was also dubbed 'The Shilling Theatre'...) and on January 14th, a chill and squally Saturday evening, the doors opened for the first production. A flyer distributed to the public announced, 'It's not going to be an art theatre, presenting 'highbrowism' – it's not going to be a training school for amateur players and authors - a club or a philanthropic institution. Clever business brains have shown that it is possible to run a theatre of a certain size successfully at prices never dreamt of, in or outside of the West End...'. Fine words; Bob might have wondered why those 'clever business brains' had never tried it for themselves. He was about to find out why.

The opening was a big night for Newton, and, for a man of just twenty eight, a massive achievement. Patrons were greeted with a foyer that was hung, like at the Birmingham Rep', with art works, all for sale and 'all under three guineas!' Aggressive in self-promotion news of the project was announced to the press and interviews were given. 'If it succeeds...' the *Times* reported, '...it will be followed by a number of similar theatres, probably to the number of eight, which will constitute a circuit on which plays organised under the scheme will be sent...'.

The 'Shilling's' opening programme consisted of four roller-coaster short works. The first was a comedy piece, *Elegant Edward*, a favourite that Newton had performed with Hutchison's troupe in South Africa. This was followed by *The Olive Orchard*, then *Always Apologise*, finishing with a nautical comedy *In The Zone*. Newton himself walked out to thunderous applause in three of the works. "Every seat was taken..." The *Times* raved. The quartet ran for two weeks, until February 6th, when the bill changed. Newton now desperately needed a breathing space and a touring group of players over from Ireland was hired in to put on a more than authentic rendering of Sean O'Casey's *Juno and the Paycock*.

Without time for thought or introspection the theatre was up and running. A mixed herd came in through the doors every night; working men and women, the students and artists from Chelsea, journalists and critics. The Gargoyle cronies rolled in along with the pleasure seekers attracted away from the perhaps too familiar glitz of the West End, all looking for Newton's unique brand of racy pleasure.

Once again Bob immersed himself in the topsy-turvy, nocturnal theatre world. Close of show meant drinks and there was always a party to go on to, always music, always dance, always the reeling swirl of delirium. Night once again became his day, and day his short night.

May 1st saw a new production, Patrick Hamilton's *Rope*. Premièred in 1929 and based on a true case, the work looked at the anatomy of a motiveless murder. It was a brilliant snapshot of a post-war generation that wallowed in privilege, booze and a shallow obsession with fashion and film, yet was drowning in a desperate inner emptiness. Alec Guinness was in the audience and judged the performance as one of 'wit and urbanity which managed to combine decadence and moral fervour; it was also very dangerous'. 'Dangerous' lay not in the concept of murder but in the work's touching on the edgy subject of homosexuality. Newton appeared on stage alongside an old friend from his early days and the abortive production of *A Perfect Fit*, the outrageous and flamboyant American-Jew, Ernest Milton. Significantly Milton was freshly blooded from a spell of theatre management; having taken a lease on the twelve-hundred seater St James he had presented his own idiosyncratic brand of *Othello* and *The Merchant of Venice*. Seats had remained stubbornly empty and the venture had spiralled into financial disaster.

A rich character, much in Newton's vein, Milton had a disconcerting penchant for gerrymandering and was loathe to exit a stage unless it was, mid-play, to pop out for a 'quick one'. He had agreed to appear in *Rope* in return for leading a production of his own choice; in this case it was agreed that he would take the lead in a later production, *Lorenzaccio*.

The Shilling's following production was a safe, sure-fire crowd puller; a profitable trip down memory lane; a lively rendering of *Her Cardboard Lover* yielded good press reviews and satisfyingly full houses.

The months passed and to everyone's surprise Newton's theatre seemed to be proving more than a one-week-wonder. The *Observer* wondered why; '...in a time of "cut price" theatres its finances have remained something of a mystery. West End 'stars' and companies have played there. The level of drama has been high. The natural assumption is that some mad Maeceanas has had a fortune to throw away on the venture...'. In his dressing room, bleary-eyed and none too well for wear, Newton patiently explained his philosophy and the mystery of his finances "If you want to know the exact weekly finances" he said, "I can give them to you... there is no mystery about them. We depend on three things, a low theatre rent, a *large* theatre and the co-operation of our actors. Also upon a twice nightly policy... We started with the idea of a shilling stall being a definite counter-attraction to the cinema. We toyed with the idea of having a few seats at two shillings, but then I remembered that I myself have often come away from a cinema because I could not get in for less than two shillings...the single exception is the gallery which is sixpence, and oddly enough we find that this is not used much. People seem to prefer to pay their shilling and to come nearer the house. The gallery is chiefly used on Saturday nights and then by people who have tried to book shilling seats and found them all sold out". With growing passion he stressed his policy of offering leading actors a minimal salary but with the option of lead role in any production they chose. Breaking down the figures, Newton continued '...the theatre holds a thousand seats, which with its shilling stalls and sixpenny gallery gives an approximate capacity of £40 a performance, there are twelve performances a week on our twice nightly system, which means a capacity of £480 a week, our expenses are roughly as follows. Theatre rent £20, lighting £10, Company salary £80/£100, Theatre staff £40, Rates £5, Printing, billing and advertisements £30, Author's royalties £20, a total of £205..."

"All in all, in good weeks, we have made as much as £30 a week profit on the theatre, which, again, is not a lot, and has to be set off against the weeks when we have only just cleared expenses...but the important thing is that at the moment we are relying on half-capacity...if we can run and keep going on this it suggests that we have a permanently workable proposition...We already have an interesting and regular public drawn from Putney, Hammersmith, Fulham, Roehampton, and the painters and students of Chelsea. We find that we have a dedicated clientèle of five or six thousand who have the *habit* of coming to us once a week, partly because we are as cheap as, or cheaper than, cinemas and partly because they like the drama which we provide. The standard of taste is on the whole very high...".

The enterprise did indeed seem to be flying. A Grand Charity Concert was organised for the Fulham Unemployment Fund which included a boy genius playing Chopin and Villa Lobos and finished with the renowned Black American Paul Robeson singing.

The big names from the West End stages, curious enough to risk their reputations, now tacked onto the slipstream. Actors who would later become household names appeared cap in hand, Alistair Sim, Margaret Rutherford, Jessica Tandy amongst them.

The famous Irish Players appeared again in February in Sean O'Casey's *The Shadow of a Gunman* and in March with *The Plough and the Stars,* Newton throwing his weight in with the latter production.

On April 3rd the curtain rose 'for one week only', presenting *The Magnet*, 'a new and original Play in three acts by Marjorie Newton'. Rather pathetically autobiographical, it was her sentimental reworking of the dreamed-for marital reunion with Algernon and lacked any form of conventional structure. '...An indifferent and badly-produced play', the critics carped, which 'in spite of some good acting it does not in any way help the cause of the theatre locally, either at a shilling or at any other price...'. 'It contains enough, and more than enough, material to fill a three volume novel...' another reviewer spluttered. For Bob it was a financial loss but it was an act of pure loyalty.

By this stage Marjorie had become, in the words of the woman who was to become her daughter-in-law, 'alarmingly eccentric'. Now a passionate Christian Scientist, she believed that Algernon's desertion was merely an aberration and that once he had been on a 'spiritual journey to find Truth' he would see the error of his ways and returning to his loving family, would be reconciled. She put all this in her play. If not well written, the play did at least authentically portray Marjorie and her children's chaotic lives...

Joan Littlewood, a woman who in later years would run her own theatre group, was at this time homeless. In desperation she had knocked on dozens of doors without luck until she arrived at Bob's place in Cheyne Walk. "What do you do?" asked Marjorie. "Well, I write, and...". "God sent you... come in!" Marjorie trilled. It turned out that God had sent Joan to translate a book Marjorie had written. "Into which language?" Joan asked. "Into a film!" Marjorie replied. Not unused to a little eccentricity, Joan would soon find her new 'family' more than a handful. Installed, rent free, in the basement, she set about knocking out the film script. Scanning through Marjorie's notes she found a delirious portrayal of the family with 'Bobbie stuffing his dress suit into the copper fire, introducing whores to his mother when she was lying in bed, and robbing the gas meter'. Unable to work the jumble of material into any kind of sense she appealed desperately to Marjorie. "God never made a woman without a shilling" was all Marjorie would say.

Dutifully Joan struggled on, then the great day came when the script was deemed as finished. Algernon was ordered to appear, as was Anthony Asquith, one of the finest film directors of the day whose 1929 *A Cottage on Dartmoor* was rated one of the finest British silent movies ever made.

Tea was issued to the select audience and the 'Great Reading' was carried through without interruption...

Bobbie (The eldest son)

Listen, family. I've found out what's the matter with Dad.

He's thirsting after goodness.

Peggy (Youngest daughter)

Like we used to after cocktails...

When the last page was read there was a long, difficult, silence.

By April, overburdened by the workload, Newton had hired a full-time manager and, struggling to balance the books, an early decision to absorb the burden of the despised 'Entertainment Tax' in the door price was overturned. Now, and indicating that the 'good weeks' were becoming fewer, it was slapped on top of the ticket price. A 'few Special Stalls and Dress Circle seats, 2/6 (including tax)' had also been worked into the equation.

The end of May saw Ernest Milton's promised production; Alfred de Musset's *Lorenzaccio*, one of the few productions in which, according to the inexplicable lore of theatre, the lead 'male' role could be taken by a woman.

Anglicised to *Night's Candles*, it was a gory tale of corruption and murder and one of Newton's favourites. Very much a grand-scale production, the work went out in three acts with Newton and Milton at the fore of a cast 'half-a-mile long, (a staggering thirty five in fact, including Margaret Rawlings, one of the new stage stars) thirteen scene changes and acres of Renaissance scenery...'

By now the theatre programmes had been contracted out to the 'Theatrical & General Advertising Co' and their 'Magazine Programme' and for their threepence the punters now got a neat little ten-page book. For *Night's Candles* there was an interview with actress Isobel Jeans shoehorned between a competition quiz, 'Our Empire Page', 'Your Hair' and adverts for Lyons' chocolates, Schweppes soda waters, and Abdulla cigarettes...

The production opened on Monday, May 29th, 'every evening at 8.0, matinees: Thursday and Saturday at 2.30'.

Set in sixteenth century Florence, the work plunged into the murky world of the Medici. The *Times* reviewed the production with reservation. Milton's lead role was described as 'developing a character of uncommon insight', '...a part of rare flexibility and colour', yet it also observed that the play was overly top-heavy and one that would have been 'greatly enhanced if there were not elsewhere in the play so many diversions that confused its form'.

The *'Observer's'* critic commented positively on the breadth of a production of 'incredible energy'...' with its huge cast and relentless scene changes 'all for the price of a shilling stall...'. It could not, however, resist a jibe about Milton's propensity for stage-hogging and a disastrously missed lighting cue in the final and decisive moment that left him holding up the poised and murdering dagger, bathed in a cheerful flood of limelight and with nowhere to plunge it...

Unfailingly, night after night, the Shilling opened its doors and a show was put on. Some failed to come up to the mark, some failed to bring feet through the door, but as Barry Jackson had found, the old standards were eternally popular and well attended. The critics, a cabal whom actors had long regarded, as the saying went, 'much as lamp-posts feel about dogs', curmudgeonly with their praise, were forced to accept that Newton's theatre project was a runner. The pressures on players and staff, and Newton in particular, were however immense. Only a half hour interval lay between the two evening shows so a room had been cleared out backstage so that Bob could snatch a few minutes of sleep. Much fatigue was, of course, self-inflicted; the party circuit was relentless and, on stage and off, Bob was always at the fore. During one afternoon rehearsal the alarm was suddenly raised 'My God, the sprinklers are working...!' 'Here...' shouted Bob from above '...I'm having a pee!'

Passion was sustained by a cocktail of booze and adrenalin, and that was what the people came to see. Every performance was an event and every event was a performance. Performances were, however, frequently delayed. The pub next door might have been deliciously comfortable but audiences were often less than amused when late, and obviously merry, the cast would stumble onto the stage. The chant of "Drunk... drunk... drunk ...!" would rattle through the auditorium but it was all part of the great game, just as it was when Bob was with Lawson in the *Henry VIII* tour; "You think I'm drunk..." he would again roar out to the sea of laughing faces, "you wait until you see....".

Bob was nevertheless as much a perfectionist as Coward and Novello. He always demanded and always gave his best; sometimes that best needed a little Dutch courage. Young actors and students of the theatre began to come from miles to see Bob at work. Tricks learnt from the Rep' were carried faultlessly onto the Shilling's stage. The creaking boards of the proscenium trammelled neither the players nor their imagination; audiences were often suddenly and uncomfortably aware of a gaping hole in continuity and a line hanging unanswered in the air. Then a voice would shout out from the stalls "This is me...I'm on!" and a figure would shamble inelegantly onto the stage. The audience would gasp, break into embarrassed laughter, but it's Newton, who throws himself into the play seamlessly...

Newton's productions were, by design, a million miles from Coward's 'Amiable Evenings', but not everyone appreciated his Rabelaisian style. One young actress, Elizabeth Monde, timorously noted in her diary, 'I started rehearsing for another play at the Shilling Theatre this morning... God help me!' But it was that style that made the theatre what it was; it was Newton himself.

Like Algernon, Laura Knight had now broken away from the formal training that had so inhibited her style and she was finding that her paintings were in demand. Working as manically as in her Lamorna days, she nevertheless found time for her prodigy's latest stage output whenever she was in London; that night, she noted, Bob was playing to the crowd, running a skirmishing banter; 'Shut up, you bastards!' he shouted back at the audience...

With a mixture of sweat and blasphemous brilliance Newton steered his theatre through the precarious weeks, aware that both friends and creditors were watching with unblinking eyes. With his usual cheek and charm he managed to talk Leontine Sagan, one of the leading woman producers of the day (and a director for Novello), into handling his October offering, *Finished Abroad*. In this light hearted and contemporary tragedy/farce, Newton was the sole male on stage and comfortably surrounded by a bevy of beauties. Brilliantly performed, the work was chalked up as another ringing success.

Coinciding with the twenty-first birthday of Jackson's Birmingham Rep', the Shilling's next production, *Saturday's Children*, was imported wholesale from the Westminster Theatre and the cast now played alongside Newton who took over the lead role from his old Rep' pal, Colin Keith-Johnston.

In line with the other London venues, the Shilling closed its doors for a short summer break, then with the population drifting back into town, prepared to open again. Inevitably, the passing weeks saw the first rush of popularity die away and balancing the books had become a battle. The run-up to the Christmas season, however, brought a gift in the form of a script that Newton knew would be a hit. The play was *The Greeks had a Word for It*, an 'extremely transatlantic' work by Zoe Akins. It was a bawdy tale of three outrageous gold-diggers and Newton knew exactly who he wanted to take the two leading roles, David Tennant's actress wife Hermione, 'Totie' to her friends, and her sister Angela.

Clutching the script in his hand, his arrival at the Tennants' home was typical. 'I was sitting on a high green bank at Telfont,' Hermione Baddeley recalled, 'looking at the carpet of daffodils in front of me, when I noticed a figure staggering up the drive. A man who looked as if he'd slept in his clothes the night before came into view, his thick black hair was tousled, his face flushed and his gait unsteady. He yelled a greeting and immediately collapsed at the bottom of my bank. I slid down towards him. Robert Newton, who had obviously called at more than one pub on the way, grinned up at me. He managed to tell me that he had a play for me to read...' Only too aware of Newton's financial straits and his inability to pay West End rates, or indeed pay at all, she nevertheless knew that for Newton to stagger this far away from Fulham he must have found something electrifying; 'If he found a reasonable play' she said 'he often got his friends to appear for nothing. And because Bobby Newton could be quite brilliant at choosing plays people did listen to him... I listened to him now...'.

Newton indeed knew where public taste lay, it lay low-down and dirty. Baddeley had become the new Bankhead and *The Greeks'* was to be her *Cardboard Lover*. She agreed to take the part and the play was hurried through rehearsals and put into production for the pre-Christmas run.

The opening night was packed. Next morning Newton blearily scanned the crabbed columns of the dailies. The critics had roundly damned the production as 'banal and crude', 'a conglomeration of drunken orgy, gold digging, debauchery and dirty work generally put together so untidily that the only thing that might be described as Greek to anybody was the plot...'. Bob smiled, the thing was a smash-hit and they loved it!

As the critics correctly pointed out, there was more than enough 'undressing' on the stage; it was exactly the sort of play and the sort of review that brought paying customers through the doors. '"Never look a gift-horse in the mouth", is the old adage, and to expect more for a shilling than a brilliant characterisation by Miss Hermione Baddeley.....' Another reviewer remarked, 'Banal and crude...', but with the lure '...even so, Miss Hermione Baddeley and Mr Robert Newton almost tempt me to have another shillingsworth. If they appeared against a more edifying background I would pay ten times as much....'

The play could have run for ever but true to word and creed Newton gave it just a fortnight's run, like all the others. Out in the real, West End, world the play was greedily snapped up...

In the illusory nocturnal world Newton inevitably gathered in his wake a cloud of yarns. As Proust had long since observed, given enough time falsehood becomes truth. The rumour that the Prince of Wales had attended an evening performance and had sat 'incognito' next to a charwoman was never substantiated, but the tales of drunkenness were true and the local police knew Newton only too well. Too often they had gently swept him up 'drunk and disorderly' for a night's sleeping-it-off in the cells. Always urbane, always charming, always full of apologies the next morning, Bob would make friends and laughter over breakfast before dashing back to the theatre, a tin mug of coffee in one hand and the latest script in the other. A regular in every pub and bar for miles around, he left hats, canes and coats, outrageous tips and bad debts. And everyone who met him was charmed, left reeling, shaking their heads, filled up with a priceless anecdote to be related and embellished.

Some tales were true: one night at the Gargoyle, Bob had taken on-board a bit more than usual. It fell to Jack Marks, the club's receptionist and kindly factotum, to suggest an early taxi home. Bob reacted badly, the situation developed into a scuffle and Jack got bitten on the hand. The next afternoon in Soho, Jack bumps into Bobby; Bobby, profuse with theatrical apologies, falls on his knees, kisses the bandaged hand, then throws himself into the gutter, wailing for forgiveness. Jack is terribly embarrassed. Forgiveness is given. Backs slapped. Hands shaken, gently...

The end came after two exhausting years. Standards never dropped off but no one had really expected it to go on for ever. Few had expected it to go on for more than a few weeks. Stages across the country were falling silent, shouted down by film; even Percy Hutchison's speculative theatre venture in York had crashed. The Shilling had been a remarkable achievement, it had opened every night for two years, two winter and two summer seasons. Forty-eight plays had been put on and Bob had led in most of them. In the depths of an international recession and within an industry in crisis, Newton had succeeded where others had failed; succeeded with a mixture of brilliance and sheer hard work. An entrepreneur extraordinary he had brought pleasure to thousands, made an enduring name for himself and perpetuated the art. It had never been about the money or personal fame, it had been about a passion for the stage.

By now Bob had more than ever become a 'name'. Aldous Huxley (Author of *Brave New World*, 1932), another man who had drunk from the muddy pool of Hollywood and tasted the bitter sweetness of the dollar, now approached Newton. .. 'I met last night the man who runs the Shilling Theatre at Fulham. He expressed a desire to look at *Now More Than Ever*, and I think it would be a good idea to send him a copy...I think he might possibly give it a show...'.

He was too late however. Bob's penultimate production opened on November 19th, a production of Edgar Wallace's play *The Green Pack*. A fast paced three acter it included in its cast, and was directed by, none other than Percy Hutchison...

The wheel had turned full circle; Newton was now employing the man who gave him his big break a decade before.

The final night for the Shilling was on February 12th 1934. A struggling Rex Harrison appeared, playing under Newton in *Anthony and Anna*. "I remember one amusing play I appeared in by St John Ervine, called *Anthony and Anna'* he later recalled, 'in which I played a chap who is allergic to work, but graciously hires himself out occasionally for luncheons, dinner, or country weekends. My co-stars were all excellent actors..." Then came the retrospective and snooty caveat, "But all this was at a theatre called The Shilling, in Fulham...". The wage packet must have compensated for the perceived lack of prestige, because he had previously taken up Newton's offer, and had appeared in an Oscar Cook play, *Division*, alongside Donald Wolfit.

The curtain closed for the last time. Bob walked out alone, and bowed. Cheers, champagne, flowers and tears. Bob was just twenty-nine. The Shilling was sold on as a going concern, a new management buying out the lease and taking over the theatre that Newton had re-launched and sailed it on unsteadily into the nights...

At the outset of the grand venture Bob had talked fulsomly to journalists about 'the first Shilling Theatre' and of his hopes that it would spawn a chain of half a dozen, ringing the capital. It was a dream and a vision he would return to two decades later, in a different country and a different age.

Out on the high streets the floodlit cinemas rolled out the latest talkie sensation, Novello's *I Lived with You*. Shot at the glitzy new Twickenham studios, the old stage cast played out the familiar routine, except that the role of Mort was now played by the young man who had taken Newton's place on the tour, Jack Hawkins. Another young player got her film break here too, Ida Lupino; like so many she swept up the press clippings and departed for Hollywood...

5. Another Brush With Celluloid

Thirties British cinema had always been the home of melodrama. Unsubtle, somehow innocent, somehow typically 'British', it served up to the masses a diet of chorus girls carved up by impeccable ex-officer types in seedy seaside hotel rooms, the doping of racehorses and a blasé obsession with foreigners. Somehow it was all as familiar and as reassuring as beer on Saturday night and the Sunday family roast. For the film industry the nervous honeymoon period was over and film-going had become a national obsession and a routine part of life.

The hung-over dawn saw Newton glance behind him and know that he had stepped out somewhere between the new royalty status of 'stardom' and notoriety. The critics' reviews, the press calls and the sycophantic friends had made him both a 'name' and a slave to that name. It was as they had said long ago at the Birmingham Rep', he was now in bondage to the telephone and his agent, to the carping critics and the applause of the crowds. The passage of his life was mapped by yellowing newspaper clippings. And already Vere-Barker from Connie's was calling, hassling, making the offers, talking big money, talking exposure...

All around him three million were waking to unemployment, to idleness and disease, misery and crime, prostitution and booze. Newton picked up the morning papers and read of the irrefutable words shouted from Moseley's soapbox stage. He read of the Jarrow March and the revolution that never was; read that far away in Cornwall the fishing town of Newlyn was at war with itself. 'Progress' had come even to that far-away place and the old was being swept away. There were the usual short-sighted protests, the artists up in arms.

And everywhere there was talk of 'the next war'.

And yet the Thirties were also a boom time; it was the decade of the car, the cinema, and the suburban semi; it was an age of self-conscious modernity that laid the foundations for post-war affluence. Certainly there was no place for gloom in the fantasy world of theatre. Pessimism was 'muck' that was spread by 'panic-mongers' to 'jitter-bugs'. Laughter and affluence, cigarettes and whisky masked the diurnal frowns.

Quickly Newton was back at work. By May he had thrown himself into the role of a dashing Irish pilot, Patrick O'Leary in *Once Upon a Time*. Put on at the suitably named, three hundred-seater, Little Theatre in the Strand and directed by Esme Percy, the work opened on the 14th. Translated from French, the plot was aptly described as 'a sort of Grand Guignol thriller with a happy ending', a satisfyingly action-packed tangle of 'blackmail, murder and nefarious schemes'. The stage was filled with barbarian but charmingly incompetent kidnappers and a disfigured heroine who recovers her beauty at the hands of her intended victim. The yarn galloped along ludicrously; the crowds seemed to love it but the critics didn't. Suddenly all war-serious and looking for highbrow intellectualism, they damned with faint praise; 'the play is essentially old fashioned', 'rather tedious' and filled with 'a great many... stock theatrical situations'. Only Newton's reviews were good; 'Mr Robert Newton was natural, easy and sympathetic...', his performance displaying his natural, off-stage, 'easy charm'.

In the run-up to the hectic pre-Christmas season, Newton shifted to the Duke of York's and a favourite comic role, Boris Feldman in *The Greeks Had a Word For It*.

After its thunderous run at the Shilling, the work had transferred straight to the West End. With the bawdy chemistry working on as well as off the stage, Newton, impeccably dressed in white tie and tails, worked superbly opposite the rich comic flirtations of the Baddeley sisters and Margaret Rawlings. Fashionably dressed by Norman Hartnell, the trio's wise-cracks came thick and fast, and the play became *the* must-see, hit of the season.

Actress Googie Withers, accompanied by some very 'correct' and 'countrified' friends who she was cautiously introducing to the grown-up experience of London town, joined the queue to see the play. Having lapped up every saucy moment, the Arcadian contingent asked excitedly to be introduced to the 'stars'. Withers was apprehensive, but Bob had appeared to be sober enough... "Backstage he was impeccable" she recalled, "and received them graciously, asked them to sit down and engaged them in intelligent conversation about the play...and then in the middle of a sentence he turned around and urinated in a wash basin..."

By the end of February the play had decamped to the capacious Cambridge Theatre before spiralling out to Bob's old patch and the Theatre Royal in Birmingham and the provinces. Night after night throughout the summer the cast delighted new audiences. Riding on a crest of delirious applause it seemed that the thing would run for ever. Inevitably, after a long year of playing the same role nightly, Newton had had enough: enough flea-bitten hotels and enough seedy towns. Looking for a change for the coming Christmas season and a return to the sophistication of London, he slipped back to the Cambridge Theatre to direct and co-produce *Success Story*, a brassy tale of New York big business and a personal favourite from his Shilling days.

That year the New Year's Eve party at the Gargoyle was one of the best ever; everyone turned up and balloons, funny hats and streamers were the order of the day. To the delight of all, a tame Palace equerry, 'Fruity' Metcalfe, spilled the beans of life behind the palace doors and the latest gossip about the Wallis Simpson affair. Champagne flowed, kisses followed and the nagging thoughts of Hitler and Mussolini were pushed to the background...

The new year saw Newton at the Arts Theatre Club in Leicester Square. Registered as a private club, its productions lay outside the stifling remit of the Lord Chamberlain's censorious eye and the venue was renowned for its controversial productions. An appearance at the 'Arts' was one which many actors, cautious of their career and reputation, turned down; Bob however jumped at the chance.

The new work was a production of Strindberg's gruelling tragedy *Miss Julie* and Bob's part was that of 'Jean', a valet and the lover of his master's frighteningly deranged and suicidal daughter. The second part of a double bill, following Helge Krog's *The Copy*, *Miss Julie* was demanding in the extreme, minimalist in style and one of sustained and grim intensity. In a small and intimate theatre and on stage throughout, unsupported by peripheral and distracting activity, it was a bravura role for Newton.

The play opened on January 25th and expectations were high, yet the mood and taste of the public had been badly misjudged; suicide was definitely off the menu. The next day's papers saw the critics slating the piece; 'Strindberg's *Miss Julie* is a fine piece of grim writing but needs to be perfectly acted if it is to have its due effect. Last night's performance'... 'fell far short of perfection'... 'Robert Newton, who played the footman, failed altogether to suggest the man's essential commonness and lack of breeding.' Suitably convinced, the public stayed away and after just two performances, played to half-empty houses, the production closed.

Newton shrugged, took some time out and at the end of March turned his attentions to Nancy Price's new production at the Little Theatre. "A programme of four one-act plays..." the Times reported, "included a new piece by Mr St John Ervine, *Ole George Comes to Tea...*". Put out as a series of matinee performances the gentle quartet seemed to please. Bob appeared in 'Ole George...' as one half of a young couple facing the surprise of imminent parenthood and produced a piece the critics judged 'a pretty sketch'. Remaining in the services of Nancy Price he moved on to a short run of W. B. Yeates' *The Player Queen*.

Tirelessly moving on Bob was quickly hired back in the familiar environment of the Duke of York's, where he welcomed a contrast from the bleakness of 'Miss Julie', *Roulette*.

A joyously frivolous comedy-farce that traded on the far away and exotic myth of Monte Carlo, the work spun around the roulette table, where a newly-wed wife is abandoned for the attraction of the wheel, husband turns rotter, cad becomes eloper and immaculately dressed vultures circled speculatively.

Taking the role of Mark Gresham, a suave philanthropic philanderer, Newton's role was that of the cad/eloper. Glittering, sophisticated, racy and a million miles from a cold and grimy London, the play, like *The Greeks...* and *Private Lives*, had all the zest and escapist ingredients for a hit. Opening in May with a cast including Margaret Railings, hot from her part in *The Greeks...,* the first night saw a packed house and closed to thunderous applause. The next morning's *London Sketch* raved about the 'brilliant, cynical, comedy'. *Stage* magazine said Newton leant 'all his quiet charm to the figure of the middle-aged Gresham'. The play was a hit; laughter came in through the foyer and stayed throughout, yet some critics still grumbled. One wrote 'Robert Newton, as the other party to Lisa's elopement, plays with sincerity; but the monotony of his delivery ends by spoiling his work'. Contrarily *The Bystander* complained that Newton was too young for the part...

Like *The Greeks* the play roared through the Christmas season and threatened to run for ever. Never one to sell out for boredom, Newton handed over his part at the end of March and took up another invitation from Nancy Price and her Peoples National Theatre company.

The new work was *Whiteoaks*, a saga of a French-Canadian family which was to become a personal favourite for Newton. Working as director he also took the lead role of 'Rene'. Staged at the Little Theatre, the quiet, timeless charm of the piece was apparent to the punters, but not always to the players. Tall, gaunt and commanding, Nancy Price forced her ideas onto her actors with her overpowering, frightening personality. One player, sick of the bullying, had already quit the cast; she had left a note stuck to her dressing-room mirror... 'Gone Mad. Gone Home..'. Bob, however, had been there before and knew what to expect.

Whiteoaks told a tale of stability to an audience troubled by uncertainty and the work captivated, ran to packed houses and broke records. The *Times* showered praise on the work, and the "clumsy, shy, tautly strung boy, and even more remarkably – for here the obvious opportunities are less – in Mr Robert Newton's portrait of the elder brother, Rene, who is more fully revealed than any other character in the piece, and is continuously interesting to watch".

Bernard Shaw was amongst the audience and afterwards wrote to Nancy Price, "Amazing! There's nothing in London like it..."

After a non-stop 832 performances the show closed. Bob left with a great affection for the piece; he also left with his 'Rene's' pet, a spaniel that went under the stage name of 'Merlin' and, off duty, had become a favourite member of the Cheney Walk household as 'Rastas'...

"I believe in matriarchy..." Bob told *Leader* Magazine in an October interview, "families dominated by the mother. That's what happy nations are made of. Happy families, like the one in *Whiteoaks*. But you can't practise the family cult if there isn't a strong woman at the head. You must have a strong woman...". At eleven thirty in the morning, Newton's volubility took the nervous journalist by surprise. "We actors are lucky people, we were born with the gift in us, my father painted, so did my grandfather, my mother wrote, there had to be a creative talent in me. Whatever form it takes is just chance. I once wrote a novel myself, rather a bad one, *Tarnished Brocade*, about the Charles II period... the important thing is the creative gift..."

Bob was right, it was 'rather a bad one'. Published by Selwyn and Blount, London in 1939 the critics however clapped politely and the public, coughing up their seven and six, swallowed it in satisfying quantity never the less. Spurred on, though never really a writer at heart, Bob was already rattling out his next work, '*Swords of Bronze*'. A roman a clef, a padding out of the bones of history with the airy stuff of the 1930's, it was pure theatre. A re-telling of the biblical story of David, it was the sort of thing Barry Jackson would have loved... the public however were not to be gulled this time and the title sank into history.

A matriarchal presence might have been a comfortable theory but the reality was less cosy. Man-about-town Bob had now taken up with one of Denham's handsome starlets, Googie Withers. Working his familiar magic, Bob had inveigled her back to his place for 'a drink'. Crashing in amorously they were confronted by Marjorie, standing at the stove and decked out in a pinafore, "Your eggs are nearly ready, Bobby" she trilled. His plans scuppered, Bob walked over to the cooker, looked into the pan, picked it up and crowned her with it...

The memory of Peta and his baby daughter and all the accompanying protestations of mature respectability had long been consigned to oblivion and Bob's life off-stage, despite his mother's interventions, was a riot. His fame had brought fortune and his well developed taste for the affectations of the wealthy, for society, for fine clothes, food and drink, was satiated. He was a handsome young actor in a celebrity obsessed city that was fuelled by greed, booze and sex. Few women were safe from his advances and few resisted, or at least, not for long. Careless with his wealth, with an utterly beguiling smile and a boyishly irresponsible attitude, his romances were passionate and brief. Inevitably they overlapped. Each encounter was lusty; some were serious but none was fatal. Until he met Annie. The meeting occurred in a Bloomsbury tavern late in the night. Their glances met through the smoke and ruck. The attraction was immediate and unstoppable, the romancing brief and to the point, "I'm in love with you..." Newton said, "what are we going to do about it?"

Annie was Annie McLean, the daughter of Sir Robert McLean, a hard-nosed, straight-talking Scot. An engineer, he was the chairman of the aircraft manufacturer Vickers. Annie was a larger-than-life character. At twenty five she was six years younger than Newton. Nicknamed 'Spitfire' as a child, she was as forceful as her father. Fittingly, at his suggestion, she was to give her pet name to the famous fighter aircraft that he helped design...

With a natural talent for accents, Annie was doing voice-overs for the BBC. She thought Newton very odd, extraordinary even. She was living in Mayfair with her parents. Newton, whose attitude to money and possessions was more than relaxed, was crashing between loaded and broke, friends sofas and grand hotels he could not afford. What they did about it was inevitable; he moved into her bed and into her life. Sir Robert was less than delighted. Annie had been schooled, trained and brought up as the son he never had. "You're going to hell, you're going to hell... all this is going to be wasted, because of sex...!" he growled. Bob, bleary and tousled, was nervously introduced to the family breakfast table. "Huh, huh, was I right?"

McLean had done too good a job of educating his daughter and he knew it. Like a none-too-clean stray, 'Bob' quickly became an integral part of the household. The amour was noisy, messy and riotous but the McLean family said nothing; their uncontrollable daughter had, at last, found her match. Then the affair took a jolt; Bob was contracted to a regional tour alongside Hermione Baddeley, and there was no getting out of it.

Saturday's Children, another first from Bob's Shilling days, opened at the Wimbledon Theatre and then, all too quickly, went out into the provinces. The farewell was tearful. The McLean family breathed a collective sigh of relief; bottles were restocked and life got back to the old order. But Annie was not ready to let go, and neither was Bob. All too soon the tour concluded and the love-nest was reinstated in the Mayfair establishment.

Throughout Newton's Shilling Theatre adventure, Lawrence Olivier, Bob's neighbour in Cheney Walk, had closely watched from the sidelines. Both admired the other's talents and both had reached the point where they were in constant demand and could pick and choose parts. With Coward's heavyweight patronage, Olivier, despite what had turned out to be a galling introduction to Hollywood, had been contracted by United Artists into a film production, *Fire Over England*. Simultaneously he was setting London abuzz with plans for a radical new production of *Hamlet* at the Old Vic'.

For Bob the weeks passed happily in the soft luxury of Annie's bed and he was joyously content and forgot about work. Annie, however, already had an eye to the future and quickly saw that she would have to take him in hand. Bobby would have to be watched, both for drink and women. Romping under the sheets may be all well and good but she saw that it would fall to her to give his post-Shilling Theatre career some kind of direction. The importance of both Olivier's upcoming film and the Shakespeare production was not lost on her and very little of her formidable charm was needed to talk Olivier into giving Newton a part in both. 'Larry...' she said, 'he's got a magnificent voice and Dutch courage, why don't we get him into Shakespeare...'.

By August *Hamlet* had gone into rehearsals and to everyone's surprise the union between 'Spitfire' Annie and 'Bob-a-job' had failed to peter out. It was looking serious and it didn't help that Sir Robert had crumbled before Newton's charm. "He used to make him laugh" Annie said. "He used to ring up and say, 'Sir Rabbit, that bloody daughter of yours is causing me a lot of pain and she's lying dead in the Great West Road' and Dad would say 'Well, pick her up and bring her home. Can't have her lying about there!'" Perhaps Sir Robert saw in his pseudo 'son-in-law' something of his own rebellious spirit. "He didn't give a bugger"... Annie recalled of Bob, "he would say to my Mother, 'Lady McLean, could I try a little of your excellent whiskey', and within half an hour the bottle would be empty. It became a ritual, Mother loved it. He was part of the tapestry of life...".

Of course the unthinkable, inevitable happened, and on Christmas Eve, with the tangled and interminable divorce proceedings from Peta finalised, Bobby and Ann Isobel Noel married. The ceremony was at the Register Office in Chelsea. Close family attended; the McLean's, Annie's sister, Marjorie of course, and Pauline and Joy, all close friends now. The timing was significant, Annie was already flexing her control over Bob and chose the date of the wedding so that it did not interrupt the *Hamlet* run. There was a lavish party but no honeymoon. The marital home was in Turville Heath, near Henley in Buckinghamshire, two game-keepers' cottages that had been knocked together and charmingly converted by Annie's mother.

Married life at 'Bicks Bottom' was good, and both Bob and Annie knew how to throw a party. On one occasion, when the Harvard and Yale teams came to row at Henley, Bob decided they would have to come back for an impromptu bash. Before long, however, it all got too much; the Yanks were taking over and Bob started losing his temper. "There are too many bloody Americans here!" he roared at Annie. "You brought them here, what are you going to do with them...?" she yelled back. "I'll get rid of them...." Bob muttered. Within minutes the place was full of pigs; Bob had let loose the neighbour's herd and driven them in through the front door and into the house. There was chaos; furniture went crashing over, snorting, honking pigs all over the place...

Gloriously happy in the throes of passion, Bobby now showed it in the way he knew; spreading his joy from the stage he shamelessly hammed-up the Sunday-sermonised voice of the Bard. Years of stage work had taught him an armoury of skills, voice control, timing, dramatic delivery; *Hamlet* went into rehearsal and Annie looked on nervously. "I was standing in the wings near the old girl (Lilian Bayliss, a woman very much like Nancy Price, and the redoubtable, if eccentric, matriarch of the Vic' who believed her mission to save the theatre was Divinely inspired) when she said 'Oh, Mrs Newton, we've never had a laugh on that line before...'" Annie sighed, "It's the beginning of a great peroration... Bob is going to fart his way through six weeks of Shakespeare." Bayliss, unused to blatant sacrilege, tried to explain "He didn't know what he said..." '...by FARTinbrass of Norway!' Bob yelled. Bang. Roar from the ninepennies.

Olivier was very much a maverick choice for the lead role, but Alec Guinness was by now an essential. Michael Redgrave had been offered the role of Horatio but he turned it down, preferring the pouting role of Laertes. Management had conceded, replying, 'Laertes by all means if you prefer, though *I'd* call Horatio the better part....'. That part fell to Newton, and the derisory wage of £20 a week.

Rehearsals had given little time for either honeymoon bliss or Christmas festivities; the full dress-rehearsals staggered on until five in the morning. On January 5th *Hamlet* had opened to a packed house. The production had been *the* talk of theatre-land for months and expectations were high. The Old Vic', its sacred boards hollowed by the footsteps of practically every 'name' in the history of theatre, was famed for producing high quality Shakespeare. It *was* the West End.

Pre-dating modern, indiscriminate Bardology, the play received a standing ovation on its opening night and the choice of cast ('a jumble of good and the insufficient' according to one critic) seemed fully vindicated. Neither a safe imitation nor one that wildly defied convention, the play was judged a critical triumph. Going out night after night to a slightly awed audience, Olivier's Hamlet was cited as 'modern in its naturalism' if lacking in 'music'. Newton's critics were equally divided '...though a trifle lacking in solidity and too highly strung, (Horatio) is spoken well and with understanding' said one, 'Horatio *ne ferra pas*, since 'won't do' sounds so rude...' said another.

Most telling perhaps was the judgement by another member of the cast, Stuart Burge. In the preamble in Act 1, the lines spoken by Horatio, despite their apparent simplicity, were formidably difficult, and were consequently often dropped:

"*Now cracks a noble heart. Good night, sweet prince,*

And flights of angels sing thee to thy rest."

Burge witnessed Bob's sensitive handling of the lines and was genuinely moved by effect.

Inevitably the production became snobbishly precious. Bob however, never so fastidious or as insecurely sincere as Olivier, soldiered on in irrepressible and irreverent form. The production closed reluctantly and triumphant and the cast, now including Vivien Leigh as Ophelia, was booked to go on to inaugurate an annual performance in Denmark. Four great actors – Olivier, Newton, Guinness and Redgrave – all destined to become stars, caught for a brief moment at an historic theatrical cross-road, were about to part. They would never work together again. Bored with his role and aware that the foreign tour was little more than a stunt for the Danish Tourist Board, Newton declined.

The British economy was now once again faltering; nearly bankrupt and with only empty coffers to offer the swelling ranks of angry jobless, the government had turned avaricious glances towards the film industry. Cinemas were booming but British audiences were showing an obdurate propensity for American imports. Bright and fresh, they were, most importantly, different. Audiences flocked to them and good British pounds winged west across the pond. Contriving to bolster an industry that could be milked for tax, and perhaps like Stoll becoming aware that the grumbling proletariat was being corrupted by 'foreign influence', the government looked to its statute books. The result was the Quota Act, the 'Cinematographic Film Act', a garbled piece of legislation that required 20% of all films screened to be 'British made'.

The intention might have been sound but the result was a spate of cash-cow, slipshod flicks that had been knocked out at lightning speed. At a budget of under a pound a foot, cheapness was everything and at a thousand feet and a thousand pounds a reel, producers naturally tried to turn out works under the £4-6000 fixed sum. Compared to the former average production costs of £30,000 for most films, the result was a string of horrors; the reviled 'B' movie was born and the very term became a negative value judgement. Audiences immediately smelled a rat, yawned and left the performance for the blind eyes of the cinema charwomen...

Thirty-three films had been shot in the UK in 1925, many of them Anglo-German productions; now, eleven years on, thanks to the Act and a growing demand for film, 228 titles, almost all quickly cobbled together, had been distributed. Audiences jeered dismissively. Soon the tabloids damned the aptly dubbed 'Quota Quickies' an 'unfortunate aberrations'. Even the Board of Trade was forced to take action. In 1936 an issue of *The Economist* stated pompously that the primary object of the Board was 'the complete extirpation of the quota quickie'. To the relief of audiences across the country the worst days of the 'B' movie were soon to be over.

The weekly programme offered by most cinemas now consisted of a newsreel, a cartoon, a 'short', and a second feature film, the dreaded 'B' picture, then - the whole point of the evening, the first, or main, feature. The whole thing lasted for over four sweltering, bum-numbing, smoke choked hours. The jury was out as to whether it was because of, or despite, the quickies, that British film was now booming. The debate raged endlessly; the 'anti' lobby held up the string of unwatchable flops, the supporters insisted that the legislation had given the industry a leg-up onto the international film stage and also given many actors valuable experience and exposure. In the production of *Fire Over England* Newton was about to find out.

First however there was a new piece of bureaucracy to add his signature to; the dreaded 'moral clause'. With a flick of a pen he was condemned for the duration of the shoot 'to comport himself both with dignity and decency in his private and professional life and not to commit or permit any act or thing which would bring him into notoriety or contempt or disgrace...'. It was a lovely idea.

A time and lens warped re-working of the Spanish Armada, the film was amongst the last of the quota quickies and, ironically, it would turn out to be amongst the best. The film was the inspiration of Alexander Korda, the producer of the film *The Thief of Baghdad*, that had chased the production of *London Life* off the stage twelve years previously. Hungarian born but 'as British as a side of beef', Korda understood that 'film' was an anagrammatic derivative of flim-flam and that fooling, flattering and flannelling people was as important to a producer as having any savvy about cinema. Britain's only film Mogul and, according to many, the saviour of the industry, it had become his mission to re-write British history through costume drama. His 1932 *The Private Life of Henry VIII* had been a smash hit on both sides of the Atlantic; now he looked for *Fire over England* to copy that success.

The age-old tradition of music-hall entertainment was still a fundamental of public taste and this was reflected in a British film industry that was, despite its popularity, effectively marking time. The height of the production boom years, 1934, saw the release of 170 UK produced films; of these 56 were comedies and 35 were musicals. The remaining 42 were variations of the tired crime-drama theme.

As 'history' the plot of *Fire Over England* skated on thin ice. Many thought the project a risky financial gamble, but as the decade drew near to a close, the inevitability of the 'next' war began to throw a long shadow over Britain. People on the streets had begun to talk about the 'Flap', the 'War Flap', and then warn each other sternly not to get 'in a Flap'. Pessimism was deplored; Europe, the government roared, was on the brink of a Golden Age. But Korda was a European and a refugee and he knew better. The people knew better too and reached, instinctively, for reassurance. That reassurance now came through the fantasy of patriotic fiction.

Infinitely more than just a film maker, Korda was a stealthy frequenter of the corridors of power. Rubbing shoulders and palms with the industry barons and politicians of London, Hollywood and New York, he was an active manipulator and a fervent anti-appeaser. *Fire Over England*, timed to be released in the Coronation year, was to be a blatant, sabre-rattling, propaganda exercise.

The chosen producer was, ironically, a German, Eric Pommer; the director was an American, the much respected, though slightly past his prime, William K Howard. Korda's masterpiece was to be shot in his new and lavish studio, Denham. Sited in two hundred acres of parkland and dubbed the 'New Hollywood', it boasted seven vast stages, air conditioning, the latest sound and lighting gear, its own power plant and a rather brittle air of optimism. Above the imposing entrance three union flags waved proudly. The standard studio joke was that they represented the three British workers employed there; all the rest were Europeans. Not for nothing was it boasted that the studio had an 'international aesthetic'.

If the Quota Act had spawned some dogs it had nevertheless also produced a new generation of home-grown film 'stars'. British producers lacked Hollywood's catalogue of contract screen talent to draw from and looked to the stage for their actors. Carried in on the tail of Olivier's new-found fame, Newton arrived at the studio complex to find a bewildering maze of draughty corridors and locked doors. And he could also see that Korda's 'Hollywoodization' had extended to the sets. The vast and airy high-ceilinged 'halls' were the exact opposite of Elizabethan architecture...

The film plot was taken from a well crafted and almost ready to film book by A E Mason, yet Korda again showed himself thoroughly tarred with the Hollywood brush and had set his stable of pet script-writers to tear the text to pieces. Newton's role was that of a Spanish Grandee, 'Don Pedro', eighth on the bill and playing opposite Olivier, who takes over from a quickly snuffed-out James Mason. Central to the production was the diva, Flora Robson. Playing Queen Elizabeth, the film was intended to be hers, and as much a queen in real life as in costume, she demanded from the outset to be treated as such.

Despite its modernity, a bewildering confusion reigned across Korda's rambling film-factory. Within his tangled autocracy the left hand was kept a mystery to the right and producers, directors and players found themselves switched, mid-shoot, from one sound-stage to another. Even Newton, new to the industry, saw that production methods were decidedly quirky. The script, the Bible for the players, was being re-written at will throughout the production; shooting often went on into the night, retake after retake being shot seemingly regardless of cost. Worse from Newton's point of view, an habitual night-bird, were the atrocious hours. Annie was now firmly at the helm and arrival at the studios for the hours of make-up and wardrobe meant waking at four a.m., even if the first shot wasn't taken until way after noon.

Fortunately a familiar face greeted Newton at the studio; Henry Ainley, one of the backers of the Shilling Theatre project and a solid drinking buddy, had also been written into the cast-list. A thunderingly imposing stage actor, Ainley relied heavily upon his inborn spontaneous talent and, like Newton, faced the inane and pedestrian demands of film work with loathing. Like many in the trade, he had his drinking demons and the interminable hours of inactivity inspired a bottle to appear in a dark recess of the studio. Cast in a small part, he was, unfortunately, dispensable, and, staggering once too often in front of the camera, he was soon duly dispensed with, fired summarily by an outraged Korda...

As the long days passed Newton struck up a close friendship with William Howard. Another man very much after his own heart, Howard started every day with a tea-pot of whiskey. Slowly he convinced Newton about the demise of theatre and the superiority of film as a career prospect.

Playing opposite Flora Robson and taking the romantic role alongside Olivier was Vivien Leigh, one of Korda's retained, £1000-a-year starlets. From the start the set was a bonfire of vanities, a disparate coalition of exhibitionists all wanting and needing to be the main attraction, and the production had its share of incident. 'We shall probably end up by fighting' Olivier had told Leigh '...people always get sick of each other when making a film'. Very much like an exotic cat, Leigh would purr and she would scratch, and looked divinely pretty doing both and Larry was hooked. Beset with the boredom, their 'friendship' erupted into an unashamed, passionate and very public love affair. Both separately married, their behaviour was judged, even by the contemporary dual-standards, as outrageous. Wild rumour and speculation about their movements began to dominate studio life. The worst kept secret since the Wallis Simpson affair, their every action was spied on, yet they did little to hide their clumsy liaisons.

As the days passed and the actors settled into the alternating routine of tedium and feverish activity, Olivier began to look tired. The exhaustion was not caused by the work, but by Leigh; '...she's bloody wearing me out!' he complained to anyone who would listen. In the background, Korda, calm, patient, the eternal gentleman, the Svengali and matchmaker, nodded approval. Already manipulating both of their futures, he understood the power of scandal and did everything to see that the illicit union of 'his' stars prospered.

Inevitably the affair took over the set and with the smouldering passion between the two driving the on-screen romance, Robson saw both the film and the plaudits being snatched from her. Resentment burrowed into her heart. Sitting hour after hour in her heavy Elizabethan costume, feeling the sweat coursing its subtly tortuous way down the inside of her putty nose, she fumed impotently. Newton, playing his scenes opposite the stunning 'Spanish beauty' Tamara Desni, faced his own challenges. Annie could only look on.

Co-conspirators in the Olivier/Leigh affair, Bob and Annie were hardly surprised when the couple turned up late one night at their cottage in Turville Heath. Red-faced, complete with suitcases and their beloved bull terrier, Marney, they breathlessly announced that they had run away together. The escape from marital boredom was as clumsy as their liaison however. Champagne and congratulations were hurriedly suspended and the giggling elopes concealed behind a sofa when Olivier's wife, smelling a rat, appeared and hammered on the front door. With denials on Bob and Annie's lips and disavowal of any knowledge set out, the hound sprang out into the room and all was lost.

Shooting was completed in September, after an over-long fourteen weeks. The Leicester Square première on February 25th, 1937 was a typically lavish Korda affair, attended by tame royalty and a squadron of reluctant admirals. As the new centrepiece of the work, Olivier and Leigh's romance came across rather manically and was decidedly outshone by Newton's more subtle seduction of Tamara Desni. Nevertheless the film reflected the bullish public mood, received roaring popular approval and overnight the names associated with the picture became table talk. 'One of the most notable pictures of the year…' *Picturegoer* said. '…a really finely produced and directed history.' Critics of course bitched and bickered; one called Olivier's acting 'too theatrical'; Newton, who had played his part with a calm understated maturity, drew praise and only a little censure.

Graham Greene, ever vitriolic and not yet sold out to the enemy of film, reviewed the work in the February release of '*The Spectator*' magazine; 'Mr. Korda's great National Coronation-year picture of Elizabethan England (has) done one remarkable thing; caught the very spirit of an English public schoolmistress's vision of history…nevertheless it is the best production to come from Denham yet'.

The Hollywood launch at Grauman's Chinese Theatre was another of Korda's 'hospitality offensives'. Despite its supposed 'Britishness', the film was blatantly geared to American tastes (after early Hollywood trial screenings, 'trying it on the dog', scenes that met with displeasure were promptly snipped) but even the usually undiscerning Americans pointed out that the 'quintessentially British' film was in fact 'presented' by a Hungarian, produced by a German, and directed by an American with a Chinese cameraman, a Russian art director and co-writer, and a French costume designer. Nevertheless *Fire Over England* was one of the major British film successes of 1937.

Newton left Denham with a sigh of relief and turned back to the West End and the familiar antiquated home of the stage. Film work had nevertheless been extremely profitable and his weekly salary of £100 had amounted to a small fortune. If he was exhausted by the deadly dullness of it all, he was forced to reluctantly admit that it was where his financial future now lay.

Life within the Newton family continued with the eternal round of love/hate encounters. Algernon, happy in his new life, forever abstemious and grand now with an affectionate appellation of 'The White Knight of Hampstead' was working out of the Birch Hall Inn near Beckhole and had become a sought-after figure. The winter of 1936/7 saw him happily working and travelling, on-board a cruiser in the vibrant winter sun of the Dutch East Indies. Just previously, he had travelled to America and Arizona, accepting a staggering £5000 commission (the average working-class man made £5 a week and £300 would buy a tidy three bedroom home...) to paint a Chicago millionaire's faux palace. Later, allotted a room in Buckingham Palace, he had painted the Mall. 'The King and Queen didn't disturb me...' he commented.

Marjorie however was floundering. She clung to the memories of the past, her cigarettes, brandy, her own crazy brand of religion and her children. 'Bobby' was of course the spoiled favourite; Nigel always the underdog, the stay-at-home problem. Pauline, with all the bohemian morality of her brother, had moved on from the philandering Basil Murray and was trying a spell as 'Mrs Silvester Gates'. Joy, similarly, had sloughed off Igor Vinogradov, with whom she had a daughter, had moved on to briefly marry Dennis Craig and, bouncing gaily through a second divorce, had now crashed into the life of a new man, Bernard Penrose.

Known since childhood as Beakus, Bernard was a dashingly handsome adventurer and blue-water mariner who had been drawn to the bright lights of London, the Bloomsbury set and the elite of society. With the added attraction of an inheritance, a Cornish pedigree and home in the Duchy in the shape of a beautiful creekside house that had long since been infiltrated by the artistic set, the appeal was irresistible. Dora Carrington, hopelessly entangled with Lytton Strachey, had always taken his heart, but Joy had unfailingly snatched it back. Bob and Annie had met and appraised the new lover and had come away with a firm friend. Finding approval, a registry marriage between Joy and Beakus took place in February, and the couple retreated to a sailing honeymoon along the south coast. The creekside house and the unsuspecting locals were left in the hands of Beakus' brother, Roland, and a host of his arty friends. Lost with his paints in the West Indies, Algernon wrote an affectionate little card to his favourite, hoping that the newly-weds 'were both flourishing'.

Despite his allegiance to the stage Bob was now quickly re-called to Denham. The film was *Twenty one Days*. The work was designed as a blatant Leigh/Olivier showcase, and, Korda decided, was to be the one to establish Leigh as a major star. The screenplay was blown up from a Galsworthy short story entitled *The First and the Last* and had been adapted for the cinema by Graham Greene. Formerly one of the most vehement critics of the British film industry, Greene had U-turned faultlessly when offered the chance to turn his hand at a film script. His presence alone brought the work a degree of respectability. Overseen by Basil Dean, the plot played on that classic, suspenseful, saving grace of countless films: the courtroom drama. Newton was cast as 'Tolly', a young lawyer.

A typical 'gaslight' genre work and set in the smoggy, 'Sherlock Holmes', London streets so beloved of Americans, Bob's was a relatively small part, but one which recurred throughout the film. Appearing in four courtroom scenes, his developing style was instantly recognisable; rich voiced, keen eyed, his acting was utterly natural and deliberately restrained so as not to draw attention from the Leigh/Olivier drama.

Leslie Banks' lawyer character formed the mainstay of the drama. Promised promotion to judge he sees his prospects blighted by his brother's (Olivier) entanglement with a foreign married woman (Leigh) and the accidental killing of her brutal husband. The titular 21 Days was the time spent in prison by an innocent man accused of the crime and the time the fate torn lovers had together before Olivier's doing the 'decent thing' and giving himself up.

Going into the shoot, Dean's directorial style quickly proved problematic. Very much the irascible and pompous headmaster, his cracking whip however had little effect on Olivier and Leigh. Still ploughing through their steamy passion they treated him with total disregard. Mid-shoot they plunged the studio into chaos by flitting off unannounced to Denmark for a long weekend to put on the promised Hamlet production. Their beloved bull-terrier was dumped on Bob and Annie who were staying in a hotel near the studio. With Bob busy on set and Annie busy watching him, the dog was locked into the hotel room, and through the long, lonely days occupied itself by ripping apart the mattress and most of the furniture...

True to form, Korda could not resist taking over when he saw things going badly. Interfering with the already complex screenplay he promptly shot an additional scene. The final takes were not done until late June; the completion deadline was overshot and the result was a studio thrown into chaos. Despite this, production costs were kept under £100,000.

A frisson of excitement saw the completed work screened in-house for the first time. Still being coached by Olivier, Leigh's acting was far from adequate and, as Newton suspected, the work was a complete turkey. Even Dean saw that he had been a victim of Korda's interfering machinations; 'It was a public relations exercise to please, as well as publicise, the young lovers... I was certainly the fall-guy in that merry plan!' Greene, who had thrown up his job at the *Spectator* to work full time on set, was likewise little pleased. Only Korda was satisfied; the film cans were sealed up, dispatched to the vaults and set aside for a later day.

Celebrating his new-found fame, and more importantly his new-found wealth, Bob lunched with Annie at Rules along with Peggy Ashcroft. Mid-meal Bob slipped out with an air of mystery. He returned minutes later accompanied by a suited and white-gloved flunky loaded down with Georgian silver. "This is a present, madam..." the man said obediently, "there's about five thousand quid's worth of stuff on this tray...". Bob stood back, beaming Annie a glow of loving satisfaction. Annie was not amused "I'm afraid it'll have to go back, I am so sorry..." she said addressing him. "Bob" she snapped, "pay for the taxi!". Annie was in no mood for frivolity. Talk of war was now everywhere and crept into every conversation. Conscription had begun and a dose of 'war fever' was being handed out with every gas mask. In the parks the immaculate lawns were being cut up for slit-trenches and air-raid shelters.

Bob was now recalled for his third production at Denham. Despite being under pressure from Connie's to become one of Korda's stable of 'tame' contract actors he signed up for a film-only deal.

Directed now by Victor Seville, the film was another typically British production that pandered to the irrational public taste for garbled espionage. Gritty and grim, *Dark Journey* was a typically murky spy film with a labyrinthine plot that read as a portent of the coming conflict. Bob's role was small, that of a German U-boat officer. Raw boned and clipped, he appeared for just two minutes, right at the opening of the film. First seen barking at his crew in a bastardised German accent, he then turns to interrogate a glamorous 'French double agent' in neat Chertsey English. That double-agent was of course Vivien Leigh, Korda's gold-mine. Her role was to play the sex-interest opposite a suave and monocled Conrad Veidt (making his first film at Denham) with whom she manages an implausible romance.

Graceful and restrained, Veidt was an old film hand, having seen the silent years in Hollywood. Working alongside Cecil Parker, the quintessential Englishman and eternally baffled civil servant, Leigh, despite Olivier's best efforts, only managed to stumble hopelessly in Veidt's wake. Newton did his bit and quit the set as quickly as he could.

Screened against film competition that was now drowning in gooey sentimentality, general release came on March 23rd. Despite being a very much second-rate work, it was the sort of solid xenophobic sabre-rattling the public wanted and the press notices were good. Graham Greene's review was, however, less flattering; 'Abandon life all ye who enter here!' he opened his piece, addressing the 'pedestrian unreality' of this 'most Denham of pictures'. The Gordian plot wrinkled the brows of even British audiences, and it was agreed that before shipping the film to Canada as *The Anxious Years*, and presuming that proximity to Hollywood was no guarantee of sharper wits, an extra, de-fogging reel, would have to be added to the work...

The film industry was still in its formative age; it was forgivably easy to make a 'bad' film and this was undoubtedly one of them. The plot structure had been snatched wholesale from the stage and the result was an unmistakable excess of dialogue and a dulling lack of motion.

Unable to inveigle him into a long-term contract, but convinced of his screen appeal, Korda had contracted Newton, along with most of the cast from *Fire Over England*, for his next production. This was the United Artists financed *Farewell Again*.

Directed by Eric Pommer with American Tim Whelan, the work saw Bob appear as 'Jim Carter', a British soldier afloat. Basically the work was a recruiting poster for the British military forces; overflowing with patriotic zeal, it was a barrack-room ballad of Tommy Atkins, the ubiquitous British soldier. The troopship 'Somersetshire', loaded with the officers and men of the Twenty-third Royal Lancers, complete with their assorted chattels and families, is homeward bound after five years in India and all aboard dream of warm beer and good old Blighty. Tensions and conflicts come to the boil when within sight of the white cliffs of Dover the regiment is ordered east again. The film tracks the six desperate hours of Southampton shore-leave granted to the soldiers.

With a bravely realistic directorial approach the film was a series of episodic character sketches; somehow it was even more 'British' than *Fire Over England*. Working alongside Flora Robson and Leslie Banks, Newton pulled himself out of the deadly 'Denham' apathy and played his neurotic, knife-waving character with relish, effectively dominating the plot.

Public release came in November and reviews were good; 'a first rate script... that had the sense of timing, the sense of filming bits and pieces about it, necessary to story-telling on the screen'. Gratifyingly, *Picture Post* quoted Newton's performance as stealing the picture. Fearful that the King's English would not survive the trans-Atlantic voyage, the film was re-titled *The Troopship* and dispatched west... where it was once again pointed out that a 'British' film was essentially the creation of a gaggle of foreigners.

Whether the domestic studios provided it or not, there was little doubt that the 1930's British public, whilst obsessed with war, now also had an appetite for American style riches and glamour. Society might still be sub-divided along class lines but the old hierarchies were loosening; glossy magazines now sold the myth that the kind of glittering lifestyle previously reserved for the toffs was available for all. Even the upper crust wanted a piece of the glamour action, and blue-blooded beauties were selling their faces to *Picturegoer* to peddle cold creams and soaps.

Grand with his name printed large on cinema posters on both sides of the Atlantic and pocketing over £150 a week, Bob accepted the tedium of the studios and learned to laugh at the petty squabbles. Annie was at his heels and once again he set his alarm-clock and staggered out bleary eyed into his next film, another Denham/United Artists production, *The Squeaker*.

Previously filmed in 1930 and now enjoying a London stage version, the work was a product of the prodigiously prolific Edgar Wallace. (Wallace was to clock up 175 novels, 24 plays and numerous newspaper and magazine articles.) Walking out nightly in the stage version, Alistair Sim, playing a crime reporter, simply translated his evening role for daytime filming. The American star, Edmund Lowe, took the leading role as a moody Canadian detective. With twenty films already to his credit, he had reluctantly come over to England to film a work entitled *Seven Sinners* and employing a mixture of cunning and temptation, Korda had persuaded him to stay on to do *The Squeaker*.

The budget for the work was limited and the script suggested a more modest production than Denham's previous efforts. Played out on the ubiquitous grim and smoggy 'London' set the thing was however sure to be popular. Having been reared on a diet of Conan Doyle, 'Sapper', John Buchan and Agatha Christie, the British contrary appetite for assassins, adventurous international jewel thieves and detectives was insatiable. Characterised by an obsession with murder laced with sexual undertones, the genre's popularity was aptly summed up within the industry as 'News of the World' culture.

Working alongside Eric Maturin, an old Shilling player, and Stewart Rome, now in his decline and taking bit-parts, Bob was centrally cast as the doomed 'Larry Graeme'. A suave but hard-pressed jewel thief, he wants 'out' of the crime game to live with his new love, a night-club singer played by *Fire over England* sex-pot Tamara Desni. Bob makes his exit an hour into the film when 'done for' by the bad guys.

Signifiacntly Bob's character called for him to once again adopt a strong regional accent. Accents, dialect and 'class' intonations were all throwbacks of stagecraft; deemed difficult for 'foreigners' to understand, many directors saw them as out of place on the modern screen, certainly if spilled from the lips of the lead character. Whilst Olivier's bland received pronunciation saw him steered into the 'leading man/romantic' class, Bob's predilection for dynamic roles and accents began the channelling process that saw him become labelled as a 'character actor'.

The film hit the screens on November 6th and turned out to be predictably popular. Suitably translated for the American market to *Murder on Diamond Row* it saw its US release a month later.

Olivier and Leigh were now called away for work, and Bob and Annie found themselves again saddled with their hound. Remembering the hotel room incident, the brute was shipped down to Turville Heath where its energies could be safely used up in the countryside. Unversed in the country-code, however, it went native, savaged the local livestock and got plugged by a gamekeeper. Breaking the tragic news to Leigh was fraught...

A frigid January, 1937, saw Bob turn out for Denham's next project, *Four Dark Hours*.

In another sleazy little Soho thriller, John Mills, a vaudeville trained comedian/dancer, appears as a Cagney-like all-singing, all-dancing character and Newton plays his brother, 'Dave Connor', a cocky spiv with the heart of gold and a weakness for family. Yet another murder victim, the film's opening sees Bob dripping gore on Platform One at Paddington Station. Brutally knifed by the racetrack gangsters he has betrayed, he was out of the picture inside of twenty minutes yet was very much the focus of the story.

The plot, a manifest British version of American gangsterism, was one pennen by Graham Greene. With little love for Korda, Greene had long labelled him a destroyer of British film and routinely trashed his productions; relations between the men were little improved as, inevitably, his screenplay was churned into an impenetrable mess by Korda's hacks. The result was put through production at breakneck speed. Too drearily realistic and lacking in glamour, it failed to enthral his chosen studio audiences. Weighing in at just under sixty five minutes it was utterly unremarkable. Seeing that it wasn't going to make the blockbuster he desperately wanted, Korda held the film back from general UK release and the reels were sent down to the vaults to sit on top of *Twenty One Days*; another of his long-term 'passive investments'.

These investments however cost a lot and earned nothing and Korda was desperate for the big money-spinner that would compensate for projects that had spiralled out of control. A previous work, *Knight without Armour* had been costed at a hundred and seventy eight thousand pounds but topped out at almost double that amount. Now he bought up the film rights to Robert Graves' best-selling novel *I, Claudius*.

No mere parochial work, this was going to be a big-bucks sex-flick with classical aspirations. To Graves' horror, sixty skimpily clad 'Vestal Virgins' had been slipped into the script; this, it was announced, was going to be the studio's 'greatest film'. Under the banner of London Films, a company that had a damaging reputation of turning out rather bright and over-sophisticated pictures, the project was a collaboration with United Artists, in which Korda was a major shareholder. After interminable planning, negotiation and delay, studio work commenced on the 15th February.

The pivot of the piece was the emerging genius, *the* only genius in the whole profession Olivier was to say, of Charles Laughton. An agonising perfectionist and merciless self-critic, he was cast in the central role of Tiberius Claudius.

An 'American dance hostess' turned film-star, Merle Oberon, was expensively imported from Hollywood to take the part of Messalina, his wife. Oberon's story was a cameo study of racism and the cruelty of a life in film; a pseudo American she was also claimed to be Britain's only glamour star. The reality was birth in Bombay as Estelle O'Brien Thompson; her father was a British engineer, her mother a part-Sinhalese nurse. As an incipient luminary, this dusky past was studio transformed to a Tasmanian origin, her voice into pure Mayfair RP and her skin whitened in a daily make-up ritual. In her Hollywood roles a special skin-whitening light, the 'Obie', had been created for her.

Flora Robson was given the part of 'Olivia', the wife of Augustus, and Newton, 'Cassius', a Roman guard and Caligula's murderer.

As ever, shooting got under way with the familiar tangle of conspiracy, liquor, tedium and gossip. Rumours that Laughton was setting up his own production company with Eric Pommer and the incessant death-by-whisper rumours of the studio's financial meltdown infiltrated the set. Inevitably there was the usual stew of sexual intrigue; this time it was Korda that was tangled in the web. Infatuated with Oberon, he began manipulating the production in her favour. 'Part-owned' by both Samuel Goldwyn and Korda, she had been called away from the Hollywood hotbed and was soon bitterly frustrated both by the very British delays in shooting, with her script and her role. Wailing loudly to anyone who would listen, she complained that appearing alongside the pastry-faced and lumbering Laughton was not the kind of exposure she needed. Desperate, she cabled Goldwyn; 'Messalina nothing. No acting opportunities. Heavy old-fashioned vamp. Secondary to Laughton. Feel miserable. Think 'Claudius' would undo everything you have done. Do not want do picture. Need your friendship, and advice badly. Would be confidential. Awaiting reply. Not spoken Korda yet'. Goldwyn, a master manipulator in Korda's vein, turned a deaf ear. Korda however was now putty in her hands and responding to her perfumed tears, whole scenes were scrapped and re-written. The other players bayed in protest but reels were binned. History was being rewritten to give Oberon a sexier role.

Graves saw his work being effectively transformed and condemned the whole thing as 'a great joke'; the choice of Josef Von Sternberg, the man who had invented Marlene Dietrich, as director seemed only to make things worse. Autocratic and caring more for style than content, he was very much a woman's director. Interpersonal relations were not his strong point and his bullying methods inspired universal loathing. He asserted his power by staring at those under him coldly, under heavy, snakelike lids, his mouth twisted into an expression of utter contempt. Like Korda, his fortune was on the wane and he looked desperately to *I, Claudius* to revive his prospects. Aware of Laughton's artistic sensibilities, Korda had instructed Von Sternberg to handle him with kid gloves. Unfortunately no two individuals more opposite in temperament than Laughton and Sternberg could be imagined; Laughton had put Korda through hell and back on previous works and the choice of Von Sternberg as director looked like an act of pure revenge.

A RADA top scorer, a dithering homosexual and a temperamental genius, Laughton's *Private Life of Henry VIII* had almost single-handedly granted rebirth to the British film industry. Now, struggling to evolve from his previous film character, Rembrandt, he needed sympathetic handling and room to find a new persona but conflict with Von Sternberg was immediate. Always a tortured soul, and particularly paranoid at this time in his life, Laughton began to feel increasingly martyred as he set out for the studio each day. Sulking and prevaricating endlessly, he was totally unable to perform; in response Von Sternberg fumed and swore. The set became a war zone. Everyone lived in a fit of nervous jitters. 'It was not a nightmare, it was a daymare' Von Sternberg raged. Oberon's career ambitions and the needs of the other actors became secondary to the two men's personal war; day after day the made-up cast sat impotently by and watched the on-set drama dissolve into farce.

On March 16th and with little more than half the script shot and the budget already massively overspent, production was halted. On the previous evening Oberon, ever the diva, had been 'involved' in a minor car crash and had been taken to hospital with a few cuts and bruises. Rejoicing, the studio inflated the episode into an expedient crisis and wailed that the production could not go on without its 'star'. In the following days, with the insurance companies infiltrating the studio, very public efforts were made 'to find a suitable replacement'. Then, after an appropriately attenuated period, and with a suitably long face, Korda declared the project dead in the water. The joke went around the set that Korda himself was driving the car on the fateful night. The insurance pay-out was safely banked, creditors were momentarily placated and the studio staggered back onto its feet. The great manipulator had survived for another day.

Hindsight has shown what a great film *I, Claudius* could have been. The photography was superb and Laughton gave everything he had to the part, certainly as much as he was allowed under Von Sternberg's militaristic dictatorship. Release would not have harmed Newton's career either. A BBC television programme was made of the film in 1965, entitled '*The Epic That Never Was*'. It showed Newton performing magnificently in three key scenes; at Claudius' farm where he is sent to summon Laughton, in the anti-chamber of the palace, and in Caligula's private chamber where, humiliated by a kick from the Emperor, he departs, glaring back at the mad ruler wrathfully.

This was to be Newton's last film with Korda. The world was changing and cinema was changing. A 1937 Parliamentary Commission recommend that the following year's review of the Film Act should, despite the dramatic increase in British film production and cries of 'unfair' from Hollywood, increase the 'must be British' quota to 50%. Korda had however worked his magic with Newton as he had done with others; Bob had now become a 'name' in film.

For both Newton and Laughton the *I, Claudius* fiasco had been seminal. The new legislation and Government backing spelled the opportunity for freelancing and both realised that they must now use the new cult of personality and take their futures into their own hands. The rumours had been right. Since the spring of 1937, Laughton, his wife Elsa Lanchester, another ambitious motivator like Annie, and director Erich Pommer had been working secretly towards creating their own film company, 'Mayflower Productions'. Crucially they had attracted the encouragement and financial backing of John Maxwell. A solicitor and entrepreneur, Maxwell was the owner of the distribution company, Wardour Films. Running a string of provincial cinemas he had created ABPC (Associated British Picture Corporation) taking over from British National Pictures and gaining control of the huge Elstree studio complex at Borehamwood. Like Korda, Maxwell had a unerring eye for talent, an almost bottomless pit of funds and the drive to use them. Operating with a fraction of American budgets, Elstree had flourished under his control and was invading the territory dominated by Hollywood.

Laughton was delighted at the prospect of being in charge of his own project; financially backed to the hilt he was free from insensitive directors. *Vessel of Wrath* was one of three scripts that he and Pommer were working on and it was decided that it should be the first to be shot.

Worked from a popular Somerset Maugham castaway-in-paradise tale, the plot mixed clashing personalities, a love story and a return to stolid British values and it was an ideal vehicle for Laughton and his wife to work on together. American scenarist and playwright Bartlett Cormack easily adapted the story for film and Laughton found that his dream became a reality with frightening speed. Bob and Annie were called to the Laughton's home for a 'meeting'. "Your wife is staying with mine..." Laughton purred to Bob "we'll head out to the tree-house...". It was the old Noel Coward situation all over again; nervously Bob and Annie stuck together. Business concluded they refused the offer of drinks, backed towards the door, made their excuses and fled....

At preliminary meetings it had been decided that as Europe was on the brink of war, filming on location in the West Indies would be impossible and that the south of France would have to do. Laughton was impressed with Newton's work and during *I, Claudius* the two had indeed secretly discussed the project. Now Newton was contracted to play the world-weary 'controleur', a leading role in the film. He was to exemplify the stuffy face of colonial bureaucracy playing opposite Laughton's beach-combing reprobate 'Ginger Ted'. Tyrone Guthrie was to play the Bible-bashing Reverend Jones, Lanchester was to play his sister, 'Ginger Ted's' love interest. By early May, Laughton was throwing himself passionately into the project; incessantly on the phone, interfering everywhere, he even personally selected the costumes to be worn on set. Almost as an afterthought Bartlett Cormack was offered the job of director.

Autumn approached and the cast, crew and various 'natives' recruited from London agencies, set off south to the Mediterranean. Potential locations were viewed in the unspoiled landscape between

Nice and Cannes and eventually Laughton and Pommer settled on St Maxime.

The days were long and flawlessly sunny and the nights mild. The location proved ideal and filming began in the sub-tropical gardens of Château Robert. Though hot and sweaty, Laughton played the perfectionist and deemed it not hot enough and not sweaty enough and along with the other actors Bob found himself sprayed with water and daubed with oil and dirt. Filming struggled through the tough days and laughed throughout the good. Laughton played his role as only he could; perfectly. Nevertheless take after re-take was shot. Each was good, each seemed indistinguishable from the last, but Laughton could not be satisfied. Progress stalled as, almost predictably, 'Ginger Ted' evolved way outside the lines of the script. With the constraints of planning, budgeting and organisation secondary to Laughton's uncompromising search for perfection, cast and crew shook their heads and looked towards another *I, Claudius* disaster. The budget might have been big, but was, nevertheless, bracketed and Laughton's fanaticism looked set to try both Pommer's limited patience and Maxwell's purse. Bartlett Cormack withered under the strain of Laughton's incessant interference and the pressure of his first location shoot; slumped in the shadows with Newton, he broke down and took to the bottle, happy to let Pommer direct. By September all hands were thoroughly blistered and burnt; the first stage of shooting was completed and the circus began decamping daily for shoots on a small island off San Tropez. The unfortunate Cormack had now cracked completely; twitching violently with a nervous tic of the face he had to be gently repatriated.

Production continued; Newton, bundled up in a murderously uncomfortable uniform, played his character with infinite patience. Employing a suitably nebulous foreign accent, he played his part as world-weary and restrained. Laughton however, always delightful company off set, became impossible in front of the camera. His search for perfection had become a blight. One day a quick scene was planned to fill a few minutes before lunch: Pommer was filming a sequence where 'Ted' was misbehaving. Guthrie, the missionary, was called to 'slam out' and 'Controlleur' Newton was to have a rare tantrum. It was an easy two minute take. The take went 'in the can' smoothly and all hands set out for the shade and a well deserved drink. But Laughton wasn't satisfied and asked politely for a re-take. Pommer of course agreed. By eight in the evening Laughton was still not satisfied. By now Newton had done the take so often that he was acting on auto-pilot. The next day the agony continued, take after take. Then Pommer snapped; stamping off set in a fury he screamed that the very first take would be the only damned one he would use.

The onset of winter saw the weather closing-in. Location work was reluctantly wrapped, though inevitably not to Laughton's satisfaction, and the crew turned back to England and Elstree.

Another faceless industrial plant and dubbed 'The British Hollywood' Newton soon saw that its alternative label, 'The Incestuous Village' was more apt; it was the 'Porridge Factory' where 'Jock' Maxwell ruled with an iron hand. Two large stages had been combined and decked out in suitable jungle shrubbery. The players were again sprayed with oil and showered by rain machines and the filming process was anything but comfortable.

Eventually the film was spliced together and, to everyone's surprise, proved to be visually stylish and rather beautifully shot, the characterisation believable and the plot coherent. The spring première at the Odeon in London's Leicester Square was stupendous. The first night saw five thousand screaming and idolatrous fans clawing to see the 'stars' arrive. The critics said all the right things and Newton got good reviews; 'One of the biggest hits' said *Variety*, 'of an altogether competent cast is Robert Newton as the controller'.

The film might have been charming but it was never going to set the world on fire, and despite the initial hysteria and the plaudits, it failed to live up to its financial expectations and did only moderate business.

Duly dispatched to America, the work underwent the pettifogging process of censorship and was scissored to comply with the Hayes code. Then it was re-dubbed *The Beachcomber*. The launch was graced with a promotional tour by Elsa Lanchester but again the work failed to create any great impact; Laughton was accused of 'overacting' and 'hamming'. Sixteen years later in the remake of the film, Newton would receive the same irrational broadside. The film was however recognised in 1938 by the American National Board of Review Awards, getting a third place slot in the English Language awards (after *The Citadel*, and *Snow White*) and Laughton and Lanchester awards for Best Acting Awards.

By the early summer Newton was joyously back in his native Cornwall. Contracted to star in a film adaptation of the famous Eden Phillpots play *Yellow Sands*, he was based at Sennen Cove, near Land's End, just a few miles from Lamorna.

A sunny comedy-romance with a political twist, the play had seen a record 610 outings at the Theatre Royal, Haymarket and a long provincial run, becoming a favourite of Repertory companies across the country. Another ABCP picture, the film cast was prestigious and Newton's role was *the* central figure, 'Joe Varwell'. A fisherman and a firebrand socialist, he finds himself embarrassingly rich from an inheritance. His character might have been the central figure of the plot but the 'star' performer however was Dame Marie Tempest. An actress of vast experience, always exquisite in her appearance, she was the standard bearer, if a decidedly dated one, for good taste and dress. Perpetually the centre of attention and now putting a tentative and genteel toe into the lucrative world of film, she was billed to play the matriarchal 'Aunt Jennifer'. Wilfred Lawson had been hired in, cast only too appropriately as the village drunk; Newton knew that his stay in Cornwall promised to be a riotous pleasure.

Almost an island within Cornwall itself, Sennen was divided by a steep hill into 'village' and 'cove'. Unflinchingly facing the raw blue Atlantic, cold and dangerous in the winter, wind smitten and sun bleached in the brief summer, it was a beautiful, remote and hard place. The Monday evening arrival of the lumbering studio lorries that ground down the hill and clogged up the narrow streets, seemed to the locals an invasion and the prosaic plod of village life was brought to a standstill. There was uproar; lorries would not fit into the garages, there was nowhere to store the masses of gear and there was not enough accommodation. And suddenly the village was awash with high fashion, painted glamour and star faces the locals had only seen in their newspapers. Cast and crew, some 41 in number, comprehensively took over the Cove Hotel.

The word was put out that a number of fishermen would be needed as 'extras' and the next morning almost every man and boy was lined up outside the roundhouse, ready for inspection.

To the delight of the locals, filming seemed to infiltrate every part of the area, across to St Levan and nearby Porthgwarra, and at Newton's suggestion, down in Lamorna valley, just along from 'Bodriggy'. The script included scenes shot on the water and a makeshift raft was quickly lashed together to hold camera and crew. A rickety and dangerous affair consisting of a section of staging crudely lashed on top of two punts, it caused much mirth to the watching fishermen. The local newspaper, *The Cornishman*, covered the vexed and fascinating filming process blow by blow. Filming dominated village life for the better part of a month and the fine weather made the technically difficult task of outdoor shooting and sound recording relatively easy.

Outside working hours, all social life was led by the irrepressible Wilfred Lawson. True to character, he wore the same ragged suit on set and off and faultlessly maintained a state of inebriation. A confirmed and unrepentant alcoholic he was at the helm of every drinking foray; the Cove Hotel was unlicensed, so all drinking was done at the Old Success, the only pub, and truly the village was drunk dry.

Resplendent in his Armstrong-Sideley limousine and driving back to Sennen for a late shoot, Newton stopped for a lunchtime pint at a pub in Long Rock, just outside Penzance. By now he too was adopting, full-time, the character he was playing and in sea-boots and grubby smock he looked none too respectable. Certainly the landlord thought as much and Bob was abruptly ordered out. That evening cast and crew descended on the pub en masse. Scrubbed up and dressed in suit and tie, Newton was unrecognisable. Drinks were ordered for all in the house, then Bob turned to the landlord, reverted to 'Joe Varwell' and growled 'All except for you, you ...!'

Rain or shine, the evening close of shoot saw Newton drive back to spend the night in Lamorna. Sennen's tourist hotel was not for him, he was a local! By now Nigel had married into a Cornish family and his in-laws had moved into the valley. Conveniently Algernon's new mother-in-law was ensconced next door, and these were considered family homes.

For Bob the glorious Cornish summer had been a revelation; too long away, too long in dirty London, his return to the Duchy was like homecoming. Off-set hours were spent rediscovering the simple world of his childhood. Bob was ever of the people and it was the company of the working Cornish men and women of Lamorna, Mousehole and Newlyn that he sought. Drink was always the catalyst, laughter the reward. A protracted and boozy session at the Wink in Lamorna saw him challenged to walk to Newlyn, backwards; it was a challenge he, of course, took up. Yet Bob also showed himself often to be the family man. With a child-like delight he was drawn to the company of children; ever generous with his wealth and invited into the home of a Newlyn fisherman he paid the man's daughter the outrageous sum of ten shillings for the privilege of plaiting her beautiful long hair.

Bob looked enviously at Joy, who was now happily established with Beakus in their beautiful Lambe Creek home. With more money in his pocket than even he knew what to do with, and seeking to replicate their happiness, he impulsively bought a house. Gear Cottage was a pretty little bungalow on the north coast between St Just and St Ives, set in a landscape untouched by time. It was a magical place; hidden amidst an untamed, pre-historic and numinous land, it was cut off from the cosmopolitan world by a stretch of wild heathery moor. Six miles from the bustling market town of Penzance it was the perfect fantasy hideaway. The cottage was however run-down and sadly neglected and it needed work. Annie, who had rumbled Bob's plans too late to stop him, was far from amused. She could do little about it however; certainly Marjorie was little help. Unable to settle, unable to find a new relationship and a new life, she was dividing her time between meddling in her children's lives and her own brand Christian Science. Exasperated, Bob and Pauline planned to dispatch her out of London. War was looming, and now that Bob, like Joy, was grand with his own country seat, she was persuaded to move south, away from the expected rain of bombs.

The town of Newlyn suited her taste and a pretty fisherman's cottage, situated up a steep little side street that boasted its own artist quarter, was rented for her. Gently Marjorie was repatriated to the county that she had known as home.

All too soon the Sennen shoot wrapped and Newton said his goodbyes to the mass of locals whom he had befriended; the fishermen, the children, the coy local girls. Especially he said his farewells to Tom Pender, the gentle giant coxswain of the lifeboat. A close bond had grown between the men, something close to Bob's always yearned for father-son empathy.

The circus stopped off to shoot a few scenes at a farm in Higher Pudsham, near Ashburton in Devon, then headed north again for Elstree and interior shooting. In Sennen Lawson and a local donkey had become inseparable companions and a feature of life on set; now, facing the soulless tedium of studio work, Bob livened life up by buying a donkey of his own, riding it into the studio and installing it in his dressing room...

By February the film had been brought through post-production and as a thankyou, the Sennen locals were bussed the few miles to the Savoy Cinema in Penzance for a special preview; a real treat and an adventure for many of whom had never ventured so far from home!

Burned out by the monotony of studio work, Bob decided a holiday was called for. The Gargoyle Club was the centre of his and Annie's social life and hearing tales of David Tennant and Hermione Baddeley's exploits in St Moritz, a skiing trip seemed the ticket. By now a happy four-way relationship had formed between Bob, Annie, Beakus and Joy and a winter jaunt seemed the antidote to a country gripped with pre-war blues.

In Kitzbuel, Austria the party took to the slopes; whilst Annie, who had skied for Scotland, handled it all with ease, the Cornish contingent floundered hopelessly. Convulsed with laughter they were often unable to move. Stiff and bruised they floundered back to their hotel where the long evenings ran into the nights; the hospitality was excellent and the party threw themselves wholly into the exciting new experience of continental cuisine and wines. Relations with the German guests were, however, problematical;

hard words were said and someone spiked Beakus' drink. It had little effect on his iron constitution however and the party resumed with sneering jibes of 'Nasties' thrown across the room.

The release of *Yellow Sands* came in July at the Piccadilly Cinema, London, and like the play, it was an immediate hit. Calculated to appeal to a nostalgic American market, it was called 'charming and witty' by the Motion Picture Guild, 'the cream of entertainment'. The work also read as a social documentary, showing a special place that had shaped Newton's life and that was vanishing fast. This was Newton's first stab at a leading role and he carried his part with passion. An angry and convincing screen character, he utterly dominated the film and made it his own. For the first time he showed his undoubted talent. Rightly, '*Variety*' overlooked Marie Tempest's cameo and lauded his performance as 'the most legitimate' in the work.

A world away in Hollywood, Newton was now beginning to be noticed. Sam Goldwyn and director William Wyler were planning the year's prestige production, the first film version of Emily Bronte's *Wuthering Heights*. To take the part of Heathcliff, Goldwyn's first and immediate thought was for Ronald Colman, the ubiquitous 'English costume actor'. It had already been decided that the part of Cathy would be given to Merle Oberon who had been shipped back from England, 'on loan' from Korda. In her baggage was a print of an unimaginative little piece that had been knocked out some time back, *21 Days*... the bait was laid.

Finding Colman bound to an unbreakable contract and unavailable, Wyler looked at *21 Days* and Olivier with interest. A flurry of telegrams flew across the Atlantic but failed to elicit any response from Korda. Goldman expressed doubts about Olivier, condemning his acting as too aloof and stating that he could never deliver a sufficiently coarse and ruthless performance; Wyler was, however, dispatched to London.

Olivier had previously taken a nibble at Hollywood, but Hollywood had bitten him back, and, now embroiled with Leigh, he was reluctant to return. The lure of Hollywood's jingling purse was nevertheless persuasive, and he travelled back with Wyler. Initial test shoots didn't go well; Larry was missing Leigh, and the demanded 'on-screen charisma' between him and Oberon, who was herself reluctant to be away from Korda whom she was planning to marry, was not in evidence. Goldwyn, looking on from the wings, was less than impressed with Olivier, that 'damn ugly English actor'. Olivier, equally unimpressed with Hollywood, hurried back home to Leigh. The shooting date was imminent and Wyler gave chase. Olivier however was obdurate. Growing desperate Wyler screen tested Newton. His response was ecstatic. On June 7th he cabled Goldwyn, 'Have 'found' Heathcliff.... amazing young English actor.... much better than Olivier...' adding that Korda thought Newton ideal. Bob's screen-test reels were dispatched to Hollywood, but Goldman was not persuaded. A frantic crossfire of cables ensued. Goldwyn grudgingly suggested that Newton have a moustache and, still determined to have Olivier, replied 'Newton out of the question.' Wyler pushed harder, swearing that 'Newton is a magnificent Heathcliff... has strength and power which Olivier lacks....'. Goldwyn wavered and Wyler again cabled - 'Olivier has unavoidable weaknesses... Olivier admits Newton is better Heathcliff... why can't you believe me about Newton.... am your agent not his....'. But now, riled by the nagging, Goldwyn had dug his heels in. Eventually, worn down by the relentless pressure, Olivier agreed to take the part and the purse.

Had Bob been hired into the Hollywood project his position would have been problematical; by now he had contracted into another ABPC production, *Poison Pen*.

The roll-call of professional actors within what was still very much a fledgling industry was small; everyone knew everyone and, arriving on set, Bob found that he had the pleasure of working again with Flora Robson and Belle Crystal, one of the *Yellow Sands* cast. Also roped in was the willowy figure of Wilfred Hyde-White. The predictable routine of studio work got under way and a bottle appeared in a quiet corner of the studio and the inevitable card game sprang up. This time it all got out of hand; on one occasion both Bob and Hyde-White held good hands and neither would fold. The kitty went up and up until there was over five hundred pounds and a fist full of IOUs on the table. Sweat trickled and the tension became unbearable, then Hyde-White cracked. "This is ridiculous!" he shouted and stormed out. The debts, which Bob could never have covered, were never settled and on this occasion he got away with it.

Another work that had been adapted from a stage play, the film was again squarely aimed at the American market. Demonstrating an innovative use of exteriors and 'natural' backgrounds it was another pretty tale of rural life, murder, jealousy and drink. Set in a picturesque 'Devon' village that was torn apart by anonymous hate-mail, Bob appeared as 'Sam Hurrin', a broad village character. In a scattering of scenes, he was on-screen for just ten minutes or so in this sixty-five minute piece. Released in the spring, the film passed in front of the acid eye of Graham Greene who was rightly scathing; 'a deplorable example of an English film which tries to create an English atmosphere... the dialogue is appalling, the ignorant patronage of men who have spent their lives among the sets of suburban studios is thickly spread over the English countryside.'

Unsurprised by these reviews and with Annie at his heels Newton seamlessly rolled out of his bed and on to his next work. This time he was taking the starring role; the film was *Dead Men are Dangerous*. Directed by Harold French (taking his first stab at life behind the camera) Bob was cast as 'Aylmer Franklin'. In a typically inane plot where, as a bankrupt novelist, he changes identity with a murdered man and is in turn pursued by the killer, he then becomes the chief suspect in another killing. Brilliantined and bespectacled in a seventy minute work of many guns and little entertainment value, Newton did what he could and managed to raise the work above the floundering and pedestrian. *Kinematograph Weekly* was generous saying Newton's 'wide emotional skill not only invests the character with conviction but enables it to evoke sympathy...'.

Laughton's production company's second film, *St Martins Lane*, had garnered little praise and less cash and 'Mayflower Pictures' was in trouble. With the inevitability of war driving the British public into a quasi-delirious state, cinema was booming and with an estimated 40% of the population attending weekly, yet ironically, as in the formative days of British film making, money was now becoming desperately short for actual production. In a last-ditch effort to save his company, Laughton called on an old friendship and pulled off a tremendous personal and professional coup; he persuaded the emerging genius, Alfred Hitchcock, to direct his next picture, Daphne du Maurier's *Jamaica Inn*.

The work was a radical departure from the modern thriller cycle upon which Hitchcock had built his career, yet he agreed to direct what was very much a 'retro' work before even glancing at the script. Too late he found that the thing was a travesty of the classic book and an utter mess. This was inevitable as the part of the villain was a devil in a dog-collar, a vicar; this would have been utterly unacceptable to the Hayes Office diktat and release in either the UK or America would have been impossible. Hitchcock desperately tried to get out of the contract, but Laughton, who knew that this was his last chance, pleaded and begged. Hitchcock demanded a total re-write; Laughton argued against it. Hitchcock was a technical perfectionist and for him film was all about meticulous preparation. He also liked a happy set where teamwork meant a light-hearted, friendly and fun working environment. Unfortunately Laughton's dithering, dictatorial attitude was diametrically opposed to Hitchcock's. A team of writers was hurriedly called in to work on the script. The great Elstree feud had begun.

At the head of a star-studded cast Laughton, of course, took the lead role; Newton took the second billing. His was the cooked-up and appropriately 'Cornish' character-part of Jem Trehearne, an eighteenth century 'insurance investigator' who was trying to rumble a gang of cut-throat wreckers. A strong supporting cast was led by the growling Leslie Banks and one of Connie's new actors, nineteen-year-old Maureen O'Hara. Laughton's chosen protégée, it was her first major film. Blushing and racked with nerves, she was to play the leading romantic interest in the more than welcoming arms of Newton's Jem Trehearne.

In the depressing knowledge that the home film industry was entering another of its doldrum periods, shooting began on September 1st. Once again Newton began the six-days-a-week process of dragging himself to the studios, clocking in at four in the morning and often reeling out twenty hours later.

Unlike the beautiful exteriors filmed for *Yellow Sands*, Bob saw that this was to be another stagy, 'porridge factory' production. There were some, token, location shoots in Cornwall but the studio sets and the mocked-up 'Cornish' scenery were utterly bogus, full of two dimensional composites, creaking façades and phoney seas stirred up in a large tank. Bob groaned from the sidelines as Laughton and Hitchcock began to fight. Hitchcock thought actors should be regarded like dancers, always carefully choreographed and always humoured; Laughton was no ballerina and his sense of humour had comprehensively deserted him. Quickly the spats reached monumental proportions. Each man blamed the other, and each drove the other to distraction. Laughton, still obsessively 'methody' in his amateur way, was now doing to Hitchcock what he had done to Von Sternberg in *I, Claudius*. The fact that Hitchcock and Eric Pommer detested each other didn't help a situation that was spiralling into chaos.

Watched despairingly by a cast and crew that stood idle for hours, Laughton now began experimenting with the 'walks', the leers, and the voice of his character, the porcine 'Sir Humphrey Pengallan'. This was a big budget picture, and as both star and co-producer, Laughton had too much power and too much at stake. Life in the studio degenerated into an inner circle of hell. Unnoticed amidst the maelstrom, Newton and O'Hara, however, worked well together, their scenes flawless and empathetic. Laughton could see that he had a rising star in O'Hara, yet, desperate to finance what he knew could be his last attempt as producer, he had already secretly sold-on her contract and a five picture deal to MGM in exchange for a financial bail-out.

Picking up every morning from the night before, the bickerage continued. Hitchcock was now preoccupied with his imminent departure to America to work on another du Maurier book, *Rebecca*, and, more a film technician than a personal psychiatrist, he threw in the towel and let Laughton have his way. Ruefully he remembered Korda's advice; 'With him (Laughton) acting was an act of childbirth, what he needed was not so much a director, as a midwife'. Nevertheless Laughton's skill was, if costly, unquestionable and Newton observed his technique closely; only

Laughton could possess the utter professionalism to accurately load and cock an antique flintlock pistol.

In the end Laughton's screen histrionics were challenged only by those of Leslie Banks, who growled, bristled and slammed throughout. Newton, by comparison, played his part staid and straight-laced and with considerable fortitude. Filming wrapped in the middle of October and everyone walked away knowing it to be a disaster. Running to 108 minutes the work saw its première at London's Regal Cinema. The stars were herded in and out in regulation Hollywood style in flashy limos to the now familiar screams of fans and autograph hunters. The next day's reviews dubbed Newton's Jem Trehearne 'a dyed-in-the-wool hero' who 'contributes sturdy support' to a film that was a 'box-office miracle'. *Variety* called it 'excellent entertainment' and 'a typical Alfred Hitchcock direction job'. Perhaps not. Other, more honest, reviewers, called a spade a spade. 'Mr Laughton's Laughtonism has slowed things down...overplaying unashamedly...it doesn't seem like Hitchcock...'.

Both Laughton and Pommer knew that Newton's 'sturdy support' only helped to prop up a work which was little more than a mess, and only rarely hinted at Hitchcock's directorial skill. Yet somehow the film packed cinemas for five weeks, broke records and received unwarranted levels of press attention. British audiences however, more attracted to American output, were becoming decidedly sophisticated and the inadequacies and glaring continuity errors were not lost on them. Graham Greene, representative of the sniffy new-intellectual middle-classes, penned a fittingly vitriolic review and the word got out that the thing was, as everybody had suspected, a turkey. 'It is more difficult to know why Mr Hitchcock embarked on this bogus costume piece and submitted himself to a producer. There is only one Hitchcock incident here in embryo...'. He even found ink to damn Newton's saintly Jem Trehearne, '...with his gasps and glittering eyes' he was dismissed as 'particularly unsympathetic'. Done to death Mayflower Pictures folded; O'Hara, one of the few who enjoyed good reviews, had attracted the eyes of Hollywood and left for the States in Laughton's baggage train.

DuMaurier wept bitter tears over the botched production and Hitchcock struggled to distance himself, physically and morally, describing it as 'a ridiculous thing to undertake'. He followed on behind Laughton, a $40,000-a-picture contract in his back-pocket courtesy of Myron Selznick. Dubbing the film merely an 'apprentice piece' he got away with it; public memory was persuaded to be short, and the debacle did little to dampen his growing status. Nevertheless the work he had turned out was undoubtedly one of the worst films of all time. Perhaps the only thing he took away from the set was a deep respect for Newton.

In Hollywood Hitchcock scored a remarkable success with *Rebecca* and went on to triumph with a string of other great films. Selecting the cast for his 1947 film *The Paradine Case* he had doubts about the stage presence of the lead actor, Frenchman Louis Jourdan, who had been chosen to take the central role of the valet. This was only Jourdan's second film, and Hitchcock feared him to be too Gallically smooth, too suave, to be able to successfully carry a part where great repressed passion was needed. His ideal casting was Newton, 'with horny hands, like the Devil!' Perhaps Newton would have thought otherwise. Laughton had followed Hitchcock onto the set, and once again made his life a living hell...

By this time war had been sold to the British public as inevitable and minds were being carefully kneaded into a state of selectively xenophobic fervour. Once again Bob staggered into the 'porridge factory'. Recycling material from an earlier French failure entitled *SOS Mediterranean*, where an international maritime coalition displayed an unfashionably chummy co-operation between French, English and German officers, a new film plot was muddled out. The Germans had now been excised and replaced by a more contemporary ally, Russia. "Enemy navies forget war and battle a new horrible menace to civilisation!" the posters screamed. Perhaps they were self-referring.

Sponsored by the Ministry of Information and retitled *Hells Cargo*, the plot served the usual entrée of murder, before moving on to an unpalatable main course of a 'mad sea captain' with a contraband cargo of poison gas, which is, naturally, released. The triumvirate coalition of seemingly equally mad sea-dogs then save the day and the innocents on-board a passenger liner in the path of the gas. Reconciliation, international harmony and much hearty back-slapping close the story.

Directed, rather loosely, by Harold Huth, Newton played a suitably clipped and 'foreign sounding' Ruski, 'Commander Tomasou'. UK release was in May; the American version, dubbed *Dangerous Cargo*, followed quickly. Whilst far from being art, the film depicted what was unmistakably 'the Hun' getting a drubbing, and was a popular success. *Kinematograph Weekly* wrote warmly of Newton's performance, '...his is a fine piece of character drawing.'

On September 3rd 1939, Chamberlain glumly announced that Britain was once again at war with Germany. Like everyone Bob heard the announcement without surprise; comfortable in a Chelsea pub the horrible reality of conflict was blurred by drunken patriotism. Without thought he gathered up the sweepings of the bar and headed down to the nearest police station; en masse they signed up. It was a fine gesture; they were applauded as heroes, hands were shaken and backs slapped; the 'public commendation' was in the post. Doubts and recriminations were left for the following morning.

Annie might have protested but there would have been little choice in the matter; the war was only a few hours old when Parliament passed, almost without debate, the National Service (Armed Forces) Act. Overnight every fit man between the ages of eighteen to forty-one was deemed liable for military service. Unlike in 1914 there was no widespread rush of volunteers. By the end of 1939 727,000 had been conscripted, in 1940 4,100,000, and in '41, 2,222,000. The nation braced itself. The deadly effects of conflict on the centres of population had already been only too well depicted, ironically on film. The 1936 production of H G Wells' *Things to Come* had dramatically and portentously shown the reality of mass civilian death at the hands of the dreaded bombers. The most shocking scene showed a packed cinema taking the first, deadly blow.

On September 4th, the day after war had been announced, the government, fearful of such an onslaught, shut down every one of the four and a half thousand cinemas in the country. It seemed to be a death-blow to the film industry. Only Korda and a handful of clear thinkers could see that it would also be a death-blow to public morale. He pressed his case; film would be a vital war weapon, he insisted. To prove his point, he abandoned all his projects and turned the whole of his production empire to producing the first 'war-film'. Eight weeks later *The Lion has Wings* was screened. It was a stunning piece of propaganda. Spitfires and barrage balloons drove back the aerial attackers. Confident and brisk, it gave the assurance that Britain was 'ready' and that 'we were going to win'. Government conceded, cinemas reopened and the people flooded in at a rate of thirty million a week desperate to see the war that was happening.

Within six weeks of being invaded France had fallen; then the disaster of Dunkirk unfolded. British optimism perished on the bloody beaches and the nation reeled in a state of shock.

Seemingly now an almost permanent fixture at Elstree and fast becoming desperately bored with the whole thing, Newton turned up dutifully and September saw the release of his next film. A typical produced-on-a-shoestring Ministry of Information propaganda work it was a war-melodrama entitled *Bulldog Sees it Through*. Initially entitled 'Alias, the Bulldog', and sneakily hinting at the eternally popular 'Sapper' character, the film was, in fact, hashed up from a novel by Gerald Farlie. A yawn-worthy tale of German spies and saboteurs in London, the work laboured under the censor's usual constraints; 'the use of the name of the deity in any form is prohibited: also such words as 'lousy', 'blasted' and 'damned' etc.'. The plot warily followed the usual line, and as the studio blurb put it... 'A test pilot and his secret-agent butler unmask his ex-fiancé's husband as an armaments' saboteur...'. Inevitably there was a corpse that has, naturally, disappeared. Once again directed by Harold Huth, Newton appeared as 'Watkins', the 'secret-agent butler'.

Taking the lead role of the 'Bulldog' was Jack Buchanan. A debonair and immensely popular song and dance performer, he was a stage and screen star who had briefly run his own film production company. Now aged forty-eight, this was his second shot at the famous 'Bulldog' character.

The work ran to seventy-seven minutes; obligatory screen glamour was well supplied by one of Bob's old paramours, Googie Withers and a rapacious twenty-four year old Norwegian blonde beauty, Greta Gynt. Modelling herself on Tallulah Bankhead, Gynt's social and sex life, even within the acting profession, was considered outrageous and Bob, forever with a roving eye, was smitten from the start.

By now Bob's relationship with Annie, strained by his relentless drinking and unapologetic womanising, was becoming problematical; Sir Robert had proved to be right and it was 'going all to Hell'. Early in the marriage Annie had suffered an ectopic pregnancy and had been told that she would never be able to have children. It was a bitter blow for them both, one that opened an emotional gap that had widened into what was becoming a slow drifting apart. Bob was up to his neck in film work and emerging only to crash-out; Annie was shuttling between the studio, Turville Heath and her parents home. Meetings were infrequent and dissolved too often into rows, but Annie was still addicted; there was little wonder. The Bob she loved still occasionally appeared; looking out of the window at Bicks Bottom one day, she saw a horse drawn cart standing outside. The back was laden with flowers; "I don't know what I'm doing here..." the man grumbled, scratching his head, "...you know, madam, there's no insanity in my family!". It was another 'Bob' escapade. "You've come to the right address..." sighed Annie with a smile.

On the 'Bulldog' set Newton had quickly formed a close friendship with Buchannan. 'Jack showed an extraordinary patience and understanding' it was recalled, 'which was often necessary in getting a performance from Robert Newton who was a colossal imbiber and led a Rabelasian life. One evening after they had completed their day's work, Bobby invited 'The Master' back for drinks at the elegant house he had rented in Cheney Row, Chelsea. There was no furniture and no light. Bobby invited his guest to sit on one of the mattresses which were his only creature comfort. He lit a candle in one of the many bottles which surrounded them, exclaiming 'There, it's a lovely light, isn't it'. A moment or two later he started a fire by tearing out a large section of the superb Regency banister....'. One of the lasting, if expensive, legacies of Bob's time with Buchannan, very much an advertisement for British male fashion, was a predilection for classic tailoring and Rolls Royces.

By now Newton's dream cottage in Cornwall was taking shape. Friday evenings would be spent thundering down the A30 on his motorcycle, south and west into the setting sun. The Gurnard Head Hotel was just a couple of fields away; the Tinner's Arms was down the road and the weekends were well supplied with good company and booze. One Sunday night, well beyond 'last orders', someone casually asked Bob if he was filming on Monday. "Christ!", Bob bellowed. Staggering out he clambered on his motorcycle, kicked it into life and roared back up north. Riding all through the night he arrived at the studios at dawn, chilled to the bone, bleary and unshaven. He staggered onto the set and waved to Buchanan. "Couldn't let you down, Master...", he croaked, then passed out.

January 1940 saw the long-delayed release of Korda's Oliver/Leigh sales board *21 Days*. By now Hollywood had moulded something like fame out of the raw clay that Korda had sold across the Atlantic; public interest in the couple was intense but nothing could disguise the fact that it was a poor work. Graham Greene reviewed the work for *The Spectator*; 'Perhaps I may be forgiven for noticing a picture in which I had some hand, for I have no good word to say of it...'. Detecting a strong odour of 'cooked ham', he dismissed the story as one 'particularly unsuited for film adaptation'. 'Slow, wordy, unbearably sentimental, the picture reels awkwardly towards the only suicide censorship allowed – and that, I find with some astonishment, has been cut out. I wish I could tell the extraordinary story that lies behind this shelved and resurrected picture, a story involving a theme-song, and a bottle of whisky, and camels in Wales... meanwhile, let one guilty man, at any rate, stand in the dock, swearing never, never to do it again.....'. Famous last words.

Greene was right about the plot's total unsuitability for film. Early in the formation of the industry it was seen that, like theatre, some kind of agreement would have to be cobbled together between producers as to just how far they could push the boundaries of taste and decency. In 1912 the British Board of Film censors was set up by the industry itself. Ten years later its authority was legally recognised and censorship officially came to the screen. Falling into three basic categories, the rulings looked to protect the authority of the church and state; Rule One was there was to be No Blasphemy. Politics of course reared its head; there to be no rattling of the cages of the docile working classes. It was decreed that there was to be absolutely no upsetting Johnny Foreigner either. Swearing was taboo; even Shakespeare was tidied up. Nudity was, of course, banned; except for 'Negroids'. 'Orgies' were out. Contempt for the State and the Kings Uniform was a no-no. 'Lascivious behaviour' could not be screened; nor could gross drunkenness, childbirth, venereal disease, 'sexual relations between white and coloured people' (half-castes were OK'ish), drugs, cruelty to animals and children, prostitution, incest, realistic epilepsy...or suicide.

A million miles away back in England, and despite the half-hearted and interminable business of phoney-war, Newton knew that he would soon be called up. Remembering his childhood dream, he hoped for service in the Navy. It was a hope he was to come to regret.

September however saw a temporary deferral and yet another film. A new genre of film had sprung up in the forties, one that Newton was to portray in many forms. It commented on and reflected the realities of a bewildered and rapidly changing society catapulted by war into an uncertain future, and somewhere between condemnation and nostalgia, it re-evaluated the past. Looking at upper middle-class Victorian households, the genre dramatised the common conception of nineteenth century 'hypocrisy', where the surface appearance of an established social hierarchy clashed with a hidden 'reality' of tyranny, intolerance and familial stresses. 'The mixture of banality and *haut gout*, naturalism and eeriness, which pervades the nineteenth century can arouse a certain nostalgia...' one social historian wrote, 'the interiors of this age, with their gloomy light, their heavy curtains and carpets, their dark wood, and their horror of the void, breathed a particular warmth and disquiet...'. Very much a critique of the family structure, the old inherited mores were now put under the spotlight. Suddenly marriage and the bonds of family were being portrayed in terms of confinement.

Adapted from a play by Patrick Hamilton (author of *Rope*), *Gaslight* was directed by Thorold Dickinson. Centrepiece of the work, the vaguely 'foreign' Anton Walbrook (another Anglicised German who had fled Nazi repression) plays 'Mallen', the sadistic and lunatic husband who was trying to drive his wife, Diana Wynyard, into a similar lunatic state by various sinister knockings and scrapings. On the cusp of the action Newton made a lightning appearance as 'country cousin, Vincent Ulswater'. Almost an extra, he appeared only at the end of the film, after the dirty deeds had been done. With superb sets and with one foot firmly in the creepy Gothic, the work was a masterpiece, certainly one of the most visually striking films ever made in Britain. Pulling in the crowds, it set a new gold standard for British cinema. An outstanding success, some critics rated the film as 'perfect', certainly the best film of the year.

The piece was shot in only nine weeks. M.G.M's David O. Selznik was so impressed by the result, already recognised as a classic, that he offered Thorold Dickinson a long-term directorial contract. War and call-up was however imminent, and Dickinson, to his enormous credit, refused.

Shipped across the Atlantic with high hopes, the work was re-titled *Angel Street*, snapped up by M.G.M, withdrawn from circulation and slammed into a vault. Rumours of the destruction of the prints infiltrated the industry... (this was in fact true; Thorold Dickinson fortunately succeeded in saving a single copy) but all soon became clear; a glossy and poor quality Hollywood version was in the pipeline. 1944 saw Charles Boyer and Ingrid Bergman appear in the same roles and the work was re-exported to the UK under the title *The Murder in Thornton Square*.

Britain was now on a war footing, shortages began to hit the film industry and it was obvious that some kind of rationalisation would have to be enforced. Film production was nationalised and fell under the not unenlightened control of the Ministry of Information, which vetted all film project proposals and apportioned available film stock.

Newton's last picture of 1940, *Busman's Honeymoon*, was produced under the remit of the Ministry. Directed by Arthur Woods and produced by M.G.M., it was a development from a popular Dorothy L Sayers drama seen on stage at Comedy Theatre four years before.

Again Newton played the 'yokel' character, handyman 'Frank Crutchley', a murder suspect. A character at the side of the action, but one that keeps ducking in and out of the plot, 'Crutchley' leers and squints throughout, employing a bona-fide 'west-country' growl to prove that he is 'up to no good'. The lead part of the quintessential Englishman, Lord Peter Wimsey, was taken, somewhat strangely, by an American, the Hollywood leading man Robert Montgomery. A pretty and old-fashioned little who-done-it, the film was screened in November, then exported across to America as *Haunted Honeymoon* and turned out to be a minor success. Perhaps demonstrating the gaping rift of understanding that lay between the two nations, American reviewers praised the film's quaint charm and marvelled at British fortitude in making such a charming little work when 'Norway was being invaded and the Low Countries overrun'.

That 'quaint charm' had, however, now paled for Newton. He found the film process utterly boring, but with the West End virtually closed down by the summer's deadly air-raids, it was, at least, work.

Released at the same time as *Busman's Honeymoon* was a little eight minute, one-reeler knocked out for the National Screen Service; *Channel Incident*. Worked up from a screenplay by Dallas Bowler it was a recycling of the already near-myth of Dunkirk, and turned crushing defeat, incompetence and horror into palatable heroism and victory. Directed by Bob's old friend, Anthony Asquith, the work was spliced with some real naval sequences, and told the story of a woman, played by Peggy Ashcroft, struggling against Naval bureaucracy. Dressed as a man, she takes her 'little boat' across the Channel to rescue 'her man' from the beach. Working alongside Gordon Harker, a notorious Cockney, Newton's character took a fatal bullet playing the role of a brave Bren gunner.

Having languished in the vaults for three years, *Four Dark Hours* was at last released, now retitled as *The Green Cockatoo*. Premièred in the US, the work seemed creakily anachronistic, nevertheless *Variety* magazine rated Newton's performance 'good as John Mills' no-account brother, around whom all the action revolves'.

During June, July and August 1940, the bombs had been falling ever closer to London. In mid-August, on a sunny Thursday evening, there was a sharp attack on Croydon; sixty-two people were killed in less than half an hour. Then, on Saturday, September 7th, a full year after everyone expected it, London itself faced the onslaught. It was one of those rare, beautiful, autumn days which felt like spring and made even the drab city streets appear fresh and bright. There was hardly a cloud in the pale blue sky. When the sirens shattered the silence that afternoon, the Blitz had begun. London was not to know a single peaceful night for nine months.

As the blitz was unleashed a besieged government at last fully grasped the vital propaganda value of its home-grown screen stars. Those not yet drafted into the services suddenly found that the morale industry needed them. Now established as a top-rank screen personality, Newton's military call-up was placed second to his film commitments and he was contracted into a new work, a film version of Bernard Shaw's cutting political satire, *Major Barbara*.

Despite being written back before the Great War the work was in tune with the issues of the day. Dynamic and controversial it looked at class, the troublesome and invisible world of the working masses, the role of the Salvation Army and the dream of a Utopian future. The genius behind the film was Gabriel Pascal. Another enigma of the Korda mould, extraordinary in every way, 'a Romanian, who claimed to be a Hungarian, and who looked like a Himalayan', he was an Anglophile giant who routinely butchered the English language. He had previously made a film success out of Shaw's *Pygmalion*, now, the story went, he had arrived again at Shaw's door and offered all he had in the world: ten shillings, a dream and a wallet full of promises in exchange for the film rights of *Major Barbara*. Mixing charm, charisma and bravado, he had bluffed and bullied Shaw into acceptance. But perhaps it was all too easy; Shaw was no fool and was an avid cinema-goer. A founder member of the London Film Society in 1925 (along with Augustus John) he believed that 'a good film was a filmed play' and, presciently, that cinema was 'going to be the mind of England'.

The director of *Pygmalion* had been Anthony Asquith, but Asquith was unavailable, so Pascal turned to the next man down the ladder, the man he had planned to be the film's editor, David Lean. Pascal titled himself producer and director but had only the vaguest idea of how to conduct the making of a film; like Korda however he did have an eye for greatness in others and knew how to delegate. Lean became both his right and left hand man. 'Assisted' by the fanatically punctilious Shaw and master cameraman Ronald Neame, Lean set about the business of putting together a script and mustering players. The chosen cast was strong, Wendy Hiller took the lead role, Rex Harrison, suitably annoying, was cast as her fiancé. (Weirdly Harrison's film character was based on one of Shaw's close friends, the classical scholar Gilbert Murray... the father of Basil Murray, Pauline's ex-husband...) Robert Morley was given the role of the Father. Donald Calthrop, Emlyn Williams, Penelope Dudley-Ward, (an old flame of Bob's from the *Hell's Cargo* days) and Sybil Thorndike filled up the gaps along with Deborah Kerr, ("...her name rhymes with 'star'") who at just eighteen was appearing in her first film having been picked up almost by accident. Billed underneath Harrison and Morley it was Bob, however, who scooped up the prize part. A pivotal figure, appearing mainly in the first section of the film, he took the stand-alone role of Bill Walker, a tough, snarling, wife-beating Cockney whose calloused soul Wendy Hiller was determined to save.

Korda's days of empire were now over and Denham had passed into the hands of J. Arthur Rank. The routine of filming commenced in late May with a sense of urgency; the vast studio complex had been requisitioned by the military and Pascal had been granted only ten-weeks to complete the film. Two of the vast studios had already been taken over for food storage and Pascal was assigned the one remaining stage and no more.

Production and the blitz went into full swing simultaneously. Caught up in the chaos, Pascal, a noisy, excitable egomaniac, chose to throw himself into the co-director's role with a passion. 'You are ruining my picture... you are crucifying me!' he would scream at any passing cast member. For him this was going to be the film that won the war, yet by week two, production had fallen behind schedule. As filming went on things got steadily worse.

Denham studios lay uncomfortably close to the RAF's frequently targeted Northolt Aerodrome and nerves on-set quickly became jittery. To make matters worse rumours began to circulate about some kind of secretive war installation in the studio's grounds and suddenly Denham was seen as the prime target for the entire Luftwaffe. Every time an enemy bomber crossed the coast, the studio alarms would sound and all hands would hurriedly decamp to the shelters. 'Bloody air-raid!' Lean would rage. Newton and Donald Calthrop showed more mettle and would sit the raids out in the comfort of the set.

"We had some wonderful actors in the film" Rex Harrison noted, "including some notorious drunks... a watch was kept on the dressing rooms for odd bottles of scotch, but nothing was ever found... and yet darling Robert Newton and Donald Calthrop seemed invariably to carry a heavy load. Eventually we discovered that each of them had a hidey hole on the set, where he kept a supply of nectar... and instead of retiring below to the air-raid shelters, they sat chatting and imbibing, oblivious to danger, until the rest of us came back to work..."

Battling with Pascal's rowdy paranoia, David Lean steered the shoot with a delicate touch. A Quaker and a man who abhorred liquor, he nevertheless had a great liking for Newton and something clicked between them. Like Bob his family roots were in Cornwall, his family coming from the great mining centre of Redruth; strangely he also had links with the Salvation Army, his predecessors having worked with General Booth to set up the organisation.

Although officially merely the 'cutter', Lean saw that Newton and Calthrop's scenes were pivotal to the work and quietly directed them when Pascal was away from the floor...

A break from the maddening chaos came as cast and crew decamped for a six-week location shoot at the idyllic Darlington Hall estate in South Devon. Pascal, ever the domineering tyrant, did his best to destroy the idyll; the whole set-up was imperiously recalled for a few wasted days before being driven back to Devon again. Pascal's irrational wrath was everywhere; firing and immediately re-hiring, no actor or technician was spared. A petty spat over the way a cigar was handled ended with him resolutely refusing to speak to Robert Morley. Bob was warned for his drinking on-set, put on suspension, fired, reinstated and fired again. Yet Pascal too had come to adore

Bob; like Lean, he had come to see in him the extraordinary talent upon which his whole picture would hang. *Major Barbara* was very much Shaw's ideal of a play filmed and the work dependent on dialogue. As filming progressed Newton and his character took over the film and Shaw carefully wrote in whole new scenes to embellish his role.

Racked by bombs, union troubles and domestic spats, filming ground on. Eternally haunting the set, Shaw demanded that every word of his script was not only spoken, but spoken correctly. The ten-week deadline was passed, extended and passed again. Tension mounted to an extraordinary degree. Nervous breakdowns resulted in the appearance of new faces, the film's editor, Charles Frend, tried to beat his brains out against the cutting-room wall...and Bob got his call-up.

On a dark and squally morning, glowing with farewell libations, Bobby Newton stepped up smartly at one of the Royal Navy's anonymous manning depots.

Along with the faceless gaggle of newbies he was quickly stripped and showered and screamed from shack to shack; his hair was butchered into the regulation short-back-and-sides and he took his place, rigidly to attention, amongst the old and the young, the bullies and the mothers-boys. Naked and shivering before the medic, Bob duly coughed and duly forgot to mention his asthma.

Poured into a boiler-suit, he was issued his pay book and driven, shivering, out onto the hallowed parade ground for an introduction to square bashing. Bewildered and bemused, he suddenly found himself eating on 'mess decks' and sleeping in hammocks within barrack blocks named after the naval heroes he recalled from his school days.

Taught by tough petty officers who were the backbone of the navy, Newton learned when to keep his mouth shut, when to shout the streams of approved naval oaths and how to attach the word 'Sir' onto every statement with intonations of infinite subtlety. He learned to respect the ragged yet sacred stretch of gravel called the 'quarterdeck'. If he wanted to walk out of the gates he had to wait for 'shore-leave'; then a 'liberty-boat' would be 'alongside'. It all seemed rather absurd at first, but the ingrained 'navy' attitude infected Bob like everyone else. Soon he was absorbed into the esoteric world of the seaman and began to regard himself, as seamen always have, as distinct from landsmen and vastly superior.

The navy was now desperate for men. Rated Ordinary Seaman, the lowest of the low, Newton was posted to *HMS Raleigh*, the Royal Navy's Plymouth shore base. Petty officers, hardened to the task of turning the streams of raw recruits into something like sailors in a handful of weeks instead of the usual months, wearily appraised the new bunch. Newton, swaying slightly, eyed them back cheerily. Bugle for 'lash up and stow' blared out at six in the morning and three months of dawn-till-dusk 'more-army-than-bloody-navy' saw Newton sweat out the land and some of the liquor.

Given special leave and thrown hurriedly back onto the film-set Bob found more tragedy. Donald Calthrop had been informed that both his sons had been killed in action; utterly broken and unable to go on he took to the bottle and quickly ended his life. A moment of silence was held on the set. His rather sad part in the film was finished by a body double.

Ironically, it was to be Pascal's incompetence that saved Denham studios. Production ran so far overdue that the military gave up and looked elsewhere for premises. Eventually, and after an incredible six months, the work put through to post production. The original budget of £125,000 had now soared to over £300,000 and the film's backers braced themselves for a substantial loss. Perhaps it was inevitable; the troubled UK film industry was always going to lose out against the might of Hollywood.

America was now the undisputed leader within the industry. Worldwide it controlled 65% of the market. In the period 1937-38 the US produced 545 films, Britain only 162. In the almost five thousand cinemas now operating across the UK, eighty percent of film shown was American; little wonder that by the end of the war Britain was to owe £22 million in rental fees.

The transition from phoney to real war signalled a period of fundamental change in Britain. The changes began after September 1939. Some were abrupt, some were gradual, but nothing was ever going to be the same again. Remarkably the film industry, like much of the media, produced little that could be interpreted as a comment on the world situation. As tight-lipped as the appeasers, hardly a single film had been made about the Nazi menace before the war. Only the American *March of Time* series produced any journalistic account of events inside Germany, much to the displeasure of the British censors. Cinema steadfastly remained neutral and turned out bland escapism from wherever they could buy it; mostly it came from America.

The British public knew only too well what war was to bring and dreaded it; retrenching into the immediate present they were perfectly happy to live in ignorance while they could. Escape from the nagging worries came cheaply in film, in music and colour, in wealth and in facile romance. These were products that the American film factories produced in abundance and the British public consumed them voraciously. And it was easy to see what was right with the technically superior American imports and what was wrong with so many of the British pictures. Over-written, wordy, unctuously polite and deadly slow, too many home produced works still smacked of proselytising and the creaking traditions of the stage. *Major Barbara* was without doubt a 'superior' film, a thinking man's work where 'truth' was the objective hunted down throughout. It had all been done in a thoroughly British way; realistic, orderly, the film was still, in essence, a series of photographed vignettes and for many it represented the apogee of boredom.

The 1930s had seen British film mature but the set-up was still a very un-Hollywood-like mixture of studios, amateurism, genres and legislation. Ironically it was the war that was to provide the industry with a stable, if temporary, environment. 'Britishness', class identity and the all-embracing idea of consensus were to become central concerns. The decade had seen the ascendancy of the middle class and its values, yet despite the politicians' flannel and the spread of wealth, the landed gentry and the traditional elites were still as powerful as they had ever been. Fragile and fearful of rebuke, middle-class values had come to film but few offered a complex analysis of society. Public expectations of cinema were high, but the social changes hinted at would take a decade and a war to come into effect.

The winter of 1940 was exceptionally harsh. Snow fell early and thick and as the days shortened, turned to ice. Many actors had already fled to America, amongst them some notable screen faces. All were labelled with the cruel jibe, 'Gone with the Wind Up'. As *Major Barbara* wrapped Bob at last received the dreaded buff envelope and call-up. The easy life was done. In the bitter darkness he packed his bags and reported for navy life.

6. An Extraordinary Seaman

The year of 1940 was one of miserable military defeats for Britain. Thoughts of a swift victory were replaced by ones of mere survival. Radio went into overdrive, came into its own, and Tommy Handley's 'ITMA' ('It's that man again...!') changed the nation. A background noise that was louder than the bombs, it lampooned the enemy mercilessly and achieved the seemingly impossible. Carrying millions on a wave of simple laughter it helped make light of their predicament and the horrors around them.

Hot on the heels of the Ministry of Information's disingenuous 'No propaganda' guidelines for film, the desperate and subliminal crusade to bring America into the war saw a subtle moral side-step. A campaign to simply show 'what Britain was fighting for' was initiated. This was a risky tactic. Obtuse or not American audiences were now extremely aware of overt propaganda and contra-suggestible to it. Anything that came with a whiff of moral pressure was immediately regarded with suspicion.

A protracted war had now become inevitable, and the British government turned its mind to the problem of 'the actors'. Whilst keen that they too should be seen to be 'doing their bit' like everyone else, they saw that it was the cinema screen, and these 'star' actors, who would sell the vital message to the Americans. A list of key actors to be reserved from the general carnage had been mulled over but, in the labyrinth of Whitehall, no one had ever actually got around to tackling the matter. Now actors were being called up. Olivier and Richardson were already drafted into the Fleet Air Arm, as was Rex Harrison; Kenneth More was destined for the navy... but Newton, like his father and reluctantly facing Churchill's war, was ahead of them all.

As an island nation, Britain had always placed its faith in its Navy, yet the First World War had revealed serious problems in the Senior service. Flaws in ship design had become disastrously evident in action against the German fleet, yet for much of the inter-war period government had shown itself unwilling to address the situation. It was partly a matter of economics, partly a move towards a hoped for peacetime economy, but by the time 'the next war' was spotted on the horizon, the long delayed military expansion had come almost too late. Even then, the Admiralty dismissed the threat from the air and dictated that the war would be decided by naval action. At high levels it was also decreed that the 'U' boat threat would be neutralised by the new under-water detection system, Asdic. All too quickly this too proved to be a deadly mistake.

Sucked back into the navy and graduating from seamanship training to gunnery, Bob was assessed as ready for further instruction and dispatched to Portsmouth.

There after more bawling and screaming, he and his mess mates received the dreaded notice of their postings. Those with influence got cushy numbers at shore bases. The lucky ones were assigned to the slick destroyers or the big battle wagons. The unfortunate sods got the tiddlers and the minesweepers. With trepidation Newton opened his draft-chit; he had drawn Special Services, the bloody minesweepers, and was ordered north to the Mine Sweeping and Torpedo School at the icebound Scottish shore base, *HMS Lochinvar*, a 'stone frigate', located on the Firth of Forth.

By the end of 1939, Nazi mines were having a deadly effect. In a single week in November, 60,000 tons of shipping had been sunk off the east coast. The navy had been forced to move on quickly. Suddenly maritime war had become a deadly and technical game and it was no longer possible to dispose of mines by simply peppering them with rifle fire whilst standing well upwind. Five weeks of wire splicing, frozen hands and the endless 'pulley haulley' of warps and sweeps made Newton ready for sea service, or at least, as ready as he was ever going to be. With his pay-book in his pocket, a railway warrant in his hand and laden with gas mask, newly stamped kitbag and hammock, he headed south to Greenock and His Majesty's Minesweeper *Britomart*.

One of the new 'Halcyon' class sweepers, *Britomart*, 'J22', looked and was tiny. Built at Devonport in 1938, she displaced 875 tons. Running to just two hundred and forty five feet on the deck she nevertheless packed in a complement of six officers and seventy men, all under the watchful eye of the 'old man', Lieutenant Commander Spencer Shelly Stammwitz. A 'Fleet Sweeper', designed for fast mine clearing, she was lightly armed, with just two four inch anti-aircraft guns, four .5in machine guns and depth charges aft. Narrow, shallow-hulled and light, her decks cluttered with gear, *Britomart*, like all of her type, would prove to be dismally unstable, pitching and wallowing even in harbour. 'She'd roll on wet grass...' the old hands muttered.

The task of mine sweeping was distinctly unglamorous, but in military terms, vital. Churchill later summed it up; 'A significant proportion of our whole war effort had to be devoted to combating the mine. A vast output of material and money was diverted from other tasks, and many thousands of men risked their lives night and day in the minesweepers alone'. As a class, the fighting Halcyons had quickly proved their ability. Shortly after hostilities began, a test had been carried out in Lyme Bay; 50 dummy mines were laid and the sweepers were ordered to find them. They found 51.

Ordinary Seaman Newton stepped on-board with a thumping heart. Flushed faced, he touched his hat, stood gaping at the confusion and was bawled unceremoniously below decks. There his new mess mates accepted him with the egalitarian ease of the lower deck and pointed out his bunk. In civilian life he might have been a film-star but now he was just another wet-behind-the-ears, bloody 'Hostilities Only', greenhorn. Dutifully Bob drew his thirty shillings a week and followed the party line; "This is the sort of thing that is happening to people all over the world" he said to the newspapers, "...it was a big transformation from studio lights to the King's Navy, but it is proving a fine experience...".

Early in the spring of 1941 the Germans had changed tactics and were trying to block the vital sea-lanes in the Channel. *Britomart*, along with a flotilla of other sweepers, was transferred south, temporarily attached to the 3rd Escort Group and Irish Sea Escort Force.

Thankfully, she was never far from home. Her regular patrol was banging up and down the east coast yet her activities took her into many ports; Oban, Inverary, Aultbea, Londonderry and the Clyde. Tying up in Gurnock was a regular occurrence; navy discipline in wartime was relatively relaxed, the crew were given all the shore leave possible and Bob became a regular face in the local bars. Routine boiler cleaning always took a wonderful three days and shore leave was richly welcomed. It gave time to sleep, wash and shave and write home, yet for smokers and drinkers like Bob, wartime privations were becoming noticeable and increasingly hard to take.

Early in the war the well-known cigarette brands became scarce; by May 1941 the joking definition of a millionaire was 'a man who smells like an onion and smokes the cigarettes he likes'. By August *any* cigarette seemed a luxury and manufacturers were appealing to smokers to 'show a little restraint'. Odd-looking packets began appearing on shop shelves and were eagerly snapped up, but there was little enthusiasm for these obscure brands. The hated 'Pashas', an unpopular Turkish brand with an unpleasant smell, were everywhere. 'Walters' simply tasted foul. Drinkers also faced problems. In the first year of war, beer production fell by a tenth and whisky by two thirds. The invasion of France had cut off supplies of wines. Government cashed in on need and successive Budgets hiked prices; by 1941 a pint of Luke-warm Wallop (mild ale on draught) had shot up from a shilling (5p) to one and seven a pint. The doleful sign saying 'No Beer' was too often seen displayed outside pubs. Many bars didn't open until eight at night, or only on alternate nights, and then often rationed customers to a pint, or a half, a head. Spirits had doubled in price to 1/6 (8p) a nip, often more. A bottle, if anyone would sell you one, would now put you back twenty five shillings and ninepence (£1.29p). By 1943 Scotch was almost unavailable and 'vodka' became the popular, patriotic, drink; even then a bottle would set you back over two pounds.

The soft luxuries of a cosy berth and shore leave were rare however, and *Britomart*, like every navy ship was hard pressed; mine sweeping duties were endlessly carried out whenever she was not required to act as an escort or patrol. By mid-September she was operating out of Belfast, then Liverpool.

Subsumed by Service life, Bob's earnings had diminished and he had quickly sold his Smith Street house in Chelsea to a Gargoyle chum, John St Aubyn, (the Fourth Lord St Levan, of St Michael's Mount in Cornwall) for the princely sum of five hundred pounds. With the call-up universal and morally unavoidable, Annie was now doing her bit and volunteering for the American Red Cross and she desperately needed a base in London; the solution seemed simple...

By now Lawrence Olivier and Vivien Leigh had gone public about their relationship. They had blown their earnings from *21 Days* on a pretty little love-nest in Chelsea, Durham Cottage. Very much the sophisticate, Leigh saw that it would fall to her to elevate the uncultivated Olivier and had re-decorated in exquisite taste. The domestic dream was short-lived however. Olivier had been transferred to Hollywood for the filming of *Wuthering Heights* and *Rebecca*; simultaneously secretive talks regarding Leigh's involvement in *Gone With the Wind* were progressing. They looked for a tenant and were only too happy to leave their cherished hideaway in Annie's safe hands...

By now the war was going badly for the Allies. Across Europe the Nazi war machine seemed unstoppable and the British army, reeling from its mauling at Dunkirk, was still struggling to recover. The situation was desperate and the British government now saw that it must grasp at whatever allies it could, no matter how unappealing. Attacked in its turn, Russia had staggered back punch drunk. The toll of her casualties was enormous; she could only give ground, of which she had a premium, and hope for a miracle. Churchill knew that if Russia fell all the might of Nazi Germany would be turned on Britain. War brought about strange bedfellows and now the Russians, the brutal bogeymen of Europe, yesterdays rapists of 'Gallant Little Poland', were, in a sudden about-face, to be counted as 'comrades'. Russia would have to be supplied with fuel, raw materials and munitions to fight the common war; the question of 'how' was faced as an afterthought. The only feasible way lay in a northern sea route, above Iceland, through the Arctic fogs, ice and storms. As always, the problem was laid at the door of the already beleaguered Royal Navy.

Built to fight a two-ocean conflict and lacking modern equipment and numbers, the Royal Navy was already extended far beyond its limits. At the end of '41 Japan had come into the war with a series of devastating naval victories. Now the British navy was fighting in the China and Java Seas and the Indian and Southern oceans and, in the northern hemisphere, it was engaging both German and Italian forces. All the Admiralty's arguments against the northern convoy routes were simply ignored in the face of political expediency; Soviet Russia must be supplied, no matter what. Britain's tired warships would now have to face the oldest form of marine conflict, the convoy battle.

Sailing north, the convoys would have to cross the Norwegian and Barents Seas to the Soviet port of Murmansk at the head of the Kola Inlet, the only ice-free anchorage on the Soviet Union's northern coast. During the summer months the convoys could also use the ports of Archangel and Molotov on the White Sea. The high latitudes through which the convoys were to pass were notorious for monumental gales, sea-ice, deadly colds and blizzards. In the winter there was little or no visibility, in the summer daylight was almost perpetual.

The navy knew that the routes of the convoys would be dictated by seasonal fluctuations of the polar ice-fields. Summer would allow a safer northerly route, but the winter would force the ships nearer German air force bases in occupied Norway. As if to make matters worse the warm waters of the Gulf Stream which ran north-east along the Norwegian coast created both blinding fogs and a poor environment for Asdic. Summer or winter however, blizzard and gale or flat calm and crystal clarity, there was no avoiding interception by air, surface and by U-boat.

Convoy work, more than any other kind of war, was a life of acute discomfort and interminable monotony, yet one which might erupt at any second into a savage crisis. For desk bound strategists the operation was tactically unsound; for the seaman it was to be hell on earth.

The Halcyon Class minesweepers were never designed for Arctic conditions, but they now had a vital role to play. With a proven capability of anti-submarine warfare, there was little choice. On board *Britomart* there was no announcement; both officers and men were kept in the dark as to their fate. As ever, the rumours began. The first real hint came in a sudden flurry of training. Such was the shortage of escorts that 'working up' the ship was cut to a minimal five days. Every daylight hour was spent in gunnery, anti-aircraft, torpedo and anti-submarine practice. Then the rumours were effectively confirmed; the ship underwent the rudimentary process of 'Arcticizing'. The majority of the crew had never set foot aboard a ship before 1939, now they had to learn fast; there was to be no more easy coastal work. Soon they would become battle-tried veterans.

On the 21st September *Britomart* steamed out of the Mersey and headed north. On the evening of the 23rd she anchored in the vast, deep-water harbour of Loch Ewe, northern Scotland, where a ragged assortment of merchantmen were battening down for dirty weather. Early the next morning, as the first flurries of snow fell and the cheerless dawn broke, *Britomart* and a rag-tag naval escort herded the merchantmen of convoy PQ1 out into the churning Atlantic to begin the two thousand mile voyage to Archangel.

The first leg of the journey was the seven hundred mile run up to the relative safety of Iceland and Hvalfjord, the 'fjord of the whale', or universally to British sailor men, 'that God-forsaken bloody place'. *Britomart* was 'going Foreign' for the first time and through the mind of every man ran the name that had already been slapped on the operation, 'The Suicide Run'.

The steam north was relatively easy and the convoy anchored in Hvalfjord, an irregularly shaped eighteen mile long inlet, on the 28th. Just two miles wide, it made an ideal place for the convoy to lick its first wounds and regroup. Already the place was crammed full with drab naval vessels, depot ships, oilers and store ships. Ringed by treeless shores and backed by precipitous snow dappled mountains, the place could have been beautiful, yet, now, was utterly forbidding.

The respite was brief. Steep seas met *Britomart* as she cleared the shelter of the coast and she buried her bows. Shipping green and taking on-board tons of water, her handling quickly became difficult. Below-decks was turned into a slopping shambles. The convoy comprised ten wallowing merchantmen. Hidden by the darkness and the filthy weather, the passage was mercifully free from enemy attack; the conditions were dreadful but were as bad for the stalking enemy. Stuck in the undignified and dangerous position of the 'tail-end-Charlie', *Britomart* could only watch helplessly as the gale split the little convoy and the merchantmen vanished into the darkness.

Now, for the first time, with fear chewing his guts, Newton really understood what he was facing; freezing Arctic gales, black waters that would swallow a man in minutes and perpetual darkness. And always there was the enemy; silent, waiting to kill him. Like all the new hands, he wilted in the bitter cold. Tortured by the maddening, pitching rhythm, he suffered all the agonies of seasickness. Each watch brought another unbearable and deadly period. Naval issue clothing was good but the sub-zero wind cut through the layers he had piled on as if they were paper. Numbed and reeling, even old hands found movement almost impossible on decks that were slick with ice. Each crew member wore every scrap of clothing they possessed, long-john's, sweaters, woollen mufflers, balaclava helmets, duffel coats and sea boots stuffed with long socks. Ontop of everything went the inevitable Admiralty pattern inflatable rubber lifebelt. Shouted orders were answered with muttered curses. Ice constantly built up on decks and superstructures and had to be hacked away; the thought of capsize was on everyone's mind. Pulling and hauling with deadened fingers and feet, the routine of de-icing with steam hoses and picks was endless.

The misery of foul weather was of the worst kind. Newton, like the other hands, spent hour after hour on deck, drenched with spray. Seeping its way through his oilskins and the thick woollies underneath, the icy wet contacted his skin and trickled down into his boots. Too often the weather was so foul that there was no possibility of going forward or aft on the upper decks. There was water everywhere, boats were smashed, gear was torn away; if an enemy had been spotted there would have been little chance of getting off a shot. Below decks there was little relief, only the stench of sweat and vomit and latrines, the eternal spiralling, pitching madness, only the damp misery of leaking decks, sweating bulkheads and chill miasmas that penetrated every corner. Food was of the most basic kind and the long-suffering and much abused cooks fought their own galley battles. But the food, when it came, was usually hot; tinned sausages, soup, thick Irish stews with 'dough boys', eaten with a spoon out of mugs and the ubiquitous pannikins. Ironically, and to Newton's amusement, 'Tiddy Oggies', navy for Cornish pasties, were always popular.

The passage was agonisingly slow and 'action stations' a perpetual order. Steering as far north as the winter ice allowed, the sweeper's seventeen-knot cruising speed was cut to a deadly eight knot crawl by the panting merchantmen. Just once, in the company of her sister-ship *Harrier*, and in a glorious burst of activity, *Britomart* raced ahead, ordered to investigate reports of enemy activity off Spitzbergen. Nosing into Isfjord, they discovered a German party just arrived by air and setting up a meteorological station. All guns blazing, they forced the enemy to abandon their equipment and scramble to escape. It was a glorious, minor victory.

Eventually the bleak snow-capped headlands of Nova Zemlya hove into sight and, on October 11th 1941, *Britomart* cautiously entered the mouth of the Dvina river. At first they nosed their way through the crusted sea ice with infinite care; then one of the experienced officers pointed out that this was nothing compared to what would come later. Soon they took to driving contemptuously at full speed, crashing through the 'bogey' along the tortuous 24-mile course that made the approaches to Archangel.

The merchantmen were discharged and *Britomart* berthed adjacent to the bombed-out shambles of Miamaksa in the mouth of the river, just downstream of Archangel. Curious locals stared distrustfully from the dockside as if the arriving foreigners were from outer space; only the local kids showed any spirit and fights broke out over the chocolate bars and cigarettes that the sailors handed out.

Granted shore-leave *Britomart's* liberty men spilled onto a land that looked colourless and uninviting. Expecting a diminished grandeur they were faced instead with a few stunted trees and a handful of squalid shacks; the place was an utter dump. The local people looked hungry, apathetic, dirty and destitute, they didn't even beg, just stared listlessly, ignoring the rowdy, goodhearted greetings from the invading sailors. But of course there were always the permitted bars. Bursting into what passed for a restaurant Bob beat the rush... "He had quite a lot of money on him and ordered caviar and vodka all round..." one of his shipmates remembered. The party was riotous. "However when it came to paying, the Russian waitress wouldn't recognise English currency..." The official exchange was supposed to be twenty roubles to the pound but this time the sailors hit a typically Russian brick wall, "...the situation looked like brewing up into an international incident. There was a lot of argy-bargy on both sides before the matter was settled somehow...".

Convoy PQ1 had slipped unnoticed past the nose of the enemy and began handing over its cargo of tanks and fighter aircraft. Winning through to Russia didn't, however, bring a safe haven. German bombers followed the convoy into port. As the dock workers struggled to discharge cargoes, their efforts were all too often brought to nothing as merchantmen were blown to bits or consumed by fire. Lethally close to enemy airfields, air-raids occurred as if by clockwork, three times a day until it all became routine; Archangel took a terrible blitzing and the packed waterways became scenes of pitched battles.

Mercifully orders for *Britomart's* return to home waters came almost immediately, and by the 23rd of October she was back in Hvalfjord; three days later she anchored at Scapa.

The first convoy run up to Russia had been a salutary lesson for the navy and had shown many deficiencies in the little Halcyon class sweeper. At Scapa, *Britomart* was hurriedly put through a further 'Arcticizing'. From here she headed south to relatively warmer waters, steaming into the teeth of the first real gale of the winter. Sea conditions were atrocious and *Britomart* was forced to seek shelter in the Tyne before finally tying up at West Hartlepool. There the refit was continued; twenty three days tied up against hard and twenty three opportunities for Bob and his mates to take a run ashore.

For the film industry the outbreak of war had spelled disaster, but now, with all social normality seemingly suspended, film, like booze, tobacco and casual sex, was classed as a vital distraction. When cinemas re-opened their doors there was a stampede. People just didn't care about risk of being bombed. There were casualties of course. One film, with the ominous title *Opened by Mistake*, acquired in the cinema circuits the sort of albatross reputation that Macbeth had in theatre; three cinemas showing it were bombed. Undaunted, the public demanded entertainment and any film, no matter how bad, could be shown. Standing, or sitting uncomfortably on the floor, throughout a whole four hour showing was not uncommon. Much of the material shown was blatant propaganda, but nobody cared. Newsreels were always a hit, so much so that they were often screened after the main feature. Footage showing 'the destruction of the enemy' was cheered; captured Italians were greeted with hoots of derisive laughter and when Spitfires and Hurricanes sent the enemy 'crashing to earth' there was often a standing ovation. For most people going to the 'pictures' meant a long, cold wait in a queue, and a packed house that was stiflingly hot and thick with tobacco smoke. Yet it was pure escapism.

In early November, as *Britomart* was preparing for her next run to Russia, Bob received orders to report to Denham studios. Despite the almost obligatory nature of the summons, his agent was able to demand a hefty £12,000 fee. He was engaged to appear in Anglo-American's production of A J Cronin's novel *Hatter's Castle*.

The piece was a grim morality play and Bob the central character; as if to follow his thuggish role in *Major Barbara*, he was now to play 'James Brodie', a towering, bullying Scot. Following in the genre pattern of *Gaslight* where the drama centres on the husband's tyranny over his wife, *Hatter's Castle* further echoed this scenario by emphasising the authoritarian rule of the father over his children. Backed by Paramount and produced by MGM British, the work was bang up to date, radical and bold. The plot centred on Brodie's daughter, played by Deborah Kerr, a girl whose naivety results in pregnancy, and is brutally turned out of the family house. James Mason was to take the role of the family doctor, and Henry Oscar, an old friend from *Fire Over England*, the part of Brodie's business rival.

Going into rehearsals under the directorship of Lance Comfort, a man as mild as his name suggested and one renowned for getting the best out of any actor, Newton immediately demonstrated that he had been influenced by Laughton's 'method acting'; he had now to 'find' someone to base his screen character on. "I had some difficulty finding 'Brodie'..." Newton told a reporter, "Quite by chance I met him on a golf course, just the man, pots of money, no culture, power gone to his head. I bought him six golf balls on the spot, I was so glad I'd met him!" Perhaps less enchanting was his penchant for taking his screen character off-set. Like so many others, the war was taking its toll on his marriage. Bob however relished his new role, and he soon came to regard *Hatter's Castle* as his 'favourite film' to date. "We were all like one big family on the set" he said. As if to prove this point, walking into the studios one morning, he was informed that one of the bit players, the diminutive Scot, David Kier, had just been laid off. Outraged, he found Kier, picked him off his feet, tucked him under his arm and stormed back onto the set. "As long as we are filming, David gets paid....!" he bawled. That evening, out on the town and celebrating this triumph for British Justice, Newton stumbled across Dulcie Gray, ('Gracie Dull' according to typical theatre humour) a pretty, twenty three year old brunette who had also just broken into film. Bob's chat-up was as seamless as ever... "He invited me to a drink which I could resist, but a lift home, which I couldn't... we both went to the pub next door. He became involved in a fierce argument with another customer and eventually swapped his car for a horse. He offered me a ride, but I luckily refused as he wasn't seen again for three days...'.

Three days were little enough for Bob, however. Ever the Lothario he had already set his sights on Enid Stamp-Taylor, one of the minor players in the cast of 'Hatters'. At the age of just thirty-seven she had successfully, and briefly, married into money. Young, free, newly single and decidedly a beauty, she faced Bob's romantic assault with assured and worldly ease. Comfortably shmoozing in a swanky Park Lane restaurant, autograph hunters and secrecy were the last things on their minds...

By now alcohol had come to dominate Bob's life. He had experienced war first hand and neither he, nor any serving man, could have endured a life of day-to-day survival and the constant threat of sudden, bloody death without some opposing reaction. Ashore, in the heaving stew of pubs and bars, and at the bottom of a glass, the antidote to all the horrors of the last cruise was so often found.

Newton's unexplained absence threw production into chaos and a rankling conflict developed between Bob and the film's producer, Isadore Goldsmith. With an eye on the American market Goldsmith now dictated that 'Scottish' accents would not be used, and that all parts were to be spoken in the best King's English. Having already 'found' his 'Brodie', Newton could not change. Perhaps he had learned more than method acting from Laughton. With the devil in him, he fought back, slipping in a Gaelic burr whenever he could, and bringing the studio and Goldsmith crashing down around his head.

Co-director on the set was Laurence Evans, "...There comes a point towards the end of the story when Bob says "I built ye up and I'll burn ye down" and he cavorts around the set with a flaming torch in his hand. The fire department weren't mad about it but they allowed it to happen. During filming Bobby was living at a pub called The Water Mill in a village near Denham. He had a caravan in the garden at the back of the pub, a gypsy caravan, and of course he spent most of his time in the pub and at night would go back to the caravan and sleep it off and get to the studio early in the morning. On this particular night he had obviously had a couple of drinks too many and he decided to rehearse the next days shooting. They found him with a torch in his hand, saying "I built ye up and I'll burn ye down...", having set fire to his caravan. It was not popular... but all the really funny stories about Bobby were about his drinking... he was renowned for his drinking, but always in the nicest possible way".

Part of Bob's gipsy lifestyle was, once again, a donkey, now his customary morning transport to the studio gates. Once there and 'in character' he became a monster. Deborah Kerr, who had already played the terrified victim of Newton's rages in *Major Barbara*, began to face his new character with a very real terror. One scene demanded that 'Brodie' slaps her across the face and then kicks her; she begged that the scene be done in one take...

Hatter's Castle was completed and released before *Major Barbara*. The work saw its première, with credits suitably citing both Newton's and Kerr's appearance 'courtesy of Gabriel Pascal', and it was a roaring success. Once again it truly *was* Newton's film. James Mason admitted, "We all stood back, he carried everyone before him and was magnificent". Even the curmudgeonly critics applauded. *Variety* called Newton's work a 'superlative performance' and that 'his name should be displayed above the title!' Another critic raved, "We have witnessed some of the best acting since Laughton left these shores". For the *Observer*, Newton's Brodie was 'a stunning tour de force...'. The critics were right, but unaccountably it took five years for the work to see its US release.

The film was an individual success story, but the British film industry was struggling to survive. In the vacuum of competition, Hollywood reigned undisputed and all eyes were upon it. In Hollywood lay fame and fortune for actors, directors and investors alike. MGM's forthcoming production of *Gone With the Wind* was now being launched with a massive pre-emptive publicity strike and the casting of 'Scarlet O'Hara' lay at the centre of the artificial media frenzy. Korda, the consummate manipulator, had long argued for his rising star, Vivien Leigh, to take the role, and Selznick, convinced of her screen value since seeing her in *21 Days*, had quietly signed her up. With the contract in his pocket, Korda continued to sit on his earlier work and wait. Stashed away for two years, it had almost been forgotten, only seeing a glimmer of daylight when it was sold on to Columbia in '39, who in turn suppressed it. It was only when *Gone With the Wind* and Olivier's *Wuthering Heights* had hit the screens, that it was at last released. Confusingly it was variously labelled *21 Days Together*, *The First and the Last* and *The Twenty One Days*. In America Leigh and Olivier, incognito and giggling, attended to watch themselves. But the film only showed them as the unsophisticated, callow actors that they had been; ashamed, they slipped out before the end.

They were not the only ones to slip away from a film screening. Wendy Hiller was holidaying in Anglesey in Wales and a private showing of *Major Barbara* was held for her in the tiny cinema in Bangor. "Gabby had been cutting and cutting..." she said "and I made him keep several speeches which were absolutely necessary. When I realised that those vital speeches were not in the film, I went to the ladies and wept and never saw the end of the film...". The official première was a grander affair, held on March 20th 1941 in Nassau in the Bahamas. Organised by the exiled Duke and Duchess of Windsor, Pascal appeared, larger than life and complete with Katherine Hepburn draped on his arm. The London opening took place a month later at the Odeon, Leicester Square.

Even hacked down by sixteen minutes to 121 minutes, it was obvious from the start that Newton and Hiller *were* the film; Bob, with a virile, yet simple and poignant naivety, simply out-acted everyone. April's issue of Picture Post, the leading British popular magazine of the day, captured the mood of audiences exactly, 'British films find a new kind of man; Hollywood has its tough guys, Robert Newton is as tough as any of them, but in a new way.' 'Robert Newton for the tenth – or is it the twentieth time? – has stolen a film from the stars. He's been doing it for years in a quiet, effective way. The parts cast for him are never particularly large or particularly interesting – until he gets in front of the camera and begins to act them. By the time the film is shown, Robert Newton's performance is the one the critics single out, and the one the audience remembers after they leave the cinema. There was his neurotic soldier in 'Farewell Again', his Dutch controlleur in 'Vessel of Wrath', his secret agent in 'Jamaica Inn', and any number of other characterisations which jump to life in films that often lack quality in other respects. And now he has done his spectacular piece of limelight stealing in the £250,000 'Major Barbara ...'. Film Weekly echoed these words, 'The magnificent performance of Robert Newton as Bill Walker, the Cockney tough, is the keystone of this faithful adaptation of Shaw's play...'. The *Sunday Dispatch* wrote; 'It is as much Robert Newton's film as Wendy Hiller's...', the *Sunday Times*; 'Robert Newton as the tough, brings a warmth and reality to the film which I do not think Shaw put there...'.

In his foreword for the written work, which included a chunk of classics courtesy of Gilbert Murray, Pauline's ex-father-in-law, Shaw had said, with a hint of self-deprecating irony, that no doubt his work was safe from discovery by the American viewers; 'You have sent us some of your old destroyers, and I am sending you a film version of some of my old plays'. He was wrong. His film was not only 'discovered' in America but promptly dragged through censorship; fearful that it might 'offend any of the religious community' it underwent a thorough snipping. The work was however well received and the paradox not utterly lost in translation; 'a manifest triumph', the reviews crowed, 'a more triumphant picture than any the British have yet sent across'. Pascal had been sure that his film would make his name but amazingly, and despite the rave reviews, the venture proved a financial failure. Perhaps the Cockney accents were too pronounced and the dialogue too fast for the dullard yanks. 'An Englishman cannot open his mouth without making another Englishman hate or despise him' said Shaw; perhaps he should have said '...an American hate or despise him'. Even he lost out to the sum of £20,000.

By the middle of November Bob's part in *Hatter's Castle* was completed and he returned to navy life and two shillings a day. A letter now came from his father; with news of the family working its way north to the inn at Becks Hole he had heard of his son's successes.

November 17th 1941.

'My Dear Bob, I have been reading wonderful notices of your two last films, Major Barbara and now Hatters Castle. I wish I could see Hatters Castle. I expect I shall have to wait a long time to see it up here. But perhaps it may be on in London somewhere when next I come up. I am so pleased & proud of your success. I felt I must write to you and tell you, you have certainly had your chance at last & made the most of it. I am hard at work on a country house for Lord Tredegas, when I have done that I am doing painting of Dytchley Park for Ronald Tiree, the member of Parliament. I wish you could come down here for a week end, while you are doing the Amy Johnson film, but I suppose it's quite impossible. I should like to see

you & for you to see our little pub. I have no licence but I can role (sic) up the barrel?!

With the best of luck & much love From Dad.

The Ministry of Information had a backlog of film projects and Bob's time was indeed already booked; summarily ordered another twenty-one day special leave he come straight back from his ship and in full navy rig rolled into Denham Studios to appear in *They Flew Alone.*

The screenplay, written by Viscount Castlerosse, one of the Shilling Theatre's backers, told the life of Amy Johnson, the 1930s air ace. Placed in the context of British imperialism, her courage was now portrayed as a part of the collective national war effort. An early victim of the war, Johnson was hailed a heroine and her story seen as a priceless piece of propaganda. Now, for the first and only time in his career, Newton was to step into the shoes of a living person, Amy Johnson's husband, Jim Mollison. Johnson's competitor in the air, Mollison was every bit the debonair playboy and Newton was ideal as his double.

The film was the initiative of Herbert Wilcox, a true-blue, white-collar, pillar of the British film establishment. His wife, Anna Neagle (an ex chorus-girl destined to become a 'Dame') was to take the part of Johnson. Bob might have been the ideal casting for Mollison, but Connie's had foreseen trouble and Willcox had been squarely warned, "Bob is a genius, you must make allowances...". They were right. Pillar of society or not, Wilcox came across as a stuffed shirt and represented everything Newton detested; the two men clashed from day one.

Struggling to cope with wartime restrictions, material and staff shortages and black-out regulations that ruled out night-time exteriors, the filming process got under way. Neagle's first studio meeting with her co-star was something of a shock. "Bob was given three weeks leave to make the film, this was quite common practice during the war. Actors and actresses who joined the forces were frequently given short periods of home leave to make films: it was the only way to keep the industry going and turn out entertainment for both troops and civilians who became increasingly under fire and strain... I can still recall his first arrival at the studios, straight from a mine-sweeping voyage... still wearing his uniform as an able-bodied seaman. I innocently believed at the time that his nautical roll was the result of a recent voyage on rough seas..."

Bob had by now fully developed a penchant for 'becoming' the character he was playing and he threw himself willingly into the Mollison role; the two men were introduced and telling them apart became difficult. Immediate pals, their lifestyles made them long-lost brothers. Adopting Mollison's drinking habits and style of dress, Bob quickly took to living his lifestyle on set and off. At 3.00am and in the middle of a blitz, he appeared at a cab-man's shelter in Sloane Square. He was wearing 'a pearl-grey topper' one of the cabbies remembered, 'grey morning suit and slung round his neck, binoculars. He stayed two hours. For the first hour he ate his way in silence through two helpings of Spam and chips. Then, pushing the plate away, he delivered a running commentary on a mythical Ascot race which, the cab men agreed, was better than anything they have ever heard from the BBC'.

Perhaps constrained by the fact that the man he played and the events he portrayed were so recent and real, Bob handled his screen role with an admirable subtlety. The actual process of shooting film, however, was a struggle. Very much Jack ashore, Bob, along with Annie, had taken up residence at the Savoy at the studio's expense and both were determined to make the most of leave and luxury. Working opposite Newton was an education for the prissy Neagle. "I little realised how many rough seas lay ahead of us together! But he gave an extraordinary performance. He was a most original actor and all his characterisations made a great impact on audiences....". Wilcox also remembered Newton, "Newton had recently appeared in *Major Barbara* and was a really great actor. But he was also an incurable alcoholic, his meetings with the real-life Jim Mollison cannot be recorded here. Both were extraordinary and extrovert characters and had no respect for law and order, women or the conventions. After any night they had together, I was lucky to get Newton on the studio floor at all..."

Unaccustomed to the rigours of naval life and the constraints of discipline, Bob was both exhausted and restless. Enjoying his freedom to the full meant that he had to be physically dragged onto the set each day by an agent worried about his own percentage. "One day, with a crowd of two hundred extras" Wilcox remembered, "I waited two hours for Newton anxiously and had almost given up hope when, with great relief, I saw the hired car that always picked him up from the Savoy. I looked in as it passed, but to my dismay – no Newton. The car stopped. The driver opened the door and out fell Newton. 'Get him to his dressing room', I told the assistant director. 'Strip him and douse him with cold water. Then give him some black coffee and dress him'. 'Me and how many?' asked my assistant. However, we got him on the floor where Anna as 'Amy' and the crowd of extras had been waiting. Anna was patient. The extras were not. The war was on, rations were tight, and to see a highly-paid star hold up the production and waste time and money did not amuse them. Bob came on, his face bloated and the colour of beetroot. His eyes were glazed and he made straight for me, starting to weep as only a drunken man can. 'You are so wonderful, Herbert. The greatest director in the world. I'll never let you down. I'm here – to act!' he declaimed in old-fashion Lyceum style, with extravagant gestures. I could see the angry mood of the crowd. 'Then act, Bob', I answered. 'That's what we've all been waiting for, and what you are paid for'. 'Herbert, darling' he went on 'I don't want the money. I love you and will act for *you* for nothing'. Anna on the sidelines must have been at the end of her patience. She also sensed the crowd was becoming more hostile. I took a chance. 'I've never kicked an actor before, Bob, but if you don't shut up and get on with the scene, I'm going to kick you in the backside'. (Backside was not the word I used!) 'You wouldn't do that to me, dear Herbert' he whined. I did. The effect was electric – on Bob, the crowd, and Anna. With an attitude of outraged dignity, Bob did the scene first time and to perfection."

That was Wilcox's version of the tale. The truth was that Newton had bile in his soul. He had lived war and he had seen sudden death; he had heard the death-cries of his friends, and the taste was bitter. His dislike of Wilcox and his easy-living, establishment cronies had turned into an outright aversion. The next day his car turned up on time, complete with passenger. Bob had come the whole way clinging to the roof. Time and resources were limited and filming proceeded with mechanical haste. In three weeks Newton's job was done. Quitting the soft luxuries of the Savoy and the Sloane Court hotel, where, mid-blitz, and playing himself, Bob had blithely recited Shakespeare to the nervous punters, he stepped back into his Navy rig. Then a phone call from Connie's saw him take a quick voice-over job...

The offer came from America; Columbia Pictures wanted Newton to do a voice-over for a character in one of their animated cartoons. Bob shrugged, he thought that was Annie's line. In a work entitled *A Battle for a Bottle* he found himself locked into a sound-recording studio with a still bruised Deborah Kerr. The script followed the recognised cat versus dog plot, Bob the growling bulldog on the porch, Kerr the purring feline using up her nine lives in pursuit of the titular bottle of milk. Released as No 17 in Columbia's 'Phantasy' series it was shown in America on May 29th 1942.

Unsteady and glowing with farewell drinks, Bob fell out of Annie's arms, out of the Rolls and through the dockyard gates at Hartlepool. On-board *Britomart*, officers and crew welcomed their celebrated mess-mate back with cheers and rough good humour.

They Flew Alone passed through post-production and Jim Mollison was invited to a special preview. Asked his opinion he replied, "I thought you (Neagle) caught Amy's spirit exactly". Asked about Bob's screen rendering of his own part "Well... he lifts it a bit, doesn't he?" he replied, raising his hand to imitate drinking. "Well, didn't you?" he was asked in return. "Well, yes, I suppose I did!" Newton's casting as Mollison seemed to knock Neagle, squeaky clean and very much the lady, off her stride. Perhaps he was too much of a real man for her. Wilcox, aware of Newton's uninhibited attitude towards women, had grown reluctant to submit his own wife's fragile morality to close contact. "Throughout the picture, Anna never played one of her close-up scenes with Newton. I decided to leave them for the sober period. As it never came, she played them all to me, with the back of my head in the foreground of the camera". Running to 104 minutes the work was premièred at the Odeon, Leicester Square, and was an instant hit. Once again it was Newton who had stolen the show.

The film quickly saw its US release; presumably it was another part of the unsubtle 'No propaganda' assault. Retitled *Wings and the Woman*, the audiences flocked to the film. The critics perceptively judged Neagle's performance as 'prim and proper' and 'at times, just a shade too prettily got-up for belief'. Another reviewer called Newton's Mollison, 'rambling and sketchy', but 'seems to come to grips with it in a manner particularly his own'... 'Mr Newton, though not invariably easy to understand as regards his diction, makes a splendid Mollison, catching the right sense of the man's conflicting impulses, erratic brilliance, and need for affection... Mr Newton plays Jim, the self-styled "playboy of the air" with genuine sympathy, conceiving a man of strange impulses which he can neither express nor control. His characterization of Mollison is a fine, compassionate, piece of acting'. In a work riddled with competing discourses some saw a proto-feminist agenda. Perhaps there was, even if Neagle played her character tempered with an antiquated modesty.

Bob's return to his ship coincided with orders for her departure; she was to proceed north to Scapa Flow and then onto Seyoisfjorour, on Iceland's east coast. She arrived four days before Christmas; on the 25th itself festivities were carried out and the men allowed the luxury of a run 'ashore'. There they were greeted by wind, snow and an intense cold, but the luxuries available in a country relatively unaffected by war were more than welcomed.

On Boxing Day *Britomart* made rendezvous with two ships of convoy PQ7A which had left Hvalfjord and proceeded north through thick ice and into the teeth of a howling easterly gale. Suddenly one of the merchantmen was torpedoed and sunk; there was little anyone could do; rescue attempts were out of the question. It was a depressing start.

Foul weather and frostbitten fingers and toes now became the standard. Decks were black with ice. Temperatures plummeted and every man jack knew that anyone going overboard was as good as dead. Two minutes were reckoned the maximum endurance; even if rescued, immersion inevitably led to the horror and shame of amputation.

Ten long days later, on January 5th, 1942, Britomart struggled into the Kola inlet. There, after a brief rest, and in the company of her sister-ships *Sharpshooter* and *Salamander*, she began the task of sweeping for the German mines that were now being laid by the hundred and posing a growing menace for incoming convoys.

Sweeping with 'all her knitting out', 250 yards out and 500 yards astern, eyes were eternally divided between the dark face of the waters and the grey sky. The front line and the Luftwaffe's airfields were just a few miles inland; air attacks came daily, even at sea, and lookouts aloft perpetually scanned the gloom for sight of the devastatingly effective Stuka dive bombers. On the 24th of January there was a fierce air attack; *Britomart* shot down one Ju 88, yet in the mele was hit by two bombs. Fortunately both failed to explode and damage was only slight; one able seaman was killed and another was badly wounded.

Even at night, during the middle watch, the weary midnight-till-four slog, there was the danger of a U-boat attack. Only the thought of the noon grog issue kept many of the shivering men going.

The onset of winter plunged the land into an almost perpetual darkness and life was dreary enough for homesick sailors. Relations with the Russians had deteriorated drastically since the first convoy and shore-leave was problematical. Inevitably standards onboard dropped off and frictions festered in the hours of boredom. There was, however, always spit and polish. Uniform across the navies of the world, when in idleness, when in doubt, the command went out, "Paint ship!"; the navy's answer to everything, it passed the weary hours. Off watches were filled with dhobieing, letter-writing and sleep; the evenings saw the eternally popular and utterly inane rituals of tombola, uckers and darts. Sunday morning brought the refreshing orderliness of Divisions; all hands turned out in their best rig, two shivering ranks facing inboard, at attention on the fo'c'sle, the only space large enough to accommodate the whole company. All stood bare headed for prayers. Afterwards came the Captain's rounds, an inch by inch inspection of the entire ship. Only later came the longed-for cry of 'Up Spirits'. At 11.30, tot by tot, the grog was doled out, then came 'Pipe Down' and a Sunday calm would fall over the ship.

Mine clearing was now seen as vital to the Arctic convoy system and the whole war effort. Without the efforts of *Britomart* and her sister ships the White Sea would have been an impassable death-trap for the Allies and the northern route rendered unusable. Typically the crippled and antiquated Soviet fleet possessed none of the latest sweeping gear. Even when equipped the Russians were not sufficiently sea-animals to use it properly without supervision and had to be taught the technicalities of degaussing. In desperation the Soviets offered to buy *Britomart*. Whilst the teaching went on so did the daily sweeping; the Nazi war machine saw that air-dropped mines were constantly replaced.

The monotonous routine was broken in late January when *Britomart* was ordered out into deep water to intercept the incoming seven ship convoy, PQ8, and escort it in. Bogged down in the impenetrable fog, her position was however helpless. Perhaps it was a lucky escape. *Sharpshooter* and *Hazard* made it out but a U boat lay in wait. At 19.45 U454 loosed off a torpedo and hit one of the merchantmen, striking in the No 1 hold. Badly damaged but not sinking the ship stalled, and was ringed by a flurry of naval vessels. At 22.00 *U454*, frustrated and without a kill, loosed off a fan of torpedoes at an unidentified vessel it had picked out in the frail light of the lighthouse on Cape Teriberski; the salvo missed the intended target but by a fluke struck *HMS Matabele*, one of the fleet's crack destroyers. One torpedo hit her magazine and the destroyer disappeared in a blinding sheet of flame. Two men were picked up out of the bitter water, barely alive; two out of a complement of two hundred.

The miserable winter saw harbours and waterways clogged with Allied merchantmen; the Soviet Union was fighting for its life and could supply nothing to fill their cavernous holds. Rumours of a dash for home were eternally rife but the new year saw no sign of the longed for orders. In February *Britomart* saw a break from the slogging routine, dashing out she joined the force escorting in the ten-ship, joint convoy PQ9/10, bound for Archangel. Detaching at Murmansk she turned around to briefly join a homeward-bound convoy, the lucky devils of QP7. Ringed by ice, sea conditions were a flat calm, but plummeting temperatures created an impenetrable blanket of fog. Navigation was a nightmare; breaking out into the Barents Sea *Britomart* hooted her farewells and reluctantly turned back again.

Relations with the Russians had always been difficult, the locals suspicious and cowed. Gradually Russian xenophobia deepened and the British navy found itself regarded more as an enemy than friend. There was no more 'Rule Britannia'; all shore leave was suspended and the Commissars screened off the jetties; Russian sentries were everywhere on the docks. Usually they were women, massively-built, clad in sheepskin jackets and armed with rifles and lethal looking bayonets that were lowered aggressively on sighting any British sailor ashore. "Angliski matros!" was the recommended reply. For homesick sailors it was a bitter blow; the locals were imbued with fear and even the black market dried up. Viewed with deep distrust by Communist Party officials, any encores of international friendship were now rebuffed and every conceivable obstacle was put in the navy's way. Standing orders saw ships and crews isolated and moored mid-stream and Soviet 'security officers' stationed on-board every ship. The romance with the capitalists was definitely over; Stalin was already planning how to carve up post-war Europe. The message was clear, 'intellectual' fraternisation by any Russian would be followed by exile and death. In something of an understatement Churchill was to comment, 'The Russians showed neither appreciation of our efforts nor understanding of our difficulties...'.

By the middle of March and with no end of the deadly chill of winter in sight, supplies on board *Britomart*, now stationed at Murmansk, were running dangerously low. The NAAFI store had long ago been stripped bare; hot food was just about the only comfort left but supplies from the shore were mean. There was always the inevitable boiled-to-death tea and cocoa; only the corned beef seemed endless. By now the ship was in poor repair; spares were running perilously low and rumours circulated endlessly. Then the long awaited announcement came; *Britomart* was homeward bound at last.

As part of an overall strategy, convoys were now timed so that they passed each other in mid-ocean. Now, with the incoming convoy behind schedule, officers and men could do little other than obey the amended last line of the minesweepers' theme-song and '...bloody well wait'. Then, on the 23rd, just outside the Kola Inlet, *Britomart* tucked in to her allotted station astern of 19 ship convoy QP9 (always an unenviable position; U boats, unable to approach a convoy from ahead would tend to fire off shots at the stern-most ships...) and headed west and then south.

The convoy was well escorted, but the weather was foul and the fleet plunged into the teeth of a screaming force nine sou'wester gale. The empty-bellied merchantmen riding high in the water pitched and yawed, struggling to keep position. The home run was agonisingly laboured; every ship was coated with ice and looked in danger of turning turtle. By the dawn of the 24th conditions had moderated and news from the fleet brought a ragged cheering; one of the escort minesweepers, HMS *Sharpshooter*, had sighted a shadowing U-boat, U655. Hiding in a snow-storm, she had thundered down, rammed and sunk it. It was a small victory but clawing south, the convoy battled against that more obdurate and invincible enemy, the sea. In the season of the equinox and with the barometer dropping, sea conditions became appalling. This time *Britomart* survived. Others did not.

Rust streaked and battered, *Britomart* discharged the merchantmen at Reykjavik on the 31st, picked up her skirts and crowded home southwards with all speed. Tying up in Leith on 2nd of April she faced a comprehensive overhaul and a half-yearly docking. Annie was at the dockyard gate in the Rolls Royce, with a bottle of champagne to welcome her hero home.

By now Marjorie was comfortably established in Newlyn and settled amongst fisher-folk sturdily indifferent to eccentricities. Nigel, married and divorced, had followed her down and was now working out of a dark little studio in Boase Street. The pair made a permanent, if slightly bizarre fixture. 'Clodgy Cottage' stood hard alongside the little school in Trewarveneth St that Bob himself once attended and now it became the focus for a generation of children who came to recognise their own local celebrity home on leave. All were thrilled when he tossed apples from his mother's prized trees, along with handfuls of coins, into the school's playground. The town's little cinema, the *Gaiety*, was of course showing all the latest films, and when Bob's came around, Marjorie, hob-nobbing with the local fish barons, would be there, standing in her crumpled finery to applaud 'her boy' as he appeared on-screen.

By now no part of the country was untouched by war and Cornwall felt the impact. German bombers, often unable to locate Plymouth's naval dockyards, would swing south to dump their loads on the little coastal towns and harbours. Newlyn took its share of death and the old coaling hulk that lay grounded in the middle of the harbour was hit time after time, bombs thumping through the hull into the soft mud; 'The sunken wreck of the Ark Royal!', crowed Lord Haw Haw. Enraged, Bob would shake his fist at the evil silhouettes high above, shouting obscenities as Nigel hassled him indoors. Marjorie's home was close to the harbour and she often heard the wail of the sirens and felt the blast of high explosives. On one occasion Mornie, Lamorna Birch's daughter and an old friend, was visiting. The air-raid sirens suddenly sounded and they hurriedly took shelter under the stairs, Marjorie stopping to snatch up a bottle of brandy. "Pray and drink..." she advised. "...Pray and drink!"

Civilian contractors now struggled under the constraints of wartime shortages and building work on Bob's Zennor hideaway ground to a halt. Desperate to escape the madness of the blitz, he and Annie now crowded in with Bekus and Joy at their idyllic Lamb Creek house. Joy knew how to put on a party, even in wartime; it was Nigel, himself forever living under the shadow of sexual trauma, who coined the phrase 'Let your Joy be unconfined', aptly summing-up a sister whose morals came straight out of a Restoration comedy. In something of a 'Swallows and Amazons' dream-world, Bob's leave became a delirious rediscovery of his childhood. A constant stream of artists, writers, sculptors and casual freeloaders passed through. Lee Miller, having heard of the place when she was doing a series of studio portraits of Bob for Vogue, came to stay. Ever on the edge of social acceptance, even Nigel came across to paint. All sought the West Country magic and most possessed a more than relaxed attitude to relationships. Despite the hardships, life was good and lived to the full; parties inevitably spilled over from lunch and into the evening and then up the winding lane to the Punchbowl and Ladle pub, or over the river to the Park Inn. Late night raids for more liquor and cigarettes were the norm; the thunder of Bob's motorcycle pulling up in the early hours outside the Punchbowl' announced another casual break-in. Bottles clattered into the side-car and a handful of crumpled notes were slapped on the bar and it was just another night. Wartime life was presumed to be short and much of the time was spent painting the town red; any town, any shade. The nearby town of Helston provided a plethora of watering holes and 'The Angel' also provided a billiard table; Bob would tip the landlord a crisp fiver and he and Augustus John would drink and play the night away. Rowdy and grand, 'profitable nuisances' like the Lamorna artists, these exotics filled the hotels and bars; distributing largesse and laughter, they enriched the lives of the locals and sowed the seeds for a generation of fireside yarns.

Bekus was now serving in the Royal Navy and Joy, left home alone and bored, meant that trouble was never far away; Googie Withers, an old friend since *Busman's Honeymoon*, heard from Bekus ashore in Athens... "He met up with a fellow naval officer, from another ship, whom he did not know. Over a few drinks his new-found friend told him that he had just returned from leave in England, which he had spent, very enjoyably, in Cornwall. He told him that he had met a very attractive woman in a pub in Truro, who had suggested, at closing time, that they return to her house for another drink. To cut a long story short he said, her husband was away at the war and he stayed the weekend. The only thing that marred an idyllic weekend was the fact that they had run out of booze on the Saturday night. But she told him that her husband had an excellent selection of vintage port locked away in the cellar and fortunately, he said, he knew something about locks and had managed to open the cellar door... That was too much. 'My wife!' Bekus had exploded. 'But what's more, my bloody port!'"

In Lamorna, Boskenna Manor had been passed down from the Colonel to his daughter, Betty, and runs down south were part of the social circuit. Betty too could always put on a great party; Augustus John and his daughter Poppet were frequent visitors.

For Bob , leave was richly relished, this time it was cut short...

The Admiralty was facing a chronic shortage of officers and was scouring the lower decks. Having perpetually haunted officers' bars and wardrooms, Bob now faced poetic justice. Rated 'C.W' he was required to report to barracks at Portsmouth for twelve weeks intensive instruction before an appearance in front of the dreaded Officer Selection Board. Fellow actor Kenneth More was also called in on the same grim business... "Newton was then at the height of his fame as a British film star, and with one of his films actually showing in Portsmouth. Newton was a very heavy drinker and an equally amusing raconteur. Every evening, although only an ordinary seaman, he would hold court at The Goat public house, surrounded by officers of all ranks who felt honoured by associating with someone so famous. The Officer Selection Board did not share this view. There had been several occasions when Newton would drift off when the pub shut, and carry on drinking elsewhere. Then, rather than pass the sentry at the barrack gates, he would climb over the wall into his quarters. Several times he had been caught and hauled before the Officer-of-the-night for his behaviour. At his interview with the Selection Board, Newton had intimated to the Admiral in charge that he would be doing the Navy a favour if he accepted a commission. He did not wait to be told he might become an officer, Newton said that if asked to accept a commission, he would consider the matter...".

David Niven, in his inimitable style, also recounted the yarn, if somewhat differently, starting with Bob's 'excellent degree from Oxford University'... 'The mysteries of navigation eluded Bobby Newton, and after four months of intensive coaching, he viewed with apprehension his final exam. He saw to it that he was suitably 'relaxed' when a stern-faced Master-at-Arms called out his name: 'Able-bodied Seaman Newton!' Bobby shuffled forward and found himself on a 'mock-up' of a ship's bridge. Awaiting him was the Selection Board, two Admirals and a captain. The imitation bridge was fully equipped with a wheel, engine room telegraph, compasses, callipers, pinnacles, radars, depth sounders, log book and gadgets for shooting the sun and when in great difficulty oneself. The Captain blew down the tube and issued brisk orders to a non-existent engine-room staff, rattled off a lot of information about Rhumb lines, GMT, Nulls, Fixes, Lorans and Sonars, then he spun the wheel. 'Newton', he said, with something of a flourish, 'that is the situation- what is your course?' Bobbie peered dazedly at the maze of sophisticated hard-ware, the helpful possibilities of which largely escaped him during his tuition. The Admirals consulted their notes and leaned expectantly forward. 'Well', said Bobbie, trying an engaging smile, 'I should hazard a guess... that we... are... heading...roughly...er...West?'. 'Thank you,' said the Senior Officer present, 'report back to your ship'. Or as Kenneth More remembered it '...you would be better employed in your chosen vocation... amusing people!'"

Grand tales, and perhaps something near the truth; back on-board *Britomart* Newton weathered the jeers of his messmates and tumbled back into his old bunk safe from the lofty ranking of Acting Temporary Probationary Sub-Lieutenant. He was never officer material and he was to sum up his philosophy years later in words spoken out of a film script: "I'm the perfect private soldier, no worries, no responsibilities... I can't even be demoted!"

In the early years of the war the fear of aerial bombardment had a far greater mark on theatres than on the cinemas because people were basically reluctant to go far from home in the blackout. Many London theatres had simply closed down and transferred productions to the provinces. Only the Windmill, a great wartime institution, stayed open during the Blitz; the proud inscription 'We never closed' was amended to 'We never clothed'. By May '41 however, desire had overcome reluctance, people learned to cope, theatre got back to normal and plays that had been launched in the provinces moved back into the West End. Performances now started early, at six, so that everyone would be safely out again by nine. Another change was the emergence and vogue for serious 'talk' plays and works looking at the brave new world 'after the war'.

The spring of 1942 brought another low point for the Allies. The Japanese seemed unstoppable. Singapore had fallen in February, Java in March, Rangoon was under their control and the fate of India hung in the balance. In the Western Desert the British and Commonwealth forces had taken a bloody beating and the Navy had suffered huge losses in the Mediterranean. The battle for the Atlantic had now entered its most deadly phase. The U-boats were slaughtering the convoys and Britain faced starvation. In London, as in the rest of the country, the public mood swung from blithe gaiety to black depression and all the news seemed to be bad. Fearful of a collapse in public morale the government turned to the entertainment industry to distract minds from the whispered thought of defeat. The Ministry of Information had the power to veto even the Navy, now it summoned Able Seaman Newton; he was informed that theatre guru George Black had short-listed him for his new stage production, and he was expected to co-operate...

The play was *No Orchids for Miss Blandish*. This however was no serious 'talk' play. Based on a best-selling pulp fiction novel by James Hadley Chase it was an out-and-out, no-holds-barred, sex shocker, a sordid tale of an American heiress kidnapped by a gang of lowlifes; sadism and brutality, rape, torture and perversion were its principal themes. 'Most of the women are sluts and most of the men are vicious murderers...' the moralists moaned. The Nazis were so concerned about its content that they banned it from British PoW camps...

Having played the bully in his last two films, Newton now had a reputation and had been cast in the central role of Slim Grissom, 'vicious as a black mamba, a degenerate, homicidal, imbecile'. Playing opposite him and taking the part of the kidnap victim was Linden Travers. With a Cornish connection and stunning good looks framed with masses of flaming red hair the components for another off-stage drama were assembled. Bob was already entangled with one girl and another affair was the last thing Annie needed...

Rehearsals were brief and the play opened on June 29th at the Grand Theatre, Blackpool, running twice daily (5.30 and 8.00). The opening night didn't go without a hitch; one pivotal scene sees Bob's character feeling along a mantelpiece for his gun...but the gun was not there. Not to be daunted Bob reverted to improvisation... "Where the fuck's the gun!" he howled. There was a roar of laughter, it was Newton at his best and the audience loved it; somehow the work exactly reflected the moral mood of the time and every performance was a sell out.

After a final night on July 25th the show decamped to the capital and the Prince of Wales Theatre. Five days later, at 7.30, a howl of approval came from an audience thoroughly bored with drab wartime utilitarianism and intellectual highbrowism. Falling back to a nanny-state routine of two early performances, one at 2.30pm and another at 5.15pm, the show was a thorough hit.

Laura Knight was working in the city and was approached by a friend. "You doing anything this afternoon…?" he asked her, "No, like to go and see your protégé at the Prince of Wales Theatre?" 'Because I happened to get Robert Newton his first job in the theatre by introducing him as a boy of promise to Barry Jackson', Knight explained, '…Bobby always told people he was my protégé!' Delighted she agreed; the invitation was however tempered with a caveat, "I warn you, *No Orchids for Miss Blandish* is the worst play ever put on in London, but the public love it, real melodrama! Whatever do you think your protégé did the other night? When the audience should have been crying their eyes out, they were roaring with laughter instead and that Bobby of yours just walked down to the footlights and yelled out at them, "Shut up, you bastards!"'

The play rolled out on a wave of applause; every evening Bob's character developed into a wilder extreme and audiences brought the ceiling down with their whistles and cheers. As he had done with *Hamlet* he now began to improvise; glassy-eyed and drooling, he presented a horribly real characterisation. Breaking away from the script and leaving the other actors standing open-mouthed, he would suddenly swing out from the proscenium and hurl abuse at the audience. Ad-libbing obscenities he brought management running and the production almost to a close. The pace of work, like the pace of the play, was relentless, and the part Bob was playing was intense; inevitably he carried 'Slim Grissom' off-stage...

The critics denounced the work as trash, 'a farrago of nonsense', but the audiences, the ultimate critics, queued up. It was not all love back-stage however. The part of Ma Grissom was played by Mary Clare, an old hand and a distinguished actor. She and Newton clashed angrily, she condemning him for his ad-libbing, he condemning her for taking the farcical rubbish too seriously. Billy Milton was in the theatre and witnessed Newton's response; 'Bob, intoxicated, climbed into the flies above the stage and, while she was playing a quiet scene below, delicately urinated on her....'. Consistently packed houses meant that demand outstripped supply; George Black rubbed his hands and the show was transferred to the more capacious Apollo Theatre.

Crashing into Newton's dressing room one afternoon, Milton saw Bob, complete with the walking stick which had now become a permanent feature, practising grimaces in the mirror. "Billy, one day I'm going to be a film star" he proclaimed, then, breaking into his nightly vocal warm-up routine, "Oriana... life without you, is just dust and ashes, I must have you!' he swept out majestically and onto the boards and into the embrace of Linden Travers.

Thrown together on stage and straying out afterwards for drinks and dancing was a fatal combination and the inevitable, inevitably, happened. Annie, ever eagle-eyed, saw the thing before it even happened; Bob had strayed, ended up in Travers' arms and in her bed. The fling turned into an affair and once too often Bob didn't return home. The showdown came backstage; Anne, proud, hurt and ever the spitfire, slapped Travers hard across the face, twice. "That's not for seducing Robert... that's for not satisfying him". Not for nothing did Travers cite 'No Orchids...' as her 'favourite part'.

The play ran through the 1942/43 Christmas season and into the new year. Then the party was over and Newton got his navy recall. By now *Britomart* was again stationed in Russia and Bob's weeks were spent pointlessly ashore, the days filled up with parade, sentry duty, spit and polish.

Far south in the Mediterranean, 110 miles off Algiers, a ghost from Newton's past, the mail ship *Windsor Castle*, now a troop transport, was sinking, ripped apart by a German torpedo.

The bitter, war-impoverished February saw Newton get another release from duty; this time he was to work on a film production. As in *Hatters Castle*, he was once again to play a father figure. In the former he played the tyrant, now he was to play an 'ordinary and respectable' man, everything he had so capitally failed to be in real life. The film was Noel Coward's *This Happy Breed*.

After four long years of war Britain was weary, the people bored of lives steered by chaos. Film now moved to reflect this. A counter-movement of social realism had sprung up, challenging the old, failed, system of paternalism and the people were looking towards an extension of social franchise and consensus politics. It was all looking dangerously Red. If film re-examined the dynamics of family life, the examination was one done at arms length, constrained by censors who were themselves leashed in by an elaborate set of rules and guidelines. It was argued that this censorship had constructed a cinema that failed to address social and political matters, or at least, rendered it unable to present them in a truly critical perspective. World shaping events such as chronic domestic unemployment and the rise of Fascism abroad, it was said, failed to find clear and obvious expression in the pictures of the day. The industry, the critics cried, was merely a 'dream factory' that simply peddled opiates for the masses. Some saw the more sinister motive, that it was a form of organised social control.

Perhaps the much derided Americans had got it right; back in 1915 a judgement in the Supreme Court had defined motion pictures as a 'business, pure and simple, originated and conducted for profit'. European academics may have cried out for film to become a force for good, but the majority of Britons simply wanted an evening out after a hard day and a few hours of easy-viewing eye-wash. Yet even that plea now came with a caveat, one at last advantageous for the British industry. 'We're sick and tired of having American films (chiefly second-rate) rammed down our throats...' one film fan wrote, '...they may be slick of production and technically sound, but they are filled with oomph-oozing women, their bodies covered or uncovered to stimulate the sexual rather than artistic senses...'.

First conceived as a play in 1939, *This Happy Breed* had almost become a casualty of the war. However, with the worst of the blitz over and theatres reopening, it was simultaneously to be staged and worked into a film. Looking at the tumultuous period between the wars and through the eyes of an everyday London family, it was both an examination of change and a cosy and reassuring assertion of the continuity of life and the passing nature of conflict. Propaganda or not, Coward had once again come up with the right goods at the right time. In a flagrant piece of social buttressing, solid middle-class values were held up as beacons in the darkness and despite challenges, the old status quo was shown to be the stabilising factor in changing times. It was a reassuring and comforting lie and just what the establishment wanted the people to need.

In the stage version Coward, of course, took the lead part of Frank Gibbons. Frank, however, was a middle-aged, middle-class Londoner and Coward's accent and manner were uncomfortably out of key with his character. He managed to carry the character on the stage, just, but it was obvious that he was not the right man for the unforgiving film role. Despite strong hints from Coward that he would like to take the film role, David Lean, the chosen director, resisted. Coward offered the part to Robert Donat, but Donat turned the role down because he 'did not believe in the things Frank believes in'. Newton had no such scruples. He had attracted an enviable reputation for character acting and Lean, having seen his acting skills in *Major Barbara*, pressed for him to be given the job. Quietly, Coward was rejected by his own people. Still carrying his vicious instinct for revenge, he now re-inked Newton's name in his notorious little black book, his bitter little 'List' of those to be stabbed in the back whenever possible. Rather fittingly his own name was simultaneously being inscribed in the Nazi's 'post-invasion hit-list'...

Blithely Bob became 'Frank Gibbons' who was, of course, Noel Coward. It was an easy task; Coward always wrote learnable dialogue. With many writers the players didn't bother to learn the lines verbatim, because it was a gilt-edged certainty that the script would be re-written on the set. This was not Cowards way; always there was a hallmark deftness and confidence.

Cast to appear as the harassed housewife to Bob's 'Frank' was the star-that-would-rather-not-be, the unwilling diva of *Brief Encounter*, Celia Johnson. Ever the 'Staunch British Housewife' type, she had been showered with rave reviews for her part in Coward's first film *In Which We Serve* (where she worked alongside another of Bob's cavalcade of lovers, Barbara Waring...). She professed that she was unable to understand how 'knocking the world sideways as a cockney mother of three' would help win the war and it took all of

Coward's powers of persuasion to get her to work on the film. David Lean's wife, Kay Walsh, was cast as one of the daughters. Merle Tottenham, one of Coward's little favourites, and an old friend 'done to death' in the 1936 *Dead Men are Dangerous*, played her usual servant role. Amy Venness, a familiar face from the *Yellow Sands* shoot, was chosen to play the brilliantly crabby Mother-in-law. John Mills, another of Coward's chosen band of 'little darlings', was cast as the sailor-boy-next-door and the son of the always endearing Stanley Holloway (...who had briefly appeared in *Major Barbara* as a policeman). The new work was very much a spin-off from Coward's nostalgic naval piece *In Which We Serve*, and Johnson, Walsh and Mills each transferred their film characters pretty much wholesale and intact. Mills again played the sailor in love with Walsh's 'Queenie', and Celia Johnson the faithful wife.

At the film's conception, David Lean, with typical prescience, and despite the interior nature of the piece, had decided to shoot in Technicolor. First seen in 1917, the process had been greeted with the same mulish resistance that heralded the arrival of the talkies. It was not until 1939 and the release of *Gone with the Wind* that opinions changed. In 1943, there were only four Technicolor cameras in the UK. "Why on earth are you doing it in colour…?" the bosses of Denham howled, clutching at their wallets. "Why not… it's new and it excites me!" Lean replied. Exciting or not, the process was also exacting; the heavy and cumbersome three-strip cameras were a technical nightmare; it took a full twenty minutes to reload them. For actors the process was an attenuated, sweaty toil; the standard studio lights give a yellow glow and colour filming demanded the use of ferociously hot arc lamps. The result was a hellish working environment and an intensity of colour that was garishly bright. Lean understood that the tale he was telling was one of ordinary, often dull, daily life; this was not high drama that cried out for brilliant tones. Mixing form and meaning the studio technicians washed the set with high-tech dirt. Actors, already plastered with a peculiar pale blueish slap that made them look like rather prematurely aged ghosts, now faced a further daubing.

Studio time was booked at Denham and shooting began in late February just as the stage production opened at the Haymarket

Theatre. Despite a grudging mutual respect for their professional skills, personal relations between Newton and Coward failed to thaw. Coward sporadically haunted the set, resentful that Lean had given 'his part', the best in the film, to Newton. Once again the two men grated uncomfortably against each other. Coward could never countenance indiscipline, unless it was his own, and he had little patience with weakness. Remembering Bob's past, a stinging caveat was tacked onto his contract. "Bob had been told by Noel that he must not drink..." Lean noted, "and that any time he was drunk on set he would forfeit five hundred pounds of his salary. It was in his contract. His salary for the whole film was, I think, nine thousand pounds, and this was very serious for him, so he didn't drink at all during the first weeks....".

Margaret Williams, a peripheral member of Coward's little social circle, wrote to her husband, the actor Hugh Williams, who was overseas on active service; 'Bob Newton is working with Celia and John Mills in '*This Happy Breed*'. They all send their love, specially Celia. Bob is looking very fat and very much on the wagon!!! I think Celia has him under control...'. Little did she know.

David Lean directed in a subtle, light-handed manner, and brought the work to life. Intuitively Bob understood the ethos of the work, found his character, and played his part opposite Johnson with a brilliant and understated naturalism. On-set he was the archetypal, doughty, self-depreciating Everyman. Obediently on the wagon he was, however, closely watched on all sides. Shooting progressed smoothly, but it was too good to last. With only ten days of work to go, no fines and a clean slate, he took a 'phone call from Joy down in Cornwall. Marjorie had been in poor health for a long while and it had fallen to her to act as nurse. Now he was informed that his mother's condition had taken an ominous turn for the worse. The news came as a shock and Bob was quietly devastated. Stuck on the set and unable to get out of his contract, he hit the bottle. Duly reprimanded and fined £500 by a finger-wagging Coward, he played it clean for a couple of days, then did it all over again.

John Mills recalled the scene... "One Sunday, half way through the shoot, I was mowing the lawn at Misbourne Cottage when I saw what appeared to be a dirty-looking tramp swaying down the street towards me. When he got nearer I realised it was Bobby Newton, paralytic. "Hello there, my hearties, I've come to visit you...!" Newton cried. Now David's (Lean's) house was only ten yards away so I yanked Bobby into the cottage and Mary and I poured coffee and bacon and eggs into him. At one point he staggered out into the garden, took about two hundred pounds out of his pockets and threw it up into the air. Juliet was running all over the place trying to stop the money being blown into the river. Anyway we managed to sober him up and sneaked him out of the village. The next day I saw him in make-up and he looked like a ghost, awful. 'Morning, darling boy' said Newton, '...I hear you had a bit of a party last night, how do you feel?' 'Fine, Bob...' I replied, 'how about you...?' 'Never felt worse...' Bob replied, 'but I'll survive... now I know who my real friends are'. That evening a case of champagne arrived at Misbourne.

As the shoot neared completion and the stage play moved towards its final night, Coward threw a swank party at the Haymarket Theatre to celebrate. Everybody who was anybody in the theatre world was invited, along with the actors and production crew. Everybody, that was, except Bob. The party was charming; Joyce Grenfell was doing her little act, it was all very pleasant, all very informal, a lovely party, when suddenly Bob crashed through the doorway, absolutely plastered. Red-faced and with his hat askew, he staggered into the room, spotted David Lean and his circle and staggered over, "Bob, for Christ's sake, don't come in here now..." Lean hissed. "Why wasn't I invited to this..." Bob roared. Spotting Coward cosy with Gielgud and doing one of his risqué little ditties at the piano, Bob started across the floor "I'm not going home until I talk to this effeminate man...!" The crowd parted, open-mouthed with horror "There they are..." Bob roared "with their jock-straps full of promise!", "Oh..." responded Coward, "we're all so *terribly* bohemian, aren't we." and goes on playing. Things went downhill fast and afraid of a fracas, a group started half carrying Newton to the exit; "I'm not leaving without my hat..." he bawled, "I came with a hat and I'm going with a hat!" By the time he had been dragged outdoors the police were waiting. Peace restored, the party returned to its sibilant pleasures. Several hours later a large crowd was spotted gathering around a shop doorway. Sure enough there was

Bob, now stripped down to his trousers and struggling furiously against the combined force of no less than three burly coppers. Shoved into a van he was carted off to the Bow Street lock-up.

Celia Johnson, who had started working with Newton under the simplistic impression that he was merely 'nice', gave her own account of this classic Bob performance. "On Saturday night, Noel gave a party at the Haymarket to which everyone was invited, Bob had not been invited it turned out. I didn't go, wanting to go home, and I think on the whole it's as well I didn't. Getting to the studio today I asked how they all enjoyed it and everyone said ' Oh v much', rather vaguely, and then Bob appeared at lunch with a terrific gash on his cheek (this necessitated shooting him from only one side and then in the dark)... and I, still a little innocent, thought vaguely, oh, he's been on the booze and fallen over and said lightly 'How did you enjoy the party, did you go'. He said unblushingly, 'I just looked in...' which turned out to be the understatement of all time; it seems he went and got stinking and while Noel was singing one of his songs he stood up, took off his coat and shirt and fairly let fly. Ronnie Neame and Tony and William got him out and he was last seen almost naked being hustled down the Haymarket by the police and spent Sunday day and night in the cells. He had only just got out after being charged and fined and had come hotfoot from there to the studio just in time to shoot this afternoon. They managed to get the charge of nakedness shelved and he only got done for being drunk and disorderly and we trust and pray it will not get into the papers. Ronnie and David hadn't told me, to show him they were not telling tales, so of course I jumped in with both feet, tomorrow I am lunching with Joyce Grenfell who was at the party and shall hear the rest...!" Of course Bob remembered nothing of the incident....". Witheringly, but perhaps with a motherly affection, Johnson signed out of her diary, "....he is an idiot!"

The next day Annie bumped into Coward on set. "How can you deal with this situation?' he asked. "Noel," she replied, "what else have I got to deal with...".

On July 15th the news came through that Marjorie had died. Her passion for the Christian Scientists was undaunted and she had stubbornly refused medical treatment for sclerosis. She had died at home after suffering a cerebral haemorrhage. 'She died, silly bloody woman, because she wouldn't let anyone get a doctor for her...'' Bob raged. Ironically one of the central characters in *Happy Breed*, Sylvia, the spinster sister, was also a Christian Scientist. Granted compassionate leave, Bob and Annie travelled down to Cornwall and Lambe Creek. Petrol was now almost unavailable, and the days of driving down were over. The Rolls' was laid up and they booked onto the Cornish Riviera train; Joy was at Truro station to meet them. Pauline arrived shortly after.

The funeral began and ended in farce. Pauline had dressed to kill and appeared in black, complete with veil and dripping in jewels; Joy, exhausted from her weeks of nursing Marjorie without any family help, had hit the bottle early. She rounded on her sister in fury, then, looking for a further opportunity to let off steam she turned on Annie; "Family only!" she hissed. "I am family..." Annie returned, "and I've known Amelia Balfour as long as I've known him!" nodding at Bob. The spat continued in the car; hip-flasks and a cathartic acrimony traded all the way to Newlyn. There Nigel appeared, dressed in a shabby old corduroy suit. "This is hopeless..." roared Bob, "could you not get a decent suit to turn up to your mother's funeral!" Reaching for his wallet he bundled Nigel into the car, dispatching him into Penzance and the first tailor's shop. After a long wait the car and Nigel reappeared, with a new suit that was as ill-fitting as the corduroy. "You're not going to have another one, unless you want to strip me!" Bob shouted. The weather was stiflingly hot and on the long hot drag up to the church in Paul village things didn't improve. Surrounded by God-fearing Newlyn folk, the family wondered what they were doing there; Marjorie was no Christian and despite her flirtation with the Christian Scientists she had no belief in Gods and Devils.

Weeks later, with some of the pain forgotten, Bob remembered the day; "I had purple lines on the palms from clutching my hand to stop me laughing at Mum's funeral, it was so 'ugh'. If you didn't laugh you would have cried. You didn't know what you were there for...!"

"Bob had several brothers and sisters" Googie Withers remembered "and when their Mother died they decided at the funeral that it would be a fitting gesture to take her on a last visit to all her favourite pubs. The hearse was a horse drawn one. Bob somehow managed to clamber up on the driver's seat and took charge of the reins. The others climbed onto the roof and a memorable journey began, lasting all day and half the night. Which has become part of the folklore in Cornwall. The story goes that they took the horse into several bars, and that he made his way into several others. No-one seems to know to this day how Mother came to be safely interred…!" Marjorie, herself a secret, heavy drinker, had always ticked off her Bobby for drinking; Annie remembered that Bob had growled, tears in his eyes, "I've taken you to all the haunts you would have hated....!"

Somehow the actual interment took place; as the coffin was being lowered however, Bob grew exasperated by Nigel's teary histrionics; delivering a hearty slap on the back, snarling "For God's sake, Nigel, stop snivelling!" Caught off balance, Nigel stumbled and teetered forward, nearly following the coffin in. The gasps broke down into giggles and the vicar's final words were lost. The ceremony over, the party preparing to decamp to Newlyn where the obligatory tea and cake get-together had been arranged; Bob, still reeling from the pub-crawl, clambered into the back of the hearse, lay down, and singing loudly, demanded to be taken back to Trewarveneth Street... "*I've* paid for this bloody funeral, so I'll travel home how I like!"

The final location shots for *This Happy Breed* were left until July, but the sun, in true British fashion, refused to shine and the whole thing became a trial of endurance. Celia Johnson: "We did a scene in Hyde park, and the entire population of London tried to get in front of the camera. Bobby Newton and I had to stroll along together, he saying "This is the first time you and I have been out alone together for years…" and every time he said 'alone' the crowd bellowed and whistled and by the time we reached the camera we had a mob of several thousand strong pushing and giggling and peering out from behind us to try to get their silly faces in the picture, I can't think that the shot will be any good but it is done, and that's all I really care about…".

With just one last location scene to shoot and Bob's promises of staying sober gone out of the window, Johnson was longing to finish the whole dreadful thing. Remembering Bob's penchant for exhibitionism and 'artistic nudity', she was more than a little tense, "R Newton had 'slipped a bit' and we were all a little nervous particularly as the shot was at a church door in Clapham, it would hardly have been the place for a strip-tease performance, he started rather aggressive, but finished giggly....".

In the end, and mostly because of problems with the Technicolor process, the film took far longer to carry off than anyone envisaged, ten months. The final price tag was over £220,000. The first studio showing however revealed that Lean had tamed the vexatious and garish Technicolor process and the results were simply stunning.

Laurence Olivier was hired in to narrate a little prologue, and the film was released. The kitchen-sink story line was one that every Briton could empathise with and the film was a box-office hit. Britain's top film money earner for 1944, it was justly rated 'perfectly made and played, one of the greatest films ever to emerge from the British studios'. The *Times* saw the film as 'yet another proof of the excellence of work British studios are now doing...'. Aware of his screen shortcomings, Coward had always been dismissive of film; "I'd rather play a bad matinee in Hull than do a movie..." he spat petulantly. Like Bob he had become quickly bored with the technicalities. Nevertheless he took his bows, and the credits; the piece was always properly entitled 'Noel Coward's This Happy Breed'. The musical score was always his, but no-one had the courage to point out that in the crucial 'death' scene, the background radio jazz piece, Mischa Spoliansky's 'Dusty Rhythm', was heard in one of Bob's old films *The Squeaker*...

Variety magazine gave the film a resounding thumbs up; 'The story, about a typical British family, living at 'Number Seventeen, Sycamore Road', flows seamlessly through twenty one years, tear jerking, heart warming and endearing. Robert Newton is a superb presentation as the steady, earth-bound, but intelligent Britisher...' 'Nearly two hours of the pleasure of recognition' crowed *Punch*. Lean was delighted and took his modest bows along with the cast. Coward took his in a grander style and thanked all of his players by name; except for Newton.

In a terse letter to one of his 'little darlings', he hissed 'I have already told you in my cable about the Trade show success of "Happiers", and the excellence of the Trade notices. Although nobody seems to have rumbled Bobby Newton, at least the majority have the grace to like his performance less than those of the other principals...'. The rift between the two men had now become unbridgeable. Perhaps it was because Bob had achieved what Coward could never have done and made the film into a classic. Coward could never bring himself to mention Newton's name, certainly not in his autobiographies. Lean, however, remembered Newton with a real warmth, 'I had a great weakness for Bobby Newton, he used to drink too much, and when he had a couple of drinks he would speak the absolute truth, which could be horrifying. I remember him talking to a friend of mine after lunch, when he'd had a couple of drinks, and he leaned across the table and said "Now I'm going to tell you about you", and he did, bang on the dot, you know. Withering. He could be cruel, but what he said was undeniably true. I loved him".

With a logic that was no doubt clear to the industry but to no-one else, certainly not groaning British audiences, *Four Dark Hours* was now re-released. Re-titled *Race Gang* it was screened against the latest American colour works and looked hopelessly tired and antiquated.

In the middle of December, Bob, complete with a parrot, reported back for duty on-board *Britomart*. She had just returned from ten months in Russian waters. Battered and rusted, she desperately needed a refit. Now Newton heard first hand the whispered news that the government had hushed up, the apalling truth about the deadly run he had missed, PQ17.

In the whole of the war there were to be three convoy battles that, in terms of sheer atrocity, stood out from all the others; Operation Pedestal, the deadly Malta run was one; PQ17 was another. Little did the men who survived it know that the next Arctic convoy, PQ 18, was going to be the third. The thirty-five merchant ships that had formed PQ 17 had set out from Hvalfjord in late June. *Britomart* was part of an unusually powerful escort. Mid-way between Iceland and Murmansk news had flashed through of a suspected enemy interception, including a powerful surface fleet. Orders were issued for the convoy to 'scatter'; each was to make his own way as best he could. A terse signal had been sent from the naval escort to the convoy, 'Sorry to leave you like this. Goodbye and good luck. It looks like a bloody business'.

On the night of the 4th, *Britomart* and the escort had withdrawn. The Germans realised that the convoy was defenceless and the 'bloody business' began. The image of the naval escort clinging together for mutual protection whilst the unarmed merchantmen were slowly picked off one by one was not an edifying one. *Britomart*, another sweeper and an AA ship, had briefly joined four lumbering merchantmen, but spotted by an enemy plane had made off at speed. The mood below decks had turned near mutinous; the British Navy never turned tail and ran. *Britomart* had made it to Murmansk. Only eleven of the convoy followed her in. Stuck rotting at anchor until November, filthy weather and a succession of screaming gales had given *Britomart*, acting as part of the escort to convoy QP15, a hellish passage. Thirty ships had left Murmansk, twenty eight had made it home.

Back in the uncomplicated, rough-house of navy life Bob felt a happy sense of relief and homecoming. But it was over too quickly. *Britomart* was patched up and licked over with paint. She received her sailing orders. Such was the debacle of PQ17 that the Arctic convoys had been postponed and *Britomart* was dispatched into the English Channel for routine sweeping; she was spared another Arctic run, yet she was to face another, more terrible fate. Then Bob again received orders calling him back to London for film work.

The Oliviers returned from the States and Bob and Annie were obliged to decamp from Durham Cottage. The transition was not a happy one. The place had taken a knocking in the blitz, but it was the wild parties, parenthesised by drunken domestic rows that had reached monumental proportions where items of furniture frequently ended up out in the street, that had done the damage. Leigh's pastel retreat was in tatters, and hardly a window remained intact.

Months before, Olivier had spoken to Bob about the forthcoming film production of *Henry V* in which he had the lead role. David Lean had been offered the director's job, but had turned it down;

Olivier now found himself pressured into taking the role of director as well as lead actor. True to human nature he was gathering about himself the comfortable old faces he knew and trusted. Bob had been first on his list. His appearance was essential, and his part was obvious. Newton however had been reluctant, and was even more so now, feeling that he had spent enough time away from his ship and his shipmates.

Strenuously promoted by the Ministry of Information, the work was the familiar David and Goliath tale, almost a re-run of *Fire Over England* and had, of course, tremendous propaganda value. The Yanks were now at last on side and the tide of war was turning. The end seemed almost in sight; armies were poised along the coast for the secret D-Day landings and every effort was being made for the desperate, final push. The worst of the blitz was over, but much of London lay in ruins. Now it was facing the dreaded V1 rockets.

Across the country the victory "V" symbol was chalked everywhere; it may have been stirringly patriotic but it didn't fill any empty stomachs. Echoing the preoccupations of 1594, *Henry V* was to be the morale boost that was now so desperately needed.

Along with Bob a huge cast of familiar names had been commandeered onto the project, most of them proven Shakespearean actors; Newton's part was small but central, the swaggering 'Pistol'. All fired up with liquor and Dutch courage, the character was the classic comedy foil. And it came with a bona fide Cornish link. King Harry wandering the English camp in disguise, announces himself to Pistol under the name 'Le Roy' "Ah....!" growls Newton's 'Pistol', "a Cornish name, art thou of a Cornish crew?" Bob was persuaded.

Mainland Britain was effectively a military zone. The land bristled with the detritus of war and the skies were filled with the waspish droning and the long white trails of fighters; filming the expansive Agincourt battle scene exteriors promised to be a logistical nightmare. The answer lay in neutral Ireland, in the south near Dublin, on a vast private estate near Enniskerry. There, Olivier juggled his starring role with herding, feeding and lodging seven hundred unruly Irish extras for a thirty-nine day shoot. Studio work was a simpler affair. Shot at Pinewood and Denham work started on

August 9th and was completed on Jan 3rd 1944. All the old familiar faces turned up, Ralph Truman, Leslie Banks from *Jamaica Inn*, John Laurie, George Cole, even Roy Emerton, one of the Shilling Theatre backers. Significantly there was no Leigh, her 'owners' considered the part she was offered, too small...

Working in front of sets that had been scaled up from the exquisitely illustrated medieval Book of Hours, 'Les Tres Riches Heures du Duc de Berry' and with squished perspectives and enamel rich colours, Newton's part was indeed brief and relatively quickly shot. His mop-haired 'Pistol' was a farcical self-mocker, the other side of the coin to Olivier's theatrical and Kingly passion, and Bob played it expansive. Dynamic and outrageous, his 'Pistol' was the counterpoint to the whole affair and Bob threw himself into the thing wholeheartedly. He mocked the war, to raise a laugh and to be different. For he was bored with it all now, bored with film, worn out by navy life, worn out with the half truth about the war that he knew to be a damned, bloody, lie. "Wildly eccentric" muttered a disaffected James Mason. But Shakespeare lovers knew better; Newton's rendering of the lines "Doth fortune play the housewife with me now..." was declared 'the true rendering'.

With an unsubtle foresight Olivier had given Bob a personal chauffeur cum minder; "You're going to have to get him here" Olivier warned him. "It's no good us sending a car if he doesn't wake up!" Laurence Evans retorted. Evans, one of the studio crew in *Hatters Castle* and an old friend (he was later to marry Bob's old flame, Barbara Waring), was a permanent fixture on the Denham set. Grand with the title 'Production Manager', the reality was that it was his primary task to get Bob into the studio every morning. Pinning him down to a fixed address was problematical because at this stage Bob was having an affair with at least two girls. "On one occasion... I went first of all to Bobby's house, no reply, I went to the next house where he should have been, no reply, I'd better try Linden Travers' place. She had a third floor flat somewhere in Chelsea, so I pressed the third floor button and the third floor window opened and this beautiful red-haired girl called out "What is it?" So I called out "Is Bobby with you?". "No he is not!" and slammed the window down. Later that morning he rang the studio, "How are you dear boy... Oh, it's wonderful here, it's warm and dark and louche. I wish you were here!" Bob was two hours late for make-up...".

In the midst of filming and rolling out of the studio late one evening, Bob unexpectedly ordered his car south. "Portsmouth." he demanded. The driver knew better than to argue. At the naval dockyards Bob bullied his way past the sentries, stamped down the dock, climbed the gangway and went on-board *Britomart*. At dawn the next morning he re-emerged and staggered back to the car. "Pinewood" he croaked. Bob had spent a night with his shipmates.

The process of filming at Denham was fraught; every conceivable light blazed in the middle of the blackout. Neither the air-raid wardens nor the jittery neighbours were impressed. Of course special permission had been issued by the War Office but with strict conditions; if a purple warning came, which meant an imminent air raid in the area, every light had to be doused in two minutes flat.

Wilting under the burden of both directing and starring, Olivier's friendship with Bob was stretched to breaking point. Once again Evans was there; "We had a wonderful set built of a beach and the sea and ships coming ashore and the sailors jumping out, and Pistol was up the beach behind a large boulder. At a certain point, given his cue, Pistol was to run down the beach waving a huge sword and shouting. It took ages to set up. Extras on the boats, people making waves, people on the beach. We didn't get to shoot it until the afternoon. Unfortunately that was too late for Bobby; he was behind the boulder with his sword. Larry said "Camera, action!" and it all happened; the boats came in, the sailors jumped ashore and at that moment Pistol should have come running down the beach. He didn't because 'Pistol' was asleep behind his rock! They all had to go back. The sailors got back into their boats which had been taken out of shot, and the cameras re-set. And blow me if it didn't happen again. Larry was incandescent with fury. Finally we managed to get a prop man to crouch out of sight and on cue send Bobby running down the beach....!" Fantastic; but the sequence never made it into the finished work.

Ironically, and typically throughout the industry, Bob's best sequences didn't make it to the screen. Bob would put everything into his work, but by the time the sound equipment had not worked, or the lighting was not right, and there was a call for "Camera re-loading" and "Sound re-loading", he was on to the tenth take and his patience long since spent.

The frustrating grind of studio work did not, however, stop Bob from finding a little time for city high-life. Forever profiting from fear, the clubs and cabarets of Soho and the theatres were booming. "The play was '*Lottie Dundas*'...", recounted Dulcie Gray, who was appearing at the Vaudeville "...and I was playing my first big star part. The audience was suitably silent and, I hope, enthralled by my performance, you could hear a pin drop. I walked down to the footlights and with my arms outstretched started a long, moving, speech. I got to the middle, when suddenly I heard a loud male voice in the audience shout 'Sh, sh, please be quiet and listen to this great artist'. Astonished I stopped speaking. In the stalls, standing with his back to the stage was a man waving his arms about. He began to shout again. 'Do you hear what I say, be quiet!' Furious I raised my voice to a high pitch, continued my speech, successfully swamping him. There was a scuffle and finally the man was removed. After the play was over I was sitting in my dressing-room taking off my make-up, when there was a knock at the door and before I could answer Robert Newton almost fell in. "My darling" he said, "...how disgraceful, it was the audience making all that noise, but I silenced them..." He came over to take me in his arms, and received the best double smack that he ever imagined. To my surprise he fell on his knees to the floor...".

The summer air-raids of '44 had momentarily paralysed the entertainment industry, but now that the worst was over, and even if it wasn't, the people wanted entertainment, anything to forget the bloody war for an hour or two. Borrowing heavily from Eisenstein's '*Aleksandr Nevskii*' (a film where the 'flick, flick, flick', montage technique was first perfected), a fusion of Bakelite radio, old Vic' and celluloid trickery, *Henry V* was brought to completion and released. Two hours and eighteen minutes of blazing Technicolor Shakespearian Renaissance, it costed out at £3,260 a minute; the most expensive British film ever made. Not bad for a director's first attempt. At £80,000, one sixth of the final budget, the horrendously complex Irish battle-scenes made just 16 minutes and 46 seconds of the finished film. The momentous realisation of D-Day was now on everyone's lips; before their eyes history was made into contemporary propaganda. The film's rousing patriotic theme was teasingly hinted at for weeks before its release by posters simply bearing the cross of St George.

The première was at the Carlton Theatre in November. The first night ran the usual gauntlet of critics' gripes and a degree of public antipathy. Worried, Rank made a patriotic appeal. The rallying cry worked and Britons packed into cinemas with wild enthusiasm for an uninterrupted five months; at the fore were a generation of school children. Entertainment had evolved into a history lesson. Swallowing hard, the critics reworded their columns; 'Easily the most spectacular triumph of the British studio' roared the *Daily Herald*, 'easily the most important film ever made', the *Sunday Pictorial* echoed.

Screened to the uncouth American distributors, the work was received with a stony silence. 'The factory workers of northern England had booed the film off the screen... the steel workers of Pittsburg will never understand it.' the Americans carped. Agincourt may have been won again but the film lost the battle against the Hays Office. Duly castrated of its glorious 'bastards' and 'damn's' the film was road-showed in America and suddenly it was away. The Americans loved it; it screened for eleven months. On Broadway it went on to net over a million pounds in the first year. 'No wonder the British films are so good these days' one newspaper complained 'Look at the screenwriters they've got, William Shakespeare and Charles Dickens...'.

A work that had almost died stillborn was now nominated for seven Oscars. Promoted by Churchill himself, the film may not have single- handedly won the war, but with the 1927 Quota Act about to expire and niggling doubts about the viability of British film, it did relaunch the whole British picture industry. Very much the product of cultural upheaval and an industry galvanised by the propaganda imperative, the work, despite its stage origin, was far more than a play that had been filmed. Like *This Happy Breed*, *Henry V* was quoted as a new generation work, very much a cinematic production.

The ironic reality was that the work was amongst the first British films inspired by television. Dallas Bowler, the central screen writer, was one of the producers who had worked with Olivier on a BBC series entitled *Scenes from Shakespeare*. Broadcast in the late '30s, there were fewer than five hundred TV sets in England.

Dedicated 'to the commando and airborne troops of Great Britain...' the film achieved its purpose, stiffened backs and spurred on the invasion of Europe. It also announced Britain's re-invasion of Hollywood. Newton had by now clambered to the top of the British 'star' heap. Interviewed, he was asked about the film and his role, then asked about his navy career. "This is the third film I have made since I went into active service" he said "and each time I return to my ship I find new inspiration, I am among men from all walks and see their reactions in danger and in trying times of monotony and inaction, which bring temperament to the surface, I am happy now they are convinced that actors are human and can live in the regular mess, the same as they do. It was not easy to win them over, at first they doubted me as a seaman... but after I scrubbed the decks like fury and stood my turn at everything, I passed the test."

Certainly he had passed the test; ever generous, ever popular, ever up for 'defaulters', he had nevertheless shown his worth. Whilst other actors had quietly transferred to America he had stepped up to the line and done the duty that was expected of him. He had shown courage, taking the worst that nature and an extraordinary theatre of war could throw at him without complaint. Mucking in he had mixed with officers and men with egalitarian ease, and even through the haze of the worlds worst hangovers, all had loved him. His days in the service were almost over. The war was dragging to its inevitable conclusion and with public demand for film entertainment at its peak, the actors who had survived were firmly put out of harm's way and back on their stages.

Surprisingly the navy had an enlightened view of the nature of alcohol and addiction, and they could see that Newton needed help. Suffering like many with lung and breathing problems brought on by smoking, his asthma and the intensely cold and damp living quarters, Bob was 'Honourably Discharged' on health grounds. He had 'done his bit'. In a single voyage he, like all the men who sailed the Arctic convoys, had faced more danger and hardship than others faced in six years of war. Churchill called it 'The worst journey in the world'. The battle for Stalingrad was partly won by British sailors. Bob had done his bit and survived to tell the tale, but how much use he had been to the war effort was debatable. He had probably never done one jot of damage to the enemy, but the goodwill he had generated was priceless. Actors could, and often did, claim exemption from conscription; for Newton this was never an option. Discipline was relatively relaxed in wartime forces made up of pressed men. Perhaps it was a good thing, yet there was still the eternal growl for 'aft with caps off' and Number Eleven punishment. But Bob had responded by always showing willing. Cheerfully he had demonstrated the ubiquitous British phlegm and been a good comrade. At the dockside and in the bar he said his emotional farewells. He was no warrior, but he had come to know war and hate it silently. He had lost dear friends. He coughed thickly now, and the asthma that had always plagued him had worsened Bob waved his last goodbyes to the laughing, familiar faces and turned to face the same devils that had haunted his father after his war.

By August *Britomart* would be a grave, lying on the ocean bed, filled with its dead. Slaughtered by 'friendly fire' off the French coast. Bob would never know the truth.

Another victim of the war, perhaps, was the love that tied him and Annie. Recovering his health, he had rented a pretty five-room cottage in Sussex, Ticherage Mill. Here, away from the London smogs he could rest and indulge in his passion for fishing. But this was not all; for him responsibility had never been easy, monogamy an impossibly dull prospect. Laurence Evans summed it all up; "At a very glamorous dinner party Bobby met a famous, titled gynaecologist surgeon, the most famous one in London. Bobby sidled up to him after dinner; "Sir Ernest, will you ever do an abortion?" "What an extraordinary question" was his reply, it being illegal in those days. "I understand" said Bob "but look, we can hypothercate. Just suppose you *were* to do an abortion, how much would you charge?" "The most ridiculous question I've ever heard in my life... but I suppose a thousand guineas...". "How much for two?" Bob leered.

After the raw excitement of navy life, existence on civvy street tasted flat. Night-life in the Gargoyle filled the gap but the temptation of female flesh, fluttering by, wafting perfume, was always too great. Looking to flee temptation and be back amongst the 'ranks', Bobby signed on as cook in the Merchant Navy's Small Vessels Pool based at Plymouth. Temporary, four-man crews were needed to pick up and deliver auxiliary vessels from the builders yards. Trips hugging the English coast were, in comparison to his Arctic cruises, joy rides. "There's no better place to dry out than on the briny!" Bob insisted, trying to persuade David Tennant to sign up. "They're always looking for cooks in small vessels. The galleys are tiny, but you don't mind. You love to cook, why not come down with me and try it out, sign on for a few weeks?"

The fractured nature of the Jim Mollison/Amy Johnson marriage that Bob had played out in *They Flew Alone* very much echoed his relationship with Annie. The affair with Linden Travers had dragged on after *No Orchids* had closed. Stamping out with his bags Bob, had moved in with her. That was bad, but there were also rumours about him and Marjorie Rogers, and that she was pregnant. But then he *always* had someone pregnant. Only not Annie. She'd had an ectopic pregnancy early in the marriage and had been advised that it was unlikely she would ever have children, and that hurt. Even though Bob adored her, needed her, he was infatuated with Travers. Despite the pleading and the incessant rows, he refused point-blank to give the affair up. He demanded a divorce. Annie, however had seen it all before, one infatuation after another, and refused...

One of the scenes in *This Happy Breed* sees 'Frank' give his son some fatherly advice on the morning of his wedding; "... Put your wife first, always... anything that's liable to bust up your home and your life with your wife and kids... well, it's just not worth it... just remember that and you won't go far wrong!".

Sound advice, but advice Bob could never himself follow. Soon his life would crumble into another disaster.

Figure 1: Bob, Pauline and Joy, Bodriggy, Cornwall, 1913. (Jill Garnier)

Figure 2: Oil of Bob by Laura Knight, 1922.

Figure 3: Charcoal sketch of Bob backstage at the Rep, 1922.

Figure 4: Newton's only silent film, The Tremarn Case, 1924.

Figure 5: Bob portrait photographed in 1934. (Dominick Penrose)

Figure 6: Bob and Annie at Killiow, 1938. (Dominick Penrose)

Figure 7: Filming Yellow Sands, Sennen, Cornwall, 1939. (Family archive)

Figure 8: Bob on the set of 'Major Barbara' in Navy rig, December 1940. (Private Collection)

Figure 9: On stage in 'No Orchids for Miss Blandish'. (Private Collection)

Figure 10: Publicity work for Obsession, 1949

7. Temptation Harbour

At midnight on May 9th 1945 the British people staggered out of the darkness and into peace. The previous day they had done the cheering and yelling, Churchill's 'brief period of rejoicing'. Now, in the bleary morning-after, war was officially over. The war. And in the place of the sirens, the thuds and the shakes, there was a silence that was too sudden and too hollow.

All around there was destruction; a quarter of a million homes had been destroyed, millions of lives ruined. Many spoke of the war as a 'civilian war' but throughout it had been far more dangerous to be in uniform. The total number was never known but official estimates put the losses at nearly half a million.

Anger followed the rejoicing, filling the void. The grim reality of the cost of the war became apparent; America had retrenched into isolationism and pulled the plug on cheap loans and Britain, like Germany, began to pay her reparations. Britain was bankrupt and her recovery from victory was going to be more costly than Germany's recovery from defeat. The message from government was unequivocal; the future was going to be all about 'coping'.

Stroppy, unsentimental and unpredictable, the British soldiers, airmen and sailors home from war threw Churchill, their yesterday's hero, out and voted in Atlee's Labour lefties. The real hard work was now beginning, grim days, grim years. Six years of war were going to define the next decade.

But that was tomorrow and for now there was noise and light and all the bright immediate things that had been so longed for. The people poured into the cinemas and theatres, into the throbbing clubs and dance halls, lived out the fantasies that took them away from the past, bypassed the present, and into a future of plenty that they knew was far away. Like so many, Newton faced a peacetime world with uncertainty. So much had happened; so many friends had died. He sealed up all the yesterdays in a bottle and learned not to hear the cries of the dead.

The war years had effected a momentous and all-pervasive impact on British cinema. The call-up had left studios with only a third of their staff and most of the studio space had been requisitioned for storage. In 1939 there had been sixty five sound stages at the disposal of the twenty two studios, by 1942 there were just thirty, divided among nine studios. Raw materials for costumes and sets had been, and would be, perpetually in short supply and film-stock severely rationed. Little wonder that production had dropped from 222 films in 1936 to 116 in 1938 and 60 in 1942.

In critical, ideological and stylistic terms, as during the 1914-18 conflict, British society had been profoundly influenced by the demands of war. Now, in the aftermath, film, even if it was mostly imported from America, had to be interpreted in new ways. *Henry V* had been a passionate paean to finish the war; now it formed the foundation of a new industry. The peak demand of austere war years had seen box-office takings treble and income continued to rise even in the bleak post-war years that followed; thirty million cinema tickets were now being sold every week and suddenly the protectionist Quota Acts were rendered obsolete.

The war years had produced a preponderance of film about individual males and their experience of conflict; times and society might have changed, but the importance of film still lay in its ability to act as a vehicle for nationalistic propaganda. Throughout *They Flew Alone*, Neagle, as 'Amy Johnson', presented successes placed within a context of patriotic self-sacrifice; "I want to try and do something for England...!" she cried. During the war, film had made the masses feel that they were part of a cohesive social unit and that 'class' differences were a thing of the past. This, of course, was a falsehood that their masters were happy to perpetuate. Now government and film-makers colluded again to produce images that carried on the ideal of national collectivity. Everybody was shown as still 'pulling together' in the face of national emergency; individual sacrifice was shown to mean the sublimation of personal desires that conflicted with the needs of the country. It was all terribly convincing. The reality was that the long-term concept of 'nationhood' depended on the reaffirmation of traditional, pre-war, patriarchal and class values. The ideal of individuals from different social and regional backgrounds, all happily bonding, was once again peddled. Somehow it was all rather 'Red', but everyone pretended not to notice.

As film addressed the people, encouraging him and her to 'do their bit' for 'us', the struggle to re-erect the old barriers was silently active. But if pre-war public consensus had been perceived as a docile satisfaction with the status-quo, there was now a more progressive element where class consciousness was being re-defined; Britain was pregnant with the Welfare State.

The most dominant film genre during the latter years of wartime had been, of course, the male war film. Post-war audiences were, however, sick of conflict, and they were also sick of the pre-war tradition of hare-brained fantasy and gung-ho adventure. Peace brought its challenges to the British film industry; the war years had seen record cinema attendances and audiences full of patriotic good will, now tastes were changing. The penchant for drawing rooms and stately mansions, the vapid meanderings of the idle rich, affected accents and public schools had been left far behind. People were also tired of the synthetic Hollywood gloss; now they looked to their celluloid screen gurus for guidance and tangible realism. The focus now was on the old obsessions, with unhappy marriages and the inequitable division of property. They looked for real British people, real situations and real emotions and they found it all, not in the genteel drawing-rooms, but in the squalid back kitchens.

1945 brought a flood of sex and infidelity to the screen. The question that every ordinary serving man had silently asked when far from home was addressed through fiction; what had home life really been like and what had their wives been doing when they were away? John Mills and Stuart Granger, the soldier-who-come-home and the despicable spiv, the universal metaphors, battled it out in *Waterloo Road*. The good-guy won, reconciliation was effected, marriage rebuilt and society was stabilised. It was the comforting lie everyone wanted, but they knew that the reality had often been very different.

Bob's relationship with his agent had always been problematic. Theatre business had ever been run on tradition, cash, a handshake and a gentlemen's agreement. Eternally dismissive of the mundane routine of life, the best Bob could ever do in terms of officialdom was a pencilled note forgotten on the back of a fag packet. By now Annie and Bob had become strangers and their very real love had transmuted into periods of bitter sniping and then frigid stand-offs. Stepping in as a reluctant partner-substitute, Edward Vere-Barker, Connie's boss and left hand, now became Bob's life agent as much as his professional pimp. It was all part of the job and they both knew it. Unfortunately Vere-Barker had made the mistake of not only living in Chelsea, but living just a few hundred yards from Bob...

Bob's life was in ruins; he missed Annie badly, his life was going terribly wrong, and he was determined to make everyone's life hell. Annie had blankly refused to resolve the muddle her absentee husband had made of his career. "Right..." he shouted down the phone at her, "I'll bloody sort it out myself!" Straight out of the bath, and with only a towel around his waist, he slapped down the street. "Come out here, you bastard!" he yelled. Vere-Barker was used to this sort of thing now. "...You get down on your knees and thank God for all the good things I've brought you!". It was all part of the trade, part of the routine, but this time Vere-Barker held an ace card. He knew Bob was tired of film work and was desperate to escape the eternal chaos in his personal life; joyously Bob grabbed at the offer of stage work. The production was Walter Greenwood's sparkling 'Cornish Comedy' *So Brief the Spring*.

Despite the impact of cinema and radio and the advent of the rich man's toy of television, amateur drama held a huge potential for agonising self and social re-examination and was gaining enormous popularity. Semi-pro theatres were springing up all over the country. The intellectual set of Oldham, having found themselves short of a legit' venue at the outbreak of the war had quickly opened their own and rattled out their first show within a month. Now it was flourishing and had secured the provincial opening for 'So Brief...'.

Local-girl-making-good Dora Broadbent, later Dora Bryan, had grown up in theatre and like Newton had learned her trade as an assistant stage manager. An emerging 'name' as the Northern tart-with-a-heart she was engaged to take a part in the Oldham opening week. At twenty three she was a looker, if an innocent one, and Bob, ever the philanthropist, was delighted at the prospect of working with her. Offering to waive his fee he swore he would work for expenses only.

The play was set in a summery garden on the cliffs above 'the Cornish Fishing Village of Trelooe' and 'Outside the "Three Jolly Sailors" on the Harbour side'. As a bona-fide Cornish man, Newton was to take the lead part, that of 'Randy Jollifer', and as in *Yellow Sands* he was to tread the sand-strewn boards barefoot, dressed in denims and fishermans jersey. Rehearsals began well, but things, somehow, quickly went awry. Bob would fortify himself with a '...sustaining amount of drink,' Dora Bryan noted, '...and at times was so incoherent that he couldn't really be understood, and invariably I found myself having to say his lines as well as my own. He took it upon himself to arrange the plot of the play. I was playing the part of the hussy, and he took quite a fancy to me, making wild grabs at me on stage, instead of lavishing his attention upon the character who was supposed to be his true love. This made no sense of the production at all and when dear Walter Greenwood came to see his play for the first time he wondered what on earth had happened to it...".

What had happened to it was that 'Jack ashore', Newton had taken to the local hospitality with a vengeance. Almost continuously inebriated, his stage appearance had turned the comedy into a farce and his roving eyes had turned on Dora... "One night after the show Bob offered me a lift home in his taxi. He was staying at the Midland Hotel in Manchester. We drew up at the gate just as Mum and Dad were going in with fish and chips, so Dad invited Mr Newton in for a cup of tea. The taxi was disposed of and we went inside. Bob said he didn't like tea very much and added that he was actually allergic to it, so instead he worked through Dad's bottle of Drambuie. Just after the war that was a luxury saved for Christmas, but for Bob every day was Christmas and the bottle disappeared in one evening. I left them to it as I had to be up early for rehearsal next day... I had switched off the light and was about to go to sleep when I saw a large figure in long naval underwear silhouetted against the doorway making its way towards me. Fortunately Dad had heard someone moving about and came to the rescue, intent on preserving the chastity of his daughter. "No, Mr Newton..." he said kindly but very firmly, "You are sleeping in here..." and he propelled Bob towards his allotted bedroom".

By early December a bitter winter had struck; Bob had been pulled back into line, the play back to the authorised script and cast and crew on to Nottingham. Attracted to a star name who could turn out a proper Cornish accent, audiences crowded in and the work received rollicking reviews, but as the show rolled on to Wimbledon in February, closure drew near. Ever the inventive raconteur, David Niven rolled out one version of the tale...'It could have been brought on by over-work or a longing for the play to close so that he could indeed 'head west', (to Cornwall) but one Saturday night in the St James' Theatre, the curtain did not rise; the audience became restless, then impatient, and finally, from the gallery, a slow hand clapping started and spread to the dress circle, and the stalls. At last the middle of the curtain wobbled uncertainly and a pair of shoes appeared beneath it. Sensing an announcement, the audience hushed itself into silence. Unsteady hands pulled the curtain apart just enough to frame the purple countenance of the star. "Ladies and Gentlemen...." roared Bob, rolling his eyes at every corner of the house, "the reason this curtain has so far not risen... is because the stage manager… has the fucking impertinence to suggest that I am PISSED...!".

As within theatre, the cosy pre-war semi-professionalism of the film industry had perished. A muddled re-hash of the Quota act now effectively dictated a base-line production cost of a pound a foot, up to £7000 per film. Bogged down in post-war gloom, and despite the boom in demand, the industry was finding that times were tighter than ever. The drab accountants had taken over and decreed that there was no time for amateurism.

Reports of Bob's heavy drinking had gone before him and this was a worry to many producers; with fresh new faces back home from the war and clamouring at the stage door, many were reluctant to contract him. The screening of *Hatters Castle* and *Major Barbara* and a re-release of *Jamaica Inn* had however, seen his popularity soar. Reluctantly investors started to understand that the public were attracted by his name and that Newton was a 'star' personality and a popular face.

With British film beginning to experience a popular renaissance Connie's agency was suddenly receiving more offers than their troublesome star could handle. There was talk of him taking a role in the period drama *Hungry Hill*, director Jean Renoir wanted him to star alongside Chaplin's ex-wife, Paulette Goddard, as the lecherous man-servant in his *Diary of a Chambermaid* and Pascal, flushed with the success of *Major Barbara*, wanted him for his next Shaw adaptation. However Associated British Pictures and Rank were also interested and came up with an offer that, despite the rumoured £10,000 offer from Renoir, couldn't be ignored.

Annie was now snapping at Bob's heels and threatening to bring the legal trade down on him; worse news came in the form of the Inland Revenue who were rattling their pens and demanding money and Bob found that his financial situation was unusually precarious. Reluctantly he admitted that his dream of a Cornish hideaway was unsupportable; Gear Cottage was put on the market, but the Rolls had to stay. Signing a two-picture contract, he prepared for another grim term at the 'Porridge Factory'.

Before that, and perhaps because of professional pride, or guilt, March 16th saw him back at the Oldham Rep' and a brief star-appearance, playing opposite Dora Bryan in the Anton White play *Semi Private*. There was time for just one dress rehearsal before the big opening night but Bob played his part sober and with consummate professionalism. The audience was enthusiastic and success was toasted with champagne. Late that night, and with a glint in his eye, Bob once again asked his co-star if she would like a lift home...

The first ABP production was entitled *Night Boat to Dublin*. Flicking through the script Newton saw that it was yet another work that bowed to the ongoing 'realist' obsession and was laden with post-war Nazis, spies, 'A' bombs and kidnapped scientists. Filming was at Welwyn Studios and all the usual suspects had been roped in; Leslie Dwyer, an old friend from the days of Gladys Cooper's *The Letter* tour, a rather pretty Muriel Pavlow, and the impeccably English Wilfred Hyde White, who was making the briefest appearance as a taxi driver...

Struggling with a typically British style and a labyrinthine plot that dragged against a flat monochrome backdrop, Newton knew that the film was not one in which he could let rip. Direction came from Lance Comfort and Bob sailed through comfortably enough, playing his part of 'British M.I.5 officer, Captain David Grant' walking-stick and all, very much as himself. Bored to death, Bob maintained his habit of 'becoming' his part. Each morning he would turn up at the studios, very military, very soberly dressed and carrying an immaculate new brief case... that contained nothing but a bottle of brandy.

Public release came, appropriately on April Fools Day, 1946 and despite the above average production-values and Pavlow's dollop of foreign glamour, the reaction of the cinema-going public was muted. By this time however the Rank Corporation had bought a share of the 'Universal' conglomerate; suddenly there was a British foot in the door of the huge American market and *Night Boat to Dublin* sailed across the Atlantic.

Off-set, Newton's steamy infatuation with Travers had run its course. Annie had been proved right and by September he had wandered back home, unrepentant and considerably worse for wear. Despite his promises and pleadings, she could see that their marriage was over. Perhaps it was because of the war and what he had experienced, or perhaps because Annie had just given up nagging, but Bob's drinking had by now turned from careless pleasure to a desperate need. Too often things got out of hand. Casual lunch-time drinks developed into monumental benders; the police would be involved and he would vanish for days, sometimes weeks. Crashing out then drying out, he awoke to find that he had become the newspapers' favourite fool and labelled an unemployable liability. Remorse followed regret and degenerated into bouts of self-pitying depression that could only be cured by alcohol.

Much of the problem lay in his past; as a boy he had been abandoned by his father and it was a reality he had never been able to come to terms with. Now, as an adult, loneliness and rejection was a thing he could not tolerate. Always he would seek company, any company, and seek to charm it and company was always found around a bottle. His relationship with men however was very different from that with women. Men always seemed to understand, men were always the drinking buddies; women were the eternal, alluring, frustrating mystery. Frightened, and aware that he was losing Annie, he played the loving husband and slowly won her back. Then, of course, the temptation to wonder became too great and he found himself in love and infatuated all over again. This time the new darling was Natalie Newhouse.

A peripheral member of the Gargoyle Club, Natalie was twenty-five, sixteen years Newton's junior. From German Jewish stock she had gravitated like so many to London during the war, and like a stray, through the doors of the Cavendish Hotel. With a fiercely independent spirit and a quick, provocative mind, she was an unstable fireball of passion. The fateful meeting had come when Bob had phoned David Tennant's daughter, Pauline, about a part in a play; a voice had answered that set his heart thumping. Within minutes he had driven across town.

Michael Luke, another Gargoyle Club member, knew Natalie only too well; 'A street-wise gamine, small, pert, pretty with rich mouse hair, extremely seductive and meant to be... the china-blue-eyed nemesis of many a member's inflated ego. Sharp tongued and smiling, she would tuck the smile beneath her peekaboo hair style and the mouth would emerge angry, a sling-shot of acid words flung defiantly at the face of the offender of her curiously strong code, a code, in its special way both moral and rebellious. If the words thus flung did not suffice their object, then a splash of drink in the face would follow. Or just as likely, laughter; mocking or forgiving. Generous and unrelenting with her favours, gregarious or seated alone with a scowl, Natalie, small in white shirt and green skirt, knew, it seemed by instinct, all that a far longer experience of life might have untaught her.'

Annie was used to Bob's indiscretions and still secretly hoped for a lasting reconciliation, but this time it was different. Home life became a nightmare of rows and Bob simply got drunk and stayed there. Annie, still the spitfire, reacted with rage and war broke out. The furniture got smashed up and the police were summoned up from the Gerald Road station.

As usual Bob made promises to reform, but Annie knew them to be lies. The breaking point came when she discovered that he had sneaked Natalie up to the cottage in Sussex. Suspicious she had called up the main house, Tickerage Mill, asking about Bob's whereabouts and was told that he was there... but with 'a Miss Newhouse'. The sense of scandal was palpable, even over the crackling line; "I don't know what he's up to..." the housekeeper hissed.

After eight turbulent years, hate and acrimony were the stale fag-ends of their love and divorce was inevitable. "Miss Newhouse..." Annie wrote to her solicitors, "has a very bad reputation; she attempted to commit suicide some years ago over a love affair and is now walking on crutches. She is a dreadful creature; takes drugs and behaves in a dreadful way...".

The truth was that Natalie had fallen through a skylight in the blackout and broken her leg; the rest was open to debate.

After a week in Sussex, Bob and Natalie escaped back to London and the Ritz Hotel. Aware that the lawyers were hunting them down they booked separate rooms, but no one was fooled. Annie's fury knew no bounds; her Scots blood was up and she had Bob on the run. Hiring private detectives she pursued the fugitives at every hotel they turned to.

By the middle of December the gloss had rubbed off Bob's new passion and he was on the phone to Annie. Maudlin, he grew sentimental and said he wanted to come home for Christmas. With the infuriating, boyish and irresistible manner he rapidly worked his old charm. "I can't go on with this creature, she's a frightful woman, can't you save me from her, I can't stand her any longer... I want some advice about my film work, I can't get any from her, she's a half-wit!" he said. "I am going to divorce you" Annie spat back. "Here, why don't *you* speak to the silly bitch" Bob suggested.

Later that night he phoned again, swearing it was all over with Natalie and that he no longer loved her and wanted to come back home... but he had to put her back on her feet.

Annie relented and met him more than half way; but the bloodhounds tracked the lovers down again, comfortably louche in Flemmings Hotel. Cornered and guilty as hell, Bob's temper snapped. In a vitriolic telephone spat he condemned Annie as 'a damned plague' and demanded a divorce. "Oh, come to your senses, Bob..." Annie pleaded, "Don't you realise what a mess you're making of your life...I won't do anything about it if you are prepared to give up this girl..." Bob was insistent. He wanted a divorce, but a friendly divorce, he said, of the kind his family always effected, without bitterness.

For ever sentimental Bob's thoughts instinctively turned to 'home' and he set off, driving south to Cornwall. A half-way stop for a hotel lunch saw him spotted by star-struck staff. In an adjoining room the 'Pirates' rugby team, up from Penzance, had also spotted 'their' local celebrity and crowded in. Too late the staff tried to hiss them back to their seats, warning them not to disturb 'Mr Newton'; Bob, however was having none of this; "Come on in here!" he roared, "My Mother used to live in Newlyn...!" Rounds were stood all around and lunch rolled on well into the afternoon...

The time was yet to come when actors had to protect their careful generated studio image and hide from 'their public'. Bob was always 'of the people'. He loved company, *needed* company. Intensely gregarious, always on first names with everyone, always 'old cock' and 'my lover' to everyone; darkness and silence was loathed and dreaded. Ever a bundle of contradictions, he also dreaded domestic boredom. Now he found himself separated from the woman who was always his left and right hand; he was also homeless. A meeting, predictably in a pub, with one of the swelling ranks of studio hangers-on, lead to a new friendship and somewhere to crash out. The new face was Arthur Colin-Campbell, a 'film extra'.

Leader Magazine carried a more than telling article in its October 1946, issue. 'Anybody who knows Robert Newton can hardly fail to know Arthur Colin-Campbell as well. They are just about inseparable for twenty-four hours a day. Colin is a furnisher of film and stage stars' houses and a dealer in antiques. He has just done a house for Kay Hammond. When Newton is busy on film, Colin acts as his valet, dresser and all around nursemaid and carries on his business by telephone or through agents. He won't leave Newton. The actor lives in his flat, talks to him about politics and everything under the sun, drives to the studio with him and hears over his lines both in the Rolls Royce and in the dressing-room. "He's got his little peculiarities" says Colin. "I've got to leave the light burning all the time in the flat, he can't bear to wake up in the dark. And during the day he can't bear to be alone. There are never twenty-four hours I don't hear from him. If he's somewhere else he gives me a ring; It may be five or six in the morning. But I can be sure he'll ring some time."

The breakdown of Bob and Annie's marriage now seemed final. Annie was out for revenge and she demanded her half of the Chelsea house which was now sold off.

Lost in his own delirious world, Bob was comfortable enough sofa crashing with Colin-Campbell but he knew it was only a short-term option. Natalie was now another permanent fixture in his life and she wanted a cut of his earnings and she wanted a home. His fee from *Night Boat* and the sale of Gear cottage bought a house; overlooking the Thames in Cheney Walk, it was also conveniently near Chelsea...

Without Annie's earthy common sense to steady him, and with Natalie living on a nocturnal overdrive that took in a constant round of parties, Bob began to pile on weight. Pale and drawn, chain-smoking and dulled by prescription drugs, he was close to collapse. Looking into the mirror he could see that his life was starting to unravel. The chest complaint he had inherited from the navy returned and the nagging of early onset angina was a constant presence. Sleep had become a nightmare of feverish delirium and was filled with terrors. Too often he would be found unconscious on the streets; too often found wandering around Soho half-naked and incoherent. For the newspapers it was all good copy, but the reality was a hellish drink-dependent derangement that was coming close to madness. Even Natalie began to see that something had to be done.

The April trip that Connie's window-dressed as a 'brief holiday to Switzerland to visit old school friends' saw Newton checked into the Santa Agnese Clinic, a private sanatorium. High up in the Alps it wasn't only the mountain air that was dry; closely watched by eagle-eyed nuns and far away from liquid temptation he sobered up, dried out and rested. Moving south to Ascona and then on to the Grand Hotel on the shores of Lake Locarno the nightmares retreated and sleep was found without the horrors of hallucination.

On October 19th 1946, Sally, Newton's daughter by Peta, had her sixteenth birthday. Now, true to the letter of the law and with a punctuality that verged on obsession, she and her father were to be reunited.

It had all been arranged by the lawyers; they were to meet in the neutral ground of a London hotel and the date was set for a Saturday. Duly delivering her daughter to the door, Peta, unable and unwilling to meet a man who would perhaps no longer recognise her, hurried away. Sally, very much the innocent, sat and waited nervously. A long hour passed. Her father was late.

When Bob had headed off to America for his part in Coward's *Private Lives*, his marriage to Peta had simply faded out and Peta and her daughters had been forced to survive on bitter family charity. Rootless and constantly moving on, they had been bombed out of their home in Romney Marsh in the early days of the war. Like refugees, they had retreated to the bleak Welsh mountain where Peta herself had been born. There Sally had been incarcerated in a boarding school that she quickly grew to hate; ironically escape had come in drama classes. By the end of the war both mother and daughters were utterly sick of the vacuous monotony of rural life. Newton's growing fame and rising earnings had boosted her monthly alimony to £40; that was enough, they packed their bags and headed back to the bright lights of London.

Sally's reunion with her father had been fifteen years in the coming, and it was an event that Peta had dreaded. Divorce had been perverse, protracted and costly; seeing Bob's name up in lights whilst she struggled merely to survive had been a galling experience. Now, as she dropped Sally off and walked away, she knew that the man who had so blithely seduced her would now steal away her daughter.

'I shall never forget my 16th birthday,' Sally recalled, 'I was sitting alone on a bench seat in the foyer of Quaglino's Hotel...' Natalie came in first, Bob was parking the Rolls, '...of course I didn't know her. How should I know her. I didn't know he'd got a mistress. So she comes in and comes up to me and says 'Is your name Sally Newton?' and I said 'Yes'. I was so gauche. And she said 'Oh, because I'm Natalie Newhouse'. And I said 'Oh...', I didn't even know she was anything to do with Bob. The swing doors from the street turned rather faster than usual and a wild-looking man catapulted inside. This was my birthday present, this great bearded thing comes round the door and says 'Oh, you've met have you', and then he said 'I'm your father'. He didn't know whether to shake hands or kiss me. In fact nothing. Nothing. 'Oh, let's go and find a drink'. You know. I didn't know about drink in those days. We sat down to lunch, just the three of us, Bob, Nat' and me and then, when we got to the coffee stage, Pauline and Joy walked in. They must have been in tune with the fact that Bob was meeting me for the first time and they all came in to see what was going on...'.

With an age gap of just thirteen years Natalie and Sally could have been sisters; Sally was bowled over by Natalie's self-assured vivacity and an instant empathy was formed. 'Afterwards all I remember was going back to Cheney Walk, because Pauline said 'Let's all go back to Cheney Walk'. That's where they were living then, No 5, where a great tea was produced by servants, it was a great day, and darling Nat'. She had such guts! Bob and Nat' had this incredible love-hate relationship. Bob really loved Nat', but he couldn't cope with her because she was so volatile, so abusive and aggressive...'

Sally returned home to her Mother, late, tipsy and glowing with happiness. She faced an angry inquisition. 'Oh...' she blurted out, 'I've just met Bob's mistress, Natalie, she's only twenty nine...'. Connie's gave *Leader Magazine* a different, sanitised, version; '...I heard she wanted to act so I arranged to meet her last Sunday (sic),' Bob was quoted 'Our meeting proved my other point, how women dominate every situation. I was scared stiff, but she put me at ease. We had lunch, went to the zoo and got on famously. I'm arranging now for her to go into the RADA or a good repertory company...'.

The winter of 1946 was severe; snow fell endlessly and the Thames froze over. The 'Great Frost' set in and the country was paralysed. Coal shortages and a rigorously enforced regime of daily five hour power cuts combined to make life a misery. March brought a temporary thaw and burst pipes, and then the worst blizzard of the year. The weather seemed to reflect the state of the country. The economy was in chaos and locked in the grip of post-war privations. These were the 'austerity' years, the low-point of an England defined by two million unemployed, by 'sweet points and clothing-coupons, margarine in plain packets, kids in balaclavas and hob-nailed boots'. Industrial production had juddered to a halt.

Blowing his earnings to escape the grim winter, Annie's wrath and post-war society where it seemed that the only thing that wasn't rationed was gloom, Newton and his new lover had flown out to spend the Christmas holidays in Bermuda. Under flawless skies and in a multi-coloured playground for the rich, they immersed themselves in a society untouched by war and basked in the luxury of guiltless decadence. Mixing with the beautiful people and rubbing shoulders with the American rich, Bob found himself, suddenly, on the brink of a new life; a meeting with a film executive from Universal Studios, now linked with the Rank empire, lead to talk of a collaboration with the rising star, Burt Lancaster, in his next film.

Bob duly set his daughter on the bottom rung of the rickety stardom ladder. After an April holiday with Natalie in Cassis in the south of France, he set to work on another 'Two Cities Films' production, *Odd Man Out*.

Lifted from a novel by F L Green, it was a bleak British take on *film noir* and a piece that perfectly reflected the introspective and self-obsessed mood of the day. Very much a critique of masculinity, the work was set in post-war Belfast and tracked the final hours of a wounded and dying IRA gun-man, who, feared and shunned, wanders the slatternly streets, a Christ like figure, on the way to his own Calvary.

Directed by Carol Reed, a man whose abilities Newton knew were comparable to those of David Lean, the film focused both on the almost silent victim and the kaleidoscope of grotesque figures attracted to him. The script was gritty, brutally realistic and cliché free. Rejected after a quick glance by Stewart Granger, because he didn't have enough lines, the central role of the dying man went to James Mason who was to give an outstanding performance and was to build a career from it. Newton was to share top billing with him though his was almost a cameo part. His character was the wild and bearded 'Lukey', a deranged and tormented artist, a drunken scarecrow, who seeks to portray the dying man's agony and the coming darkness of death.

Stark and monochrome, a classical tragedy with an emphasis on prestige and 'Art', the work was filmed in Denham Studios and in the unmistakable, bleak setting of bomb scarred Belfast. Newton's character was an extreme one and the studio machine quoted him as finding his inspiration in the rags of clothing that he gathered from East End barrows and in the paintings of Richard Dadd and Louis Wein, artists who both ended their days incarcerated. Perhaps there was some truth in this, but Newton needed no second-hand inspiration, he had grown up amongst artists; it was said that the half-complete painting of a Christian martyr on 'Lukey's' studio easel was one done by Bob himself.

As a sign of his standing, and despite his equal billing with Mason, Newton did not appear on-screen until the last half hour of the film. Working out of a bedlam set, feral and crazed, Newton's 'Lukey' was another consummate character incarnation and one that cemented his name for playing the barbarian. His appearance came not a moment too late in the picture, which for many a viewer, had already begun to drag; he walked on and the whole thing began to sparkle. Inevitably there was press talk of his 'drunken' character being portrayed by a drunken actor. Bob reacted angrily, '...it is harder to play a drunk when really drunk than to play it when sober' he insisted. Working opposite some of the same renowned Irish Players who had filled up his Shilling Theatre stage and immersed in his character, Bob didn't even notice Dora Bryan, now playing a bit part and lost in the crowd...

If the passing years have made the work look dated and the views of critics less kind, it was nevertheless ahead of its time. Expressionist values and noir stylistics abounded; blurred images, tilted camera angles and harsh lighting. A tapestry of jagged shards, of sounds, shadows, silences and blinding light, a fevered delirium, the film was enormously ambitious. It was a portrayal of a modern 'dance of death' where innocence and evil are juxtaposed and the wide-eyed child looks into the soul of the dying man. Reed's directing style was unique; an artistic experiment, an explosive reaction to the carnage of war, it showed much of the inventive and intense technique later to be used in *The Third Man* and established his name as a first-rate director.

The *Spectator* called the film 'the first masterpiece ever produced by a British studio'; the *News Chronicle* said 'Newton is the brilliant core of an interlude of sombre fantasy placed in a beautiful, decayed rococo setting....' Only the *Times* carped, '...but there is one character whose bizarreness strikes false: the drunken artist who carries the half-conscious fugitive off to his studio to paint the lineaments of pain and dissolution. Is it perhaps that Robert Newton plays the part in a style over-reminiscent of Ancient Pistol?' At a time when the home-produced film was automatically regarded as inherently inferior to that churned out by the production-line 'star-making' film-factories in Hollywood, the outstanding quality of the work was widely recognised and it was instantly hailed a classic.

Mired in technicality, the project had however overshot its budget by a third. Packaged up and edited for American audiences it was sent abroad with high hopes and, unsurprisingly, totally misfired. No one understood the accents, few grasped the deeper meanings and Newton was slated for 'overacting'. Condemned as two hours of unrelieved gloom, the new 'Americanized' title, *Gang War*, summed up the utter cultural mis-translation. But in the 'star' game, however, a day was a long time.

Prosperous America, both maternal and paternal, having brokered an interest in the concerns of the whole of Europe, now had a finger in every pie and was taking a predatory interest in the growing British film industry. The *Sunday Times* reacted in its Feb 2nd edition, 1947... 'Last Tuesday a throng of beaming film executives and less receptive newspaper types learned that a British film company, Associated British Picture Corporation, was to join with an American company, Warner Brothers, in producing in this country six films 'similar in quality to the best now being produced in America....'; above the sounds of hospitality I heard that Warner's would supply their leading stars, directors, and producers 'to ensure that these pictures are of the highest quality, suitable for World Markets'. The following day I saw *Odd Man Out*. The director and producer of this film is English, the players are English, Irish and Canadian, the director of photography is Australian born. The piece is not, indeed, if we are to judge by the work which reached us during 1946, "similar in quality to the best now produced in America". It is not similar because it is better...'.

Plodding on the old treadmill routine, Bob rolled back into the studios to fulfil his second ABP contract picture and was relieved to find *Temptation Harbour* was a more comprehensible work than the heavyweight *Odd Man Out*.

The chosen director was the easy-going Lance Comfort, and the plot a traditional and approachable contemporary thriller. Bob took the pivotal role of dock railway signalman 'Mallinson', who stumbles across a corpse, a stash of smuggled banknotes and a moral dilemma. Tracked down in his Denham dressing room dressed in 'striped pyjama trousers, a woollen vest, a pair of bright blue socks, and bedroom slippers' Newton, now the fans' darling, gave an effusive interview to the *Leader Magazine* for its October edition; 'If you meet Robert Newton on the film set... he will probably greet you as some long-lost member of his family. He will 'dear' and 'darling' everybody all the time; he will pat you on the back, put his arm around you and clasp your hand for minutes on end. In fact he has a hunger for personal relationships. All this in spite of his distaste for being written about. "If I wasn't such a good Christian, I wouldn't say a word" he says "but I'm always willing to help my fellow men...". At this point he considers what would happen if anyone tried to glamorise him in print. "Suppose you came to me one morning to describe my elegant breakfast" he says "you'd probably find me not very well, just having had a row with somebody, and drinking black coffee from a cup that has no saucer to go with it". He glowers at the idea of glamour-publicity. For the signalman he plays in *Temptation Harbour*... his model was the man who helped him with all the technicalities, a respectable, quiet, S.R. signalman, who, from his post high-up, above the station and port, sees what's going on underneath. He taught Newton how to handle the levers, for instance. "They'd rust if they were touched with wet hands, so all signalmen have an old handkerchief in the signal box to catch hold of the handle with. Did you know that? Well, the man who showed me all that, and much more about signalling, is a quiet and pleasant widower, just like me in the film". Newton is taking a special interest in this film, *Temptation Harbour*, because he himself found the story, a novel called 'Newhaven-Dieppe' by the French novelist Georges Simenon, and interested the film people in making it. When he was in London, Simenon saw Newton, but the two men never actually met; Simenon and the director were in a West End bar. Newton came in. The director pointed him out to the novelist. But before any introduction could be made, Newton had left. The bar was sold out...'.

In a challenging and thoughtful work with some good location shots taken at Folkstone, Newton developed a character whose honest and uneventful life is slowly torn apart. Human and gentle, 'Mallinson' was a complete opposite to the demonic Lukey, and one with whom audiences could cosily empathise. Drama came in the form of the murderer who tries to grab back the loot, and who in turn is accidentally killed by Mallinson. The sexual charge, with surprisingly saucy bedroom scenes, scanty costumes and a rare Newton screen kiss, comes in the form of thirty three year-old French actress Simone Simon who played Camellia, the scheming fairground baggage, and who leads 'Mallinson' into the titular temptation.

Premièring on February 17th 1947 British reviews were good, calling the work 'outstanding' and 'realistic'; the American contingent, ever uncomfortable with British regional accents, characteristically grumbled that Newton 'inclined to strike poses and declaim in an orotund style'.

The onset of another bitter winter saw a post-war normality of power cuts, fuel shortages and rationing becoming seemingly more stringent. Newton, with a new woman in his life, an agent momentarily satisfied, money burning in his pocket and a lawyer's letter telling him that Annie was divorcing him on grounds of adultery, found a life that resembled normality. Glowing with accolades for his work in *Odd Man Out*, which received a British Film Academy Best Film award, Newton was now at the peak of his career. Rated, and waged, No 3 box-office draw in the country, the year brought a frantic flurry of film work.

The first was *Snowbound*. Sucked almost seamlessly from Hammond Innes thriller, 'The Lonely Skier', it was a chilly melodrama set in the Italian Alps very much in the vein of Stevensons 'Treasure Island'. Newton took the role of 'Derek Engels', a film director and ex-wartime intelligence officer. Working alongside Dennis Price, a young Herbert Lom, the always amusing Stanley Holloway and French glamour import Mila Parely, the plot wound around the usual mêlee of good-guys and double-crossing villains seeking the new-mythological post-war El Dorado of Nazi gold. Another piece of meta-theatre that doubled up as self-promotion, the work opened with film-studio extras piling into 'Gaumont British Studios'. Once again Bob appeared very much as his off-screen self as the director of a piece being shot there. Recording took place at the Gainsborough studios and began in the middle of a summer that saw scorching heat-waves mirror the films winter's chills.

Bound up in Alpine clothing and working take and re-take under the studio lights was draining. *Picturegoer* magazine's September issue reported on the process.... 'In *Snowbound* Newton is again playing with Stanley Holloway, and is delighted to be back on the set with the man who more than anyone else has the knack of keeping people in a state of perpetual merriment. It is typical of the film business that during one of Britain's hottest summers Newton should have made a film set in the snowy Alps. Warmly dressed, with Perspex shavings of snow on his Swiss hat, and perspiration on his brow, he rehearsed his scenes in a beautifully reconstructed Alpine hut. One detail worried him. Although the look of the film will be authentic, and there have been many delightful location shots taken in the French Alps, obviously the players cannot control their breath so that it billows before them in the usual way when the temperature is very low, seeing that they are acting in an exceedingly warm studio indeed!'

The film was released in March '48; Newton got top billing although his screen appearances were sporadic. Complete with his usual walking-stick, Bob pops up briefly at the opening and again some ten minutes in. Only in the final half hour does he join in the action, just in time to perish in the flames. Shot in black and white, the work simply rode on Newton's name. The Germans got a good bashing and the Italians were bracketed as ingratiating buffoons and the thing hung together well enough; certainly it did the Alpine tourist industry no harm. It was a cheesy piece of hokum and was well received by the punters. The critics' gave an approving nod, but the work contributed little to the world of quality entertainment.

Newton's disentanglement from Annie was a repeat of the Peta divorce; separation finally came through in April. The process had been anything but the friendly legal goodbye Newton wanted, Annie burned with anger and jealousy, worse, she still wanted him. In court and in the papers both of their private lives were dragged through the mire. Natalie's previous suicide attempt was raked up and photographs of Bob and Nat', a woman sixteen years his junior, taken in Bermuda were produced, juicy examples of his 'infidelity'. Damningly Annie announced that nothing from Bob's earnings had been paid into the bank, and that he was squandering his money on 'riotous living'. She asked for £1200 to pay off a mortgage; the court awarded £700.

Pressured by an agency that knew that its 'star' had gathered too much negative press, and despite denials to a media industry which now hounded his every move, Bob and Natalie were manipulated into a quick August marriage. Robert Guy to Natalie Hazel Cochrane

Newhouse, of Framfield, Sussex, at Crowborough, Sussex. The event was 'supposed' to be quiet and low-key but of course the press had a field day and the drama they wanted was handed to them on a plate by Connie's. The story hit the daily rags the next morning; both bride and groom arrived late, having hitched a ride from their broken down car. Arthur Colin-Campbell, the socially androgynous third person in the uneven relationship, was best man and had to sub Bob the twelve shillings and seven pence registration fee...

With his next film contract safely in his pocket and the promise of more work to come, a months honeymoon had been arranged. Copying Bekus and Joy's nautical jaunt, *Tresca*, a modern and fully crewed sailing sloop, had been chartered. Along with a gaggle of merry hangers-on, the plan was to sail north to the Hebrides but as the reception at Cowes on the Isle of Wight went into full swing the weather started turning foul. Next morning, with sore heads and queasy stomachs, the plan was changed and a course set for the Channel Islands. The long term weather-forecast looked grim and the venture north was abandoned in favour of an expedition to Ireland. Doubling the Lizard and crossing Mounts Bay, sailing within sight of Bob's childhood home, *Tresca* duly beat around Land's End and sailed up the Bristol Channel. Crashing out into the Irish Sea they met conditions that had worsened and one by one breakfasts were lost overboard. Under threat of passenger mutiny *Tresca* motored back south to the calmer Cornish waters, and hauling into 'Achy Bay', dropped anchor off St Ives.

Staggering ashore and blithely unaware that they had been reported 'overdue' in Waterford and that the media, sniffing drama, had alerted the coastguard, the tousled sea-dogs headed straight for the comfort of the nearest pub, the Castle Inn. "I'm on my honeymoon..." Newton roared, "Where's the best hotel in town?" "The Tregenna Castle!" the locals roared back. Fuelled with 'drinks all round' the crowd escorted the happy couple on their way.

Remarkably the hotel was just over the hedge from the charming country home of Linden Travers...

The next morning the sun had broken out and the party, breakfasted and restocked with bottles and cigarettes, prepared to decamp to the boat. Brushing aside protests that it was illegal, Bob, cashless as ever and living on promises, wanted to pay the hotel bill by cheque. For a moment things got awkward; Bob got upset, and called for the manager. "I'm Robert Newton!" he shouted. "*I* don't know who you are..." pleaded the manager. In the end it was settled; hands were shaken, backs slapped and peace restored over more drinks. "A nice chap..." the manager muttered dizzily, "but crazy... just like in the films!" With obituaries sketched out and Connie's on the point of nervous breakdown, *Tresca* headed out for Waterford and the charity of the locals...

Smitten by the beauty and peace of the Irish landscape, Newton's mind turned once more to the dream of his own rural retreat. With his Mother now gone, a place in Cornwall was discounted as too far away across the misty moors to make a weekend hideaway. Always captivated by the unspoiled, old-world beauty of the Welsh Borders however, he had taken to motoring west out of town and exploring the rolling hills and valleys. When an opportunity came to buy land there, complete with a working farm and out-buildings, he did not hesitate.

West of the old cattle town of Hereford and in the lea of the great whales-back of the Black Mountains, Olchon Farm consisted of one hundred and forty acres of hills and soft dells. Lying above the ribbling stream that meandered down the Golden Valley, the farm was overlooked by a crumbling Norman keep. The air was clean and peopled only by the bleat of lambs and the cawing of the black crows; Bob had once again found his paradise. Sheep on the hills, fat kine in the green valley bottoms; this, at last, was his place, the farm he had always dreamed of. It was to be a home, a tranquil refuge from the grubby, thumb-marked chaos of London.

Soon the timeless valley was filled up with excited talk of the millionaire actor who had bought Olchon. He bought a tractor, the first in the valley, and Newton, soon everyone's mate, rubbed in amongst the locals, the old farmers and the hard-handed labourers. Incongruously loud in his bright yellow and red socks, with his cane and trilby hat, he drank in the old pubs and joyously rough-housed with the locals. Natalie was always alongside, as outrageous as he, and they caroused in the Court House and The Greyhound. Soon they were a familiar sight in Hay-on-Wye and at the Three Tuns, a little sinking-into-the-earth cider pub that hung onto the end of the bridge that led to Wales. The indomitable Lucy Powell was the landlady; "Clear or cloudy?" she would demand. She served cider, and nothing else.

Bob, ever the eccentric in his voguish city clothes, was now sprouting a grubby stubble for his next film.

Hot from his 1946 success with *Great Expectations*, David Lean was looking to his next film. The arts had now turned all post-war guilty and were filled up with a fashionable a-la-mode introspection and flagellating self-examination and Lean's announcement that he was going to shoot Dickens' *Oliver Twist* was greeted with hoots of derision. Lean was however obsessed with Dickens and understood the emotional power of his works, perceiving the classical moral semeiotic that transcended both time and fad. He had a budget of £1.5 million and in collaboration with Stanley Hayes, the production manager on *Major Barbara*, he had produced a condensed film script and a heavily trimmed dialogue.

Casting the central chameleon character of Fagin was however problematical. Alec Guinness, a stage actor noted mostly for his lightweight charm, desperately wanted to get into substantial film work and applied for the part; Lean thought he was mad. Robert Donat was another actor who was finding himself stereotyped as the 'quiet man'. He deeply regretted turning down the part of 'Frank Crutchley' in *This Happy Breed*; now, with Guinness selling himself successfully and landing the Fagin part, he vied with Newton for the other strong character role, that of Bill Sikes. "I did a test with Robert Donat" Guinness said later, "who wanted to play Sikes, so we were both seeking after something. I got mine by the skin of my teeth and Robert (Donat) didn't, he looked very good and he was a beautiful actor, but I didn't think he had the vitality to cope…". Lean had worked with Bob and understood his quality; Donat had neither the aggression or the vocal range and Newton's casting was a fait accompli.

The rest of the cast was impressive; Kay Walsh took the role of Nancy. Amy Venness, an old friend from *This Happy Breed* got a part, as did Diana Dors (Diana Fluck... yet to become a nationalised blonde sex-symbol). A young John Howard Davies got the peach role of 'Oliver'.

Top billed, Newton, as usual, did not make his entry into the film for about half an hour, but when he arrived, he did, it was with a bang. The scene was a crucial one, set in Fagin's loft, where a furious row was taking place. Cameraman Guy Green recounted the event, "Fagin throws a pewter mug of beer, the door is opened and Bob Newton appears and Bob had to say a line which he couldn't get right. So we kept having to play the beginning of the scene, pan across, hit the door, and Bob would fluff it and we'd do it all over again, it went on for hours, it was a simple line "What yer gin' to do, Fagin?" but he kept raising the inflection at the end and ruining it....". A lesser man than Lean would have let the thing go, and carry on, but he was a perfectionist. "David had trouble with Bobby Newton, he was inclined to ham it up, and David was always battling to keep him down, Bobby didn't think that was right and he kept hitting the bottle and David had his work cut out coping with that, I must say he handled it very well... once or twice he would say "Bobby, I think you'd better go home and have a rest", he never accused him of drinking...".

Inevitably the English summer turned to rain; outdoor shooting became impossible and as cast and crew sat idle the devil found evil work for idle hands to do. For Newton the 'evil' was of course, drinking. Lean, however, knew Newton's habit; "In the later stages of the film he used to get very fuzzy, I never knew whether he was drunk or not, he used to stand there in a kind of dream, I used to go up to him and turn the camera over and I'd tap him on his leg and say "Do you feel that?" "Yes, I'm beginning to feel that". And I'd tap a bit harder and get ready. I'd tap him on the other leg and he'd say "Yes, Yes", I'd say "Get ready, Bobby. Action!" And Bobby would go straight into the scene and he would be magnificent". Despite these 'play' lapses Bob was always word-perfect; always the pro', he played 'Sikes' in his own unique way and set the all-time standard. With a guttural Cockney accent, unshaven and hollow-eyed, his portrayal was grotesque and utterly brutal. 'Sikes' companion was his dog, the equally brutal 'Bullseye'. Bob was always a dog lover and was accompanied on set by his long-haired Dachshund, Pistol; now he spent long hours getting to know his canine co-star. He need not have worried, 'Bullseye' was another disciplined old film professional, going under the name of 'Rely on Jake the Rake'...

Shooting went well but Lean could see trouble looming; Bob was still drinking heavily and concerns were voiced as to safety during the shooting of the final rooftop scenes. The problem was overcome only when Bob agreed to wear a trapeze harness. The take went into the can and things seemed to be going swimmingly. Then a nasty little spat blew up over precedence and J. Arthur Rank himself was obliged to intervene, negotiating through the panels of Bob's petulantly bolted dressing-room door. The affair was settled and Newton's name appeared suitably large on the hoardings.

The work was previewed at Uxbridge Cinema on June 20th, then received a Royal première at the Odeon, Marble Arch. The critics loved it. Lean's direction was declared 'inspired' and the work 'a superb achievement'. Newton, the pivot of the work, was declared 'a natural for the brutish Sikes... and gets every ounce out of his opportunities.' Certainly the crucial murder scene where Sikes kills Nancy was chillingly interpreted and beautifully shot; some critics were, in retrospect, to call it Lean's finest directorial moment in his whole career. Flawlessly produced and with a mass of talented yet unaccredited bit players (among them the recently demobbed' Spike Milligan, Harry Secombe and Peter Sellers..) the film earned an unequivocal thumbs up, audiences flocked in and applause was unstinting.

Shipped over for a pre-release showing in America the film however faced competition from a new phenomenon; the great American public had discovered the flickering glories of television. As sets glowed into life in thousands of living rooms the cinemas emptied. The film moguls shuddered in horror and went into panic mode; now the industry was facing an influx of outstanding foreign imports.

The press, manipulated by Hollywood overlords fearful of any competition, now obediently howled in protest over Guinness' depiction of Fagin, 'the worst caricature of a Jew ever depicted in an

English-speaking film...'. The public, led by the bible-bashing radicals, obediently rose up in riotous protest. Inevitably general release was delayed. With the populace persuaded to wax paranoid over anti-Semitism, suggestions were made about 're-shooting' the film to make it 'fit for American consumption' in full knowledge that the cast had been scattered and sets torn down. Lean smiled; he knew that Dickens himself had faced the same irrational barrage and had bowed to it. Twelve 'offending' minutes were duly cut and the work was eventually, and reluctantly, cleared for release in July 1951. Ironically the film did poor business. So much for the maxim that *any* publicity is good publicity.

In the midst of the storm Lean was interviewed; asked to define the difference between an 'actor' and a 'star' he replied unhesitatingly; "I can't tell you as a director but I can tell you as an editor. When a good actor finishes a line I cut, but when a star delivers the line I leave it four extra frames. In those four frames there is the difference between actor and star; an unknown difference but it is defiantly there...". For him, Newton always gave those four extra frames.

Escaping the studios, Bob raced joyfully west and threw himself back into his new life as a farmer. The transition of ownership had not however gone smoothly. The legal trade, smelling film star wealth, got involved and sucked blood. The local papers ran the story. 'Claim By Film Star. For Possession of Farm at Llanveynoe. The only civil action for hearing at Hereford Assizes on Monday, Mr Justice Stable, M.C, was settled out of court. Mr Robert Guy Newton, Of Eaton Place, London, the film star, claimed possession of Olchon House Farm, Llanveynoe, Clodock, as owner, from Mr Alfred Leslie Griffiths, the vendor, who was still in possession. Mr G G Baker, OBE, appearing for Mr Newton, said the parties had been able to settle the case out of court. It had been agreed that possession of the farm should be given on 24th June...'. A fat wad of notes had settled the matter and Bob turned to business.

Realising that he could never turn farmer full time, Bob knew he would need a manager. The main farm house, a great gabled and dormered homestead that was the centre of operations, was turned over to a bailiff, a tenant farmer, and a pretty barn, Sheeds Barn, lying half a mile away across the fields was converted into his private home. Complete with a telephone and bell-pulls and a star-box down in the kitchen, the place was the quintessential country retreat. Oak beamed, punctured with massive fire-places and riddled with solid oak doors, the two bedrooms were approached by a quaint winding stone staircase. Gloriously happy, Bob leaned on his five-bar gate and looked out across the rich green sod down to the river. It was all his; he had his farm, had his chickens and pigs, his sheep and cattle. He was forty three.

Barry Jackson, busy with his Malvern Festival, found a moment to write to Laura Knight about their shared 'protégé'. Newton's foray into pastoral life had hit the papers. 'I thought the enclosed might be of some interest. It caught my eye in our local paper and being of an inquisitive nature I looked out the place on the map. It is about fifteen miles beyond the back of nowhere, and how Bobby found it is beyond my fervid imagination. The farm lies on the north slope of the Black Mountain...'.

The farm might have been beyond the back of nowhere but Bob was soon tracked down by the press. With mock pathos, he bemoaned his fate as an actor. He was doomed, he claimed, to go endlessly from film to film, and 'because of high taxation' never be able to retire to 'the comparatively unlucrative life of a sheep farmer...'. Taxation, like marital fidelity, was a lost world for Newton; but it was one that would soon come to his door.

Problems also lay closer to home. Annie was still seething; now she saw her ex-husband's name once more up in lights and splashed across the papers and raged with the anger of a woman scorned. She had, perhaps with justification, always claimed credit for his break into film and his subsequent success; now she fumed and plotted away the lonely nights. Her response was perhaps predictable. Sensing Annie's hurt and loneliness, Joy had invited her down to the tranquility of her Cornish home, plied her with hospitality and the shared sympathy of a woman who too had experienced rejection. In the blissful spring days Joy, Annie and Beakus made a happy trio. Perhaps too happy. Annie quickly seduced Beaukus. No saint in sexual matters, this act of treachery by an old friend cut Joy to the quick, "How dare you do it..." she raged, "we were such good friends." "Joy..." Annie replied, "I did it out of spite...".

As the lives of the two women foundered in anger, Sally, taken under her father's wing and into his life, found that hers was blossoming. Two happy years of drama school had led to the Embassy Theatre and the same back-stage jobs and silent walk-ons that her father had done at Birmingham. The late developing parent, Bob now displayed a keen interest, taking her to the studios when he was working. Sally's final year saw the traditional end of term exam stage production. Bob and Nat', of course wanted to be there, but so did Peta. The dilemma was terrible; ignoring each other in a small theatre was impossible and the awkward reunion was unavoidable. Sally faced the ordeal of her performance with the added stress of seeing both her parents sitting stiffly and uncomfortably together.

Newton was now at the top of his career ladder and the film world lay at his feet. Thirty percent of the UK population went to the 'flicks' at least once a week, spending £100 million at the box-office. For leading players like Newton, one-off fees for single picture deals of £10,000 was now the average going. Compared to the average weekly wage for adult males in the UK of just £8 6s, this was a fortune. All that London, all that the world could offer, was now his. He had his London house, his servants, his dream farm and by contemporary standards huge wealth, but too often he found life an empty, desolate place. Always there was something missing. Burnt out, lost and angry, drink was always the cure, 'to drown the buggery of life' he said. But the equal and opposite side of the drunken euphoria was a black depression. Vere-Barker found that the angry flak still came his way and bowed to it, but in Natalie Bob had found his match. A companion who could more than hold her own at the bar, and, as with Annie, one who was able to return his anger with interest, drunken rows were monumental, protracted and violent.

Always emotionally unstable, Natalie had her own demons. Her use of drugs had edged rapidly towards dependence; Bob became worried and suddenly found he couldn't cope. Annie, who had now stolen Beakus from Joy, was now happily settled in Cornwall, and she was, of course, the person that he looked to for help.

Counting her an 'old friend', and considering her stealing of his sister's husband evening up the scores of infidelity, he decided that an impromptu visit might clear up any old resentments and get things back on a good 'family' footing. Combining his reconciliation mission with a holiday, he once again chartered *Tresca* and cruised south to Cornwall. With time on his hands and the devil always at his shoulder, a slight navigational deviation east saw him slip quietly ashore in France for a little casual piracy...

Those gathered at Lambe Creek heard the developing story on the wireless. Apparently Bob had been arrested by the gendarmes for landing illegally from a small boat. Laden with booty, like the Cornish smugglers who had filled his childhood dreams, his escape had been a theatrical escapade of disguises and bribery. Googie Withers was there, on holiday with Annie, and recounted the story.

By this time, she recalled, Annie had picked up "a very independent and rather villainous-looking dog called 'Twisty'. He used to disappear at regular intervals for several days at a time to visit his girl-friends in Truro, and when he came back he was always starving, generally wounded, and more cantankerous than ever. He had just returned from one of these expeditions and was coming down the drive when Bob arrived. At first we thought he must have escaped from gaol, because he was wearing what looked like a French convict's outfit. It transpired later that he had swapped his Savile Row suit for a Breton fisherman's overalls. Needless to say, although it was only eleven o'clock in the morning, he was well and truly under the influence. Bob fell out of the taxi on top of Twisty, whom he greeted as effusively as a long-lost friend. Twisty reciprocated by biting him right through the hand. Bob was so anaesthetised that he didn't notice, and kept on patting blood all over Twisty's head. Then he suddenly looked up, saw his ex-wife, and clasped her to him in a passionate and bloody embrace. After she had changed her dress and we had patched up Bob as best we could, he didn't feel the iodine either, he insisted on coming to the beach with us. This was a mistake, because, apart from attempting to rape his ex-wife on the back seat of the car on the way, he had obviously had to answer the call of nature while we were swimming because when we returned to the car we found him sprawled half in and half out of it, the lower part of his torso completely exposed and being solemnly contemplated by a group of about twenty curious children, who were being hurriedly collected and taken away by their horrified parents, some of whom had recognised Bob. We zipped him up, took him back to his boat, and handed him over to the tender mercies of his crew, all of whom were in the same state of blissful euphoria as Bob...".

Unrepentant, Bob sailed for home. Picking up Natalie he drove north-west to the glories of Buxton, where Sally was working under Joan Littlewood. Having progressed from her first film job, a bit-part in *Adam and Evelyn*, she had moved on to her maiden stage engagement, an appearance in *Day of Glory*.

Back in London, Connie's agency was eagerly following up the tentative approaches Bob had made in Bermuda, and a UK meeting was arranged between Newton and Burt Lancaster. Hollywood was now basking in its golden years, and it seemed impossible to back a loser. The European war had equated to boom years for the industry and despite the inroads made by television, a staggering eighty million Americans were still hunkering down with their sodas and popcorn in their local cinemas each week. Lancaster, with seven films already under his belt, was one of the new-style Hollywood marvels; brimming with confidence, mortgaged up to the hilt and with a fleet of backers, he had formed his own film company and the planned collaboration with Newton was to be its first production.

Newton greeted Lancaster as an old friend; slapping him on the back, he swept him into his Rolls and out into the dubious glamour of West End night-life. Signing into one of the more exclusive clubs, Newton directed Lancaster to the bar with a casual "ask the barman for my usual..." The barman poured Lancaster a whisky and proceeded to pour half a bottle of brandy into a large tumbler... "There must be some mistake..." Lancaster protested. "This is Mr Newton's usual, sir..." the barman replied without a blink. That night Lancaster came to understand a little more about what working with Newton would involve. Both were booked into the Savoy: at four in the morning Bob stumbled into his suite. Having said goodnight to Lancaster, he had returned to the bar. Now, thoroughly drunk and dressed in his pyjamas, he insisted that seats had been booked on a flight to Paris and that they were going to sample the night-life there...

After some more sober negotiations, an April start to filming in Hollywood was agreed. For Newton this was a massive career break, one he had been waiting for, and the prospect of a dollar-rich trip persuaded him and Natalie to take in another holiday. In early March they flew out to Nassau in the Bahamas. Bathing in the blessed sunlight and the warm seas they seemed to have landed in paradise. A visit to the resort of 'Treasure Island' rang some bells in Bob's head and sealed to redundancy the plan to return home before the trip out to Hollywood. The pair now engaged on a stately and boozy journey to California via New York. This was an old stamping ground for Bob, and he took delight in showing Natalie his own footsteps. The train journey across the vast continent was undiluted luxury and stepping off in California, Newton allowed himself a smile. Eighteen years before he had been told that there was 'no place for Limey actors'; now he had been head-hunted!

In 1947 the *Film Daily* had sent out a questionnaire to film critics and radio commentators across the USA, asking if they would give a ready welcome to 'foreign' pictures. The result was a shock for the industry; over 53% responded with a resounding 'yes'. More importantly for Newton, what they wanted was British film. The British film industry had always been Hollywood's poor relation and successive British governments failed to see the value of the industry and give concrete support. Studios seemed forever bedevilled by a chronic lack of funds; scraping by and compromising seemed the only way to survive. The consequence was that grand-scale productions were rare and actors pay, by Hollywood standards at least, was relatively poor. The statistics spoke for themselves. In 1947 the UK could only boast 42 sound stages compared with Hollywood's 160; Britain was struggling to turn out one picture per stage per year, Hollywood studios produced more than double that. "You can't be famous unless you go to Hollywood" one struggling Brit' player whined "... a sprained ankle in Hollywood and all the world knows about it... in London we get nice notices if we do nice work, and there the subject ends". Bob understood; already the press were glossing up his image; '...in real life Newton is a nice fellow who likes to breed race horses...'.

Down in the San Fernando Valley at the glitzy Universal studios, Newton scanned through the long-awaited film-script and what he read came as a shock; once again he came face to face with *film noir*.

A dark American place with a fancy French name, *noir* portrayed a society where the sun had died and people got by with neon, where the only pleasures came from liquor and the knowledge that life was a cheap little game where everyone played dirty. Pure pulp fiction, a skewed reaction to the American dream that had been bloodied on the battlefields of Europe, the genre was the bitter child of the Californian nights and represented expressionism at its darkest. Rotten with paranoia and self-doubt, it was a monochrome world where nothing was black and white.

Bob saw the script through a strangers eyes and was appalled; this was *film noir* a la London; Lancaster's chosen screenplay was an adaptation of the book and stage play *Kiss the Blood off my Hands*.

Previously run on the Broadway stages under the title of 'The Killers', the script was far from the genre classic and was simply yet another sleazy crime thriller. Newton was experienced enough to see that it was a disastrous choice; audiences had turned away from mindless killing. Despite both British and American producers' penchant for the underside of human existence, violence was now thoroughly outdated. Imported 'lowlife' crime films had even begun to irritate British critics; 'Hardly has Hollywood decided to put the gangster film into cold-storage for a spell', lamented *Picturegoer*, 'than British producers are sweating blood and tears, and pouring out thousands of pounds, to finish films about spivs and molls and all the rest of the underworld...'. Lancaster's chosen script was simply riding on the tail of an outdated trick and ignored the reality that moralist realism was now in vogue in Britain, and that American audiences were following suit.

Planned to go out at the same time as the film version of *No Orchids for Miss Blandish*, the work nevertheless had some commercial promise. Lancaster's film character had been modernised from the book's immoral thief and con-artist type into that of a disturbed ex-POW; perhaps that alone leant the plot some kind of social relevance.

A quick glance showed Bob that his part was that of the dark counter balance and that he was to once again play the bad guy, this time 'Harry Carter' a clichéd, generic, city low-life. It all looked very much like a re-run of *The Green Cockatoo*. With a long theatrical tradition, the bad-guy character however held an honourable place in the British heart and if money talked, American dollars shouted.

The plot was set in London and the work cried out for extensive UK location shooting; but it had already been decided that the $1.1 million budget would not stretch that far. Most of the work was to be shot in front of stage sets. The only concession to realism was that some location shoots were planned to be made around Los Angeles and Griffith Park Zoo.

The shoot commenced on Stage 12, in early April. There was a bustle of American-style efficiency but the script was still undergoing constant re-writes and was far from complete. Under the direction of Norman Foster, a man described as 'a bouncy little guy who likes to think that Hollywood is not the centre of the universe', the work looked as if it might somehow manage to raise itself above the turgidly formulaic. Bob went into auto-pilot mode and slipped seamlessly into the familiar old caricature of the 'Cockney Villain', an old stereotype that the Americans loved. As the yarn progressed Newton's character evolved from confidante to blackmailer; all the while he played the cad to Lancaster's 'girlfriend', Joan Fontaine, the quintessential 'English rose'.

Bob's old Rep' pal Colin Keith Johnston, dipping his toe into Americana, was cast to appear as the Judge. It was to be a fortunate decision.

Off-set and indulging blissfully in an American VIP lifestyle, Newton was endlessly interviewed. Journalists found him willing to wax loquacious and sentimental for his theatre days. Admitting that he now preferred film work, even if it was a 'lazy' trade, he talked of ambitious plans to bring the stage to California... "four Repertory Theatres sponsored by the film companies in Hollywood, Beverley Hills, Santa Monica and Los Angeles! The plays would go around in a circle', he said, 'one full week in each spot. You have the writers; they could try out all these new plays they are forever writing, or talking about writing, besides the standard classics. As for the young players, the eager young girls and boys whom the studios put under contract and then forget about, what happens to them now? They wait around and watch, and the waiting and the watching slowly breaks their hearts. I have a daughter, Sally, by my first wife. She is eighteen, has finished her schooling, and is just starting in repertory at home. Why shouldn't America give its youngsters the same opportunity...?" The suggestion fell on deaf ears; the Yanks might have needed this Limey's acting skills but they didn't want his sermonising.

The rains that plagued the outdoor shoots in *Oliver Twist* seemed to follow Newton across the Atlantic and days were wasted waiting for the legendary Californian sun to emerge. Even the finalised shooting script was endlessly delayed; eventually it was handed around but even then the film crew had to muddle their way through a screenplay that was effectively a fleshless skeleton. Worse followed; a week into the shoot the totally mis-cast and reluctant Joan Fontaine, unable to hide her morning sickness any longer, had nervously announced that she thought she was pregnant; now she collapsed with a cold.

More used to the plodding and comfortable illogicality of the Porridge Factory, Newton found the maniacally driven yet stop-and-start pace of Hollywood studio life hard to handle. In London Lancaster had been a charming drinking buddy and every bit as much the womaniser as Newton, but on-set he was utterly different. Complex, obsessive and secretive, he held the purse and playing the Hollywood big-shot to the hilt he made the studio into a living hell where cast and crew were reduced to emotional wrecks.

Script delays meant that Joan Fontaine was overdue for her next film and her sequences were hurriedly shot back-to-back and the filming schedule was thrown into disarray. Unable to play second fiddle, Bob took to the bottle and further fouled up production. "He was hopelessly drunk..." recalled screenwriter Leonardo Bercovecci, "sometimes you had to wait it out. Sometimes he came very late. And sometimes he had to leave early...". A crisis loomed, one even Natalie couldn't handle and Colin Keith-Johnston was obliged to intervene; somehow he managed to persuade Bob not to walk away from the project...

By late May, Bob's 'Harry Carter' had copped it with a nail scissors in the belly and had flapped to a watery death in the company of a goldfish. His part had been shot inside four weeks, but it seemed a lifetime and his parting from Lancaster was less than cordial. Talk of Bob's drinking had quickly spread throughout the Hollywood machine and the grandiose promises of work had dried up. Lancaster's film now struggled through post production and it was the lurid title that was causing the most problems. It had been squarely rejected by the Motion Picture Association of America from the outset. Lancaster now fought the judgement in order to tie the film in with the book. Surprisingly he won, then, inexplicably, opted for less graphic titles, *Blood on my Hands* and *Blood on the Moon* before settling on *The Unafraid*.

By now Bob had grown thoroughly sick of Hollywood. The new 'Reds-under-the-bed' obsession was everywhere; somehow the wartime spirit of 'working for the common good' was being interpreted as subversion and the film industry seemed to be drowning in paranoia. Only too gladly he and Natalie quit the fools paradise of tinsel town and set off for New Orleans; there they booked onto the ex-American WW2 military steamer '*SS Alawai*'; by June they had crossed the Atlantic and landed in Italy and the older, more understandable, civilisation of Genoa.

Kiss the Blood off my Hands was previewed in-house on August 11th, and on the 12th in Studio City. There, complaints from the chosen audience produced a return to the original title. The film, however, still came over as diabolically studio-bound and the London street scenes totally unconvincing. Certainly Lancaster's choice of material was judged as ill- advised. The film was released and there weathered faint praise and the expected criticisms. Even the film-hungry audiences failed to turn up to see what was basically a depressing drama. The work faced a dim future and slipped unnoticed and unmourned into history. *Variety* magazine however found the good grace to commend Bob's work; "As a heavy, Newton is properly oily and detestable....".

The Green Cockatoo and *Odd Man Out* had been screened the year previously and *This Happy Breed* and *Hatters Castle* were now successfully doing the rounds in America. Now, in Lancaster's film, it was Newton's name that attracted audiences and it was his performance that was the show-stealing one. With the title toned down for decorous British tastes to *Blood On My Hands* the work was exported to England.

Lancaster later disowned the film as 'pure pap'.

If the work was a retrograde step in Newton's career, and one that a more cautious man, mindful of his public image, would have avoided, Bob didn't care. A cautious man would have also made friends in the right places. Certainly Newton had squandered the priceless patronage of Noel Coward and Ivor Novello. Now, with exaggerated tales of his drinking following him back home, studios faced a dilemma. The accountants were increasingly gaining control and underwriters baulked at insuring works that included him. Working with Newton was working with fire; yet the bureaucrats understood that it was a fire that attracted audiences.

Perhaps the war had shot a hole through the lies, but now Newton didn't care. He was sick of film and bored with the stage-work. Drink always gave the familiar oblivion, the temporary escape, but it was wearing him away, eating into him and taking him over. Time spent at Olchon, foreign holidays and fishing trips to Scotland and Ireland seemed to be a short-term cure, saw him returned dried out and full of zest. But then the boredom set in again and with it the booze.

A hint of promise came in a story run by the *Los Angeles Times*: 'One of the elaborate stories planned for the Festival of Britain next year is a picture about the British inventor of the movie camera, William Fries-Greene, in which various British stars and perhaps a few from this country will appear, if the arrangements can be made... on arrival here Laurence Olivier indicated that he would probably play a small part. The understanding is that as well as Sir Ralph Richardson, Robert Newton and others will be seen as important life characters...'

Tired or not, Newton was an actor and act he must. The offer of a new role, one that looked refreshingly different from the succession of maniacs and mono-dimensional baddies, took his interest. Developed from a short-running stage play entitled 'A Man about a Dog', (itself a loose piracy from Edgar Allan Poe's 'The Black Cat') *Obsession* was a tight psychological suspense drama. He was cast to take the leading role and to work opposite Sally Gray, his much younger and very glamorous 'wife'. Naunton Wayne, the archetypal British bluff cove, was contracted as the police sleuth.

Newton faced a challenge that demanded a total character reinvention, one in which, for the first time, he was to play the older man. He was to play 'Clive Riordan', an elegant Harley Street doctor who plans the perfect, acid-bath murder of his wife's lover. Significantly the lover was an American. Britain was coming to terms with its post-war relationship with the United States and was now facing the bitter reality of Marshall Plan war-debit repayments and the film seemed to address the love-hate relationship Britain had with its trans-Atlantic neighbour.

Bob's entry into the Pinewood studios coincided with a furore of ill feeling; mercifully this time he was not the centre of it. The usual early publicity material had been released to the industry but somehow with incorrect title and a muddled story-line. On top of this the chosen director, Edward Dmytryk, once one of the hottest directors in Hollywood, had been studio blacklisted there having survived a six month imprisonment after the McCarthyite pursuit of the 'Hollywood Ten'. Believing in the American dream of personal freedom, Dmytryk had submitted to a subpoena and appeared before the witch-hunting 'House of un-American Activities' committee the previous year, where he had found the courage to admit his earlier Communist sympathies. The rumour mill had circulated the story that he had only reluctantly agreed to direct *Obsession*, and the deal he had brokered had given him a free hand in his own project later.

A thorough professional however, Dmytryk had reviewed the shaky film-script and performed radical surgery on it, cutting out the problematical murder and instead skilfully accentuating the events leading up to a climax. Work got successfully under way and locations were filmed in Mayfair and bombed-out Church Row in Hampstead.

Shot in very much the Hitchcock vein, the work went well. Then the project hit the rocks. Incredibly a succession of real-life acid-bath murders had just been carried out nearby and as the perpetrator, John George Haig, awaited trial with the grizzly details classified sub judice, Pinewood's publicity department sent out its pre-release packs. There, for all the world to see, the vengeful Dr Clive Riordan, complete with his little bags of acid, was ready to do the business. Almost unable to hide its delight the *Daily Mirror* threw fat into the fire and splashed the pictures and story across its pages, and with barely concealed joy received a writ for contempt of court. Less welcome were the threats of legal action issued throughout Pinewood and the total ban on any media exposure for the film.

Shooting went on under a cloud yet was completed well within the £150,000 budget and in just thirty-three and a half days. It was obvious however, that public release was impossible. Lengthy negotiations with the censor resulted in compromise: the film could be shown when the trial was over and a provisional release date was set for April 21st. Then the case collapsed and the release date set back until the retrial was over. With the court case still fresh in the public mind giving Obsession a quasi-biopic air and boost that no amount of studio hype could have generated, audiences flocked into cinemas on August 3rd to view the film now luridly sub-titled '*The Acid Bath Thriller.*'

Very much a classic 'gaslight' genre picture, the set lighting was beautifully done and gave a three-dimensional lustre that took it beyond the monochrome. Set amidst the familiar battered ruins of a war-scarred city, the work shouted Art and whispered *noir* and was an instant success. Audiences watched Newton play his part as if in direct response to criticisms of overacting. Chilling, suavely sophisticated and utterly controlled he was the epitome of the calculating killer. Throughout the shoot Bob had played it sober, and it showed. Tense, almost explosive, his chilling calm hid a monster. The work was basically a 30s film, yet it was also a transitional work, teetering on the future and full of contrasting styles. Packed with British phlegm and Americanisms it had a icy, fairy-tale, quality.

Dmytryk unstintingly praised Newton's performance, "He could be the finest great acting talent. He often plays broad, lusty roles, yet I found him a sensitive man. Given the utmost understanding from a director, Newton can stand in a class by himself...". Critics and reviewers unstintingly endorsed the film; *Picturegoer* said 'I have not seen Robert Newton to better advantage for a long time...' another review described Newton's character as 'ruthlessly polished'. Re-titled *The Hidden Room* for American release the film went out in 1950; there the *New York Times* described Newton's character as 'not a simple mental case, but a polished, brilliant man, who, driven to crime, approaches it ruthlessly but scientifically..."

Obsession came to the Savoy cinema in Penzance on September 1st.

This time there was no Marjorie in the audience to cheer and clap for 'her boy'.

8. Treasure Island; Buccaneers And Bitches

The decade that had seen the death of millions came to an end and the western world seemed to be on the brink of a new era. Just as the Great War had rendered Victorian morality obsolete, the 'fifties saw another period of social revolution. Economically Britain was beginning to get back on its feet; shattered towns and lives were being rebuilt from the top down with the eternal capitalist ploy of 'trickle-down prosperity'. As the old Empire fragmented, British hands and minds instinctively reached westward across the Atlantic and the pound was devalued to bring it into line with an American economy boosted by Truman's 'Fair Deal' and a higher minimum wage. Britain's continuing obsession with America brought its own problems however and the flip side of the coin was the 'Dollar Drain'.

The vexed issue of Britain's massive war debt to America dominated domestic political debate and Whitehall looked longingly at English pounds as they migrated across the Atlantic. For once both Parliament and the press were singing in tune and almost daily criticised the twenty seven million pounds spent annually on importing American films.

Robert Boothby stood up in the House and, having learned a trick or two from his time with Bob's Shilling Theatre, displayed his understanding of the theatrical power of a good pithy quote, declaiming that it was a question of 'Bogart or bacon'. Inevitably Atlee's government looked to taxation and hurried through legislation that slapped a 75% levy on imported film and effectively impounded the profits from work produced in the UK by outside investors. Unsurprisingly the Americans bayed in protest, but the British government insisted that the legislation was 'not intended to grant the British film industry a protectionist advantage'. Unconvinced America retaliated with tit-for-tat reprisals and British cinema-goers faced a famine of Americana.

The *Times*, following the old Tory line, looked to turn the loss into a benefit and picked up the story in October, '...there is, in fact, only one Hollywood product for which no amount of ingenuity can ever provide a substitute, only one loss which we must steel ourselves to write off as irrecoverable, and that is the Hollywood version of life in Britain...'. Such acid comments surfaced regularly in the British press. Back in March 1945 the *News Chronicle* had pronounced that Hollywood was churning out 'film after film about Great Britain, mostly from books by British authors...'; perhaps imitation *was* the most sincere form of flattery.

The short term result of the embargo was a boom in UK produced films and an industry where Bob was able to pick and choose his own roles.

Among the many foreign studios who found themselves ambushed was the Disney organisation. Having lost a protracted and bitter union dispute with his cartoonists, production of the lucrative Mickey Mouse animations had become almost economically non-viable. With creditors at his heels and the whole studio set-up on the brink of collapse, Disney's thoughts turned to its hard earned dollars (over a million) now effectively banged-up in England. The result was the film *Treasure Island* and the retrospective creation of another tinsel town myth.

Ironically the film, like the book, started as an aside; neither was ever envisaged to endure, the book had been written to entertain a child on a rain sodden holiday, the film made to spend up frozen pounds. "I have been fascinated by *Treasure Island* ever since my boyhood...." Disney would crow to the press. The unvarnished truth came from Byron Haskin, the man he chose to direct his film.

Cashing in the proceeds from *Snow White*, Disney had built his Burbank studios, sat back and waited for 'something' to happen. The 'something' was his fascination for weird animals and a discount truckload of scientific film footage shot in the Arctic. With a flash of genius he saw the potential; "I'll tell you what, we ought to get a real literate writer, not one of these damn Hollywood screenplay guys, but a novelist or something, and let him look the material over and write a documentary about seals, something with dignity...". The 'literate writer' picked out of the hat was Professor Emeritus Lawrence W. Watkins, who just happened to be in Hollywood having a go at knocking out screenplays.

Watkins was set to work; the result was *Seal Island* and a surprise Academy Award. Redundant, but still hanging onto a cosy payroll, Watkins took to hiding out in Burbank's story department vaults. There he stumbled across a dusty script for *Treasure Island* and, simply for something to do, wrote up a new sixty-page 'treatment'.

'Walt had always been in love with *Tom Sawyer*,' Haskin recalled, '...there was an agreement among major producers for story material in the public domain. If a company was first in line with a claim, they were given priority. Each year they must maintain a certain amount of expense for story development, securing the rights. Walt had always wanted *Tom Sawyer* in the worst way. David Selznick had prior rights as producer for MGM. MGM also had rights to *Treasure Island*, as well as a lot of other things. Walt put in a kind of shotgun claim for all material not claimed or delinquent. MGM carefully maintained rights for *Tom Sawyer*, but one year they slipped and didn't develop *Treasure Island*. Suddenly Disney becomes possessor. "What the hell do I do with this?" he asked "I want *Tom Sawyer* not *Treasure Island*!" They threw it in the vault...'.

Disney now glanced at Watkins *Treasure Island* efforts. He had always seen the work as a kind of antique gangster movie and his interest was kindled. He thought of making it up into an animated work, but it was his brother, Roy, who came up with the idea of shooting it as live action. "Do it in England with those frozen pounds...we *should* do it there, with all those fine actors and the British scenery...". Walt resisted stubbornly but he had little choice; the banks effectively owned his studio and called the shots. They could see the financial sense in the project and forced the decision. Things moved quickly and it was agreed that the film should be shot in full colour; it was to be Disney's first fully live production and represented a make or break moment.

Having liked his last work, predictably a gangster film, Disney picked the hard-nosed, straight-talking Byron 'Bunny' Haskin as his director. Crucially, Haskin knew how to do movies on the cheap; Disney gave him a brief outline and dispatched him trans-Atlantic. To keep him company, and drive him to the brink of despair, he also sent along his pet factotum, Perce Pearce, as token 'producer'. With $1.8 million in his back pocket and thirty-two speaking parts to cast, Haskin turned to the theatre, sitting in on eighteen stage plays in eighteen nights.

Disney's publicity machine now kicked into life; the 'star' names of Donat, Guinness and Mason were media-linked to the prestigious Long John Silver lead role and dragged out as part of the usual pre-publicity hype. But it seemed that Newton's name was on the top of Disney's list. "We have many fine character actors in America..." Walt told the British press, "of course it would have been possible for me to cast *Treasure Island* in Hollywood with British actors... when I saw Robert Newton in *This Happy Breed* and *Odd Man Out* I was determined to try to secure him. His personal enthusiasm for the assignment and the tests we have already made of him in character have convinced us that he will be ideal for the part...".

That was the yarn; the reality was that, once again, it was Donat's name that had come top of the wish-list. Haskin's meeting with Newton, his second-choice 'star', was less than propitious. 'He was hung over when I first met him, I said "Well, there will be about eight weeks before we shoot. Why don't you go fishing? When you come back you'll have the job of casting the most delightful part of the show, Ben Gunn...".'.

A craftsman rather than an egotistical auteur, Haskin saw from the outset that he would have to let Newton carry the film. "I knew his reputation when I went over there" he said, "he was a British actor steeped in the full tradition of Rep', he came up the tough way in the provinces, right off I figured the best way to generate some personal enthusiasm in this guy was to suck him in as my helper with production problems, I kept on drawing on him for advice about production problems, and got him hunting for a real good character actor to play Ben Gunn...".

Treasure Island was an eternally popular work and had been filmed many times before; the 1912 Edison production starred Charles Ogle as Silver, Fox had a go in 1918 featuring their 'Sunshine Kiddies' and in 1920 Ogle had a second stab with the same role. The first sound version was produced by MGM in 1934, brilliantly played by Wallace Beery and Jackie Cooper. Despite Disney's bluffing, Watkins 'treatment' of the Treasure Island story had only shuffled the old cards; the deck was very much the same, and many of the lines included in the 'new' script were pirated straight from Wallace Beery's mouth and the original MGM dialogue...

Although aware that the adult movie market was effectively saturated, Disney only slowly came to terms with the rapidly changing patterns in society. He now realised that the children's market was an untapped goldmine and that *Treasure Island* could work with both adults and children. The casting of the crucial second-lead role, Jim Hawkins, the kid that would draw in the kids, was simple; Disney turned immediately to the American-as-Mom's-apple-pie star, Bobby Driscoll. Tied into a Disney contract, he was still hot from the film *The Window* (Surreally, a work which, like *Treasure Island*, sees him cornered by a crazed killer who then dies at the boy's hand...) which resulted in him receiving a special, child size, Oscar.

For Walt Disney the new production was a desperate shot in the dark; for Bob it was just another film, something of an unknown, though perhaps a foot into the door of the American market. Neither man had any inkling of the implications that the film, nor the repercussions it would bring about. For Disney it would spell financial survival, a way forward and the creation of an All-American legend; for Bob it would mean fame, plaudits and the creation of a character that would haunt him until his death.

Disney's pre-production circus put out its stall immediately. Part of an industry that was becoming increasingly oiled by loud-mouthed publicity and media attention, Newton was contractually obliged to swallow the dose of 'glamour promotion' he hated. Obediently attending the frantic press receptions, he said the pre-packaged words and set off to Ireland with his fishing gear. A fortnight later he was back, sunburned and with his enthusiasm restored. Casting continued and with an inspired, though not disinterested, brilliance, he suggested that the exteriors and the background scenes of 'the island' could easily be shot against the green fringed and unspoiled banks of the Fal estuary, just down stream from Lambe Creek...

As the complex organisational logistics of Technicolor filming process dragged into something like sense, the other 'star' of the film, the pirate ship *Hispaniola*, was created out of an old schooner at the Appledore shipyard in Devon. She was sailed down the north Cornish coast and around Land's End and the Lizard by the shipwrights who had converted her. On her arrival the Disney executives started casting about for piece-work 'pirates', but setting sight on the Appledore crew they looked no further. Hardened seamen with salt in their blood, sunburned, ragged and raw-boned, they were the epitome of all things piratical.

The cast of familiar faces was assembled (including Dennis O'Dea from *Odd Man Out*) and the three separate film units were organised; one for exteriors, one at Denham studios and one on-board the *Hispaniola*. In June shooting began with a blaze of efficiency; then ran headlong into disaster.

Just bounced into the country to a barrage of flash-bulbs, Bobby Driscoll crashed into the brick wall of the law. Grassed on by a disgruntled Denham ex-employee, and facing the same legal snare that tripped John Davies in the making of *Oliver Twist*, he was dragged into court and had a deportation order thrown at him, first for being an American citizen without a work permit and second for being under age, which ironically would prohibit him from getting a work permit anyway. The studio went into panic mode, fired off a broadside of dollars and the British Education Bureau was persuaded to look the other way for a short period. Driscoll was catapulted down to Cornwall and panic shooting began. Bad weather however caused delays and Driscoll was forced to stay longer than was promised. Hauled back into court, his lawyers argued furiously that Driscoll was an American citizen and not subject to British labour laws. The judge snorted derision and gave a six-week stay of execution, *not* so that Driscoll could work, but to prepare his appeal. Shooting resumed with frantic haste on July 4th; Driscoll was again thrown on stage and in front of the cameras and Haskin desperately tried to finish his scenes, shuttling him desperately between the first and third units. Six weeks later he was back in court; the lawyers said their bit, a fine was slapped on both the studios and Driscoll's parents and he was summarily deported.

The bulk of the close-up work was by now, however, safely in the can; Haskin sighed with relief and looked for a long distance double. Way down in Cornwall the local rags busily covered the drama... "Aged 11, Ian Martin, a visitor from 44 Bhylls-lane, Merry-hill, Wolverhampton, has just returned home from Falmouth after his most thrilling holiday. No doubt a visit to the Cornish coast suggested smugglers and pirates to his youthful mind. He was staying with his parents at the Royal Duchy Hotel where some of the film executives are also staying. Mr Thomson was impressed by his resemblance to Bobby Driscoll and a suitable boy needed as a 'stand in' so that Ian found himself playing a part on the *Hispaniola*, emulating the idol of almost every boy – Jim Hawkins."

Location shooting in Cornwall meant for Bob, as a matter-of-course, crashing in with Annie and Beakus at Lambe Creek. They were, after all, now one big happy family. Natalie, reluctantly in tow, was dragged in through the front door and breezily introduced. The meeting between the two women was less than easy.

A private motor launch had been hired to take all hands daily down to the *Hispaniola* and the sun-drenched set, then on to the Falmouth pubs every evening and Bob and Natalie found that 'work' had turned into a second honeymoon. Things were on the up all around. Newton's agents were getting offers of film work from all sides and negotiations were in hand for a role in a biopic of the famous French actress entitled '*Rachel*', to be shot in Paris. Now, and rather miraculously considering the drink and drug abuse they shared as a couple, Natalie was discovered to be pregnant. Bob was ecstatic. Annie, barren and bitter, found that her home had become the centre of nightly entertainment for the cast and crew, and could only bite her tongue and suffer in silence.

On location the tricky job of daily piloting the *Hispaniola* out to the various locations was entrusted to the retired coxswain of the Falmouth lifeboat, Jack Snell. "She was a lovely vessel..." he said "they did a bit of filming up the Helford River, but mostly they used the entrance to the River Fal, at Turnaware Bar opposite Feock, and further up river near the King Harry Ferry. I remember one day they discovered the battleships *Ajax* and *Achilles* anchored there. And they had to be moved further down river so as not to appear in the shot...."

The spellbinding techno-chaos of filming created a minor economic boom for Cornish traders; taxi companies, despite struggling with rationed fuel, were block-booked. Bob, of course, had his own reserved taxi, picking him and Natalie up every evening from the Greenbank Hotel. His return journey was not always so orderly. After rowdy evenings in the Chain Locker Inn, fares would too often be forgotten or simply spent. But payment always came eventually.

Down in the harbours crowds flocked to witness the arrival of 'their' home-grown film-star each day and boatloads of sightseers bobbed in the wake of the *Hispaniola*. If the onlookers were thrilled by the piratical cannon fire, simulated enthusiastically with pyrotechnic 'depth-charges', the local fishermen were not quite so impressed; the fishes were scared off and the quiet denizens of Flushing were rudely shaken out of their Sabbath beds. Bibles were shaken and only a generous scattering of crisp, new, five-pound notes warded off police intervention...

The dense wooded banks of the River Fal did indeed make a grand backdrop and looked every inch the tropical island... even if one shot featured a golden corn field. Waving palm trees were all that were needed and these were added afterwards, painted onto glass with the old trick of matte painting. One of the closing shots of the film, where Silver escapes across the lagoon in a punt, was shot against the yellow sands of Carbis Bay, near St Ives. Haskin however was a demanding director, loud, abrasive and suffering no fools. "We often had to shoot the same scene over and over again until it was absolutely perfect," Jack Snell remembered, "they wanted one shot of the *Hispaniola* turning at sea, the weather was all wrong and it took over two weeks to get that particular shot...!"

The Cornish climate may have been unpredictable but Haskin also found that directing his star actor presented problems; Newton had now developed a psychological trauma which saw him 'freeze' in front of the camera. "Bob generated lots of enthusiasm and interest in the picture" Haskin remembered, "and he became a good member of the team. Throughout the shooting he came to work sober and full of interest, but he was unfortunate, the booze had really taken an advanced hold on him. He was unable to portray his concepts fully when the camera was rolling. Something going on in his subconscious, and when the camera turned he stiffened up and became a bit mechanical, losing the charm of the role, the fantasy of Long John Silver. Long John Silver was a complex role, all the early scenes with the little boy were like Father and Son. They were tender, sensitive scenes. In rehearsals, I would just drool. I lived in the expectation of getting some outstanding scenes; but the minute the camera would start, he would stiffen, and the charm vanished; he gave a performance, but never one with that original genius shown in the rehearsals....".

Himself a secret heavy drinker, Haskin more than understood Newton's problems and stubbornly worked around them. "I tried to trick him during the scenes around the inn with little Jim, where he gives the boy the little pistol. They're charming, pure, enchanting Stevenson. I would start up the camera unbeknownst to him and walk in and say "All right, let's rehearse this thing....", I would drift aside to get out of the camera range. I'd say "Let's see how it looks...". He knew subconsciously, and he'd tighten up. He couldn't break it... I had to become one with Bob Newton as Long John Silver. I could actually out-ham the ham, which helped a lot because he'd look at me and say, "Holy Christ, I'd better cool it off a bit...!"" Cooling-off came on Wednesdays, market day in the nearby city of Truro and a day off for all hands. Work was abandoned and Newton would set off into the town's pubs with Beakus' brother, the artist Roland. Mounted on his horse-drawn trap, Bob would declaim impromptu Shakespeare to the cheering crowds.

Autumn drew in; August saw the first winter gale and the summer tourists were blown away. Location filming wrapped and the cast turned north to Denham Studios. Here Uncle Walt had taken to lurking in the wings; an air of paranoia crept onto the set and Newton found himself spied on. Bosses, worried by his reputation trawled up by the press, started wagging fingers and hinting darkly at 'penalties'. Bob however was not to be beaten. Finding a friendly local hotel in Denham village, he arranged for a room to be available for the usual evening card school. Conspiring with the landlady, a ginger ale bottle would be quietly filled with whisky... "Ginger ale please Betty!" Bob would call. Days rolled into weeks and the deception was carried out flawlessly. Then, late one night and after a considerable amount of 'ginger ale', Bob remembered that he was due back down in Cornwall the next morning for a late location shoot. The table was overturned and he staggered downstairs; he was going to drive down there and then and nothing was going to stop him! Shoehorned into his car, his hands were put on the wheel, the engine was started and he was pointed in a sou'westerly direction. Early the next morning he phoned the pub and reported his safe landing...

After nine hard months, filming wrapped and the cosy family unit of cast and crew disbanded. Eight and a half thousand feet of film footage was safely in the can. Captain Flint, the parrot, was retired to a London pub, The Prospect of Whitby. The good ship *Hispaniola* went on to other film roles before being grounded in a muddy creek and destroyed by fire. Driscoll also went on to other films before the saleable magic of childhood left him. A has-been at 20, he fell into drug addiction and was arrested more than once on vagrancy charges. Left high and dry, he too burned-out. Foundered in a mire of addictions he was dead at the age of 31. His rotting corpse was found in a New York slum and was dumped in a paupers grave.

Returning to America, Haskin viewed the first cut of the finished work. Bob's performance and that of the supporting cast was magnificent but the cutting process had effected nothing less than a massacre. Haskin was furious and laid the blame squarely at the door of the inept Perce Pearce and the haste in which the film had to be shot, "My problem was Bobby Driscoll being deported, I actually shot the picture twice; on seeing the film later I thought it could have been improved by a better interplay between the principals, but in the double shooting I was never able to bring the actual relationships alive. Bobby Driscoll wasn't there when I was shooting the major version of the picture, and the little English boy was just an ordinary child actor...." Literally un-glueing the cut up film, Haskin painstakingly reassembled it chronologically before putting it back together according to the script. The final product however had a completely different effect from the one he had intended; yards of film had been binned, the most vital and expressive sequences, but nothing could be done and the film went public with what Haskin felt to be a staccato feel.

Test screenings were carried out in January 1950 and general release was arranged for July when it would neatly coincide with the school summer holidays. The two and a half hour film was premièred at the Odeon, Leicester Square. General release came with a shower of publicity that included a lorry rigged up as a pirate ship parading the streets of London and the publication of a book of the film featuring colour plates and an almost verbatim script. Like DuMaurier's *Jamaica Inn*, the work pandered to the quaintly unique British obsession with piracy and smuggling and the thing was, to Disney's surprise, a huge hit. More importantly it was a financial success; Disney raked in two and a half million dollars in the first year.

In all it was a wakeup call for Disney and one that was to change the studio forever. Such was the success of the live-action film that fans wrote to Disney in protest, fearing that he would abandon its much loved animation completely. For Roy Disney the importance of the film was obvious. "If *Treasure Island* had been a critical and commercial failure, then the studio would not have had a rich legacy of live-action movie gems. In short Walt would probably have retreated back into animation...". "1950" he said, "was our Cinderella year".

Elevated to legend and obscured by the shower of flim-flam, the 'truth' about the film, and the almost accidental making of the 'All-American' Disney dream, lay hidden. Muddled, warped and distorted by time, only the celluloid image now remains.

Newton received unstinting acclaim for his performance. Certainly the film revolved around him and would have been nothing without his input. Critic Paul Holt said of Newton, "His Long John Silver is the finest I ever saw (and I saw Arthur Bourchier)... he is as succulent as peach-fed ham, as sweet as a spoonful of syrup held high over the porridge plate, as darkly oily as a car sump, as tricky as an ageing jockey, when he winks his right eye a deep world of cunning is revealed, and when his tongue comes out to lick his blubbery lips all appetite and all evil is on the pink tip of it. Yet it is easy to love him, for he is a warm man...". *Variety* raved, "Robert Newton racks up a virtual tour de force as Long John Silver. His grimaces, piercing eyes and general villainy are the personification of the character imagined by every juvenile reader of the book". In America Bosley Crowther summed up Bob's mastery of the work, accusing him of a 'grand larceny', so completely had he stolen the film from the other players.

Bob understood that his 'Long John Silver', 'a villainous fellow, amiable and hearty...' was his greatest characterisation yet, a figure that he was 'born to play'. He had seen beyond the simplistic appraisal of a 'particularly loathsome one-legged pirate'. Stevenson himself had written 'I am not a little proud of John Silver and to this day rather admire that smooth and formidable adventurer...'. Bob had put out a performance that was rightly recognised as a classic and certainly the American trade press that made no bones about Newton being the first serious contender for the 1950's Oscar.

The film had made a fortune for Disney, even if that fortune was still a UK landlocked one, and Walt saw the light. Immediately he made Newton an offer to take a leading role in his forthcoming, live action version of *Robin Hood*.

If Newton's performance in *Treasure Island* was a triumphant one it was also a fatal step; he had walked, open eyed, into the trap that is every actors' nightmare: type-casting. It is not without irony that the film that had made Bob's future mould had been initiated by a man who had already met the character that had come to define him, Mickey Mouse. Disney knew that he was 'trapped with the mouse, stuck with the character..."; the bloody mouse was to dominate his life, become synonymous and inseparable with him just as Newton would now be inescapably linked with the leering pirate he had just created.

Back in London Bob was keen to catch up with the news from Sally. The year had brought her six stage roles and her career was beginning to flourish; now she was starting to pick up film work. Bob's own cosy home-life however had come to an abrupt halt. Heavily pregnant, Natalie had become cranky and secretive; she was no longer the fun girl he had married and partying was off the agenda. And now he found himself manipulated into an acrimonious court action.

A proposed project that had been quietly on the back-burner for some months, a biopic entitled *Rachel*, had gone badly wrong. Weeks had passed since the initial offer and Vere-Barker had smelled both blood and publicity. The concept tumbled out of control and was plainly a non-starter. Now, the *Daily Telegraph*, aware of the public's insatiable interest in the 'stars' lives, gleefully picked up on the story and ran it in its 13th October edition. 'FILM ACTOR SUES ACTRESS'.' ALLEGED BREACH OF CONTRACT'. 'Robert Newton, the film actor, of Smith Street, Chelsea, brought an action for alleged breach of contract in the High Court yesterday against Mrs. Edana Woolf, of Prince Albert Road, Regents Park, an actress and scenario writer. The dispute concerned a film in which, it was said, he would have been paid £12,500 for 10 weeks work and £1500 for any weeks in excess. His case was that a contract was made by Mrs. Woolf to employ him at that salary as 'Dr. Vernon' in a film entitled *Rachel*, but the film was not made in the time stated. It was denied by Mrs. Woolf that there was any concluded agreement. She pleaded that if there was an agreement it was subject to further terms and conditions which were not made, and no formal contract was drawn up. Mrs. Woolf's film name is 'Edana Romney'. 'The script of the film lay before council. It is understood that *Rachel* has not yet been filmed but is to be made in the future. Mr. N Fox-Andrews, QC for Mr. Newton, said that an agreement was made in September 1949 between Mrs. Woolf and Mr. Alfred Edgar Vere Barker, Mr. Newton's manager and agent. The defendant is the wife of Mr. John Woolf, a well known producer and distributor in the film industry, and it was her intention to portray the title role in the film. Mr. Newton was to co-star. On April 19th, defendants solicitors rang Mr. Barker and a Dictaphone record was made of the conversation. A copy of what was supposed to have been recorded was produced, but when plaintiffs asked to see the record and hear it played they were told it had been destroyed. Mr.

Barker in evidence said: "Mr. Newton was invited to a Sunday party at the home of Mr. and Mrs. Woolf. He was a bit fuzzy haired because he was playing then in *Treasure Island*. He was standing beside a picture by Canaletto which was above the fireplace". "Mrs. Woolf, answering the telephone, said, "We are all crazy, Bob was standing under the Canaletto and it struck us – there was our Dr. Vernon".' Bob appeared before the dry-as-dust court and, backed up by Vere-Barker, said his piece. The thing dragged on and was adjourned awaiting a judgement.

With the project bogged down in court and the small matter of another drink-driving charge for Bob to face, Vere-Barker pressed the troublesome star to take up a new offer, the lead role in the film *Waterfront*.

Turned out by independent producer Paul Soskins and directed by Michael Anderson, it was very much a 'British' work, a gritty and contemporary drama where Newton once again found himself cast as the villain. Appearing as 'Peter McCabe', he staggered out on screen, a brawling, hard-drinking seaman who had deserted his family and only turns good and endures reconciliation as he faces the gallows. A grim little moral picture, running to 80 minutes and filmed in suitably dull monochrome, it was shot at Pinewood studios and on location in Liverpool's grimy docklands. A million miles away from the richly anticipated luxuries of Paris, the work was set in the kind of squalid, post war environment that was all too familiar to him and to the audiences. 'The Desires and Loneliness of seafaring men and their women' the posters drooled salaciously, yet somehow the work smacked only of the grind of poverty and Bible-thumping morality.

Kathleen Harrison and Susan Shaw (born Patsy Sloots and soon to face a Driscoll-like death herself) gave good support, and Bob worked effectively. He might have been the star but this time the film essentially belonged to another actor, Richard Burton.

Twenty years Newton's junior and very much the new-boy, this was Burton's third film. Although far from showing the greatness he possessed, he instantly recognised the parallels that already existed between himself and Newton. For Newton, Burton's appearance was a tonic. Here was a young classical actor, utterly without affectation and with an interest in liquor and women as ardent as his own. Imbued with a bitter iconoclasm, Burton was a man with whom he could passionately discuss the arts. Like Bob, Burton had his own demons and his own relationship problems and like Bob, tried to drink them away. He drank to forget and escape, to prove his manly independence and to show his contempt for the opinion of the world. Already aware that 'stardom' came with a price-tag, he drank to escape its vexing misery. On and off stage the relationship between the two men evolved, a phylogenetic union of patricians that could happily wallow together in self-indulgent misery. For Bob he became another Augustus John, another Jack Buchanan; somewhere between a brother and a son.

Bob may have needed his tipple to keep his sanity, but the law took a different view. The drink-driving case came to court; on 24th of June two rozzers attested that they had spotted Bob stepping out of his car in central London, 'swaying cheerfully, tie awry and shirt hanging over his trousers'. Pleading a single brandy 'for his asthma', but mostly exhaustion through work, Bob found himself backed up by the police's own surgeon; the case was taken away from the jury and he was acquitted. Found not guilty he was however 'peeved' at not being recognised by the coppers...

Each day Newton and Burton would travel up to the studios together. "He would give Richard a lift in this ancient Bentley..." Brook Williams, one of Burton's pals, remembered. "This morning Richard turned up at 5.30am and Newton appeared, flask in hand, unshaven, ready to drive them out of London to Pinewood. The Bentley wouldn't start. Covered in frost. Winter. Newton hands Richard the large flask, brandy, goes back into the house, comes out with a horse-whip and lays about the bonnet! Gets back in the car: it starts. Richard starts to laugh, Newton glares at him and they drink and drive to Pinewood where Newton suddenly insists he will not go through the studio gate. He would go through the window of the security box. Finally they all have to heave him through, by this time he's late. His dresser, in a flurry and fussing about and very camp, hurries him along, puts on the frock coat, puts on the cravat and then Newton hears the bell and starts for the stage, makes for the set. The dresser rushes alongside him desperately trying to tell him he's not wearing any trousers or any underpants. Finally the poor man says "Mr. Newton, sir", they are on the set by now, technicians, directors, actors everywhere, "Oh, Mr. Newton, sir, you can't go on like that, sir" "And why not?" The Long John eye opens its widest. "Because, sir", the dresser terrified, "there's something missing, sir". "Missing, missing?" Newton bellows, looks down at his front shirt tail and then turns to his dresser and nods. "Thank you" he says "for pointing it out. Very grateful". And he lifts up his shirt and yells "Make-up!" 'Newton was bored by then, you see.... anything to break the boredom'.

The film was released in August. Burton appeared playing his part straight, doe-eyed and callow, like Olivier in *21 Days*, and was only moderately applauded by the critics. Bob, unable to take the thing seriously despite Anderson's efforts, had lazily reprised the character with whom he had spent so much time, Long John Silver. Growling and rolling, leering and cussing, he even cut in with the odd shanty. Then, almost at the end, he seems to put his mind and heart to the thing. Turning on the waterworks he snatches the show and the hearts of the audience. In a single scene he transformed the drab tale into a heart-warming saga; hands reached for pocket handkerchiefs and heartstrings were tugged, unfailingly, across the land.

Shipped over to America as *Waterfront Women*, the accents once again faced criticism. Perhaps the carping was justified; instead of both turning in a good unintelligible Scouse, Bob had growled in bastard Cornish and Burton a soft Welsh burr.

The shoot wrapped and Bob gladly retreated West to Olchon Farm. Natalie, who was exhausted, unpredictable and strained almost to breaking point, tagged along and took to her bed. Sally came to stay, then Joy joined the mêlée along with her new lover and the house was filled with family, laughter, country air and dogs. Bob was in his element.

By the end of June Bob was back on the stage, taking over the part of 'Mr Manningham' in the Vaudeville Theatre's long-running revival of Patrick Hamilton's three act play *Gaslight*. Having played a part in the film version Bob knew the plot well enough. Now, with *Treasure Island* showing and his name splashed across the papers, the crowds poured in. "The action of the play takes place in the living-room on the first floor of the Manningham's house in Pimlico, London", the synopsis ran, "in the latter part of the last century". Appearing opposite Rosamund John, herself a major screen name, success was guaranteed and Bob stepped neatly into the breach and blithely gathered up the plaudits and applause. For Rosamund John it was just a continuation of the long haul; exhausted by the pace of work and Bob's inevitable antics, she almost collapsed on their first night...

On 5th October Natalie went into labour. This was her first pregnancy and it was a difficult one. Bob did the right things and paced the hospital corridors smoking furiously. The hours dragged out into an exhausting and protracted labour. Natalie was utterly shattered and unable to go on and a caesarean delivery was performed. To everyone's relief a healthy and lusty boy was brought into the world. Bob was overjoyed, at last he had the son he had always wanted. As soon as Natalie was discharged a party was thrown to celebrate. Somehow the event seemed familiar. Over a brimming glass Bob promised reform; the drinking and the wild life were over, he roared. The memories of his abandonment of Sally were still fresh in his mind, yet, once again, he swore that he was now going to be the complete family man.

Bob and Natalie's relationship was, however, less than stable. Without the pursuit of hedonistic delights to bind them their relationship foundered. Always the Lothario, always the ladies man, Bob had quickly found his fleshly pleasures elsewhere and tales of his amorous involvements had snaked their way home to Smith Street. Natalie was now far from well; addicted to pain-killers, prescribed from the time of a fall, she had become deeply unstable. Drowning in post-natal depression and unable to cope with a mewling newborn that only reminded her of her misery, a nanny had to be hired and Miss Daley, a suitably starchy and morally unassailable martinet, was installed. Now Natalie found herself in the same position that she had forced Annie to occupy. Scorned and neglected, she battled with her fiends alone and burned with impotent anger. For Bob it was all too much of a mystery, a crisis he

285

couldn't cope with, and he turned back to the more understandable world of drink, make-believe and theatre.

With a back catalogue of characters to draw upon it was, thankfully, Dr Clive Reardon that he now emulated on stage, not Peter McCabe. Playing it cool and restrained he made the part of the demented husband his own. "He was a sweet person..." Rosamund John remembered "and unfortunately an alcoholic; one drink had a worse effect on him than a bottle of whisky on another actor. So he was either on the wagon or, when things went wrong, a completely different person...". 'Things' going 'wrong' were happening at home and Bob slipped inside a bottle and, during one performance, seamlessly from act one to act three, missing out the second act altogether, leaving his co-stars floundering. The 'completely different person' was 'Slim Grissom' from 'No Orchids...'. The theatre audiences loved it, and so did Bob. *Gaslight* could have gone on for ever, but theatre no longer paid its stars the big money. By now Natalie had been admitted to a private rehabilitation clinic and the bills were piling up. With Connie's hounding him to take up lucrative film offers and debt collectors snapping at his heels, Bob reluctantly handed on his stage-part.

In his column in the *Sketch* the master theatre critic J. C. Trewin hailed Bob 'Stage Actor of the Month', 'for making us anxious to see P. Hamilton's *Gaslight* at the Vaudeville'. It was a pretty compliment. Bob would never walk the stage again.

The film that Connie's was offering was very different from previous roles. Bob was now forty five and the part he was offered was one that suited his middle-aged mood. Spun out from the timeless Thomas Hughes story he found himself playing the saintly Dr Arnold in a reworking of *Tom Brown's Schooldays*.

Just as the British public had an enduring love of cads and spies, it also had a sneaking regard for its schoolteachers and the lost generation of blue-bloods. Robert Donat's *Goodbye Mr Chips*! had defined the eccentric pedagogue a decade previously and in 1950 another film, the superbly satirical all female comedy, *The Happiest days of Your Life*, had set the stage for a sure-fire success.

Demonstrating the economic retrenching of the big studios, it was once again a small, independent film company that came up with the offer. Renown Pictures, like Stoll's empire, was set on producing a series of films worked from the classics of literature. Previously filmed in 1938 with the great Cedric Hardwicke taking the role of Dr. Arnold, *Tom Browns School-days*, like *Treasure Island*, had a strong appeal for both adults and children.

Shooting took place at England's 'Little Hollywood', Nettlefolds Studios in Walton-on-Thames. The cast list included the irrepressible Hermione Baddeley, Diana Wynyard, (the unhappy 'victim' in the 1940 film version of *Gaslight*), Amy Venness from *This Happy Breed*, Michael Borden, Max Bygraves and a young Hughie Green (later to find TV fame as the host of *Opportunity Knocks*). The plum role of 'Tom Brown' went to John Howard Davies and the pre-publicity posters had some justification in raving 'The *Oliver Twist* team reunited in a great new British film'. With an artfulness that would have found approval with Fagin, the Renown production team had talked the National Trust into opening up the George Inn in Southwark for location shoots and the stiff-collared governors of Rugby school into permitting filming within the hallowed quadrangles; 'The authentic British version filmed at Rugby School itself' the publicity smirked.

Filming began on July 27th 1951 and Newton slipped into a role that gave him a succession of priceless vignettes. Directed by Gordon Parry and shot in black and white, the film showed Bob playing his character subtly and with considerable restraint. Acting as if to confound his critics, he sublimated the all-pervasive pirate and, calling in a touch of the paternal Frank Gibbons, showcased his genius. After twenty minutes he sweeps onto the screen; saintly, paternal and mature.

'Dr Arnold' however didn't wash at home. The joy of the new baby had quickly waned; Natalie was hooked hopelessly into her drug dependency and facing the rock-bottom depths of depression was struggling to survive each day. Meetings between her and Bob were infrequent and strained; the baby, named Nicholas, was effectively handed over to the nurse.

Tom Brown's Schooldays was swallowed enthusiastically by the British public. Bob's character was a revelation. Rather meanly, *Variety* only applauded Newton for filling his role 'with commendable restraint'; Picturegoer, the weekly film magazine, was more generous in its praise; 'Newton is a supreme character actor; all his characters are played with that vital spark which makes it a sharply cut, enduring memory. And now we have his Dr. Arnold. It has the authentic Newton hallmark, and once more illustrates the fine dramatic scope of the man, his Dr. Arnold will be remembered. That great headmaster's humanness, his belief in his calling, his high integrity, they are here woven into an entity through that sensitive Newton voice. Newton loves the words he speaks. He defines strongly the headmaster who did so much to lift public schools out of their mediaevalism with their brutal bullying, and to instil in them a more modern and humane conception....'. *Punch* summed it all up more pithily, appraising the work, or was it the old school system, as 'an odd mixture of the brutal and the solemnly improving'.

Perhaps the film reflected a fundamental theme of the British character, but overall the work was remarkably unexciting, and perhaps only memorable for Bob's input. Duly shipped across the Atlantic and, despite being tailored very much to colonial tastes eternally curious about the inexplicable nature of the British education system, the work failed to get much of an audience reaction.

Locked into a marriage that was now deadly dull and a stifling domestic regime lived under the pretence of 'good behaviour', Bob's life was now utterly bereft of the vital element of fun. Beset by a past filled up with the ghosts of old wives, and surrounded by a weary nation that was hacking through a 'flu epidemic whilst still shuffling in ration queues, Bob was rapidly becoming sick of England. The stage seemed to be dying on its feet and even Olivier and Burton were being routinely trashed by the critic Kenneth Tynan. Worse, British bureaucracy had come of age. The Inland Revenue, ever a worrying nag at the back of Bob's mind, was now on his trail and he knew his personal finances and his tax record would bear little inspection. With rumours circulating that Denham Studios were about to close reinforcing the image of a domestic industry in decline, he looked at his home land through eyes that had seen the Technicolor attractions of some other paradise. Connie's timely offer of Hollywood film work was one to be grabbed at.

With hardly a backward glance Bob boarded the gleaming Pan-American Stratocruiser. Here 'First Class' meant exactly that; champagne and caviare, steaks and fancy French wines... it was just a hint of what America would grant wealthy and well-connected. Flying across the Atlantic and on to the Pacific coast like a man on the run, Bob hit the bottle from take-off and fell backwards into his element. Joyously back in the sun-drenched inner-world of the Hollywood Babylon, a guiltless Sodom and Gomorrah that felt like home, all the promises and the nagging regrets were checked in at the hotel desk.

America had at last woken from the nightmare of war; the advertisers dream factory of television had convinced the public that everything was all right again and the economy was booming. Consumer led and consumer driven America was *the* place to be. Powered by the oil dollar, mass-production and mass-consumption now made the perfect partners and The American Dream was reborn. It was the time of individualism; each man, and each woman, could shape their own destiny, each could aspire to become the President. Built on the power of the Atomic bomb, a society underpinned by dreams, desires and credit was sprawling out into endless suburbs. Suburbia became a landscape of gilded cages and spawned a generation of manic housewives enslaved by luxury. Here, within the rigid geometry of identical, empty boxes and identical, empty lives, America gave birth to a society that was persuaded that it was good to want, good to have, good to have more and more. But the dream of freedom and self determination resulted only in an a paranoiac anxiety to conform. It was the Tupperware landscape filled with Tupperware houses and Tupperware people. Only Valium saw them through each day.

To the nation's accountants it all spelled Prosperity. Confidence was high, and as the doubts fell away, brash decadence came back into vogue. As all the things that were immediately accessible were consumed it was, once again, the things from the Old World that became *the* social hit; in all but one of the eleven straight plays running on Broadway there was an English actor in the lead, or in a featured role; the eleventh was about an Englishman. Yet if Modernity was prepared to be generous and allow itself a romantic predilection for the antiquated it also raced blindly towards the future; art critic Kenneth Tynan flew west out of New York 'with a light valise containing a wispy Dacron-Orlon suit, savage looking Hawaiian shirt and opaque, blue, glasses, which I am assured are standard cocktail garb in Hollywood...'.

Predictably fifties America saw the birth of the new-age sexual stereotype; the female ideal came bleached blonde and big breasted, the Mansfields and the Monroes, the male ideal was muscle bound and muscle brained and Victor Mature led the parade of pre-packed beef.

A rich man in a rich man's world, Bob shrugged and shook his head; his days were filled with golf, swimming and sun-bathing and his nights with all-too available seductions. Feted and dined, he was sucked into both Americana and an ex-pat Brit' community that was, ironically, homesick.

The Beverley Hills British contingent was a tight little island that revolved around Ronald Colman, the self-appointed King-of-the-Colony. The self-appointed 'Queen' was Basil Rathbone's wife, Ouida. Only occasionally did the tight-knit clique open its doors to the non-British; to be asked to the Coleman's 'house on the hill' was considered a stamp of approval. Amongst this select group were two Americans, the ravishing duo, Constance and Joan Bennett. Now, after two decades, Bob was re-introduced; the threadbare, 'lousy Brit' that they had worked so long ago, was re-introduced as a 'star'...

One of the cornerstones of the American studio system was the iron-bound 'standard contract'. For many the pay-off was the promise of steady work, but Newton was smart enough to know that the seven-year deal, renewable every six months at the whim of the studio, was a strait-jacket that was impossible to escape. Many actors, directors, writers, had fallen gladly into the net and lived to wish they had cut off the hand that signed the contract. Theoretically it was possible to freelance but the reality was very different; crossing the studio hierarchy meant being 'offered' a film that was guaranteed to ruin a career. Refusal to take any film was also the actor's right, but it was also the studio's right to suspend the actor without pay, indefinitely, or until he agreed to do as he was ordered. With the period of suspension tacked on the end of the seven-year sentence, many found their servitude to the studio lasting a career lifetime. And then, always slipped within the crabbed small print, was the 'Moral Clause'. Bound to lead a life 'with due regard for public conventions and morals' the clause was a catch-all trap that the studio knew it could always use and this was one trap that Bob was sure he was never going to fall into.

Chauffeur driven onto the vast MGM studio complex, Newton was handed his next script. The film was to be a Kiplingesque adventure, a tale of the nineteenth century British empire in India, always good news for the Brit' contingent. Predictably however, Kipling's masterly vision had been taken and Hollywoodized to the point of death and *Soldiers Three*, filmed previously in '39 under the title *Gunga Din*, was little more than a self-indulgent farce, stripped of art by a gaggle of hack scriptwriters.

Just as within the Hollywood community itself, the plot characters were divided into two distinct camps; the Respectable and the Renegades and Bob had been categorised as one of the latter. Comfortably cast as one of three hard drinking British soldiers he saw that little would be required of him but to play the drunk.

On set and in front of the cameras Newton's screen character, weirdly named 'Bill Sykes', translated to a slovenly piece of acting that was little more than a sadly slurred reprise of his Long John Silver, minus the sparkle and the charm. Cast alongside Stewart Granger, (another ex-pat Brit' who had learned his trade at the Birmingham Rep') who had been working in the States for just over a year and Cyril Cusack, an old acquaintance from *Odd Man Out*, the jolly gang was joined by fellow Brit, David Niven and the aggressively lascivious Norwegian stunner, Greta Gynt (of *Bulldog sees it Through*). Location work was booked to be shot fifty miles outside Hollywood near Lake Malibu, and Bob camped out, care of the studio purse, in the exclusive Brentwood Club, a plush bolt-hole for the stars where sin was on tap and privacy was paramount.

Prior to the shoot, Stewart Granger, one of MGM's contract players, had nervously called at producer Pandro Berman's office; Berman told him that he had got together a wonderful cast for *Soldiers Three* but Granger smelled a rat; "I knew that dear old Bob was one of the biggest drunks in the business, so life wasn't going to be dull. Tay Garnet, a real old timer, was to direct, with Yakima Canutt as the second unit director. This man's name was a byword in Hollywood for his stunts, having done the most of the doubling for John Wayne in Ford's *Stagecoach*. He had been a champion cowboy at all rodeos for years and was built like the proverbial brick shithouse. It was a pleasure to work with this big, gentle Indian... but the script! Oh dear! If Metro had planned to ruin my career they couldn't have chosen a better subject. I went to Benny Thau with my problem and asked if my first film under the new contract couldn't be something more suitable. His answer absolutely rocked me. "Don't worry, Jimmy, if it's as bad as you say, nobody will see it so it won't do you any harm, will it?" My jaw dropped as I looked at him in amazement. He couldn't be serious, could he, this was supposed to be a compliment, but it just disgusted me, the film they were pushing me into would fail. They looked at me as if I was out of my head. As I left to a deafening silence I realised I'd made a mistake. I consulted Cary Grant to see if he could give me any tips but, having read the script, he advised me to do the best I could and get it over with...".

Bob treated each morning's arrival on set as a continuation from the night before, and 'work' quickly became nothing more than a daft, tipsy, knockabout. "The director, was enthusiastic" Granger remembered "and told me it was one of the funniest slapstick comedies he'd ever read. That was just the point, I knew comedy wasn't exactly my line. Walter Pidgeon was a veteran and being under contract, had no say in the matter, but what the hell David Niven, who was playing a supporting part, was doing, I can't imagine. He must have been very hard up... work on the film was pleasant enough with Tay laughing hysterically at every scene we shot. If everyone in the audience laughed half as much when the film was shown we would have a winner, but of course they didn't. Bob Newton was absolutely impossible, bless him, and arrived practically every morning incoherent with booze. Tay was very understanding and we would shoot around him until we could pour enough coffee down his throat to get him at least half way sober. It's difficult to work with an actor who when not incoherently drunk is suffering from a frightful hangover...".

Wallowing in the legendary American hospitality and living the good life to the full, Bob's screen appearance marked a professional low. Bloated and slurring, he had come a long way from the sparkling and charming young man that Barry Jackson knew. Like Granger, Newton had quickly seen that the film was a complete turkey and he was determined to play his part for laughs, allowing his performance to degenerate into a shabbily embarrassing burlesque. The atmosphere that pervaded the shoot was aptly summed up by Niven who said, "It may be shit, and not very good shit, but we have to go through it, so let's just be cheerful about it." Echoing this laudable sentiment Bob set his shoulders squarely at pleasure. April 7th saw him tousled and unrepentant, up before the law on a charge of being 'drunk and boisterous' in a Sunset Strip nightclub. There was little he could say but 'Guilty as charged, your Honour...'.

Dragged into the debacle, Niven saw his teetering career prospects slipping away. "As he (Bob) became more and more eccentric, assistant directors watched the clock apprehensively every morning to see if he would throw the cameraman into utter disarray by arriving too late for urgently needed repairs in the make-up department. During the filming he arrived on several occasions just in time for the first shot but still in his pyjamas... throughout the long weeks of shooting on that picture, I dreaded the magic hour of six o'clock because at the close of work, Bobbie had accumulated a man-eating thirst but he hated to drink alone. "Dear fellow" he would wheedle, "...a little light refreshment this evening. A tiny tipple on the way home to the old ball and chain?" I made a variety of excuses; but they were coldly received. "Getting a little settled in our ways are we. A little sedentary perhaps. No sense of adventure any more...?"

Manfully Niven resisted Bob's blandishments; then as the shoot came to a close he made the fatal mistake. Bob promised that it would be a simple farewell libation. "I know a little bistro, dear fellow, it's just around the corner – come, let us away." Both men were still in costume as 'Soldiers of the Queen'. Bob led the way out to his car, a 1921 Rolls Royce that he had found in a Burbank scrap yard and had restored at huge expense. The chauffeur, in full regalia and with the Rolls Royce cockade in his cap was an ex stunt-man whom Bob had befriended when he found him working as a bouncer at the Gardenia gambling hall. The 'bistro' turned out to be thirty miles away in Long Beach.

Spilling out of the car, Niven warned Bob that he was broke. "My treat, old cock, and I'm loaded with the stuff" said Bob... "we'll only stay a few minutes." The 'bistro' was less than salubrious, dimly lit and evil-smelling; the clientèle were a rough bunch consisting of Russian, Yugoslavian and Japanese fishermen from the tuna-boats. "I knew you'd love it, dear fellow, full of colour don't you think?" Bob ordered them both drinks. Outside the chauffeur stood guard over the Rolls. "Can't have people removing souvenirs from old Mary, can we?" said Bob.

For the first half hour they drank quietly and Bob sentimentally recounted tales of his farm at Olchon. Then the drink started to cut in, Bob found his form and began to roar out the opening of a Thomas Lodge poem... 'Love in my bosom like a bee, Doth suck his sweet: Now with his wings he plays with me, Now with his feet...!' The locals stirred and muttered threateningly. Spurred on Bob threw fat on the fire and delivered a few lines from the Clown in *Anthony and Cleopatra*. More mutters and threats followed and things began to look dangerous. Undeterred Bob ripped out a chunk from the pen of Andrew Marvell. "Let's get the hell out of here!" hissed Niven. "On the contrary," said Bob, "the greatest joy an actor can have is to tame a hostile audience and make them his own, and now I propose to do what Laughton has lately done in a film... I shall deliver this scum the Gettysburg Address!" "Let's deliver everyone a drink first" Niven suggested, hoping to soften the impending blows. "Good thinking!" roared Bob, ordering drinks all around. Then, an incongruous figure in his creased uniform, he began pacing up and down the bar, roaring and acclaiming, whispering or giving it the full bellows. He did the speech flawlessly, and if he didn't get a standing ovation, at least there were no thrown objects. It was probable that no one understood a word that he had said, but there was no mis-interpreting the tears that had streamed down his face.

"Lets go, Bobbie." Niven begged. "Of course, dear fellow...do you have any money, dear boy?" "No" Niven hissed, "I told you forty times I haven't!" "Ah!" said Bob, pressing his finger against the side of his nose and rolling his Long John Silver eyes, "we have a tricky situation here". By this time the barman had grown suspicious and was pacing over. "Dear boy..." Newton muttered in a ventriloquists whisper, "nip outside and prepare the getaway car, then call me from the door." Not unused to such a situation, Bob's chauffeur cranked the car into life; Niven shot back into the bar where a tense stand-off was being enacted between Bob and the bar-man. "Bobbie!" Niven yelled. Bob started back towards the exit; "Barman, dear... just put it on my mother's charge account at Harrods."

It was the stuff of legend.

The experience should have taught Niven to be wary. "One extraordinary night after the shooting" Cyril Cusack recalled "Niven took me and Bob Newton out for a drink and said, "Now, look, you fellows know all about stage acting, I'm just going to make my début on Broadway, how's it done?" As though we were going to be able over that one drink to pass on to him our two whole lifetimes of theatrical experience! So we told him not to worry and it would probably be a great success....". It wasn't.

Soldiers Three went out, three bemused men watched by a bemused public. Audiences groaned and staggered out after an hour and a half of corny and second-rate trash, knowing that they had been rooked out of their dollar. More than one film reviewer saw through the thing "...actors had less trouble with hostile tribesmen than with the script; directed by the usually reliable Tay Garnett, the humour is mostly forced, which may explain Robert's nearly four dozen growls during the course of events....".

Bob could only smile and wallow in luxury; but he quickly found that enjoying the Hollywood life didn't come cheap. However, with a red-hot American agent that put Connie's to shame, he turned to fill his wallet with some easy bucks courtesy of the emerging television industry.

Prior to 1932 neither CBS nor NBC, the two leading television networks, had studio facilities in Hollywood. Warner Brothers, however, had acquired their own local TV station in emulation of Paramount, which owned a 50% interest in CBS. Now it used its nationwide clout to tout its own films and promote fledgling 'stars'. Well ahead of the game, RKO had built an affiliation with NBC and operated in a similar manner. The teeming masses of television addicts were now swallowing programming that plugged the hits from the big studios film musicals and abbreviated plots from up-coming films.

By late 1932 NBC had opened a Hollywood studio, its staff of one putting out a modest twelve hours of programming a week; four years later, and competing with CBS, the staff had increased to a hundred and the operation moved to a huge purpose built studio. Together the stations put out over seven hundred hours of programming a week. Suddenly, television was no longer perceived as the enemy by the big studios and the small-screen executives were actively wooed and studios roster of stars and their copyrighted music put at their disposal. Then the advertisers, keen to link their products with star names, came on-board. It was a marriage made in heaven. Overnight television was saturated with 'sponsors'; 'Rinso Talkie Time', 'Hollywood Nights' (sponsored by Kiss-proof), the 'Hollywood Show' (Sterling Drugs), 'Hollywood Hotel' (Campbell Soups), the 'Helen Hayes Theatre' (Sanka Coffee), the 'Leslie Howard Theatre' (Ponds Cream) and a dozen more. The ubiquitous soap-drama was born; bland, easy-watching fillers to pad out gaps between hard-hitting commercials that turned women into commodities and sold their bored husbands the trappings of 'manhood'.

Now the Lux Video Theatre hired Bob, booking him into Episode 223, *The Suspect*. With the detergent industry setting the standard, the beer barons were soon roped in; *The Baker of Barnbury*, an easygoing Christmastime yarn was shot, then *The Argonauts*, both pay-rolled by Schlitz beer.

If *Soldiers Three* was little more than a cultural farce it did however put bums on cinema seats, raked in a few bucks and MGM were happy with the result. A jubilant press release was fired off announcing that Newton was to star in a remake of the Wallace Beery-Marie Dressler success *Min and Bill*. For an eternally cash-strapped 'star' this was good news. Better news came in October when the London court handling the *Rachel* case judged in Newton's favour and awarded him £12,500 damages and costs. "It is shown that Mr Newton reserved himself and declined other inquiries during the period and therefore lost the sum of £12,500"...

It was the stuff for celebration, and with the celebration came a string of events that forced a decision Newton knew he must make, sooner or later.

By now his name was appearing in trade papers on both sides of the Atlantic. Both the British and American cinema trade placed him third in the list of top UK money-making stars for 1950 and *Daily Mail* readers voted him into the popularity top ten. Bob knew that he was not only at the top of his career tree but that tree was rooted firmly in Hollywood. But with a new baby son whose face was already half forgotten and a grown daughter who had grown very close, he also knew it was time to go home, face the music and settle his affairs, one way or another.

Arriving back in England he found that 'home' was a mess and the music a cacophony. Still incarcerated in a private clinic in Fitzroy Square, Natalie showed no signs of cleaning up. Certainly she wasn't deceived by her husband's avowals of reform and good behaviour and once again Bob found himself drowning in a marriage that was effectively over. Narrowly escaping another drink-driving charge, he took a battering from the press. Suddenly his private life was being trawled up by the tabloids, his career sold as a series of embarrassing misdemeanours, and, despite the acclaim, his name a by-word for ridicule; suddenly he was everybody's favourite fool and even his long-suffering agent was struggling to balance the popularity books. It was a turning point; Newton had had enough and his mind was made up. Within weeks the newspapers were announcing his imminent return to the US to work on a production of Gabriel Pascal's *Androcles and the Lion*. Olchon Farm was left in the capable hands of his bailiff, and in early February 1951 Bob once again set out with a one-way ticket for Hollywood.

Deep down he had known for a long time that it was going to happen and had effectively made his mind up on the set of *Soldiers Three*. Now he was treating Natalie in the same way he had treated Peta, by doing a runner. But this time he was taking his baby with him.

It had all been carefully planned. He was by now an almost routine trans-Atlantic commuter; feeding Natalie a casual lie about taking the baby out to buy clothes, he had wrapped up the child, headed for the airport and boarded a Stratocruiser with nurse, Ellen Daley. Remarkably a fellow passenger on the plane was Tallulah Bankhead... it was all something of a delicious reunion and the pair were soon making a riotous party of the event.

Blithely touching down in New York Newton looked out at the clean, blank slate of his new world only to find it lashed by a storm of newspaper controversy and his name at the centre of it. The British press had been first off the mark. February 3rd saw headlines scream "British star accused of kidnapping". Rival tabloids soon picked up the story; 'Robert Newton arrives in New York, whither he flew accompanied by his three month-old son Nicholas: the forty-five-year-old British actor declared that he brought his baby along with him for the benefit of the Californian sunshine. From her bed in a London nursing home Mrs. Newton, the actor's thirty-year-old third wife, said that the baby had left England without her knowledge. In an interview Mrs. Newton declared: "I am a sick woman or my baby would not be flying to New York. We have been unhappy for some time, and I have been ill since my baby was born three-and-a-half months ago. A month ago I had a nervous breakdown and arrived here on Monday. My husband 'phoned me on Thursday and said he was taking the baby out to buy him new clothes. Because of our domestic difficulties, I began to be worried. Nanny, Miss Daley, 'phoned me from our home and I asked her if she would bring Nicholas to see me to-day. When Nicholas did not arrive I began to worry." Mr. Newton stated he intends to return soon to England with his son'.

For Bob it had all gone horribly wrong and he saw that he had seriously underestimated both Natalie and the press. The newspaper pieces were accompanied by decidedly unflattering flash photos; slumped in the back of a cab, hatted and with his hallmark walking stick, Newton looked every bit the haunted and guilty man. His recent foray into the English courts had taught him little of the new post-war press. 'A nurse and 24 tins of milk...' the American tabloids howled; Connie's and Vere-Barker called in the lawyers and fought to keep a lid on the scandal; 'He had to choose between leaving the child without a parent to look after him or take him along. He planned to leave next Monday, but RKO Studios ordered him to go today...'.

The next day the *Scottish Daily Record* leaped into the ring; 'Star's wife sees lawyer', the headlines screamed. 'I had made arrangements for a maid and a cook to look after Nicholas...' Natalie was quoted as saying, '...I am very frightened of flying myself...!'" In a daze Bob raced on to California, hoping to outrun the press pack. He should have known better.

The 1950s had seen the birth of *Confidential* magazine. Each issue was packed with stars, smut, lies and sex-scandals; the critics predicted it would fail but the first issue sold out with a quarter of a million copies. The publication became unstoppable and spawned a generation of sleazy copy-cat rags. Created by New York publisher Robert Harrison, a man who had already given the world *Titter, Wink, Flirt* and *Beauty Parade*, *Confidential's* circulation was to peak at a domestic five million per issue and seventy five million worldwide and it plumbed the depths of filth before someone had the courage to put their heads above the parapet and fight back. That someone was going to be Rex Harrison, but for now it was all too new and too fast and the old film community, for whom privacy and carefully sanitised expose had always been the remit of the studios, reeled in horror.

In the traditionally male-dominated world of Hollywood, a small group of women had carved out a huge power-base, each with the power to make or break a career. These were the new breed of 'gossip' columnists and the names Hedda Hopper, Louella Parsons and Sheilah Graham struck fear into the stars. Each an alley cat with a past and filled with mutual loathing, they defined the new grubby underbelly of Hollywood. Parsons spat her venom out from the *Los Angeles Examiner*, Hopper from the competing *Los Angeles Times*. The people gobbled it up, the writers were untouchable and knew it.

It was worse than vindictiveness, it was sheer character assassination. "Why do you do it?" the fallen pleaded... "Bitchery dear..." Hopper smiled "just bitchery".

What wasn't true was made up and Bob was about to experience his share. During his last American stay the gutter-press had already latched onto him; "Robert Newton... left England for Hollywood the day after he became a father..." Hedda Hopper's column mewled "why, he hasn't even got a picture to show his fellow actors..."

Bob had badly misjudged his wife's mental state. She had rumbled him almost instantly, calling in lawyers first, the press second and then the police. Significantly, and underscoring her anger and indicative of the far reaching power of the sensation-centred press and her understanding of it, she had also telegraphed Hedda Hopper. February 7th saw a piece in the LA Times under the heart-rending title, 'Mother Asks News'. "A telegram addressed to me preceded the arrival yesterday in Hollywood of Robert Newton, the British actor, with his 3 ½ month-old son Nicky, whom he said he brought here to get a little sunshine... the cablegram was signed by Mrs. Natalie Newton... it was a message of a Mother worried over her baby and asked my help... on the same plane from New York was Tallulah Bankhead... but her presence was just coincidence... his wife's cable to me was fraught with worry. Mrs. Newton is planning to file a suit for divorce soon, 'can you possibly get my baby back to England' she cabled me. I am in a quandary, Bob, What shall I cable your wife?"

British journalists were happy to feed Natalie the right words and she roundly accused her husband of kidnapping. Bob went to ground and holed-up in the plush Beverley Hills Hotel, letting the well-practised studio system swing into action. His agent, Tom Somylo, fought back with a barrage of flack and RKO's well practised damage-limitation machine went into action. Assigned a personal minder cum-agent and a publicity agent, Bob was 'quoted' as calling his wife's accusations "rubbish" and "absolutely untrue", declaring that he had taken the baby to California for his health. Spinning a well crafted yarn calculated to convince Californian finger-waggers fully conversant with 'London, England's' smog and the fearful shadow of the Hound of the Baskervilles, Bob was quoted as having kissed the airport tarmac and saying to his son "'I've brought you here for the sunshine, my son, and here the sunshine is".

If the 'Androcles' project seemed a long time in materialising for Bob, it had been even longer for Gabby Pascal. For years he had been haunting the Hollywood lots, trying to bury the memory of his last debacle, *Caesar and Cleopatra*, which had almost bankrupted Rank, and drum up support for his new pet project. Holding up *Major Barbara* as a big success, he had at last found a backer in the shape of RKO. Bob should have seen the warning signs. The fact that the film was to be shot in the US should have alerted him to the very real possibility that what was another potential classic, could, with Shaw safely in his grave, founder under the same sort of 'Hollywoodization' that had almost scuppered *Fire Over England*. Only desperation had seen Pascal climb into bed with RKO. It looked like a coup, but in reality the deal was a disaster. In a typically bizarre move, the unhinged genius Howard Hughes had secretly scooped the studio into his empire. $8.8 million had bought 929,000 shares and another plaything that he never bothered to visit. Overnight one of Hollywood's big studios fell into the hands of an anti-Semitic kleptomaniac. Defined and obsessed by money, power, intrigue and sex, Hughes was defiant and self-destructive and reviled by the industry hierarchy.

Hughes' arrival, combined with the studio bogging down with union troubles and saddled with a reputation for being a hot bed for Communists, seemed to guarantee chaos. And, beyond the simple story-line, 'Androcles' tackled the hypocrisy of Christianity, desperately dangerous ground in a country where the Christian right held power. Stuck in limbo and almost in hiding, Bob filled the idle hours and took in some cash with a little moonlighting. Following Olivier's footsteps, who had provided a voice-intro for Coward's *Happy Breed*, Bob turned his hand to narration, knocking out a neat intro' for the forthcoming 1949 Cornell Wilde/Maureen O'Hara swashbuckler, *At Swords Point*.

Crushed between Shaw's ghost and Hughes' demons, and seeing his script corrupting into a sexed-up farce, Pascal knew this was to be his last chance and desperately pre-announced the work's greatness before a foot was shot. Struggling to assemble a cast, the names of

Groucho Marx and Danny Kaye were dragged in as possibles for the lead role and the friendly press was fed the usual lines; 'Gabriel Pascal is bringing over one of England's foremost Shavian actors, James Donald, to play the romantic lead with Jean Simmons...'.

Bob took to haunting the set to escape the press, and Pascal, struggling to cope with his own mountain of problems, was drawn into Bob's private saga. Forwarding a carefully composed and caveat-loaded telegram to Natalie, and making sure it 'leaked' to the press via the gaping mouth of Hedda Hopper, he wrote ..."Dear Natalie, I had a long talk with Bob and the nurse. Nicholas has lovely quarters. The nurse is very happy and believes for the child's sake these few weeks in sunny California and wonderful food, which he can get here without limitation, will do wonders. Bob gives me the honourable assurance that any time after a few weeks stay here, and you are out of hospital and you wish to see Nicholas back, he is ready to send him back with the nurse. You know how objective I am in these matters; for me a child is a holy miracle on earth, and I will do anything to keep you and your boy happy. Will you cable me that you are comforted by my statement? Love..."

A war of bitter words raged on; the press on both sides of the Atlantic leeched onto the story and drew blood. Natalie was coming over as soon as she was well, Bob's agents said, trying to cool the situation, but the story the press wanted came at last; the prospect of messy divorce was dragged into the equation.

Filmed in black and white and directed and scripted by Chester Erskine, Newton found he was to play alongside Elsa Lanchester and that the leading role had been given to Alan Young. Taken as American, but actually a British-born Canadian, Young had cut out a niche as a lightweight television comedian. 'It's a sad-clownish kind of part which should suit the comedian to a T....' the papers said. Bob shuddered with horror whilst Shaw turned in his punctilious grave. With the work revolving largely around the implausible romantic entanglement of Christian girl, Jean Simmons, (a woman Bob could never get on with...) and Roman captain, Victor Mature, he saw that he was going to be thrown to the lions in more ways than one.

Shooting got under way on February 10th and Bob, understanding the author's intended irony and humour, played his muscle-man role somewhere between John Silver and Dr Arnold. On set, however, things went downhill quickly as Hughes' minions fired off broadsides of contradictory edicts and changes were made with an illogicality that drove everybody crazy. Then, after a series of furious rows, Pascal was sacked from his own project, thrown out of the studios and denied even the dignity of clearing out his desk.

Manipulative and sex-obsessed, Hughes, (dubbed the 'anal erotic' because he was obsessed with the ending of films) now began to meddle with Pascal's script. Spicing-up the action, he had raunchy sex-scenes and an especially commissioned 'Vestal Virgins' bathhouse sequence, complete with near-naked beauties, woven into the plot. By now the shooting schedule had been lost along with the script, and cast and crew stood back and waited for the next disaster to strike. It was not long coming. Hughes' predatory eyes had fallen on Jean Simmons. For him the signing of a film contract was as binding as a marriage contract and he felt he owned an actor, body and soul. A battle of wills began. Day after day, studio consultants and make-up artists received reams of drawings and diagrams showing exactly how Simmons' lips should be created; then the obsession with her hair began... photographs, exact measurements, colour and shade charts. Simmons snapped, snatched up a pair of scissors and cropped her hair to rags.

In the face of such sustained lunacy, Erskine was unable to bring the project back on course and weeks were wasted just marking time on the set. For Bob however, it was time to play out a sub-plot; at home in England, Connie's agency was waving warning flags. Marital and personal problems might have been his private business but too many letters from the Inland Revenue, re: Mr R. G. Newton, had been directed at them. Questions were being asked; the tax man was hot on their client's trail.

In early April Bob appeared in Austin, Texas, at the Capitol Building, pressing the flesh with state governor Garland Smith, and smilingly accepting an honorary Texan citizenship. The press and the studio publicity machine were there, making the most of the moment. It seemed a first step towards a new life. As if to cast the thing in stone, the *Sphere* published a piece in its October issue, complete with a photo: 'Homework in Hollywood: Mr. Robert Newton, the British film actor, studies United States citizenship requirements on a Hollywood sound stage between takes... Newton has applied for an alien quota number as a preliminary step towards becoming a citizen of the United States...'.

On set, filming limped from one disaster to the next. Bob sighed, shrugged, and saw that once again he was drowning in a celluloid disaster that bore all of Hughes' disturbed 'stylistic hallmarks'. Escape came in Hollywood's nocturnal party life. A world in its own right, Hollywood was a magical dreamland; the Mocambo nightclub on Sunset, Ciro's, a plethora of delirious fleshpots. Friday nights always included a visit to a fight at the Legion Stadium on El Centro. The company was always good, the liquor flowed, and the leading light for unashamed decadence was Errol Flynn.

His home on Mulholland, the 'House of Pleasure' was famed; "Strange people wended their way up to the Mulholland house..." Flynn said "among them pimps, sports, bums, down-at-heel actors, queers, athletes, sightseers, process-servers, phonies, salesmen... everything in the world". It was just what Bob needed and he and Flynn became like two long-lost brothers. Another doorway and another dizzy poolside gin-fest came via an old pal, Byron Haskin, the director of *Treasure Island*.

In the midst of another perfect, perfumed evening, amidst the delirious swill of vanities, fate engineered a casual introduction in the fatal and shapely form of a blonde twenty six year old, Vera Budnik.

From her childhood Vera, like a million other kids, knew where her future lay. It lay in Hollywood and it lay in marriage to a 'star'. At the age of eighteen she and a girlfriend had fled dysfunctional families and the drabness of Long Island and arrived in the glittering dreamscape of Los Angeles. They both quickly found work with Warner Brothers.

Drink led to drink and Bob and Vera, 'Boots' to her friends, broke away from the group; Bob was 'working his old magic', everyone laughed. But Bob had met his nemesis. Ever the sucker for a pretty

304

face, especially a vivacious blonde who responded flawlessly to his chat-up lines, he had yet to realise that Vera was a force to be reckoned with and that this time the seduction was not going to be easy. Vera was wary of Newton's reputation both as a womaniser and a drinker; Bob, of course, was hooked.

As the weeks drifted by and their meetings became dates, he saw that the way to her heart was through her kid brother, Dan, who had also shifted over from the East coast, and who was officially her ward. By now Bob was living in a cabin in the Hollywood hills and Dan became a regular visitor, sharing Bob's taste for hot-dogs, if not his liquor. Aged just eighteen, Dan fell for Bob's charms just like everyone else. As ever Bob's 'home' was exquisitely shambolic; there was no toilet paper in the outdoor 'Powder room', but there was always a bottle of gin.

Bob's romantic assault was assiduous, Dan found himself the grateful inheritor of two fine tweed suits that Bob had worn on the set of *Obsession*, and Vera the possessor of a shiny, new, soft-top, two-tone, Ford Victoria. Yet the course of true love did not run smoothly. Proudly displaying his past, Bob dragged Vera into a private showing of *Oliver Twist*. It was all going swimmingly until the murder scene. Vera was horrified and couldn't look Bob in the face for a fortnight...

By June the *Androcles* farce was still dragging on, and, locked into a cast-iron contract, Bob could only look impotently on as two prime projects that he had been promised went past their sell-by dates. In April his part in RKO's *The Blue Veil* had been gleefully snapped up by Cyril Cusack, and now the peachy 'Friar Tuck' role in Disney's long-promised *Robin Hood* had gone the same way and been grabbed by James Hayter. Almost an exile from England, Bob had also missed his daughter's wedding in London... "Blonde haired bride of 21 tomorrow: Sally Newton, film-actress daughter of film-actor father Robert Newton. But Mr Newton will not be at St Cyprian Church, Clarence Gate, Marylebone, to give the bride away. He is in Hollywood filming 'Androcles and the Lion'. Bridegroom is actor Seymour Green... for her wedding Miss Newton has chosen a white lace ballerina gown, low-necked and with tiny sleeves. She will be wearing a wine-coloured Juliet cap. She has just finished making two films, "The Armchair Detective" in which she plays a nightclub singer involved in a murder and "No Haunt for a Gentleman", a comedy in which she is a young wife whose husband enlists the help of a ghost to get rid of his Mother-in-law." In the absence of her father Sally was given away by her Uncle; for Bob it was a bitter blow.

Staggering under the hackneyed sword and sandal motif, 'Androcles' looked set to echo the *I, Claudius* torment all over again. Things were about to get worse and this time he was to be the problem. By now Vera could see that her relationship with Bob needed some careful impetus; she had come to Hollywood to find herself a 'star husband' not to become simply the plaything. With a purely feminine stroke of genius she had suddenly 'grown cold feet' over the relationship; packing her bags into the Ford she 'escaped' back to an old lover in New York. It was the oldest trick in the book: Newton was devastated, he hit the bottle and was useless on set. Alarm bells rang across the studios; in desperation calls were put through to the east coast and Vera found herself with a studio job-offer she could not refuse. The die was cast; within two days she was back in Hollywood and back in Bob's arms.

Androcles staggered back into life and eventually, fatuous, sexed-up and drowning in togas, the thing limped off the set, into post production and promptly fell into the arena of studio in-fighting. For Bob it had been a depressing experience. Worse, it had damaged his career. But with his legal spat over the *Rachel* fiasco fresh in their minds, the RKO heads came up with a sugar-coated palliative to compensate for the part he had missed in *Robin Hood*, the lead in a sure-fire hit that echoed the *Treasure Island* format and a guaranteed $50,000 fee.

Bob agreed, but only reluctantly. He knew the film wasn't going to be art and it wasn't what he wanted, but things had moved on quickly in his life. The pretty blonde he had met at the party had stayed beyond the usual pally cigarette and morning-after breakfast and, since the reunion, the word 'marriage' had begun creeping into the conversation. It was all looking serious. Officially Vera was 'engaged' to her New York lover, and she didn't hesitate to tell Bob so. It was all part of the trap, and Bob was a hopeless and all too willing victim. A hard-nosed Hollywood pro, a publicity agent and talent scout, a career girl full of drive, ambition and the ruthless brand of American brio, Vera had seamlessly become Bob's new 'Spitfire Annie'. Without hesitation she told Bob that he must take RKO's offer; it didn't matter how he felt about it, it was simply a matter of cold dollars.

Bob bowed to her wisdom; it was a seminal moment and their relationship settled comfortably again. Now the only thing that stood between them was his little penchant for drink; it was a problem, but one Vera though she could overcome, in time.

It was a nice theory but the reality was that, since the repeal of Prohibition America, Hollywood especially was awash with liquor. Everyone drank, and everyone drank a lot. Just below Bob's place was a branch of Liquor Locker; customers would go and buy their week's stash of discount booze, take it outside, secure it in a 'safe' and pocket the key. All they had to do was pick it up at their leisure.

Driving her would-be husband to some sort of financial and social solvency, Vera shoe-horned Bob out of his cosy hideaway cabin and into a rental in Coldwater Canyon Drive. Things began looking up; with RKO's deal still under negotiation, Fox's flamboyant head, Daryl F Zanuck came on the phone with a lucrative offer that promised something approaching serious acting.

If the English player had seen his heyday in Hollywood, the constant influx of thoroughly stage-trained British talent nevertheless created anxiety for the Hollywood film locals. They had good cause to worry; in the first part of a lucrative two film deal, Bob was handed the script for a new production of Victor Hugo bitterly bleak classic *Les Miserables*.

Decked out as 'Javert', he was cast to play opposite Michael Rennie, who was taking the central role of Jean Valjean. Rennie's acting career echoed Bob's own. Moving on from a succession of bit-parts in British films, and a two second appearance in *The Squeaker*, Rennie had decamped to the States and shimmied quickly up the star ladder, peaking with the classic Sci-fi flick *The Day the Earth Stood Still*. On set Rennie now blithely introduced himself as an old acquaintance; whether Bob could remember him was a different matter...

The film's director was Bob's old pal, Lewis Milestone, a man whose career had now decidedly faltered. The supporting star cast included Elsa Lanchester, James Robertson Justice and Sylvia Sidney and the set-up looked promising. Very much an 'intellectual' piece, it was just the sort of thing, Vera insisted, Bob needed after the low-grade farce of *Soldiers Three*. Portraying all the bitterness of injustice, *Les Miserables* had been first filmed in 1919, then in 1927 and again in 1935, before facing a French production the following year. The 1935 work saw Charles Laughton take the role of Javert and deliver a typically masterly performance which, despite some critiques condemning him for hamming, had set the standard. The new script had been pretty much hijacked from the 1935 version, and Milestone, seeing that Technicolor would kill it, insisted on shooting in an arty black and white.

With a convincing eighteenth century backdrop and some solid, if stodgy performances, the film ran to 105 minutes, got a polite applause and sank slowly from view. The critics agreed, unanimously, that it was an out of date piece and basically tedious. Certainly Newton's performance lacked its usual dynamism, and was played bleak and cold, utterly restrained and without a hint of buccaneering sparkle. There was little wonder; with Vera now a permanent fixture at his elbow he was a changed man.

Newton might have been enjoying another cosy romp but Vera had seen Bob's potential; the transition from lover to client had begun. Vera could see that Bob's potential was being drunk joyously down the Swanee River. Twenty years Bob's junior, she was determined to save and rebuild him and his fate was sealed. Liquor went off the menu and, with an eye on the poison pen of the gossip columnists, he was forced firmly onto a regime of good behaviour. A brief escape from the pre-marital leash came with the Christmas break and a house guest who knew how to have a good time, Trevor Howard. The hospitality may have flowed but Howard found that in Bob's secret new down-town crash-out apartment, 'home comforts' were limited. It was like the old bachelor-pad days all over again; a line of empty bottles, one bed and one broken-down sofa...

A half-willing puppet, skilfully manipulated by his lover, Bob found himself driven unerringly towards success. With no time to rest on the critics somewhat mean laurels he turned out a radio production of *Les Miserables* for one of the Lux sponsored pre-Christmas broadcasts.

Bob's new image makeover may have pleased Vera but the press pack, desperate for sensation, was still at his heels. "Robert Newton, a fine actor who's careless of his appearance and his way of life..." smiled Hedda Hopper, "is wanted for *Magdalene*. Newton has many scripts tossed his way, among them *Plymouth Adventure* and *Blackbeard the Pirate*. He won't decide on anything until he reads the script, and he doesn't like to read. Says he, "After finishing *Les Miserables* I may just wait for *The Life of Gandhi* with Gabriel Pascal'. Utterly defeated by the debacle of 'Androcles', Pascal however had faded away and died. With Vera snapping at his heels, Bob now found himself once again clutching his wooden dagger and heading out for the RKO lot.

Shot and timed for the long Christmas holiday of 1952, *Blackbeard the Pirate* hit the screens with a Technicolor thunderclap. In a cheap take that cashed-in on his buccaneering past, Bob played his character hairy and crazed. Maritime history had been thoroughly re-written; no one could have done the part but Bob, and he did it with a vengeance. Veteran director Raoul Walsh, a hard-living, hard-drinker, who had peaked his career and reputation directing Bogart in the classic *High Sierra*, was used to leading from the front, but in Blackbeard he had struggled to steer the crank ship. Throughout the shoot he could only watch as Newton hacked, cussed and belched through the 'Spanish Main'. With his beard duly ablaze, Bob growled into timeless icons all the right piratical imprecations. Instead of the old Treasure Island mantra, "cut and rip..." the byword was now "sinking, burnings, kidnap, murder... but larceny above all!"

With nearly a hundred movies under his belt, Walsh, a roguish Manhattan cowboy who sported an eye patch that made him look like one of the pirate crew, was one of the industry's least neurotic directors. Famed for bringing a lusty humour and improvised naturalism in his films, he had, this time, met his match. His directorial technique became so relaxed that it bordered on disinterest. Often he seemed more concerned with rolling his interminable cigarettes than what was happening on the set. Looking up after each take he would mutter, "Is it over? Okay, cut. What's next?" Another rampant womaniser, he and Newton had got on like brothers from the start.

As ever, the drama was not confined to the set; crossing cutlasses with fellow Brit' Torin Thatcher, (another bit player in *Major Barbara)*, who was playing Sir Henry Morgan, Bob, along with everyone else, kept a weather eye on the wings and watched the sparks fly as Howard Hughes took a lecherous cut at another of his possessions, the studio's glamour-puss, Linda (Monetta Eloyse) Darnell.

Almost plotless and with a banal screenplay that utterly lacked any of the charm of *Treasure Island*, the film was bound to fail to attain classic status. However, released in the US on Christmas Day, 1952 with blaring posters that read "Thunderous adventures of the swashbuckling Sons of Satan... Produced by hit-after-hit maker Edmund Granger, who gave you "Wake of the Red Witch", "Sands of Iwo Jima", "Flying Leathernecks", "One Minute to Zero", and more!" it packed the families into the cinemas. *Variety* called Newton's Blackbeard, a 'captivating performance'. The *New York Times* was more honestly shocked. 'Mr. Newton, who is the whole picture, must be seen to be believed... sporting a beehive chin growth that transmits a volume gamut of roars, the actor wallows through an outrageously flamboyant caricature of his Long John Silver part in Disney's 'Treasure Island''.

Financially the film did well enough but perhaps the only real profit accrued was another typical Newton anecdote. One morning Bob picked up a taxi to take him to the studio. Recognising the driver as an extra he had worked with ages ago in England, he dragged him out from behind the wheel and onto the set, bellowing that a good 'extras' part must be found for his old pal immediately...

By now Hollywood's old studio system of contract-bound 'stars' was in decline and players were contracting themselves out on a self-employed basis. Suddenly actors could freelance, work wherever they wanted and strike out on their own; a sea-change had begun in the entertainment industry. Outside, in the big world, what had begun as a risible, small screen experiment had become an explosion of broadcasting; television had arrived and was being fed to a vast domesticated audience hungry for life on the couch. The silver-screen actors started to drift towards the golden television dollar, but even the flood of quickie productions could not satisfy demand. Stations were putting out anything they could lay their hands on. Now, twenty years on, Bob had the privilege of watching his performance in the 1932 film *Reunion* on the TV. In the comfort of his home he could watch his own past, now hacked up between a dozen 'commercial breaks'.

'Androcles' now at last emerged from the battle of internal politics and hit the big screens. Excised of much of the rank nudity that would have seen it stumble under the constraints of the puritanical censorship system, it was, nevertheless, seen for the mess it was and damned with faint praise. 'A decent treatment if not an entirely felicitous film' one critic generously said. The *New York Times* saw Newton's Ferrovious as a 'robust, hilarious spoof of the militant evangelical type of Christian, but slightly overdone.' *Variety* noted of Newton's work that he 'apparently enjoys himself in the role of Ferrovious, the violent, powerful Christian whose sword and strength save the devout from death in Caesarian arena.'

'Has Hollywood paid off?' *Picturegoer* magazine now asked, 'Whenever I suffer from insomnia, instead of counting sheep, I count the British stars who have gone over to Hollywood. After that I divide them mentally into two folds to separate those who have fared well from those who haven't...'. It was a question Bob now asked himself. '...Deborah Kerr is an instance of a 'miss' by Hollywood. Uninspired casting in unsuitable projects has not furthered her career noticeably or consolidated the impression made with her early British films... Michael Rennie has fared better... for him Hollywood has paid off. But can the same be said of Cyril Cusack. Cusack has had only one good character role, in The Blue Veil, and if we are to believe the Press reports, about the only item of interest that Robert Newton has inspired over there is a testimony from the Los Angeles police officer that he was the most entertaining fellow they had ever arrested...'

Despite Vera's vigilance Bob had indeed fallen off the wagon. The *Los Angeles Times* carried the story briefly on April 7th and then, realising it had the stuff of saleable sensation, blew it out into a four column leader complete with photo of Bob goofing for the camera. It was the old story, out on the town in his slippers and in a smart diner on Sunset Boulevard Bob, free for once of Vera's constrains, had hit the sauce. The staff had deemed their 'civil rights' to be outraged and had called in the law, complaining that Bob was loud, boisterous and drunk. Dragged down-town and followed by the press-pack, Bob had entertained the cops and the usual gaggle of weekend hoods and hookers with cameos from stage and screen and got an ovation. The next morning he got another; the cops pleaded on his behalf, "Gee, go easy on him Judge, he's the nicest fellow we've ever had to lock up!" This time he got away with a telling off and a $15 fine. "Really lovely people these sheriffs..." Bob said to the press, "put manacles on my wrists first, but then removed them immediately I assured them I intended no harm. They could see I'm really a very gentle fellow, you know". Nice words, but not for just the press. Bob paid the fine, said his thanks, brushed himself down and stepped out nervously onto the street. Vera was nowhere to be seen. He knew that the reunion was going to take a lot of flowers and a lot of new promises.

Far away in Bob's past and back in Britain it was announced in the national press that Natalie was petitioning for divorce, alleging infidelity on the part of her absentee husband. January 17th 1952: "Mrs. Robert Newton seeks divorce. A divorce petition by Mrs. Natalie Newton against Robert Newton, the film star, appears on the list of forthcoming undefended petitions issued this afternoon. The actor is 46 and has been married twice before. He married his present wife at Crowborough Sussex, in August 1947. A son was born in October 1950. Mr. Newton is now in the United States". Bob had had enough and did not want to contest the case. Any prospect of returning home was over, and he knew a war of words with Natalie would be pointless; his future was in America, as an American citizen and with Vera. With spies operating on both sides of the pond, lawyers smelling money and a son pulled in half in the middle, Bob however bowed to Vera and his lawyers advice and reluctantly signed a standard counter-accusation of adultery against Natalie. In February the court threw the counter-claim out and things went through quickly, perhaps too quickly for Bob. Natalie was granted a decree nisi, with costs. She also gained custody of the child. The *Daily Telegraph* report on February 20th read: "Decree against actor. Mrs. Natalie Hazel Cochran Newhouse, wife of Robert Newton, actor, was granted a decree nisi with costs in the Divorce Court yesterday on the grounds of her husbands adultery in the United States, the Judge, exercising his discretion in regard to adultery by Mrs. Newton. Custody of the child of the marriage which took place in 1947, was also granted to Mrs. Newton". Eight years of loving and fighting was over with the scratch of a pen.

Nicholas and nanny were dispatched by air back to England, arriving in London on Thursday May 17th, 1951. Sick and hysterical Natalie effected a tearful reunion, and, clutching her baby, fled back to Olchon.

For Bob it was a bitter blow. He had lost the son he hardly knew. Vera commiserated and quietly sighed in relief. Ever the unrepentant bohemian, Bob shed a tear, picked himself up and turned his back on the shambles of his past life and looked to the future. Or rather to the present; for Bob the future was ever an unknown and uninteresting world.

His desperate need for a close personal community saw him put his life into Vera's hands and her world and, like Walt Disney, wait for 'something' to happen. Dozing in the sun, he was more than happy for fate to take a hand. Vera however had other ideas; she knew that she had the stuff of a real money-making star somewhat loosely under her thumb; he was an international star, not just a British one, and she was going to effect a prosperous resurrection, even if it killed him.

Bob knew Vera was the doorway into the mystifying and inexplicable world of America and American culture. A driver and a proactive manipulator, she knew the faces and the names, knew the ropes, and how to pull them, and knew the palms to grease. And she was something new and exciting and that was exactly what he needed. Seamlessly Vera's one-woman public relations machine swung into action and Bob started doing the social rounds. Remorselessly and apparently stone-cold sober, almost like a politician, he began to attend the press calls and photo shoots, kissing babies and opening fêtes, even flying over to the east coast for a charity event and presenting the 'Tom Brown Trophy' to the Princetown rugby team.

Bob's faltering career seemed on the cusp of a rebirth. The caveat came with drink. This time, finally, Bob was to quit the booze and the wild life, settle down and become the model husband and the new American.

9. The Beautiful Prison

On a beautiful Sunday morning in the spring of 1951 the Los Angeles police raided one of the deluxe pleasure houses that nestled in the hills above Sunset Strip. It was all rather routine; beers and sandwiches were offered around, the girls flirted and giggled and everyone co-operated. With the press dutifully flashing their cameras, the tousled tarts and a suitably outraged madam were carted down-town. What nobody expected was the customer ledger.

Suddenly it all became a terrible mess. The whore-house had long been one of the city's worst kept secrets. Then it was revealed that it planned to turn into a legit' eating-house; the neighbouring swank restaurateurs didn't want competition and the cops had been tipped-off. Suddenly, with the house ledger laid out before the beak the story went headline and speculation as to the contents went wild. The book was a catalogue of the Hollywood 'A' list; clients who 'left their Oscars on the mantelpiece in gratitude for services rendered'. The film industry went into panic mode. The scandal rags sniffed blood and grabbed wildly; dozens of stars suddenly saw the need to broaden their portfolios and snapped up work abroad.

Cornered and caught with their pants down, the studios desperately pulled strings; the thing was hushed up and the stars trickled back. Almost seamlessly the Hollywood gloss was pulled back in place but the damage was done and tinsel town's veneer-thin cloak of respectability was shredded. The studio system bared its teeth to protect its cash-cow contract stars and the gutter press backed off and turned to new game. Now they were looking for the 'Lavender' boys; 'Poof' hunting was on. Bob shook his head; at least this was one cross no one could nail him to.

Hollywood retrenched into social isolationism. A ritual hand washing took place and the result was paranoid self-censorship that crushed creativity. Overnight church congregations swelled and star-spangled patriotism and xenophobia walked hand in hand down the aisle. The anti-communist campaign, spawned in the late 'forties, jumped on the band-wagon. Led by Congressman J. Parnell Thomas the witch-hunt cast a pall over Hollywood as insidious as the newly pervasive Los Angeles smog. The House Un-American Activities Committee granted the bloodhounds open season and movie-land's fanatical right-wingers emerged from the woodwork, wrapped themselves in the stars and stripes and came out punching. Generally the punches fell below the belt.

John Wayne was elected president of a lynch mob which called itself the Motion Picture Alliance for the Preservation of American Ideals. Once again 'foreigners', always the easy target, were viewed with hostility and the British ex-pats huddled for comfort behind the curtains in their mock-Tudor clubs.

Coming from an old European tradition they intuitively understood the symbiotic nature of parenthesised good and evil, the fact that they were the two ends of the same sticky stick. It was a trick the Americans were yet to learn. Across America, but especially in Hollywood, the Brits found themselves adrift in a society of delirious and self-obsessed adolescents who, led on by the baying from the mid-west Bible Belt, the Hayes Code, the Legion of Decency, the Mother's-Union and born-again Bible bashers, were trying to divorce the two. It was all about sex, and suddenly Bob, like his fellow Brits, didn't fit in. Even the stage had crumbled under the wave of sanitised inanity. Kenneth Tynan could see it happening in front of his eyes; even Broadway, he wrote, was becoming an 'intricate, stunningly resourceful and brilliantly manned machine for the large-scale utterance of carefully garnished banalities'.

Ever the Bohemian, Bob however refused to follow the speak-no-evil party line. He didn't take sides, didn't kowtow to the myth of the Founding Fathers, the Pilgrims who came to build a new Jerusalem. He just couldn't take it seriously. Backed into a corner of its own making, neither could the film industry. Its answer to the dichotomy was to cornball; to dilute everything with a dash of trash, to build in the alibi that 'none of it was meant to be taken seriously'. Film once again flawlessly performed its duty and showcased the people to themselves and mirroring an increasingly duplicitous and two-faced society. They had cornballed Shaw's *Androclese* and Kipling's *Soldiers Three* and now Newton saw that to fit in and get on, he would have to cornball his life.

Ironically it was David Lean, a man who had never manifested any inclination to sell out to Hollywood, who most aptly summed up Newton's dilemma; "You go out to Hollywood, you buy a magnificent house and you build an even more magnificent swimming pool. Then you have to pay for it. They want you to make films you aren't really keen on, but that swimming pool must be paid for. So you do the bloody film. In England we have nothing but rain and austerity, so the only thing left is to make good films..."

In a half-way house between worlds and marriages, Newton was now living, almost besieged, in a shabby-chic residential hotel on Sunset Boulevard. Solace from the mysterious world of Americana was found with Richard Burton, a man who was having his own love-affair with fags, broads and booze. "It was the thing to do... if you were a stage actor", Burton argued, "to show your contempt for the contract stars, to stay there in that stucco monstrosity, making it quite clear that you were your own man and not owned by some studio, and the minute the fucking lousy film you were in was over, you were going back to the great... theatre where you re-found your soul as an artist and real work was done". Newton understood only too well. Like him Burton was struggling to adapt to the Hollywood 'star' life and to satisfy the woman that clung about his neck. But the posturing was a lie. Both of them had sold out to the dollar, and both were aware that there was no way out.

If the drink had drained Newton of his idealism, the Hollywood lifestyle, the sterile farce that hid a seedy reality, now drowned him. Like Burton he was a Celt, a man of passion, a firebrand; California was the land of the easy luncheon and the long siesta. Like Wilde in Paris, both men found in Hollywood "the satisfaction of vanity and an inexhaustible source of fatuity". The Americans themselves joked that New York was always twenty years behind Paris in its appreciation of contemporary art and that California was twenty years behind New York. Everyone hated everything about Hollywood. Except the dollars.

Warned off from selling truths, the film-fan press fell back on the safer ghosts of the past; Newton, tabloided into 'Fig Newton' (after the famous biscuit), was the feature of the January 23rd, 1954 issue of *Picturegoer* magazine, '...the man who was tagged Hollywood's bad-boy didn't try to pretend that a past with a bottle didn't exist. In fact, once or twice, I fancied I caught a grin of shamefaced pride in some of the stories I recalled to him. After all it's not every actor who has bought a horse off gypsies, ridden it into the studio, been ordered out, and then ridden it home, up the stairs and into his bedroom where both horse and man slept peacefully. And that's not a Hollywood tale; that's an English one. It happened on the set of *Snowbound...*'

Bowing under the inanity of American morality and with an unavoidable inevitability, Bob found himself going through the ritual of marriage once again. It was all happening too fast; it was everything he had come to America to escape. As a lover, an easy-going confidante and a lever into the upside-down world of Hollywood, Vera was perfect. Both purringly feminine and a business force to be reckoned with, she was everything Natalie had never been, but marriage was a thing Bob had never considered. After the restaurant fracas he had slipped only once; being pinched for drink driving. Once again there had been a scene, the marriage was called off, and he had found himself making more impossible promises.

Vera, issuing yet another last chance, saw that the rehab' process was going to take time.

The ceremony went ahead in June, in Hollywood, and the press pack, of course, was there. The engagement, 'pending' the long-awaited divorce from Natalie, had been loudly announced through the Fox Corporation weeks before. Bob had given his address as 2020 Coldwater Canyon and found himself dangerously close to becoming a 'company man'.

Pending or not, the first legal step towards divorce didn't come until January 18th, 1952. The wedding dithered for another five months.

Then, in England the *Evening Standard* reported the story; June 16th 1952. "Robert Newton, 47-year-old British Actor, and Miss Vera Budnik, 27-year-old publicity agent, were married in Beverley Hills, California, last night. Less than two months ago, after the actor had been involved in a minor court action, Miss Budnik said their engagement was off. Later they were reconciled. It was Newton's fourth marriage, and the bride's first."

As befitting their new social status, the marital home was Bogart and Bacall's old Benedict Canyon place in Beverley Hills. Once a wilderness of scrub and dirt tracks that had served as film locations, the area had evolved through semi-respectability into an era that saw it sucked into the domain of the gin-belt new-rich. Sub-divided into suburban lots it was dotted with residences that conformed to either 'Spanish', 'Cape Cod', 'Adobe', 'Ranch' or 'Olde English' styles.

Show-offy, sprawling and ostentatious, Bob and Vera's new home, (originally Hedi Lamarr's place before the Bogarts) came, as usual, fully furnished with all fixtures and fittings, bar, and six acres. The price was $37,500. Eight bedroomed and gleaming white, it was a swanky pillared palace that seemed to fit none of the styles yet came complete with the obligatory swimming pool and rattlesnakes.

The honeymoon was held over; for Vera's work always came first and instead a grand reception was held at Benedict Canyon. All the good and the great attended and for once Bob was let off the leash. Out by the pool Bob and Burton made the most of the occasion; deep into a lengthy yarn, Martini glasses in hand, teetering dangerously close to the waters edge...

When the honeymoon came it was spent amidst the high profile luxuries of Lake Tahoe's Cal-Neva Lodge, where, straddling the California/Nevada border, casino gambling was a bonus to the gaudy fleshpots. In the place to see and be seen; Bob was back under Vera's control and played it strictly sober.

Befitting Bob's new teetotal life, the cocktail cabinet was removed from the Benedict Canyon home and was replaced by the tea-pot; carpet slippers became de rigeur and tobacco either came cork 'filtered' or gentrified into a pipe. Models of sobriety, pressing the flesh and upwardly mobile, Bob and Vera now toured the upper-crust social circuit with unerring facility. On duty, and with Vera on his arm, Bob appeared in full fig - black tie and immaculate suit, spinning out self-effacing anecdotes, Shaw and Shakespeare. At home, ever the Briton, he was the only man in Hollywood to do his own gardening. Standing proudly in his favourite outfit of faded blue trousers, flowered shirt, Indian buckskin sandals and sombrero, he weathered the derisive roars of laughter of his neighbour, James Mason.

Privacy however was not guaranteed; coaches, laden with star-struck tourists, had begun growling up the roads. "...And this is it, folks, this is Humphrey Bogart's home....". Vera and Bob were sunbathing naked on their lawn; the invasion of privacy was one thing, but saying it was Bogie's place was another. Outraged, Bob leapt up, "Here... bugger off with you!" he roared. A dozen cameras clicked as the towel he had pulled around himself slipped gracefully off....

Escape from Vera's ever-watchful eye and the tittle-tattling tongues came rarely. When it did, with Bob crashing in at parties and dressed in his beachcomber gardening rig, he always apologised with a grin, for dressing 'so formally'. In this same eccentric garb he was spotted downtown at the entrance of Grauman's Chinese Theatre, where impressions of film stars' feet were preserved on the sidewalks. Bob tried out Shirley Temple's footprints and John Barrymore's and was annoyed when he found his feet didn't fit. When he discovered that Red Skelton's feet coincided with his own he let out a yell that, the ever watching police protested, was loud even for Hollywood. "I fear I was just a bit tiddly..." Bob muttered in court.

Vera managed Bob's career aggressively. Looking to the future, she signed him up for a radio production, a less than cheery pre-Christmas reading of *Les Miserables*. "Lux presents 'Hollywood!'..." the radio roared, "Lever Brothers Company, the makers of Lux toilet soap, bring you The Lux Radio Theatre!" (Canned applause) "Greetings from Hollywood ladies and gentlemen... in many homes the holiday season is a time of reading aloud from some favourite classic..." The hour-long 'Radio Theatre' productions already had a huge following and now, reprising his film role alongside Debra Page and Ronald Coleman, Bob's unmistakable and rich voice was broadcast across America. It might not have been film but audiences for the popular radio shows were enormous, with forty or fifty million listeners regularly tuning in.

Radio 'acting', Bob found, was not easy and the trick lay in not sounding as though you were reading from an all too familiar script. Weirdly radio studio audiences had become a niche market for certain types of star groupies; lining up early in the morning, they would queue patiently for their free tickets to see their favourite stars. Radio producers were always glad to see these semi-professional audiences and knew that when the 'Laugh' and 'Applause' boards were held aloft they would obey enthusiastically.

Theatre was always the dream for Newton, and one to be snatched at any opportunity. The opportunity presented itself one evening in a downtown restaurant that occasionally put on stage shows. Bob and Vera were dining and were nervously approached by a man from an adjoining table, "I'm so sorry to bother you, Mr Newton...but I've written this play...and I was wondering if you could look through it, if you had a moment...". Bob took the script and glanced through it. "No time like the present!" he said, and walked up onto the stage. A silence fell as Bob, swaying slightly, started reading through all of the four characters dialogue. There were nervous giggles and laughter as he hesitated. Then Bob got the gist of the thing, grasped the concept of the characters faultlessly, and without faltering carried the whole thing through to the end. Applause and roar of approval from the crowd. Bob was back in his natural element.

Surreally a ghost from the past now walked back into his life. A single print of the 1940 film *Gaslight* had survived destruction; television stations were desperate to fill the hollow gaps between the commercials, and the film at last got its US release. Twelve years old and retitled *Angel Street* it was of course hopelessly antiquated and passed by almost unnoticed, lost in the sea of chaff. Only one critic picked up on Bob's brief appearance in the film and spat out a cruelly perceptive observation, '...as a token to the oldness of this picture, Robert Newton appears in a virtual 'bit', looking very youthful and determined. A lot has happened since it was made...'.

Happy with Bob's performance in *Les Miserables* the Fox studio bosses now came up with the second part of the two-film deal;

promising a tidy $50,000 purse, plus expenses. Struggling with debit and under pressure from Vera, Bob obediently signed.

In Britain the worst of the post-war austerity had ended; rationing had been slowly wound up and day-to-day life had returned to a new normality. By 1953 the paper shortage was over and the result was a flood of cheap books. Many of these were autobiographical, almost all spoke of the war which had become the heart of British identity. Cashing in on the nation's obsession with the moving image, these books quickly became films. Suddenly everybody wanted to talk about the war again; everybody had a fount of anecdotes, tales and sufferings to expiate, and the nation went through a protracted period of re-examination and re-affirmation.

If the films made during the war had been passionate ideological battles, most of those made in the early 'fifties were simply stories without sub-text, driven by greed and made purely for profit. Yet they were, for millions, a window into history. Ironically most of what people 'remembered' of the war was, and still is, created through the medium of film. Spiced up with the advances in colour stock and with dazzling special effects the old tales were sold it all over again. There were stories of the war at sea and on the land and in the air, stories of the home front. Some were tales of fantasy, some of idealism, some were brutal in their realism; most have endured and become the painted mirror in which we like to see ourselves. Now it was Bob's turn to dabble in the genre.

The Desert Rats was intended to be a loose follow-up to the financially successful yet critically condemned *Rommel: The Desert Fox*, released in 1951. Directed by Robert Wise and shot in black and white against a vast, and suitably dusty, Californian back-lot that was decked out as the Libyan desert, the star of the new film was Richard Burton. Newton took a role under him, happily playing second fiddle (some critics saw it as third fiddle) alongside James Mason who was reprising his Rommel role. This was a no-frills production and in the familiar Hollywood style, filming got under way briskly and efficiently. Location shoots were done close to the luxury Palm Springs resort and wrapped in just three weeks. Studio work took just four. Bob was now 'dry', and the process was trouble free if, by the standards of the old days, somewhat subdued. 'Dry' was however a relative concept, especially for Bob, and Vera knew it. At home she may have had her husband on a short leash but she knew that in Burton she had met her match; now she found that it was best to occasionally turn a blind eye. Besides she had other things on her mind. An uncomfortable and searingly hot location shoot was no place for her; she was pregnant and expecting an autumn baby.

In what could have turned out to be just another routine 'all-male action film' Newton put out a magnificently understated and genuinely moving performance as a terrified and alcoholic ordinary soldier, struggling to survive the madness of war and the label of 'coward'. Playing 'Private Tom Bartlett', a former schoolmaster to his now superior officer (Richard Burton) the film centred around the evolving relationship between the two men, where Burton, still calling old master 'sir', cannot find the heart to discipline his drunken subordinate. "You might at least have got yourself a commission..." Burton pleads. "I'm the perfect private soldier..." Bob replies "no worries, no responsibilities... I can't even be demoted". Perhaps he was thinking back to his Navy days. Certainly he was behaving like it. All too easily, and despite the promises to Vera, he had been led back onto the path that strayed from righteousness.

Burton was at the forefront of sybaritic expeditions and the weekends in Palm Springs were a creditable revisitation of the good old days. Riot and pillage amongst the perfumed Latino beauties were de rigeur. Goofing as Yanks, a foray over the border into Mexico and a Tequila sodden night saw them both slammed up in a flyblown jail. They may have bluffed their way across the border as American citizens, but their booming celt accents had betrayed them on their return. It was just another grand lads adventure.

Desert Rats opened with a stirring narration by Michael Rennie and posters that screamed "Here are the guys who slugged their way from Tobruk to the sea!" Film goers, seeing Newton's name, might have rolled their eyes in dread. Screened hot on the heels of his wild-man appearance in *Blackbeard*, Newton's performance was however subtle and masterly, and once again confounded the expectation of both audiences and the critics and confirmed his outstanding calibre as a character actor. The public loved it, especially the British public and the *Sunday Express* praised its 'thrilling, documentary-style realism'. Ever grudging in its praise *Cinematograph* commented "...Newton has his moments as the alcoholic Bartlett, and the exchanges between him and Burton are frequently quite moving and give a human touch to the whole..." For Fox it was another gratifying commercial success, the film picking up an Oscar nomination for 'Best story and screenplay'.

Bob's career was back on track and his 'incorrect' past was, hopefully, left behind. He also seemed to have found happiness and the security of a wife and the society he needed so badly. In an interview with the trade papers he spoke grandly of a planned theatrical tour of America, taking Shakespeare's *Richard III* to the people, possibly with Charles Laughton directing.

Vera's pregnancy had been problem free and October saw the birth of a healthy baby, a boy they named Kim. Bob was delighted, Deborah Kerr was named as the godmother and celebrations were in order. A glitzy society party was thrown; this time the booze was for guests only. Bob sipped a glass of champagne, wrinkled his nose in mock disdain, and then dutifully stuck to root beer.

Tellingly, *The Desert Rats* was Newton's only film in 1953. Across the vastness of America, television had now taken over. It utterly dominated the public imagination and, indicating what was to be a decisive career change, Bob appeared on the small screen five times in the year, including a prestigious Christmas Day prime-time slot. Like the head-shakers who had yesterday condemned actors who had deserted the stage for film work, some saw defection to television as an act of treachery, a professional low and a threat to cinema.

Television industry financing had spawned a new sub-genre, the 'soap opera'. Adopting the conventions of the realist novel, the 'soaps' served to fill the gaps between the advertisements. Aimed at a vast and entertainment-hungry population, that included a daytime audience of bored-to-death housewives, the small screen ran on the back of advertising and corporate sponsorship. Studio bound and with poor production values, the programmes were quick and cheap to produce and yet commanded a vast following. March 16th saw

Bob's small screen début; appearing in front of millions on the NBC channel in an episode of the 'Hollywood Opening Night' programme entitled *Mr Barker's Love Affair*. Before a tiny studio audience Bob played out a study in obsession, a fanatical stamp collector who, owning one rarity, is prepared to go to any lengths to possess the only other example known to exist.

Just under a month later, on April 19th, he popped up on the screen again, now on the ABC channel and in a 'Plymouth Playhouse' episode entitled *Mr Glencannon Takes All*. ABC had lagged behind its CBS and NBC competitors, and had recently thrown a lot of dollars at its image, hiring in prestige names like Newton in an effort to raise their game and pull in the heavyweight sponsors for the '53-'54 season.

On April 30th, and with some trepidation, having witnessed James Mason hung out to dry in front of a live audience courtesy of a failed Teleprompter, Bob was back on NBC. He appeared in the Lux sponsored and long-running 'Video Theatre', episode 126, a yarn entitled *The Ascent of Alfred Fishkettle*. On March 11th he was on the radio with Ruth Hussy, in a thirty minute broadcast for the 'Family Theatre' and a reading of Kipling's *Namgay Doolah*. October 12th saw him on a one hour 'Lux Radio Theatre' quasi-documentary entitled *Breaking the Sound Barrier*.

The Benedict Canyon household was laden with enough boxes of Lux soaps to last for years.

October also saw a CBS television broadcast, the General Electric sponsored 'Theatre' where Bob starred as a wife-murdering brain surgeon, in an episode called *Confession*. On Christmas Day, 1953, *The Baker of Barnbury* was transmitted. Shot two years previously and now put out as a sponsor vehicle for Schlitz beer, the 'Schlitz Playhouse' production had Bob seated in a cosy fireside armchair narrating his own introduction. With a sly wink and piratical growl he went on to appear opposite Elsa Lanchester in a charming and sentimental romantic fairytale. Fuzzy and monochrome it was nevertheless a hit; it was safe, the kids loved it and it had all the right snowy, festive motifs to make it an enduring family favourite.

Bob was now appearing squeaky clean and apparently a reformed character. He had a couple of very respectable film successes and a flurry of TV appearances under his belt and the American trade press began to sing his praises. Simultaneously British producers started casting avaricious eyes at 'their' actor; Connie's was on the phone with an offer from Rank to do a remake of Maugham's *Vessel of Wrath*. News of Newton's possible return to the UK went public and George Minter, the producer of *Tom Brown's Schooldays*, was quick with a follow-up offer. In the run-up to Christmas the Hollywood trade press was ahead of the publicity game and reported Newton's next film, 'Langley-Minter Productions is seeking an actor to play Little Billie in *Svengali* which already has Robert Newton and Hildegarde Kneff in the roles of the mesmeriser and the lady who fell under his sway.'

Very much the industry insider, Vera had her finger on the pulse of the film business and she could see that despite the international successes, the days of the big studios and the big screen would soon be over. Bob had already successfully dipped his toe into the world of television; now she could see that the future of mass entertainment lay in that still evolving industry. Like Annie she was the driving force in the marriage, and more, she was a career woman with big ideas. She had managed to pull her wayward husband out of the gutter, carve out a Hollywood career for him and shield him from the pariah status that had attached itself to so many 'foreigners'; now she could see that she needed a way to take his career onto a new level.

Then a phone call brought an opportunity and she grabbed it with both hands. The call was from the 20th Century Fox studios, whose executives were once again kicking around the idea of Bob doing a reprise of his Treasure Island/Blackbeard character. There was nothing new in this, only the vague idea of shooting the film in Australia. Intuitively Vera understood that the 'Long John Silver' role belonged exclusively to Bob and that Fox couldn't shoot it with anyone else. That equated to leverage; leverage meant power and power was as good as money in the bank. She knew that she had the studio more or less in her hands and that they couldn't refuse a deal.

Thinking on her feet, the future suddenly became clear to Vera. She would sell Bob into the Fox offer and make the film, but then go on after it was finished, buy up the props, retain the cast and crew, cash in on Bob's hugely successful 'pirate' past and, riding on the wake of the new film's publicity, shoot a follow-up series of shorts, exclusively for television, and aimed at the children's market. The vital element of the plan was to take the whole thing into their own hands and form their own film production company.

It was a bold project and a big financial risk but with almost endless offers of American small-screen work forthcoming and two UK film deals promising enough cash to kick-start the project, Vera was convinced that not only was the idea viable but that there was a fortune to be made. Quickly Byron Haskin, who had recently directed *His Majesty O'Keeffe* with Burt Lancaster in Australia, was dragged into the house and talked on-board as potential director. Also roped in were Martin Racking, a 36 year-old screenwriter, who lived just up the road in Benedict Canyon, and Mark Evans, a producer. Joseph Kaufman, an industry insider and middleman popped up, showed enthusiastic support and was contracted in. Almost overnight, and with frightening speed, the project, just like Bob's Shilling Theatre venture, developed from a concept into a company.

The commencement of the *Svengali* project was planned for early February in Britain; Vera however saw that there was time for Bob to fit in another quick film job in the States. An intense study of twenty-two nerve-racked air passengers who fret, weep and scream their way across the Pacific in a claustrophobic and bucking cabin poised to crash into the sea, Ernest Mann's best-selling novel, *The High and the Mighty*, had created a new genre. A nightmare scenario for the growing generation of frequent fliers, the 'terror in the sky' disaster epic, was born. Now the book was to be turned into a film by John Wayne.

Under the auspices of his own film production company, 'Batjack', Wayne, one of Howard Hughes' RKO contract stars, chose as his director William 'Wild Bill' Wellman. An old friend from many of his previous cowboy films and a master of the action movie, Wellman's career had peaked in directing James Cagney in the 1931 gangster picture *Public Enemy*. Battling through a messy divorce, the Duke had thrown himself feverishly into his work. Utterly lacking any sense of his own stardom and fixated only on his career, he had reluctantly taken the starring role in the work only after it had been turned down by both Spencer Tracy (vanity) and Humphrey Bogart (greed). Amongst a strong supporting cast of popular film faces portraying the now familiar lexicon of characters, including the ubiquitous pregnant woman/frightened child set, Newton took the role of passenger, Gustav Pardee, a haunted theatrical producer, who, like Bartlett in *The Desert Rats*, struggles through his own personality problems to find courage.

At the airport in Hawaii, Bob's character stamps up to the ticket desk; "I'm Gustav Pardee, I'm 47 and I was born in New York city..." His almost pretty wife, somewhat beaten, follows him; "I'm 30...". She clatters off to follow Pardee. "He looks like a tired walrus on a rock...!" the stewardess sighs to her colleague. "And she looks like she's done all right for a slender red-head...!" he replies. Somehow it was all rather cruelly true.

The High and the Mighty was ahead of its time and it was to spawn a vast new outlet for the entertainment industry. Somehow the work seemed to encapsulate and sum up the new decade. Wealthy America had shaken off the vexed memory of war and now squarely looked to a golden, man-made, ailment-free future. Prosperity and progress were the watch-words and within the acting profession 'progress' equated to Stanislavsky's new 'Method' acting.

Method ruled; Marlon Brando, James Dean, Montgomery Clift and Marilyn Monroe were all 'method' actors. Suddenly it was 'No Method, No work'. For the British contingent this was all rather upsetting; like typical 'foreigners' the yanks were cheated even in their acting, they were practising beforehand. Bob, like all the Brits', found himself out of step, an anachronism treading water in an era of self-conscious artificiality where actors willingly and routinely underwent ethical and cosmetic surgery.

The studio were now run as hard-nosed business. On set conformity was the watchword, and conformity meant lunch-breaks spent in the studio commissary, talking shop, talking 'method' and drinking milk.

This was not for the British. For them it was a mass exodus, slipping out of the studio gates and past the disapproving frowns of the security goons to The Retake Room, a rather shabby diner nearby. Lunch meant civilised aperitifs; "There was never an American actor in The Retake Room" Trevor Howard remarked, "just the Brits. And they gave the best performances...".

Shot in colour in the new mega-wide-screen Cinemascope process *The High and the Mighty* was premièred for the industry critics and took a trashing. 'Wayne's worst film ever' they howled. They were wrong, Wayne's next film was to be his worst ever, and *The High and the Mighty* was an instant hit. Over two hours long, with a thundering musical score by Dimitri Tiomkin, spitting with fire, tossing propellers and strewn with emotional wreckage, the plot built to a clammy-palmed peak of terror that kept audiences riveted to their seats. The film picked up a whole tranche of award nominations and set the world whistling its theme tune. Overnight the critics did their usual 'U' turn, broke into wild applause, and described it as a 'socko piece of screen entertainment'. The film took $7 million in the first year.

Packing a nice pay-cheque into the bank, Bob and Vera waved goodbye to their newborn baby, flew east and across the Atlantic, and on December 21st stepped out to an eagerly waiting British press. It was all very different from Newton's messy departure and the newspapers wanted their slice of the story. Under the guise of a new American, his return was emotional and touching down in the wet and chill was a nostalgic homecoming; a place dreamed of on those bland, still, perfumed California nights. It also meant a reunion with both his daughter and his father. Sybil Burton was at the airport to meet them, swept them away from the flashing press cameras and on to the Dorchester. Vera saw England for the first time and she shuddered in the chill. What she saw came as a shock. Still scarred by bomb sites, antiquated and monochrome drab after the Technicolor neon bright of California, London was shrouded in drizzle and the muddied memories of yesterday's war. For her it was an utterly alien land.

Before they had time to settle, however, crisis struck. A panicked phone-call from the States sent Vera dashing back across the

Atlantic. Baby Kim had been left in the care of Vera's mother in New York; in the early stages of schizophrenia she had been unable to cope, the baby had been neglected and had been rushed to hospital with pneumonia. Long fretful days passed before the baby was well enough to travel with Vera back to the UK.

Relishing the return of their deliciously scandalous 'bad boy', now complete with his new family, the papers reported Vera's reappearance in the country and tailed her to her hotel for the first 'family' interview. 'Yo-ho-ho Newton makes it no, no, no... Robert Newton, the rumbustious Long John Silver of the film *Treasure Island* came home to London last night - a reformed character. His friends would not have recognised the man they knew three years ago. Mr. Newton poured tea for his blonde, attractive wife Vera. Mr. Newton fed milk from a bottle to his eight-week-old son Kim. Mr. Newton refused a drink. Mr. Newton said he would have an early night. Family man Robert Newton is in England for the first time since 1951. He put a comb through his hair and said: "Must put on a tidy look, old boy. I'm not a wild character now, you know". He winked: "Not like the old days, eh?" Said Newton: "It was the full, rich life then. I caught the flavour of it when I was acting in New York in the 'twenties. I carried on the spirit of the 'twenties into the 'thirties and even the 'forties. Then, all of a sudden, when I went to America again, I realised it was time to pull in the reins. I was older. I had to settle down. I was a man of responsibilities. I married Vera and life became simple and easy. There was no need to fly around or racket about any more. Two years ago I stopped drinking. I gave it up - just like that – for Vera. I said to myself 'No more drink'. And I don't need it now." The Newton return was quiet and unflustered – unlike his departure for Hollywood in 1951 when he went off suddenly with baby Nicholas, a child of a previous marriage. Sybil Burton, wife of Richard Burton the actor, carried baby Kim into the hotel. Kim was sleeping. Upstairs Newton helped with the child's feed. Vera Newton watched her 48-year-old, thrice-married husband. "You look as if you were running for an election" she said. The Newton family will stay in England until May while father makes films... Said Mrs. Newton as I left – "*Was Bobbie so different before I married him?*" '

The story and the picture of Bob bottle-feeding baby Kim was just the sort of heart-warming stuff to win over the fans. The reality was less sanguine; the stuff in the bottle was undiluted evaporated milk; the results were immediate and disastrous.

Bob protested that he was a changed man, but decency and sobriety didn't sell newspapers and the press trawled up the hoary old past. "The subject must be worn out by now..." Newton protested; all the drinking had been just nerves, he argued, "that's why people start drinking in my profession, you find it necessary to calm yourself down. What happens is that you get the habit and it gets you. In my case it was wearing me out. I was feeling really ill. I had to give it up or give up acting".

Pouring the bemused reporter the biggest gin he had ever seen, Bob dismissed the suggestion that he had been rescued by Alcoholics Anonymous. "No, no, Old Boy, they never helped me. They do fine work I know, but they couldn't save me. My wife is the one to credit..." Slapped on the back, with his hand almost wrung off, the reporter was sent spinning out into the night. The following days showed that the charm offensive had worked and the papers were off Bob's back... "Too much has been written about Newton's neurotic ways and too little about his superb artistry on stage and screen...". Perhaps the press had younger prey to track, or perhaps, under Vera's guidance, 'stardom' was, at last, coming Newton's way.

Despite technical innovations that had seen the death of the old 1.33:1 ratio and the introduction of panoramic screens, the fifties saw the decline in cinema audiences accelerate. In 1954 twenty four and a half million went to the pictures each week. By the end of the decade that number was to collapse to ten million. Numbers were falling, overheads for cinemas were rising, and the equation made depressing reading. Inevitably, cinemas shut down.

In 1946 there had been a record 4,709 cinemas in operation. By 1960 only three thousand remained. No more was the cry 'Queuing in all parts!' heard. The biggest cinemas were hardest hit and the vast 1930s' three thousand seaters became uneconomic to operate. Of course everybody pointed the finger at television and the figures spoke for themselves. As cinema declined the number of TV licences rocketed; from one and a half million to ten and a half in nine years. 1953, the Coronation year, saw the biggest jump in television ownership; it seemed that a television set was the new status symbol. Gone was the wartime spirit where everyone would crowd into a neighbour's sitting room; closed doors and regal isolation was now the fashion.

The rise in television ownership was a decisive factor in the decline of cinema, but there was no ignoring the fact that the majority of big-screen films turned out in Britain in the mid fifties were simply dull. Retrenching into caution, it was to West End theatrical successes, novels and earlier film subjects that producers looked for safe ideas. Nostalgia was ever the easy place to hide. Minter's *Svengali*, very much of the classic ilk, was clambering only slowly through a tortuous planning process; Vera could see that time was of the essence and the order of filming was reversed. Bob found himself pitched back into the old familiar territory of Pinewood studios and the shooting of *The Vessel of Wrath* take two, *The Beachcomber*.

Directed by Muriel Box, Newton now took the central role of the deliciously drunken and disreputable 'Honourable Ted', working opposite Donald Sinden, who took the dull, alter-ego, 'controller' role. Glynis Johns was taking the 'glam' role. Again, it had been decided early in the planning process that the budget would not stretch to shooting abroad, so doubles were employed in Ceylon for distance shots. Then doubles for the doubles were employed at Pinewood. Only too late in the process did someone notice that Technicolor was being used for the studio scenes and Eastman for location work...

In what seemed a self-portrait, Newton's role said as much about himself and his own life as his characters; tongue in cheek, perhaps he meant to be whimsically autobiographical. Shot in colour, the new production was more light-hearted than the Laughton version, yet the daily rushes had a stagey feel, and Glynis Johns came across as annoyingly prim and Sunday-Schoolish.

Work began well, early rehearsals were satisfyingly efficient and most scenes went in the can in just one or two takes; then, within a week, Bob went to pieces. Worried about his marriage he hit the bottle. By lunchtimes he was effectively useless and Box had to rearrange the shooting schedule around him.

On January 14th however, busy on set, ostensibly sober, and with Vera at his shoulder, Bob gave a remarkably telling interview to *Cinematograph Weekly*; 'Television offers vast market for films' the report headlined. 'A firm belief in the vast potentials of making films for television aimed at a world market, is behind the decision of actor Robert Newton to go to Australia later this year to make a series of twenty six TV pictures. He told Kine Studio Correspondent Graham Clarke that it was already a flourishing occupation in Hollywood and he was confident it would soon become the same here... while he was in America waiting to make *Androcles and the Lion* and two other films, Bob Newton gained a good deal of experience in acting on TV. Now he has formed a company – Treasure Island, Inc...".

Operating out of a smart town-house in Thurrock Square, South Kensington, Bob spent his off-duty hours joyously catching up with London life and gently chauffeuring Vera through a censored recap' of the theatres and bars of his past. Very much a fish out of water, Vera was tentatively introduced to his old world, his old friends and girlfriends and came face to face with her husband's hoary history. Sally was cautiously introduced and thankfully the two women established an immediate empathy.

Things seemed to be going well; there were two lucrative film deals in hand and the Australian project was coming together. Yet Bob was like his old pirate alter ego; he was a man with one leg and a foot in two camps. Helplessly he retreated back into his old ways and his old life. He started to come home late, and with liquor on his breath and the nights ended with rows and recriminations. The old pattern of emotional break-up was being played out, both at home and on stage.

Bowing to a celebrity-obsessed press, Bob gave an interview to *Illustrated* magazine. The piece was run in February complete with a photograph of Bob at home and striking a dramatic pose alongside Vera and Sally. Despite Vera's efforts the story harked back to his more saleable image. 'Once he entertained fellow drunks in jail. "Now" says the woman who married him "Bob's learned sense". The man who plays *The Beachcomber* chooses home comfort now. Robert Newton – with the scrubby beard he wears for his part in a new film as Somerset Maugham's *The Beachcomber*. With his fourth wife and Sally, his daughter by a previous marriage, he studies the script of a new film... For the last three weeks Robert Newton has been wandering around a fake tropical island on a draughty film set at Pinewood Studios, acting the part of a drunk. Unshaven, and dressed in a grimy singlet, shorts and battered straw hat, he has spent his days, brawling and bellowing to the order of Muriel Box, who is directing him... Newton is a 'natural' for the role. He is playing the Honourable Ted, a scavenger who gives up the bottle and the wild life for love of a missionary's attractive sister... But a large wink, in the final fade-out, signifies that he does not regret his raucous nights and the hours he spent in the local lock-up. The 'once-bibulous Newton', as he has described himself, is enjoying the performance. The Honourable Ted's brushes with authority and rude gestures at convention have something in common with his, now discarded, attitude. The final salvation and the decision to give up the bottle parallel the latest stage in his own career, which has stretched across twenty-eight years of acting in the West End, on Broadway and in the film studios. Newton admits that his strict teetotalism, dating from June, 1952, came about because of a woman's belief in him. He says this without smugness. He dates the 'new Newton' of whom he is very proud, from the day he met a blonde, twenty-eight year old Hollywood publicist. She agreed to marry him if he gave up the drink...'

And perhaps, as he shook hands, the interviewer saw him give that leering wink again; the nice words were just a blind. Bob had not changed, couldn't change; the only difference was that now he had to drink in secret. Newton knew that Vera was as good as her word; the honeymoon period was over and that the penalty for recidivism was not just loss of wages, but loss of wife and child. '... since he married Vera Budnik, Newton has had one drink' the papers chirped 'a glass of champagne when Kim was born. He didn't like it. Is the new Newton here to stay? This, Mrs. Newton answers with a short 'Why not?' Then she adds 'Bob's learned sense at last....'

Bob may have learned some sense but it was never going to be a lesson he liked. Nagged by Vera, harangued by the medics, spied on by studio bosses, he struggled through. Yet, day by day, he put on a masterly act of the sober and decent 'family man'. He gave the image his best shot, but somehow it all seemed to lack meaning. His appearance on his return to Pinewood may have been the picture of moral rectitude but back in his old haunts things had changed rapidly. Muriel Box saw the change first hand; "Newton had cried off alcohol in Hollywood, but was so worried with domestic problems on arriving in England, that one week into shooting he hit the bottle hard and continued punishing it to the end of the picture. With the greatest difficulty we kept him sober until lunchtimes each day, after which he was nearly always useless, the shooting schedule having to be re-arranged..."

Donald Sinden saw a similar story "....Newton should have been perfect for the part – he was a born beachcomber. It is no secret that he was a very heavy drinker, and recently, but not for the first time, he had been warned, by his doctors, that if he did not stop he would more than likely pop off in the very near future. When we began 'Beachcomber' he had been on the wagon for three months, and a sorry sight he was; gone were the thrown-back head and the fiery eyes; the jerky gestures made by his arms were now limp and seemed to lack purpose. It was tragic to realise that he had now reached a stage when he relied so totally on alcohol to inject spirit into his performance. He was listless and just moped around the studio, hardly talking to anyone. He knew he was not giving his best and this worried him. Every morning we greeted each other in the make-up room, where he stripped himself down to a pair of none too clean shorts-style baggy underpants, sat down, leaned back against the head-rest and stared with his large bloodshot eyes at the ceiling. Occasionally a low moan escaped his lips. He confided to me that he was not happy with certain elements connected with the film; things were not altogether successful in his private life; he was toying with an idea of doing Shakespeare's *Richard III* in Australia, but generally his career was not going as well as he could wish. Early one morning I was seated silently in my make-up chair when suddenly the door crashed open - what the Hell? - there stood Newton, absolutely plastered, his eyes blazing. He staggered across the room, thrust his face into mine, and with slobbering lips and flashing eyes, he embarked on the most thrilling rendering I have ever heard of "Now is the Winter of our discontent made glorious Summer..." What a Richard III he would have been! From that moment he really took off in the film, but sadly there were only a few days to go...". For Bob the old temptation had been too much. He had slipped back into the good old, bad old days and he was loving every second of it.

Newton viewed the studio preview of the finished work and quickly saw the results of Rank's, understandable, budget penny-pinching. The horrible mismatching of shooting styles and values was a disaster. Released and thrown out to the public the critics however applauded politely and the people queued up in the rain, paid their half crown and wallowed in the easygoing fantasy. Of course the film was judged against the Laughton original and, like the remake of *Les Miserables*, was found wanting. Rightly the critics judged the new work 'lethargic' and lacking the original's rich humour; Glynis Johns was damned as pious instead of sexy and Bob as simply running on half steam.

In early March Newton had moved on to George Minter's *Svengali*. It was a production that he relished and one he knew had the makings of a classic. It was also a chance to render a powerful new characterisation, one he had already 'found' and honed into something between the angelic Dr Arnold and Bill Sykes at his worst.

Despite his new, sober, public image, industry insiders weren't convinced. Whispers of Bob's secret binges and his behaviour on the *Beachcomber* set had circulated quickly. Once again he found himself under strict scrutiny and the film was only underwritten for insurance after a clause was added excluding any claim resulting from alcoholism on his part. Budgets were tight and despite protestations of sobriety, he was obliged to report to a Harley Street specialist for the standard medical examination. It didn't go too well. Turning up late he took two staggering steps into the consulting room, growled a beaming "Jim, lad...!" and collapsed, face-down on the carpet.

Svengali was a lavish colour production. A glitzy press reception was held at the Milroy club, and Bob was photographed posing with fellow stars Kneff and Terence Morgan. Shooting got under way and Bob walked on carefully made-up with streaming hair and long, horny fingernails. If he had been given the title role in this two-handed work, the focus nevertheless fell to the female lead, Hildegarde Kneff. Another 'new American', tall, willowy and hard with Germanic beauty, at twenty-nine she was set to be the new Garbo and already reeked of stardom. She had just emerged from her last film, *The Sinner*, and German cinema's first raunchy nude scenes. The work had sparked damnation from the Catholic Church, riots, a juicy court action and the publicity she now trailed in her wake was priceless. Barry Jackson would have loved it. Oversexed and over here, she walked onto the set with a blast of hot, raw lust. The meeting with Bob was fateful and Vera should have seen it coming. Once again in his cups, the old Bob was back in action and Pistol's cock was up. Tumbling into infatuation, it was 'Linden Travers' all over again.

With management huddling on the sidelines waiting for lightning to strike, the first week's shooting went well and there was an audible crackle of lecherous static from the stage. Off stage and in the dressing-rooms the sweaty tangle of desires continued. Bob may have been enamoured, but Kneff, despite her reputation, was having none of it. Quickly the sexual tension became unbearable and the studio became a hotbed of rumour, hissing rows and slammed doors. Then Kneff barricaded herself into her dressing-room and refused to come out. Bob, drunk and unused to being thwarted in his passion, prowled outside hurling abuse. Minter intervened and a kind of truce was arranged; Bob took his revenge, stuffing down handfuls of raw onions before the shooting of close-ups.

Suddenly Vera could stand no more. She had heard and seen enough, and stormed out of the studios and out of the country. Clutching her baby she flew back across the Atlantic. In a state of panic Bob hit the bottle even harder and went off the deep end. All the old devils of delirium closed in; he began arriving at the studio incoherent and production ground to a halt. Reports started coming in to Minter; Bob had been spotted staggering into bars and night-clubs dressed only in his pyjamas...

Quickly things got worse. Bob could not concentrate on his work and was on the phone to Vera for most of the day. But Vera would not listen to either his pleas of innocence or contrition. Then, in the middle of a scene, a heavy studio light fitting toppled and hit Bob, breaking a rib. The next day, in pain, badly hung-over and fretting about his marriage, he was unable to function.

Then the inevitable happened. Monday morning came and Bob failed to turn up on set.

Panic struck the studio. Kneff was on loan from Fox and the contract cut-off date was already close. Then news come through that Bob had boarded a plane and was heading back across the Atlantic in pursuit of Vera. Minter's team made frantic phone calls and a private detective waited at the airport in New York with unequivocal instructions to intercept Bob and wrestle him onto the next flight back. Somehow Bob slipped through the net. At eight the next morning he was in downtown New York, and turned up bedraggled and bleary, at a friend's house. There he spilled out the whole story; the friend begged him to return to the UK and finish the film, warning that he would certainly be sued. "I can't go back...I just can't!" moaned Bob. Within hours he was on a cross-country flight to LA.

In the studios the news was received with disbelief. Lightning had struck.

10. Days Under The Anxious Sunlight

Newton's departure from Britain smacked horribly of his last. Once again his life was in turmoil; studio, press, wife, all tangled in litigation and crashing down on his back. And this time there was a new factor, one that was affecting every member of the acting profession, the Inland Revenue; the Taxman had at last caught up with him.

Driving through the monumental structure that would become the Welfare State, the post-war Labour government had laid the burden of taxation, naturally, on the rich. Alec Guinness had been hit hard with the new 'super tax' a few years previously. Always a meticulous bookkeeper, he had weathered the storm, if with bad grace. Newton, utterly frivolous with his wealth and having no concept of 'saving', knew he had no chance of paying what was in effect a lifetime's tax bill. A public examination in London had estimated that he owed £46,300. Coming back to the UK had been a calculated risk, one that Vera understood, but neither of them had expected the pen-pushers to be so quick off the mark.

Bob's relationship with his co-star on the *Svengali* set had been fiery and problematical but, despite the rumours, his sudden exit from the country was less about sex and more about financial survival. Whispers had been circulating about his gambling debts nearing a thousand pounds, a habit he had picked up from Natalie. His relationship with Vera might have weathered the unconventional politics of studio life but the disgrace of financial ruin was, for her, unconscionable.

Within a hair's-breadth of a court summons and with his lawyers desperately filing for bankruptcy, escape from the chaos lay, of course, in drink; it was a brief period of deceiving oblivion before the hung-over reality of a flurry of reporters in Benedict Canyon. "I'm not a bit disturbed..." Bob said, brushing off the shouted questions about his relationship with the British tax office. Of course he was misquoted and the pressmen gloried in the downfall. "...And what about 'Svengali?" they demanded. But they already knew more than Bob himself and delighted in telling him. "How do you feel about the court action against you... do you plan to return to England...?".

In London the next morning's headlines read: 'Newton's tax bill: "Not a bit disturbed"' and the fat was thrown onto the fire. Newton shook his head. Belatedly he had come to realise that the press now sought only to polarise opinion; in their simplistic 'readers' world' things needed to be all good or all bad; that was what sold papers. The British media ran with the story, the *Sunday Express*, making mileage out of the inherent middle-class resentment of taxation, carried the headline: "Why let these stars get away with it?". Inevitably questions were asked in the House of Commons. It amounted to a public relations disaster and Vera watched helplessly as Bob's new, and carefully engineered, image was shot to shards.

Slowly press interest died away and Bob set about the job of putting his home life back on an even keel. The reconciliation was fraught and tearful, but, as Vera found, irresistible. Newton's stay in California was however little more than a stopover. The Fox deal was still on track; worries about the *Svengali* debacle and the tax situation were put on the back burner and Bob was dispatched to Australia.

Independent film production companies were not a new phenomenon. From the silent days right up to the 'forties, the small outfits had turned out 20% of cinema production, and some of the most commercially successful films. The post-war years were witnessing a powerful emergence of what were termed 'semi-independents'. Bogart was among the first to set up his own production company and Wayne had followed close behind. Unable to fully underwrite their productions, actors looked to the major studios for finance. In return, the studios took a cut of the profits, if any, and a distribution fee. Most semi-independents, like Newton's new-born company, were run by actors, directors and other creative artists. By the mid-fifties, thanks in part to Burt Lancaster's successes, all the big Hollywood studios, keen to take advantage of favourable tax breaks, had a hand in numbers of such units.

Broiling under the relentless Australian sun and working under the ragged old 'Long John Silver' flag, the Fox plot saw Newton once again battling it out on the Spanish Main. Shooting in colour, as now demanded by the public, especially in America, Byron Haskin slipped seamlessly back into his old directing role.

Location shoots took place in Botany Bay, Garie Beach and the famous Jenolan Caves in the Blue Mountains and studio work at Sydney's booming Pagewood Studios. Bob knew what he was doing was far from art; the script was a shameless rip-off of Disney's already ripped-off plot and his character had been bowdlerised of Machiavellian evil and transformed into a merely mischievous, child-like rogue. With a shrug, he tied up his leg and went through the motions.

Setlocked in Porto Bello's 'Cask and Anchor Inn', he played the unwilling paramour to the plump and motherly 'Miss Purity Pinker' (Connie Gilchrist) and the adventure joggled along easily enough. Bobby Driscoll was way past his sell-by date and his acting career, like that of so many child stars, was effectively over. "I was carried on a satin cushion and then dropped into the garbage can." he said. He was replaced by Kit Taylor, the son of Australian actor Grant Taylor, now one of Bob's standard 'pirates', and the formulaic, family-safe structure was complete. The standard bad-guy appearance came in the form of a back-from-the-dead Israel Hands, humour via 'Long John's' perpetual flight from matrimonial bondage and contemporary screen glamour in the form of Tab Hunter, an emerging American teen-idol. Playing his role almost restrained, Bob called up his Cornish past and with an incessant supply of 'Arrs', beguiling leers and some solid nautical dialogue, turned out a performance that defined the now regulation 'pirate' lexicon.

Filled with paranoia and aware that Vera was watching closely, Bob put on the façade of best behaviour and the film went quickly in the can.

Way ahead of the media marketing game, capital was made of the fact that this was Fox's first film shot entirely in Australia and a documentary style advertising trailer was patched together. Opening very much like *The Baker of Barnbury*, Bob, seated in a plush library and reading from a copy of 'Treasure Island', related how the sequel came about. With media clips of cast and crew arriving in Sydney to a rapturous welcome from the local royalty, Bob, occasionally lapsing into a piratical growl, went on to document the logistics of the shoot.

Effectively publicised, the film was released in the US in January and was, of course, a hit. Young people crushed into the cinemas and lapped it up, but anyone looking to see a continuation of the magic that Disney had accidentally created between 'Long John' and 'Jim Hawkins' were to be disappointed. Working from a script that, by commercial necessity, allowed little of the quality of the original, and targeting an audience of TV-dinner kids, the film was carefully crafted to circumvent the ever watchful eyes of parents and censors. There was no trace of the old snarling 'cut-and rip', no pistol shots to the face, no knives joyously 'buried up to the hilt'. Learning from a PG rating belatedly slapped on the Disney original, Newton's 'Silver' was dumbed-down into little more than an overgrown Tom Sawyer. Some critics however were kind and smiled benignly; *Variety* generously and archly said, "The title part proves a natural for Robert Newton and his fruity performance is one of the picture's main entertainment elements..." but the *New York Times* blasted the film: "Mr. Newton is outrageously hammy, to the point of freakishness, with his squinting and popping of his eyeballs and growling in a bastard Irish brogue...."

Fan mail, a fat fee and good reviews were a high note in a year that for Newton had started full of promise but now seemed to be tripping from one disaster to the next. September 24th (1954) brought disastrous news from London. Already the British press was trumpeting the story from the rooftops; Newton was officially declared bankrupt in his absence at the London Bankruptcy Buildings. Taken aback, the Inland Revenue bayed for its £46,300 and Newton's lawyers, playing for time, had made the most of the tangled cat's-cradle of their client's finances. 'Delay in preparing a statement of Affairs...' the headlines read. 'Mr F B Guedella, Mr Newton's solicitor, said that in the last three years Mr Newton had worked in three continents, which made the preparation of a statement more difficult than usual. It had needed the assistance of Australian and American attorneys, helped by his English advisers. That had caused some delay, Mr Guedella said, but he had been assured that the necessary work was in hand...'.

Bob was on the run and the men of the Inland Revenue wrung their hands impotently and waited; the case became deadlocked and was adjourned pending further revelations and/or his unlikely return to the UK. Once again Newton's career looked to be unravelling and his relationship with Vera crumbling. Beleaguered with worries, he escaped into the bottle. If running an independent film company guaranteed autonomy, it also demanded self discipline, and that was something Bob had little of. He hit the town, hit the bars, and painted Sydney red. Battling to keep a positive gloss on their star, Fox's PR staff, despite the frequent run-ins with the law, somehow managed to keep his name out of the papers.

Simplistically, Newton thought that taking refuge in Australia would buffer him from the realities of his past and that he could hide behind bankruptcy. He was wrong. Mid-shoot, a suited official marched onto the set and slapped down a crisp document. The *Svengali* incident had caught up with him and he faced a vicious back-lash; two broadside lawsuits, one for $375,000, another for $325,000. Hildegarde Kneff, Minter's rent-by-the-week sex-star, had only a limited time-slot in the UK, and the producers wailed that Bob's disappearance had spelled financial disaster. It seemed to Bob a bit like the *I, Claudius*, shoot all over again.

Minter and his frazzled production team had had no choice but to hire in another actor to pick up Newton's part and try to salvage something from the disaster. In the end Donald Wolfit, the old carthorse of touring theatre, a player that Bob had contracted onto his Shilling Theatre stage, had picked up the poison chalice. With dubious legality, and some long shots looking decidedly like Bob, the film had been released, damned with faint praise and had quietly foundered.

Despite a spate of contradictory letters from Newton's lawyers, conflating his tribulations and further muddying the murky waters, the English courts had judged Newton in his absence. Deemed to have deserted the *Svengali* set in clear contravention of his contract, a writ had been issued for the full sum of almost three quarters of a million dollars. The British newspapers, still wringing blood out of the tax incident, and delighted to have the old bad-boy Newton back, joyously ran the story to a public grumpily back at work after the Christmas holidays. January 24th 1956: 'Effort to stay action fails; Film actor to pay costs. Robert Guy Newton, the film actor, who was adjudicated bankrupt in September 1954, applied to Mr Justice Danckwerts in the Chancery Division yesterday for an Order restraining Alderdale Films Ltd, and Mr James George Minter, and Mr Leonard Jefferson-Hope, its two directors, from further prosecuting an action against him in California for breach of contract. He also asked for an Order that they procure the stay of an action against him by Renown Pictures of America Inc for breach of contract, which was due to be heard in California. Mr Muir Hunter, for Mr Newton, said he was at present living and working in California. In March 1954 he was employed in the English studios of Alderdale Films, who were associated with Renown Pictures of America Inc, a New York company, to act with Hildegarde Heff (*sic*) in "Trilby and Svengali". It was alleged that he broke his contract by leaving the studios in the middle of the production and not returning. The two actions against him, which were for $325,000 and $375,000, were set down for hearing on February 9th. Giving judgement, Mr Justice Danckwerts said that Mr Newton contracted with the American company to appear in a film to be made in this country and his services were made available to Alderdale Films, the English company. So far as the American company as concerned, his application was quite hopeless, because neither the English company nor its directors had any control over the American corporation. The Court was powerless to give relief against them. The Judge said the bankruptcy was not a very satisfactory one. Mr Newton left the country when the bankruptcy petition was pending and he had remained away ever since. His solicitors had done all they could but they had not received the kind of co-operation which was required from Mr Newton to enable the official receiver to ascertain his assets and indebtedness. Mr Newton's council had suggested that he should give an undertaking to supply all the information required but, said the Judge, there was no evidence that one could rely on Mr Newton to put into effect any undertaking which might be given on his behalf. On the other hand the respondents were prepared to give an undertaking that if they recovered assets in their action in California they would account for them in the bankruptcy. The Official Receiver had been put in a difficult position as regards the recovery of assets in America for distribution fairly among creditors. To allow the action to proceed on the respondents giving their undertaking would inure the benefit of the creditors as a whole. The application was entirely unrealistic and would be dismissed, and Mr Newton must pay the costs." A heady waft of American dollars led Hildegarde Kneff to also jump on the litigation bandwagon; 'I only agreed to do the film because I would have the opportunity to work with that actor of distinction, Robert Newton...' she wailed Germanically and slipped in her own bill for damages.

Absent from the UK and America, Bob was relatively, if temporarily, safe, but the court's ruling meant he could never go home. Bankruptcy was 'just money' but suddenly he had become an exile, and that hurt. With his reputation savaged by the press the financial success of his own *Treasure Island* television project now became even more important. Vera arrived in Australia, quickly took a dynamic hands-on approach and the shooting of the first of the 26 half-hour episodes of *The Adventures of Long John Silver* commenced on March 1st.

Bankrolled by American businessman Louis Wolfson to the sum of $450,000, and with their film production company, 'Isla de Oro Productions' (Golden Island) registered in the slippery tax haven of Panama, expectations ran high. The success of the project rested on a fundamental expectation of rock-bottom production costs boosted by a strong US dollar. By recycling the Fox sets, the floating barge-galleon, costumes and props, and by using the same basic set-up in every episode, it was hoped to bring the project in at half Hollywood cost.

At home, the Fox's *Long John Silver* feature film was doing good business. Vera made the decision to grab the easy money, ride on the back of the Fox publicity machine, and string together the first three half-hour episodes into what would be marketed as a full-length feature film, *Under the Black Flag*. "The idea to make a film about the subsequent life of Silver was Newton's..." a smiling Joe Kaufmann said in a press interview, "...with his imagination and individuality he was a very stimulating presence on the set...." "I like to do that sort of thing now and then...." Bob said, "It's the stuff for kids of every age...." Indeed; even in England sixty eight percent of children dragged their parents from their couches and went to the cinema once a week or more. Like Disney, Bob had realised that there was a fortune to be made out of pocket-money.

With canny perception and despite the issues of cost and technical difficulties, Vera had insisted, early in the planning stage, on shooting in colour. Working with the same jaunty pirate crew, complete with Kit Taylor carrying on the 'Jim Hawkins' role, flawless weather made the daily location shoots a joy. Bob found his spirit and with Vera on the set and keeping him up to the mark, a glint of gold, at last, showed on the horizon. Then the bad news hit. Kaufmann's promised finance package from Louis Wolfson and his cabal of dollar sharpshooters had failed to materialise. A notorious wrecker, Wolfson's name was, apparently, infamous within the industry. $450,000 down, Vera tried desperately to find new backers. Budgets were slashed and under the watchful eye of Haskin and veteran American director Lee Sholem, the feature-film footage was shot, quickly cobbled together and released. "Enjoyably noisy..." *Variety* commended. Noting Newton's "colossal gusto" it went on, "...his buccaneer gang overact to the point of burlesque... it's a wonder there was a set left standing after Newton and his merry band of homogenised buccaneers got done on chewing the scenery".

With time ticking away and money desperately short, work continued with a renewed sense of urgency. Under sharp scrutiny Bob did his best, hoping that some kind of profit could be raked out. The trouble was that he was tired to death with the whole 'pirate' thing, and living up to the motto that dictates that all work and no play makes Bob a dull boy, hit the bottle again. Noel Coward, even within the remit of his brief screen career, fully understood why actors got so bored; "I find it terribly tedious making movies. For one reason only – the rest of it I understand very much, but the tedious thing is that you play a scene for the first time and the entire staff – congratulations! So then you do it another time for the sound, and then you do it because the lighting hasn't been quite right, or something's gone wrong, and by the time you get the actual take, they're all going about yawning and looking away and wishing they weren't there..." Bob had been in the trade for years and he was simply bloody bored. Despite Vera's efforts he once again became a familiar and celebrated sight in Sydney's clubs, bars and dives. Often drunk, frequently disorderly, but inevitably irresistible, he collected fines and friends equitably. Like the Honourable Ted, never a business man and always trusting, he concentrated on his pleasure and left the shouting to Haskin, nagging to Vera, and the dollars to Kaufmann. "He'd get drunk" Haskin laughed, "roaring around town in a car all night, how the Hell he didn't kill himself or fifty people, I don't know..."

Vera knew she was powerless and tried to turn a blind eye but Bob's renewed foray into leisure and pleasure started to affect his work, and that affected production. Shooting on a non-existent budget, there was neither time nor money to waste, but that didn't stop Bob. It was like the old Falmouth *Treasure Island* days all over again. "Newton... got to where I couldn't shoot a whole line in one take," Haskin groaned, "I'd have to break a line two or three times, and get sometimes only a word before he'd fall off the stool, he was so stiff..."

Somehow work struggled on, each individual episode a splice work of relatively sober snatches. At the outset each shoot was calculated to eat up a minimum of $75,000; now the budget was slashed and the last dozen episodes were turned out on a desperate shoestring and as little as $11,000 or $12,000. The debts mounted and with little good will left on the set, it was all going horribly wrong. "Going to Australia... was disastrous financially," Haskin said, "None of the terms of what I was to get out there were fulfilled. The terms of our participation deal were a laugh. All my efforts to get an eighteen month exemption from Internal Revenue for being in foreign residence were also a laugh, because there was nothing to be exempt from. A real disaster. I got paid a bit, but left there completely dead broke. All the extra payments I was to get for this, my living expenses, and this, that, and the other were all welshed out somehow, including a set fee for each week that they all got except me, and I don't know why..."

Dragged through post-production, each episode was prefixed by a stirring and iconic intro and a solid piratical title, '*Ship o' the Dead*', '*Sword of Vengeance*', '*Tale of a Tooth*', '*South Sea Pirates*', '*The Temple of Evil*' etc. The appeal to young people was obvious and instant, and a financial success story seemed in the bag. Bob's relationship with Vera, however, was foundering. The happy times were over and promises of good behaviour that were impossible to keep were shown to be mere palliatives. Struggling to balance his drink dependency with a crumbling marriage that pivoted on his sobriety and nerves that were worn to rags, Bob staggered to the medics. There he was prescribed the American new wonder-cure of anti-depressants; the ubiquitous, mind-numbing 'Milltowns'. "All I ever wanted was the easy life..." Bob sighed. These were words that would come back to haunt Vera for the rest of her life.

Drowning in his own delirious beachcomber world, a letter from Algernon reminded Bob of a home and a time in his life he had almost forgotten.

In the valley of Lamorna the old days and the old ways had passed into history; the artists were gone and Betty Paynter, inheritor of an estate crippled by death-duties, had sold off much of the land. Harassed by a legion of bureaucrats and desperate to save some part of the property, she had submitted a scheme to open up the valley for development. She planned a massive clearing of trees, new roads, one hundred and twenty six houses, a shop and petrol station and a hundred site caravan park; in effect a whole new village. In a passionate petition written to the Times, the artists of old had gathered to fight the proposed devastation; 'More than sixty years ago artists settled at Lamorna; many famous men found inspiration there... We, the signatories, beg that the possible destruction of this unique and lovely valley should have your kind and earnest consideration...'.

After almost eighteen months in Australia, filming came to an end and Bob and Vera flew home to California with mixed feelings and a sense of urgency. En route there was a refuelling stop in Honolulu. As the plane was taking off, Bob was handed a telegram. It was from Sally in England; Natalie had died. The news was a blow but no surprise, Natalie's early death was a tragic inevitability. In London the *Evening Standard* reported the story on Saturday, March 19th and the unpalatable truth came out. An inquest had been flatly informed that Natalie had been taking drugs for the last ten years. A ruling of suicide seemed inevitable, yet, mercifully, an open verdict was recorded. 'Natalie Newton Death Riddle: Mrs. Natalie Hazel Cochrane Newton, 36-year-old former wife of the actor Robert Newton, died in a nursing home in Ballards Lane, Finchley last Sunday, it was revealed today. Mrs. Newton, who has been in the nursing home for some weeks, was buried at Paddington Cemetery, Mill Hill yesterday. At a Hendon inquest earlier this week the coroner (Dr A. E. L. Cogswell) returned an open verdict. The cause of death, it was stated, was acute barbiturate poisoning...'.

For Bob, there now arose the question of his son, Nicholas; for Vera, seeing her husband's name linked with a drug related death, it signalled yet another damage limitation operation to handle.

Once again 2707 Benedict Canyon Drive was besieged by the past and the press; "My heart goes out to her..." Bob said "It's hard to think she's dead, I'm terribly upset about her death. The drug taking I knew about, we all did, but I don't think many people know it was never Natalie's fault or through weakness of character that she did take drugs. She was in constant pain after she fell and broke her leg at the age of sixteen and was given drugs to relieve the pain. She couldn't move her right leg and continued to take drugs during this period..." The press however told a different story of a woman's lonely and bitter end '...Before she died she wept and talked about her husband and her five year old son...' The Home Office pathologist's report had described her death as due to 'an excess of a lethal dose of barbiturate capsules' and readers were left to draw their own, damning, conclusions. 'The Medical Superintendent of the home said that Mrs Newton was very, very difficult and uncooperative... drugs were prescribed for her but they were trying to cut them down...'

Still bleary eyed from the flight and with Vera at his shoulder, Bob quickly laid out his side of the story in a phone interview to the *Daily Mail* reporter in New York: 'Robert Newton, the British actor, told me today of the tragedy of his third wife Natalie Newton, who after taking drugs for many years, died last week in a London nursing home from an overdose of barbiturates. He returned last night from Australia with his American wife, Vera Budnik. Today he put in a Trans-Atlantic call to his sister, Mrs. Pauline Gates, in England, to try to work out plans for his motherless son, Nicholas, who is being cared for at a country house at East Knowles, Wiltshire by the family housekeeper. Newton's voice broke as he talked to me over the telephone. He said: "I will do everything I can for my boy. I'm sick of all the lies and distortions that have been spoken and printed about my not taking care of him and about him being in homes and some such rubbish. In the few hours I've been back I have communicated with my lawyer in London... to try to do everything for my son. Perhaps it would be best to bring him here. I don't know. He's been in good hands in England and it angers me to have stories that he's not been cared for."

Setting her face Vera also said the right words, "We're pretty exhausted after the long flight, but Bob and I are doing our very best in every way...". But she knew trouble loomed and that once again Bob's hoary past would creep into their lives.

When Nicholas had been reluctantly returned to England in 1951, Natalie had been unable to cope with life, let alone a boisterous child and Sally had reluctantly stepped in. Struggling to forge a stage and film career, she had soon found the task too arduous and had fostered the boy out. Now, with a grim relish the press followed up the phone interview with a dilemma. "I hope to bring him up" the piece headlined. 'In Wiltshire Mr. Newton's four year old son Nicholas went for a walk in East Knowles yesterday with his foster-mother Mrs. Janet Bricknell. Mrs. Bricknell said "I hope he will not be told of his mother's death. I have been in touch with solicitors about his future and they have told me he will be provided for. I hope to keep Nicholas and bring him up". Another ghost from Bob's past, Janet Bricknell, who was part Romany, was the housekeeper for David Tennant's country estate. Cook, nanny and moral crutch she was a reassuring, feet-on-the-ground, motherly contrast to the hedonistic life within the Gargoyle club. A sturdy, no nonsense country woman with a young son of her own, she seemed the ideal guardian for Nicholas.

With the press camped almost permanently outside, the Benedict Canyon house, supposed to trumpet Bob's career successes, now became a stockade, a refuge where curtains twitched and eyes looked for figures at the gate. Shaken by the repercussions of the Svengali fiasco, bankruptcy, and the income tax affair, Newton now appeared to be facing a costly and stressful legal wrangle over the future of his son. Worse, he had been diagnosed with a heart condition. Officially off the booze, life now meant the 'Hollywood Diet': Valium, Nembutal, Seconal, amphetamines and tranquillizers, the usual crazy cocktail of cure-all pills. Racked with asthmatic problems resulting from his time in the Navy and a lifetime of heavy smoking and with liver damaged by a lethal regime of alcohol consumption, his life suddenly hung in the balance. With a startling frankness his doctor warned him that another drinking binge could be fatal.

Battling with addiction, and despite Vera's best efforts, Bob's life swung between obedient abstinence and sudden blinding excess. Without warning, weeks of restraint and recovery would be blown on a weekend of debauchery. Monumental hangovers were choreographed by the usual blazing rows, then the tears, the promises and the regrets. And the cycle would resume. Friends saw the crisis approaching and tried to wean Bob off the liquor, but for him, the draw was always irresistible. Still, even now, it was 'Helter-skelter, hang sorrow... and a louse for the hangman'.

Domestic life, once so close to happy, was now foundering and the circle of sycophants and fair-weather friends drifted away. Bob's drunken escapades, once part of the baroque fabric of Hollywood social life, once so amusing, now smacked of Catholic immorality and gilt-edged parties and industry events passed the Newtons by.

Dulled by guilt and an increasingly heavy regime of medication, Bob found that work was drying up. The word was out: he was 'unreliable'. Within a boom and bust industry where films were now shot for New York pen-pushers with a budget of millions and an accountants eye on every cent, there was no time for mavericks.

Old friends stood by and gave what support they could, rebutting the worst accusations of the gutter press and the fresh minted gibe where 'Drunk as a newt' became twisted to '.. as a Newton'. "Newton is a genius..." demanded actress Margaret Leighton, another player who had deserted the British stage for the allure of Hollywood, "he is just going through a bad patch... the fact that he has the misfortune to be an alcoholic is not a joke, it's a tragedy." The bad patch was the collapse of the pipe dream Richard III project and the loss of another promising play role. Ben Hecht, the 'Shakespeare of Hollywood', a prestigious writer and critic with screenplay credits going back to the silent era, had written a piece especially for Newton. A study of bohemian Greenwich Village poet Maxwell Bodenheim, it was a role that fitted Bob perfectly and Hecht had given Bob a free hand in its direction. With a cast rehearsed and the production ready to be premièred at the Laguna Theatre in southern California, calamity struck; out on a bender and drunk at the wheel of his Cadillac, Bob had passed out and crashed the car through a plate-glass shop-front in Hollywood's main street. The press had raced to the scene and flashing cameras had captured the moment. In Hollywood, anything from rape to hit-and-run could be, and was, hushed up, if you knew the procedure, but this time it was too late. This time there was no-one to pay off the police and the story hit the papers. Drunk and slurring, Bob had been arrested and dragged into jail. With their 'star' languishing behind bars, the play's opening was postponed, then cancelled. Bob went to ground and pulled out of the project in disgrace. When the show did eventually open it was Patrick McGee, an invisible bit-part player in the background of Major Barbara, who took his place...

If the studios weren't calling Bob, Vera was not surprised. She had long foreseen the demise of the studios' dollar-rich hayday, and certainly Bob's part in it. It was television, or more specifically sponsorship and television advertising, that was poised to shape the future of entertainment and she knew it; that was what the Australian *Treasure Island* television series was all about. Well ahead of the game, she had insisted that the series included a Christmas special episode, *The Orphan's Christmas*, that just like the *Baker of Barnbury*, had all the eternal, festive motifs and more than a touch of *Oliver Twist*.

Edward G Robinson, one of the screen greats, saw television coming... 'Two years from now television will have taken over and will be making rubbishy films on the back-lots where Garbo used to tread...'. Vera knew that despite minuscule budgets and the lack of Tinseltown glitter, television was going to take over the world. The entertainment industry had moved on and Bob would have to move with it. It was a difficult decision for Newton to make and without hesitation Vera made it for him. 'Legit' stage actors that sold-out to film 'never came back' they used to say, now, it was the same for big-screen actors who 'sold out' to TV. Stage looked down on film, and film looked down on television. "You used to be big!" wailed the little man in *Sunset Boulevard*, "I am big..., the star replies "it's the pictures that have gotten small..."

For many actors television was indeed a career end-game. A decade before, studios bridling with terror had put their names to a covert agreement that saw actors who took TV work being blocked from the big-screen. Perhaps, then, it had been an over reaction. In 1945 there were less than seven thousand TV sets in the whole of the USA; most of them were in bars and there was nothing to see on them anyway. Three years later there were a million. But by 1950 there were 11 million plus and the start of regional broadcasts in colour; suddenly there were more sets than people. The number of commercial broadcasters increased from seven to seventeen in 1947; seventy more were in the process of being authorised and smart operators began combining stations into networks...

At 8pm on September 22nd, 1955, Britain saw ITV broadcast its first television programme; the first advert was screened twelve minutes later. Vera was right.

Bob's career was faltering but his daughter's had never really taken off. Her father's famous name had equated to a small flurry of media

353

interest but the promising start had led only to some minor stage works and bit-parts in unremarkable 'B' movies; *Armchair Detective* a black and white comedy short, and *No Haunt for a Gentleman* a barely competent whodunit, in 1952. *Double Exposure*, a formulaic crime drama had been made two years later. At twenty six she found herself with a stalled career and a marriage on the rocks. A telephone call from her father seemed to offer a way forward. Natalie's pre-tax estate of just £1,043 had left her young son with little financial support. With the lawyers still bickering, it was decided that Nicholas should go to live with his father in America and that Sally would deliver him. Right or wrong Bob had decided to play the loving father, and his son, who had effectively been raised by Janet Bricknell and had known only her as a mother, was to travel across the Atlantic once again.

For Bob the reunion was a happy and emotional moment, three children from three marriages united under one roof. Nicholas, confused and more than a little lost, had a Davy Crockett hat slapped on his head, was swept off to Disneyland and into the Great American Dream. Vera could only shrug and accept the unreality of the situation. At the age of only thirty one, she found herself giving a home to her husband's son from a previous marriage and his daughter, from yet another, who was just five years her junior.

Enjoying the attention of his extended family and sitting out the media storm, Newton waited for the phone to start ringing again. The pendulum of popularity had momentarily swung against him, and once again he was only another 'Brit' actor looking for work. Times were changing in Hollywood. The Americans were finding their cultural identity and no longer looked to the 'old country' for racial stereotypes. They had their own aristocracy now, a royalty found in the scrubby hills and canyons off Sunset Boulevard. A cultural gap had opened up between Britain and America, one that now seemed wider than the ocean that lay between them. The result was a downgrading of the 'English' stars to Europeanised baddies, eccentrics and decadent stooges. "They don't like us, you know... what are they frightened of?" wailed Trevor Howard. To survive, and make a buck, the British exiles now had to become pseudo Americans; they had to learn to think in American.

Milltowns and Martinis, high white walls and golden suntans, the Americans had at last swallowed the Californian lie of a nation where the dollar and science would make everything perfect. On the studio sound stages the new generation of Method actors had taken over. For them every script was approached as a psychological document; indoctrinated with the concept that a 'truth' could be found in each, they peered deeply 'within themselves' and their own 'life experiences'. Bob smiled; it sounded just like his mother and her cult of Christian Science. "All this talk about the 'method', the Method! What method?" Olivier howled, "I thought each of us had our own method... instead of doing a scene over again that's giving them trouble, they want to discuss, discuss, discuss... I'd rather go through a scene eight times than waste time chatting about abstractions, an actor gets things right by doing it over and over. Arguing about motives and so forth is a lot of rot. American directors encourage that sort of thing too much. Personally I loathe all abstract discussions about the theatre... they bore me!"

Like Olivier, Newton employed only ordinary perception and extraordinary genius. The Method however was a persuasive idea and rang excitingly of new-age pseudo-science. It sought to intellectualise the art and simultaneously make it egalitarian. Anyone could become the President, anyone could now be a stage genius. The flaw in the formula was that most new generation actors lacked experience, and lacked it because they had never learned the basics of technique; how to stand in the bloody light, and how to be heard. And always, lighting up every room in every home, peddling the new truths, was the refuge of television. The place where the answers could be found was not in the programmes, but in the commercials. There were millions of flickering sets in a million dingy rooms, selling the unattainable dreams. One by one the stars fell to the lure of the TV dollar, and Bob along with all the rest, was scaled down from a cinema giant, clipped of his wings, and fitted into that little box. 'Who is the Father of television?' the old joke went; 'Television has no father!' the reply.

The 'Climax!' Theatre's, April 28th broadcast saw a remake of Maugham's *The First and the Last*. Bob took Olivier's lead part of Kieth Dorrant, playing the lawyer forced to protect his inept brother.

A month later he again appeared for the Schlitz sponsored 'Playhouse of Stars' in *The Argonauts*. Recorded four years previously, he played Simon Mantle, a clerk, bored with his humdrum life and his nagging wife, who dreams of escape to distant paradise islands. The following week he appeared on the 'Lux Video Theater', episode 223, in a short remake of the film *The Suspect*. Recorded in 1950, he played Laughton's old 'Philip Marshall' character in a tale of love, hate, lust, another nagging wife and a baddie outed by guilt.

On Sunday, February 5th the following year, Newton appeared in the already enormously popular 'Alfred Hitchcock Presents' series. For Bob and Hitchcock it was something of a reunion; it had been seventeen long years since the vaguely remembered horrors of Laughton's *Jamaica Inn*. In series one, episode nineteen, *The Derelicts*, he played a witness to a murder. Directed by Robert Stevenson he portrayed the very English 'Peter J Goodfellow'. This horribly accurate piece of typecasting saw him as a 'gentleman' fallen on 'hard times' who wakes, half drunk, from his park bench to witness the killing. Once again Bob reprised the Harry Carter character from 'Kiss the Blood off my Hands' and turned blackmailer. Newton's performance was one of considerable aplomb; aloof and sardonic, yet with a twinkle in the eye and never a touch of the pirate. The hacks at *Variety*, mealy mouthed as ever, condemned him for 'overplaying'. Bob could afford an ironic laugh, he knew the role better than they.

The latter part of the year found him in the sound studios again, recording for an LP release, readings of 'XVII century Metaphysical and Love Lyrics' with Cedric Hardwicke.

A shot of positive publicity and TV screen-time were a plus, but Newton's life and career were undoubtedly stalled. Alarmed by his continued drinking, the creeping debt and his frequent run-ins with the law, friends and the old guard of the stick-together Brit' community, rallied to his aid. Recently migrated to Hollywood, William Menzies Cameron, the director of the 1940 film *Green Cockatoo*, was a man who knew Newton's acting credentials. Another fish out of water, he had however landed some film work;

he had been contracted as art director for a prestigious film project, Michael Todd's grandiose *Around the World in Eighty Days*.

Another Briton who had been hired into the work was David Niven; emerging from his own string of personal and career disasters, he had inexplicably been offered the starring role.

Fearful of the 'Lilliputian Television screen' and in a desperate effort to emphasise the difference in the two media and win back audiences, Hollywood was desperately selling itself out to sprawling dramas and wide-screen technology. Todd's new project seemed to fit the bill. Previously filmed in 1920 in Germany with Conrad Veidt as Fogg, Todd's remake was planned on a truly lavish scale. Entrepreneur extraordinary, outrageous and irrepressible, he had from the outset pushed forward the almost impossible project with the weight of his personality alone. For him bankruptcy was no deterrent. "Money is only important to people who haven't got it," he would yell "...I've never been poor, only broke. Being poor is a frame of mind. Being broke is a temporary situation." A true American, born Avrom Hirsch Goldeborgen, Todd was the son of a Polish rabbi. An explosive, guttural genius, an irrepressible self-promoter, a gambler and a con man, he had broken out from the chrysalis shell of a Broadway producer and gravitated to the bright lights and the big bucks of Hollywood in the late '40s. A self-made 'expert' in soundproofing movie stages his interests had quickly moved on to experiment with film technique itself. But just as he was getting a finger into the film business, film seemed to be dying. Television had given the whole, complacent, studio set-up a nasty jolt; "Why should people go out and pay money to see bad films when they can stay at home and see bad television for nothing," Sam Goldwyn moaned. It didn't help that the stars were hedging their bets and were beginning to get a finger in each pie, or worse, start up their own film companies and sell direct to television. Millions had suddenly stopped going to the movies and attendances had crashed from eighty million per week in the mid-forties to sixty million.

Panic set in and film executives started popping pills like sweets; if cinema was dying, they shouted, resuscitation of the flagging patient must come in the form of novelty. Overnight America suffered the indignity of the 3D and cardboard specs. Even Hitchcock had a go with *Dial M for Murder*. Horror flicks that plumbed new depths were bought out, each ticket coming with free 'insurance' that covered every viewer in the event of a heart-attack brought on by 'sheer terror'. Every gimmick was tried. Luminous skeletons were dropped on unsuspecting audiences from the ceiling; people queued for hours to get wired up and take an electrical jolt whilst watching *The Tingler*. Everything got bigger and better, bigger and better than television, and new wide-screen processes sprung up everywhere, CinemaScope, Vista Vision, WarnerScope. Now it was Todd's turn.

Mike Todd knew that television had weak spots in its poor sound quality and its tiny, grainy screen. Surely, he reasoned, the film 'experience' would be more satisfying in a fully equipped, state-of-the-art cinema. The answer to dwindling numbers was simply to hit back with a better product; grander, louder and larger. His answer was the patent Todd-AO (American Optical) system. Running at 30 frames per second rather than the usual 24, and with a gauge of 65mm, twice the width of the standard, the result was a stunning clarity of image and a baffling complexity. Conceived as a vehicle for the format, the classic 'producers' film, *Around the World in Eighty Days* was indeed to herald the birth of an empire. Todd had chewed at the edges of 'Around the World...' in 1946 as a Broadway producer. Orson Welles was to have taken the lead role supported by a musical score courtesy of Cole Porter, but the thing had imploded; stung to the tune of $40,000, Todd had vowed to return to the project. Now, and never a man to do things by half measures, he was determined that his first stab at the film world would be extraordinary; this would be an unstoppable cavalcade of 'A' list personalities.

The industry scoffed, laughing that it could never be done, but Todd was not to be put off. With a script and a wallet full of promises he went about the process of assembling a vast array of stars, each to make his or her cameo appearance. Bluffing and bullying, promising huge sums of money that in the end were always slow to appear and then far less than promised, he got his way.

Technology led, the film was a radical departure from the traditional realist genre. There *was* a narrative plot structure but only as a vehicle. It seemed that in a land where the machine was becoming the master, actors were becoming obsolete. As film settings and film image grew bigger and cinemas became larger and grander, the emphasis shifted away from realism and towards raw spectacle. Plots became more and more surreal and anchored on special effects.

Handed the leading role on a plate, (Todd had battled for months to get Cary Grant for the part...) David Niven pulled a whole character genre back from what had recently faced film extinction; the 'quintessential Englishman'. The support role of servant/valet 'Passepartout' went to Continflas, Mario Moreno, a Mexican comedian, bullfighter, national hero and millionaire; "the worlds greatest comedian..." said Chaplin. A twenty-two year old unknown with just two films behind her, Shirley MacLaine was pulled out of chorus-line anonymity for the campy 'Indian princess'/romance role.

One by one the catalogue of cameo stars were reeled in. Most climbed on-board for £5000 or so, often for less than a two minute appearance. Some were seduced by gifts in lieu of cash. Tumbling down from the gods, Noel Coward took a bit-part; his name was the mackerel to catch the sprats. He wrote his own dialogue for his 'Roland Hesketh-Baggott' character, the manager of a London employment agency. "I was fascinated to see that the script described my role as 'superior and ineffably smug'. It was clearly typecasting". He took a small Bonnard painting worth about £4600 in a tax-fiddle, and £100 cash; "Mustn't grumble...." he said. Ronald Colman got a yellow Cadillac. "All that just for one day's work?" an incredulous journalist asked. "Not at all, Madam," Colman replied "...for a lifetime of experience..."

Ironically, the 'Great American Movie' that was going to 'Save the Film Empire' was obliged to do most of its casting, and shooting, in London.

Newton's way into the two-day wonder was recounted by David Niven. A paid-by-the-line raconteur, a more than competent imbiber and a prolific recycler of studio gossip, he was, in true Hollywood form, never averse to admixing and tailoring facts. He quoted Bob as 'having an excellent degree from Oxford University'. How much of his material conformed to the two dimensional ideals of 'truth' is debatable, but if Hollywood stood for anything, it certainly wasn't that. Indisputably Niven had an insider's eye for the lunacy of it all and his anecdotes read as a priceless window into the crazy world he and Bob inhabited... "...but who the hell do we get to play Mr. Fix the Detective?" said Todd, chomping on the inevitable cigar. "How about Robert Newton?" I suggested. Todd was enchanted with the idea and immediately put in a call. "But I warn you Mike," I said, feeling every kind of heel, "Bobbie is a great friend of mine, but he does drink a lot these days and you must protect yourself. Lots of people are scared to employ him, he... disappears". "I want to see Newton," said Todd firmly, "and when he comes in, I want you here in the office." "For Christ's sake don't tell him I said anything", I begged, "he'll never forgive me". A week later Bobbie Newton shuffled in. I hadn't seen him for some weeks and it was obvious that he had been on a bender of heroic proportions". Todd went into his routine. "Ever heard of Jules Verne?" "Ah, dear fellow...," said Newton, "what a scribe!". "80 Days Around the World?" "A glorious piece, old cock". "How'd you like to play Mr. Fix?" "A splendid role..." said Bobbie, rolling his eyes, "do I understand you are offering it to me, dear boy?" "I might..." said Todd and I felt like the slimiest worm when he continued, "but your pal, Niven here, says you're a lush". "Aah!" said Newton, "my pal Niven, is a master of the understatement". He was hired immediately and gave his word of honour to Todd that he would go on the wagon for the duration of the picture. He stuck manfully to his promise..."

Working with James Wong Howe, one of Hollywood's most adventurous and talented cinematographers, and juggling with a reported 'seven million dollar' budget, the film's second director (the first, John Farrow, had a massive falling out with Todd and was fired one hour into the first day's shooting) was Michael Anderson. Another old friend of Newton's from the 1950 film *Waterfront*, he had to fight from the beginning to get the thing in the can. In the process he gathered a book full of instantly forgetable statistics. The promised 'directory of prestige stars' was indeed comprehensive and included many of Bob's old friends. Glynis Johns and Finlay Currie; Melville Cooper, playing a steward on 'RMS *Mongolia*', was an old pal from the Birmingham Rep' days. Marlene Dietrich appeared as a whore; Frank Sinatra as a bar-room piano player. Gielgud followed Coward and signed up, fittingly, as a valet. Buster Keaton was a train conductor. Trevor Howard played the Snob, John Mills a Cabby, Robert Morley a Banker, Basil Sydney a Toff. In the end fifty or so major league players were lured in and it seemed not unreasonable to presume that the very term 'cameo role' was coined for this film.

Thrown out to the public with a deafening fanfare, audiences hardly dared to blink for fear of missing a 'star'; whether Fogg won his bet or not was of secondary importance. For those bored with both stars and plot, a record 140 locations, that included Spain, London, France, India, Hong Kong, Pakistan, Siam, Japan, Mexico, Egypt and of course, America, worked as an effectively diverting travelogue.

Only too aware of the damage he had already done to his health and desperate to patch up some kind of reconciliation with Vera, Newton stayed true to his promise and remained solidly sober throughout the shoot. Filming in Colorado in the early autumn, Niven and Bob would go fishing in the evenings after work. Newton, always a keen fisherman, and now fitter than he had been for a long time thanks to several months of enforced abstinence, enjoyed these hours immensely. Niven again: "Bob was a superb fisherman, who 'tied' his own flies, he went fishing with me every evening after work and... I saw him bring to gaff countless huge fighting rainbows...it was becoming cold on those high lakes so one evening, I thoughtlessly put half a bottle of Bourbon with my gear. Thoughtlessly, because I had not appreciated how great was Bobbie's struggle to keep away from the stuff. As I opened it, I caught his eye and quickly slid the bottle back into my tackle bag; "Dear fellow," said Newton, "that was very kind of you but please don't worry. First of all I daren't ask for a little nip because quite apart from having no intention of breaking my word to Todd, my doctor told me that if I really get at it again, I shall very likely leave the building for good. So please don't feel that I am tempted by the sight of it." He paused and chuckled.... "However, kindly pass me the cork from time to time so I may sniff it.... I really do *love* the stuff, dear boy....". Love it he did. Despite his promises, temptation occasionally proved just too strong; an 'accidental' fall into the lake's chilly waters necessitated a long pull from a brandy bottle...

Two weeks after the final wrap, a selected cast including Newton had been recalled for a small additional sound recording. Niven recounted the scene: "At seven-thirty in the morning, I was sitting in the make-up room when the passage outside was shaken by a roaring delivery from *Henry V*, act IV…. 'We few, we happy few, we band of brothers, For he, today, that sheds his blood with me, shall be my brother…' "I was horrified at Bobbie's blotched and puffy face when he lurched into the room". "Don't chide me, dear fellow," he said, "please don't chide me" Tears coursed down his cheeks….". Bob had hit the bottle. Tracking him down in the make-up department, Kevin McClory, the assistant director dropped a discreet reminder that he was only needed for a sound recording and costume and make-up were not needed. But this wasn't good enough for Bob. With Niven standing by horrified, he slurringly insisted that he could only work if he was dressed up and in character. Well aware of the promise to Todd, McClory and Niven desperately tried to persuade Bob to go home. Unexpectedly, Todd arrived, smelled a rat and went in search of his star. With flawless logic Bob was tracked down in a nearby bar, nursing a glass of milk. Settling down for a cosy chat Todd ordered two 'more of the same', one for himself and one for McClory. He took a big swig and choked. The 'milk' was almost neat brandy.

Niven may have been understanding of Bob's back-sliding but Vera was not. Bob's drinking had taken a serious hold again; her patience was at an end and she had seen enough. After the doctors' warnings and all the bitter rows, the promises had turned out to be empty noises. Once again things were tumbling headlong into disaster. Despite a handsome fee from 'Around the World...' Vera saw that their income was diminishing; as ever Bob was living far beyond his income. By now the *Svengali* litigation had crossed the Atlantic to the Supreme Court of Justice in California. Once again the past was banging on their door.

Addled with anti-depressants, Bob fretted about his marriage, his career and his income, but his public response was classical; "O.K, so I owe almost a million pounds, am I supposed to give up life's little pleasures?" He knew that the Hollywood 'star' game was a farce, that they were all put where they were by cold hands and could be as easily pulled down. "The 'King' business is bullshit..." Clark Gable had growled "I was in the right place at the right time and I had a lot of smart guys helping me. Thats all".

Predictably, Bob's American dream had turned out to be only that, a dream. The waking reality was as boring and sterile as the burnt out Californian hills. "Once you've been to five parties" one Hollywood columnist commented bitterly, "it's the same cast. One of the reasons life can be so dull... is that there's no mix, as there is in Paris, and to a certain extent in London, of politicians and newspapermen and actors... the only way to meet an architect in this town is to hire one...". Uncertain, fagged out and far from home, Bob reached back into his past: ever sentimental he had secretly been making long-distance phone calls to Annie in Cornwall. "Can I come back...?" he pleaded. Annie could only laugh. She was still married to Beakus, otherwise...

For Vera hope seemed to lie in the 'Treasure Island' TV series. Initial signs had been good. Still labouring under a crippling war-debt and behind the times in terms of television ownership, UK release had come in the form of cinema shorts. Along with the film *Under the Black Flag*, they had turned out to be a dollar earning hit that more than vindicated her optimism. The US television release, following a trial black and white broadcast, was on January 13th 1956 and saw the colour transmission of all twenty six episodes. The reviews were thrilling; parents approved and more importantly, the children loved it. Overnight the series became rowdy and unmissable viewing, gaudy classics that were to shape the formative years of a generation and a million youngsters. 'Enjoyably noisy...' commented the usually conservative *Variety*.

It seemed to be an occasion for celebration but the reality was bleak. Ever trusting, Bob had left the paperwork to others and somehow Joe Kaufmann had been allowed to steal the thing from under their noses and run with the profits. Once again the tedious litigation trail opened up before them. Vera was furious. Bob hit the bottle. There was the usual acrimony and tears but this time it was different. Bob came home, sick and repentant, to an empty house. Vera had taken baby Kim and left.

Newton knew that this time a considerable cooling-off period would be necessary. With Todd's hundred thousand dollar pay-cheque in his pocket he settled back with the remnants of his family, sipped his milk and waited. The old truism that an actor was only as good as his last film was one that now chimed amongst the jittery studio moguls. Bob's independently produced and mega low-budget *Treasure Island* series was proving to be a money-spinner (even if that money had spun off into someone else's pocket...) and Bob knew that there would soon be someone knocking at his door. Certainly Todd's yet to be released film, earmarked to be a sensation if only for being a sensation, had catapulted the decidedly floundering and definitely 'B' list David Niven into high orbit among the Hollywood luminaries. In-house screenings showed Newton carrying a leading role, not only stone cold sober but with considerable aplomb, and the telephone, so silent for so long, now began rattling off the cradle. Bob smiled and shook his head. Offers of radio, TV and film work flooded in; *Anastasia*, *Land of the Pharaohs*, *The Ten Commandments*, the scripts piled up. There was even serious talk of a stage role, a glorious six-week Christmas engagement in New York with the prestigious Actors' Company in a production of *The Admirable Crichton*.

As if to underscore Bob's rising status another TV soap was now aired; Bob played Dr. Thomas Walters a surgeon forced to perform an emergency operation on a boy he believes to have killed his daughter. Put out under the *Chevron Hall of Stars* banner, the piece, entitled 'End of Night', was lapped up by the public.

The Oscars ceremony loomed, Hollywood's big annual self-congratulatory night, when the stars polished up their smiles and reached into the back of wardrobes for evening suits. This was the year that Jaque Tati released *Mon Oncle*, but there was no fanfare for that piece of film mastery. Instead the National Board of Review Awards had just put Todd's *Around the World* in first place. Ironically second place went to *Moby Dick*, in which the ship, 'Pequod', was none other than the old 'Hispaniola' converted into a whaler. Suited up and crashing into the Bob's Benedict Canyon house, Keith McConnell, an uncredited 'pirate' from the *Blackbeard* days, was surprised to find Trevor Howard there, being dressed by

Newton. McConnell, a self-acknowledged dandy, cast a critical eye over Trevor in Newton's beautifully made evening suit and saw that it was too big. Why had Trevor not chosen something from the studio wardrobe? Apparently it was because the suits didn't have pockets and Trevor was a smoker. As far as Trevor was concerned, the suit was fine, the jewelled cuff links were exquisite and the patent leather bedroom slippers were comfortable. Bob was likewise dressed to kill. He gave a final tweak to his bow tie, clapped a straw hat on his head, kissed his daughter and Nicholas goodbye, and was off...

The next day, Bob was pale, hung-over and sorry for himself. His cough had suddenly become worse. Sally now took Vera's place and Bob's doctor was called. Concerned about the combination of his asthma and early signs of angina he ordered strict bed rest.

With only a slight age gap between them, Sally and Vera had quickly established an almost sisterly relationship. Sally could see that, if only for the sake of his health, her father would have to be dragged into a reconciliation with Vera. Bob sighed; he saw that he would, once again, have to go through the ritual humiliation and begging process to get Vera back.

This time Vera was playing the injured party to the full and was doing it in style. In her diamonds and furs, she had camped out in a luxury bungalow at the Garden of Allah. Built in the grounds of a swank mansion just off Sunset Boulevard, the guest bungalows fanned around a palm-fringed pool and bar. The place to be, the place to see and be seen, the place to get seriously drunk, the Garden of Allah was also a theatre of sex. For Vera, the younger woman, jealousy was another powerful lever.

Bob knew that this reconciliation was not going to be easy; Vera was angry. And Sally was angry. Haskin was angry too. So was the Inland Revenue in England. And the *Svengali* lawyers. Everyone was shouting and angry. The whole of Los Angeles had become angry. Race was hating race and 'civil rights' had become the new cause, despite the sunshine and the plenty. And everyone was hating the Communists all over again. It seemed that if Hollywood was now defined by anything, it was defined by the re-emergence of anti-communist hysteria, 'friendly' and 'unfriendly' witnesses, violence and conspiracy. The studios were gridlocked with the unions. The stars, once public faces, casual and louche in the markets and the bars and the barber shops, now hid from 'their fans'. They hid from *Confidential* magazine and the snooping reporters that rooted through their garbage cans looking for sin. Once they were public faces; now they censored the luxury of their lives behind walls and barred windows.

But the censorship was never about sin and sex, and no one cared about 'depravity' any more. Sex had always been part of the Hollywood product, the tantalising lure; the criminalisation was only part of the sham. Sin had broken out onto the streets and nobody cared. Censorship had always been about control, controlling the dumb masses, and smothering the anti-establishment 'freaks'. *Confidential* magazine read as a guidebook to '50s America, a keyhole into the nation's secret fears, its unspoken desires and paranoid nightmares. Race and sex were carefully remade into the favourite obsessions. The rebirth of the 'blue' film saw the introduction of the 'X' certificate, not to censor or restrict, but to create a new, exciting upper category for the taboo.

Bob looked around him and saw an American society that was changing fast. For the first time in the country's history, white collar workers began to outnumber blue collar workers. By the mid-fifties three quarters of adult Americans, including low-class blue-collar workers, began to *think* of themselves as 'middle-class'. America's self-image was undergoing a radical face-lift and the demographics of self-perception were changing. Now everyone was 'rich' and everyone was endlessly looking for something more to want. Out in the wastelands of the faceless 'burbs this translated into a lust for conformity. America wallowed in a cultural mire that was to father the sentimental nostalgia of the seventies. At the height of its power and precursor to the Age of Doubt, America was already entering the Age of Disillusionment.

The film industry had always been part of the establishment propaganda machine, but the industry had changed. The traditional vested interest in preserving the elite culture against the encroaching environment of philistinism, of schlock and kitsch, of TV soaps and

Reader's Digest culture, had been broken. The mission to transmit the difficult and complex skills of reading, and listening and perceiving, had quickly sold out to the fast buck. Post modernism had reared up and consumed its makers; the classics were subsumed by the para-literature of throwaway paperback romance and erotic fantasy. Wittgenstein had died, buried under the avalanche of popular culture.

"Hollywood's like Egypt..." Selznick once remarked, "full of crumbling pyramids... It'll just keep crumbling until the wind blows the last studio prop across the sands...". Howard Hughes was more bitter, "Hollywood is through" he spat. Perhaps he was right. Hollywood was supposed to be about portraying the American Dream, gold-digging, power-conscious beautiful people, all sentimental and showing off. 1943 had spawned *The Outlaw*, an unashamed celebration of lust that was 'too startling to describe!'; in '46 the dream was gloriously sold again in *Gilda*. But 1950 only gave birth to *Sunset Boulevard*. The film defined the decade; a parable told by a corpse where the dream was soured, turned in on itself. A scathingly bitter self-condemnation, it was a piece of meta-theatre that saw no hope left. The camera had pulled back and shown that the Xanadu Hollywood 'village', where everybody knew everybody, had disintegrated into a ghetto. The glittering palace turned out to be just a beautiful prison.

Like Hollywood itself, the film making industry had come a long way. Now it was all about accountants, package deals, percentages, front money and elaborate bargaining. Chandler's embittered Philip Marlowe spoke the words for many in *The Little Sister*, "I used to like this town... a long time ago there were trees on Wilshire Boulevard... now we've got the big money, the sharpshooters, the percentage workers, the fast-dollar boys, the hoodlums out of New York and Chicago... we've got the flashy restaurants and the night-clubs they run, and the hotels and apartment houses they own, and the grifters and the con-men and the female bandits that live with them... the riff-raff of a hard-boiled city with no more personality than a paper cup...".

It was a new world that Marilyn Monroe would come to understand; "Hollywood is a place where they'll pay a thousand dollars for your body and fifty cents for your soul...".

If Hollywood was clinging to the celluloid dreams of its past, it was now the mob that ran the unions and the unions ran the studios. Besieged by television, cinema ticket sales had dropped by a third and the studios were breaking up. Even the previously amenable 'justice' system was turning against them, ordering the breakup of their cinema chain cartel. The finger of blame may have been pointed at television but the reality was that the studios were out of touch with their audience. Deeply conservative, they lived in the past that had seen their birth. Even the demographics were working against the old system; women and families were beginning to stay at home and the cinema stalls had become the preserve of the young male. The end was inevitable but the studios were not going to do the honourable thing and fall on their swords; the death was to be protracted, bitter and undignified. Errol Flynn summed it all up; 'Hollywood is a lovely place to live. It's comfortable, it's warm, it's sunny, but it's filled with the most unutterable bastards."

With Sally standing at his shoulder, Bob put a phone call through to Vera. He swore that he had quit drinking, for good, and said that he wanted a reconciliation and for her to come home. Reluctantly Vera agreed; a meeting was arranged for the following day at the Benedict Canyon house.

Sunday dawned. March 25th. Another brassy, heat-drenched, beautiful, Californian morning. Police sirens sounded in the far-away distance. Pale and breathless, Bob nervously poured himself a last drink, glanced at his watch and braced himself. But it was not to be. Bobby Newton died suddenly, far from his beloved Cornwall, in the angriest city in the world.

He was just fifty.

11. Ad Captandum Vulgas: What The People Want

❝ ● ● ● I was as hollow and empty as the spaces between the stars. When I got home I mixed a stiff one and stood by the open window in the living-room and sipped it and listened to the groundswell of traffic on the Laurel Canyon boulevard and looked at the glare of the big, angry city hanging over the shoulder of the hills through which the boulevard had been cut. Far off the banshee wail of police or fire sirens rose and fell, never for very long completely silent. Twenty four hours a day somebody is running, somebody else is trying to catch him. Out there in a night of a thousand crimes people were dying, being maimed, cut by flying glass, crushed against steering wheels or under car tyres. People were being beaten, robbed, strangled, raped and murdered. People were hungry, sick, bored, desperate with loneliness or remorse or fear, angry, cruel, feverish, shaken by sobs. A city no worse than others, a city rich and vigorous and full of pride, a city lost and beaten and full of emptiness. It all depends on where you sit and what your private score is. I didn't have one. I didn't care. I finished the drink and went to bed...". Raymond Chandler. *The Long Goodbye*.

...

Robert Newton died on the twenty fifth of March, 1956. A Sunday. The next day's newspaper reports, not so bullish and condemnatory now, told a milk and water tale of peaceful release, at home in the arms of his loving wife. He was sitting in the parlour... 'He keeled over – drinking a glass of water; Robert Newton dies as wife waits at bedside. Beverley Hills, California, Sunday. Film star Robert Newton, rusty voiced bad man of the cinema, died from a heart attack in bed in his Hollywood home tonight. His fourth wife, Vera, was by his side. She said; "Robert was having a glass of water – he just keeled over. There was nothing anyone could do". Newton, who was one of the world's top actors, lived richly and robustly like many of his stage and screen characters. He made thousands of pounds and spent them. He kept homes in London and America. He loved his children – but seldom saw them. He had been confined to bed by poor health for several days.'

"It must have been the shock of drinking a glass of water..." the wags laughed.

The *Los Angeles Times* reported the event; 'Newton succumbed shortly after the arrival of his physician, Dr Francis Ado yesterday afternoon. The doctor said the actor had suffered with asthma for several years and that this may have aggravated his heart condition...'

Byron Haskin's account of Bob's last minutes was blunter and somehow rang truer. "He (Newton) phoned them (Vera and son, Kim) and said he'd stopped drinking, and he wanted them to come back. So they went back for a conference and, as he took a Milltown from his pocket and raised it to his lips, he fell dead in front of them. And that was it. The end of a great actor…"

The next day newspapers across the world carried the story; the *Times* obituary appeared on Tuesday, March 27th, "an actor of force and power…".

It fell to Kevin McClory, an old friend who, incidentally was in the midst of a protracted affair with Sally, to arrange the funeral. Vera, shocked and lost, was devastated. A cremation was held at noon on the 29th, just four days after his death, at the chapel of Pierce Brothers in Beverley Hills. The haste was almost indecent. The occasion was simple and quiet. Just Vera and Sally and a handful of close friends. No Joy or Pauline. Just 'a little foreign funeral'.

That same afternoon the faces and names gathered at the Benedict Canyon house. Errol Flynn came. A man's man who never understood women, he was very much like Newton; his time was spent with his male friends, his drinking buddies. He was never quite the Lothario that the rags painted him to be. He had learned to distrust women; maybe he too was afraid of them. He was to die within three years, like Bob, wrecked by a surfeit of drink and drugs, a surfeit of almost everything. He carried in a crate of champagne. "From one great rogue to another...' he said 'now there's only one of us left!" And somehow the solemn gathering became a wake, the drink flowed and everyone gravitated out into the sunshine by the pool. "This is how Bobby would have liked it" Flynn said. Vera smiled, but it was an act of pure theatre. She had already started the process of blaming herself for Bob's death. Racked with guilt she would never move on.

A few days later Bob's ashes were placed in the urn garden in Westwood Memorial Park. But Bob had left written instructions, however; he didn't want his remains to stay in America, he had wanted his bones to come home to Cornwall and his beloved Lamorna.

Newton's estate was estimated at just $100,000 dollars (£35,000); it was little enough. As ever Bob had trusted his business managers and had been utterly ripped off. What was left was taken by the Revenue service in lieu of unpaid tax.

On April 12th the Gaiety cinema in Newlyn, Cornwall, screened *The Beachcomber*. But there was no Marjorie there now, and only her ghost clapped and cheered him on.

A week later, when everyone had forgotten and the world had moved on, a letter was published in the *Times*; 'Mr Dennis Pelly writes':- 'I read with deep regret in your columns of the death of Robert (Bobby) Newton. I feel some mention should be made of his qualities, apart from that of a brilliant actor. He frequently stayed with me in Chelsea when he had taken the Fulham Theatre, and his enthusiasm and optimism were unbounded. "It is just what is wanted", he used to say, "good plays at a price everyone can afford". It was certainly not from lack of initiative that the venture did not prove a success. He also had that greatest of all gifts – a very strong sense of humour. His many friends will be saddened by the death of this charming and generous person.'

Premièred grandly in New York, Todd's gargantuan *Around the World in 80 Days* saw its release and the critics, sure not to be out of step with a public opinion pre-prepared for a wonder, raved. 'A smash hit, the most star-studded film of all time'; 'Extravagant! Funny! Spectacular!' yelled *Time* magazine. 'A cinema triumph. London will love it' said the *Daily Telegraph*. Squeaky clean the film was family entertainment at its best, 'Family medal award. Rated excellent.' *Parents Magazine* shrilled. At a bum-numbing two hours and fifty five minutes, with a plethora of stars and a rash of 'exotic' location shots, the work had enough material to wow even the most jaded critic. The hype raised the standard of superlatives; spurred on by previously unknown levels of ballyhoo and publicity one print played on Broadway for more than fifteen months and was worn to ribbons. The National Board of Review said "The human race has never seen entertainment such as this. Greatest show now on earth!" The *New Yorker* gave the thumbs up: "Big, splashy. The actors are all fine, and the scenic effects are tremendous!" The *New York Journal* raved "Absolutely tops.... Earth-shaking beauty. Niven is simply perfect!". Naturally the film gathered an armful of industry awards; at the twenty ninth Oscars it scooped up everything, grabbing Best Picture, best Cinematography–colour, best Film Editing, best Musical Score, and best Screenplay. Nominations were received for Best Director, Colour Costume Design, and Colour Art Direction. But ironically none of the cast harvested a golden accolade; perhaps there were just too many 'stars', and perhaps the film was great simply for being great. And Bob was not there to see any of it. *Cosmopolitan* only said, "The late Robert Newton is splendid as the befuddled detective...". In true Todd style estimates of the cost of the film ranged from an extraordinary $3 million to an astounding $7 million; it raked in $21 million on its first release.

A glossy publication was hurried out in the US extolling the virtues of the film, but Newton's death caught the editors on the hop and a glowing obit was quickly penned in. ' "Bob Newton was born to play Inspector Fix" remarked David Niven who, as Phileas Fogg, is shadowed by him in his frantic chase around the world. His Inspector Fix is the last, and perhaps the greatest, in a gallery of memorable portraits etched by the master. They'll remember Bob

Newton.... They'll remember his Pistol in Sir Lawrence Olivier's 'Henry V'. They'll remember his classic villainy in 'Jamaica Inn', and 'Odd Man Out', 'The Beachcomber', and 'Androcles and the Lion', 'Major Barbara', and 'Gaslight', his Bill Sykes in 'Oliver', and his John Silver in 'Treasure Island'. They'll remember his inimitable rich voice, his wink, his leer, his roaring laugh. He was a non-conformist, his own man on and off stage. He worked hard and played hard, he drank hard and he loved hard. He was an artist. Upper-case. His Mother was a writer, his Father, and Brother and Sister were painters. He was an Actor. Upper-case, in the finest tradition of the English stage, from his professional début at the age of fifteen with the British Repertory Company, through his apprenticeship as an actor and stage manager with a touring company in Canada, South Africa, Australia and the West Indies to Broadway, replacing Lawrence Olivier in Noel Coward's 'Private Lives', to his great years and, at last, his final scene as Inspector Fix. He was a gifted man, sensitive, warm-hearted, rebellious. Being original, he was an enemy of convention. Being an Artist, he despised mediocrity. His like will not come this way again".

Fine words. You can almost hear Newton laugh. But the truth is there. Or some of it. Newton was more than just an actor; wryly Ronald Neame commented, "Some stage actors are not good on screen, and some screen actors not good on stage". Bob was good on both. A rare thing. Rarer still was his talent; natural, easy, inexplicable. Degas observed that it was easy to demonstrate talent at twenty, what was difficult was still having it at fifty. Bob however always had it. But he never got an Oscar. Burton was promised seven, and he got none either.

Perhaps ironically it was Noel Coward, a vain man who, even at the end of his own days, could never bring himself to speak or write of Bob, who most aptly summed him up; "A star is somebody whose name over the title drags the audience into the theatre, and the only quality they have is 'star' quality! What fascinates me about acting is when a beautiful, talented actor can come on the stage and give a performance that makes your blood curdle with excitement and pleasure, yet he can make such a pig of himself, where his dressing room is, or some such triviality, for which you hate him. Intelligent actors never do that, but then they're seldom as good as the unintelligent ones. Acting is an instinct. A gift that is often given to people who are very silly as people. But as they come up to the stage, up goes the temperature...".

Kenneth Tynan defined 'star quality' as 'the ability to project, without effort, the shape and essence of a unique personality, which has never existed before him in print or paint...'. That seems almost to define Bob's skill.

Newton's complex character can perhaps be offered up against Freud's ideas. The breakup of Newton's parents' marriage had a profound effect. Certainly Bob fitted into Freud's category of the Oedipal man. Always he showed all the signs of 'unsuccessful transference'; deeply attached to his mother, he found it difficult to sustain relationships with women. In Peta he saw and found his mother; the Madonna figure, holding her baby, she was of course the literal mother.

"I believe in matriarchy..." Bob had once said, "families dominated by the mother. That's what happy nations are made of. Happy families, like the one in *Whiteoaks*. But you can't practise the family cult if there isn't a strong woman at the head. You must have a strong woman...". Perhaps inevitably his own daughter, Sally, evolved into a pseudo sister/mother figure.

Newton was intensely gregarious, but women were his weakness; he needed female company, yet he had no idea how to behave beyond the act of being a lover. The French have a word, 'Mouflerie', a concept that is difficult to translate, but meaning a form of caddishness, a callous insensitivity. Was this Bob? Perhaps. Yet everybody adored him... "With Bobby's enormous charm he could get away with things. Anybody else would have been dismissed, thrown to the dogs. Bobby had this wonderful, generous, loveable quality..." Laurence Evans said.

Bob always sought the company of men. And men fell into two clear categories; either a substitute for his own, weak, brother, or for his own dominating and absentee father. Richard Burton fell into the former group, along with Stanley Holloway, Arthur Colin-Campbell. Of the latter group one could point to Barry Jackson, Augustus John and Jack Buchanan (Bob always referred to him as 'Master'). Back in the early days it was Tom Pender, the Coxswain of the Sennen lifeboat.

Bob was of the people, not the hierarchical, career-fixated, establishment. For him 'life' meant his relationship with family, the other players, the crews, the passing, delirious, delicious swirl of faces. With his family the relationship was always one of love and hate. 'Hardly close', he called it, yet 'closely united', if apt to occasionally 'break loose'. He had a gut affection for people, and a real need for them. Loneliness and emptiness were an anathema. He was 'Bob' to everyone, and when the lesser mortals, the invisible bit players, were obliged to 'Mr' this and 'Mr' that to others, they were for him first names; the Cornish 'my dear', 'old cock' and 'old beauty'. He always knew their names and faces, remembered infallibly old acquaintances from long forgotten yesterdays, remembered their children and their interests. Always he would buy the drinks, always try to give away the useless money in his pockets.

In 1954 Augustus John published his retrospective 'Fragments of an Autobiography', 'Chiaroscuro' and of Bob wrote '... At this time Robert Newton had not attained his present eminence. His manly beauty was unenhanced by the costly accoutrements of Californian fashion which he now wears so bravely. But Bob was always brave; brave, simple and above-board, even when under the weather. This man of many parts, in his good fortune careless; with the great heart of adolescent humanity beating more quickly at his nod, may even in his heyday profit by a word of warning. Such a word of warning I take it upon myself to administer (a septuagenarian must be indulged) 'The Gods have conferred upon you, my dear Bob, among other gifts, a generous allowance of Sentiment. If you would enjoy this abundance to the full, you will do well to use it sparingly and with an eye to the stomach, for it might come back on you – or worse, on some innocent person in your neighbourhood. To vary the metaphor: when running a race, with such a horse as sentiment under you, the strongest and most vicious in your stable, beware lest you come a cropper or be run away with. Let your steed always feel the rein, dear boy, but not the spur; by keeping well within the limits of Dickensian Melodrama (though I myself favour a narrower course) you and your noble beast are bound to romp in – winners every time!'

But Bob had no need of Gods. He had the courage to live beyond the rules, to be his own guide. For him life was for living. He was his own man, his own master. The rules that corral us all were not for him. That was what made him memorable. He was the unique one-man social experiment that we look to, to see if Bohemianism worked, even if it was a sentimental sub-sect, to see if there is a viable alternative to the cretinising, routine drudge.

Of Newton's life so much is lost, so little remains. Much was destroyed by war and acrimony. So much is forgotten. He was never a writer, never a self-applauding diarist. There are a few family photos, memories of the plays, the avalanche of press material. The films. Each contain a little facet of the man. The priceless memories. But the ordinary days, his phatic life, is lost in a forgotten oblivion.

Bob showed all of his father's nature; another work obsessed, self obsessed loner; yet, ironically, desperately gregarious too.

Like so many public faces, Bob was defined, and is mostly remembered, for his 'faults'. Yet he had no time for sexual 'abnormality', no time for the Bloomsbury set's paranoias which hid under the cloak of free thinking. When they were thinking, Bob was doing. "Did you know that when he died" Gielgud purred, spinning out the new-minted lie, "they found two hundred empty bottles of whiskey at the bottom of a lake in his garden...". Newton was more than the sum of his habits, yet, undeniably, alcohol steered his life, especially at the latter stages. And it killed him.

In the late thirties Bob had bumped into Gary Marsh, the captain of the Stage Cricket Club, and remembered that he had borrowed a tenner from him years earlier. Resorting to a nearby bar, he insisting on repaying the debt and started peeling notes from a fat roll. The evening went on and the drinks flowed and Bob insisted on handing over more and more money; embarrassed, Marsh handed the cash over to Connie, Bob's agent, who had now joined them. Eventually Bob was steered into a taxi and sent home. The next day Bob was at Connie's office, and told her to the nearest penny how much money had been handed over to her. For Sally this was no surprise, she knew her father well; "He was only ever as drunk as he wanted to be," she said "...and no more".

"...All the really funny stories about Bobby were about his drinking" Laurence Evans recalled. "He was renowned for his drinking, but always in the nicest possible way".

But alcohol is a viciously addictive drug, and it hooked Bob, changed him. Drink was the fad then, they said, it showed that you were a rebel, that you did not care for the opinions of others. Drink was the 'pick up' when the depressed low hit in the days and weeks after the triumphant performance. It was the antidote to the jealousy that placed him outside the social group that he so needed to be within. Just as in his Lamorna school days, he played the fool to win the friends. Hid discretion under a cloak of folly.

So why the stage, why did it fit Bob so well? "He was never an actor, he was always like that... a little devil" the man had said. Theatre, especially the Birmingham Rep, was the substitute for a fractured family. It was another transference. Newton was honest enough to be afraid to be alone; alone without any defence from himself. Far from being a public arena, the stage was a noisy place to hide, to escape the real world that he was powerless to control. Bob hid in a make-believe world where he had control. Of course he was a larger than life personality; extraordinary, he always stood out from the crowd. Not for him rules and parameters. For him life itself was a stage and he made up his own script as he went along, constantly selecting and bringing to the fore carefully selected aspects of his personality. He needed people, needed people close, and they became his off-stage audience. Bob quoted his own bravura brand of philosophy in *They Flew Alone*... "Time, work and worry are made for slaves"...he purred; "I've got a regular habit, I live in the present". It was a good lie. Anyone with enough charm and good looks could be a 'personality', on and off stage; Bob had to tie in his own keen natural intelligence, his genius and the decades of hard work.

'How many good plays do you get in a lifetime?' Tallulah Bankhead asked. 'Three if you are one of fortune's pets. Successful plays? That's something else again. The most successful plays are commonly trashy. Merit and success are rarely mated in the theatre...'. The mythology of success ever lay in two elements, hardships and breaks, and Newton's career abounded in both. Always it was interpreted by the critics. But much opinion is subjective, criticism the distillation of bias and prejudice. Especially when spilled from the pens of those paid to have a stance.

The twenty first century has almost forgotten Bob's legacy; David Ragan's recent book 'Who's Who in Hollywood', described him meanly as an 'English character star given to scraggly characters and florid, bug-eyed performances'. But, of course, fame was always an illusive thing. "There's no such thing as a 'legend'... nearly everyone has forgotten Laurence Olivier..." Dame Eileen Atkins said in 2008. They said that Bob was going to be 'the new Paul Muni'. Does anyone remember that name? Perhaps Newton never was a film 'star'; perhaps 'stardom' was, and still is, an American construct. And despite the citizenship he was never an 'American'. He was always English. Or rather, always Cornish. He was the gentleman amateur and, defying the litmus that tested stock types; he made his timeless trademark as the exotic outsider that resisted definition. Bob's skill lay in shifting the focus from the individual to the character. He eschewed the empty rattlings of glamour and simply told stories.

Harold Pinter had his characters recall Newton in his 1971 play, *Old Times*. '... I think I am right in saying that the next time we met we held hands. I held her cool hand, as she walked by me, and I said something which made her smile, and she looked at me'... 'flicking her hair back, and I thought she was even more fantastic than Robert Newton. And then at a slightly later stage our naked bodies met, hers cool, warm, highly agreeable, and I wondered what Robert Newton would think of this. What would he think of this I wondered as I touched her profoundly all over. What do you think he'd think? I never met Robert Newton but I do know what I know you mean. There are some things one remembers even though they may never have happened, but as I recall them they take place...'.

Unperturbed and grand amidst the good and the great, Annie Penrose was one of those invited onto St Michael's Mount in Cornwall in 1988 for the Armada Centenary celebrations. Queenly, swaying slightly, seated at the head of the table, she gripped the gathered crowd with her stories and the undimmed power of her personality. She had her longed for children with Beakus, not Bob, two fine sons, her 'bull calves', that filled her with pride. But it was of Bob that she mostly spoke; "If you get this combination, awful, droll, brilliant and a gent, it never misses... they leave everyone else in the shadows. Bob did. I still miss the old bugger, you know. Life wasn't the same when I went straight..."

Post Script

After Newton's death the human comedy continued. His will stated that he wished for his remains to return to his childhood home. Sally finished the tale... "After my father's death his ashes were brought back to England by a Hollywood film producer (Kevin McClory) since he had asked in his Will that they should be buried in the little Cornish village where he had been brought up. The ashes were handed back to my father's sister (Pauline) by the producer but she refused to accept them. He took the urn and went on a pub-crawl, buying two drinks wherever he went – one for himself and one for Bobby. He astonished the other customers by talking to the ashes over his drinks. He finally got home clutching the urn. Next day, my aunt, having had second thoughts, came around and demanded the ashes. The producer refused to part with them...."

Eventually McClory relented and handed the urn over. At Pauline's home in Manningford Abbas in Wiltshire, the urn spent a week in the kitchen before being transferred, rather appropriately, to the wine cellar. It sat there for the next twenty five years. Half-forgotten it became something of a morbid cultural attraction, a family party turn; a macabre memento mori. Oliver Gates, Pauline's step-son, would invite his Oxford chums down to the family home for weekends and no visit was complete without a ghoulish trip down to the cellars to 'say hello' to Uncle Bob. Eventually Nicholas, Bob's son, inherited the urn, and it fell to him to eventually 'do something' about it.

In the winter of 1981 he set off for Cornwall. "...amidst gifts, various contributions towards the Christmas festivities, food, crackers, warm clothing, sou'westers, gum boots and assorted paraphernalia, was a heavy, unadorned, bronze casket containing the ashes of my father.

He had been dead for twenty five years. His ashes had passed through the hands of friends, casual acquaintances, both his sisters, his daughter and were now in my care. His casket had been propped in bars, bookcases, sat in drinks cupboards, on luggage racks, been under my bed – to the alarm of several girlfriends – stored ignominiously for several years amongst cardboard boxes in out-of-the-way attics until finally I had been persuaded his ashes should be returned to the place where he grew up. I had been married for a year and it was our first Christmas away from London...".

"We arrived at night. The wind was up. The house dimly lit; perched on a flat piece of land on the black rocks at the sea's edge it was all but submerged in the spray... Boxing Day dawned cold and wet. Across the bay Mousehole, Newlyn and Penzance could be glimpsed between the squalls. Even so the plan to dispose of my father's ashes gathered pace. The casket was taken off to a workshop where the screw on the underside of the casket was loosened. It was not an easy task; no one had tried it during the twenty five years and it had jammed tight.

After lunch we started for Cudden Point, first along the track before cutting away across the moorland until we found ourselves walking along a spine of land which forms the most easterly point of the bay. As the point narrows we scrambled down to the rocks below.

Although the wind had moderated, the sea swell showed all the signs of the recent turbulence. Several hundred yards out in the bay a wave would gather which even then, seven days on from the worst of the storm, could have overwhelmed a small fishing boat. I stood, look-out, bible in hand and, after several attempts when the others were practically engulfed in water, my father's ashes were tipped out onto a rock.

They were surprisingly grey, like ground-up bones, not at all like I had imagined his ashes, and quite a little pile. As much as could be easily fitted into the palms of two outstretched cupped hands. As we waited for the next huge wave to reach the shore, I tried shouting "I am Alpha and Omega, the beginning and the ending..." but the words were lost in the wind, and salt sea spray caught in my eyes.

And just in time as we scrambled up the steep bank the wave came. It surged over the rocks and took his ashes away...".

Looking out into the Western approaches, and across the tumbling waters to Lamorna, Cudden Point is the heart of the Bay. Bob had come home.

Afterwords

Concern was endlessly mooted in the British press as to the fate of Nicholas. On March 27th 1956 the *Daily Mail* had run a two column piece, "Mrs. Newton IV to adopt Nicholas. Nicholas, five-year-old son of Robert Newton, British stage and screen actor, who died yesterday is to be adopted by his stepmother. His mother, Newton's third wife, Natalie, died several months ago. He will grow up at Beverley Hills, Los Angeles, as 'a full brother' to Kim, the two-year-old son of Mr Newton and his fourth wife. Nicholas was brought over to this country last January by Miss. Sallie (sic) Newton, the actor's 23-year-old daughter by his first wife. The widow and three children are now living at Newton's luxuriously equipped house in Benedict Canyon Drive, in a fashionable film-star section of Beverley Hills. Miss Sallie Newton also plans to remain over there and pursue a stage career."

However things turned sour. By June, Vera and Sally found themselves in court facing a custody counter-claim in the shape of a well-to-do Hollywood couple who had previously acted as temporary foster-parents to Nicholas and who now claimed that they had received a verbal agreement from Sally that they could adopt Nicholas, a claim she now denied. By the end of July a compromise settlement had been reached; Nicholas would return to England and the guardianship of his aunt, Pauline. In the September of 1956, accompanied by Elizabeth Taylor, he was flown back to England...

Sally was to do another two film works, a single episode in the American 'Lord Arthur Savile's Crime' television series, *Suspicion* and in 1974, *Sommerfuglene* (*Summer of Silence*) in the UK. She then moved succesfully behind the camera.

Algernon died in 1968 having found his love and his art.

Vera died in 2000.

Annie died in 2011, gloriously unrepentant aged 100.

Nicholas is a producer for theatre, TV and radio.

Kim lectures on photojournalism.

Dan is a renowned photographer.

Bibliography

Adamson, Joe, *Byron Haskin*, USA, 1984

Anger, Kenneth, *Hollywood Babylon,* London, 1975

Baddeley, Hermione, *The Unsinkable Hermione Baddeley*, London, 1984

Bankhead, Tallulah, *Tallulah, my Autobiography*, London, 1952

Barefoot, Guy, *Gaslight Melodrama*, New York, 2001

Belton, John, editor, *Movies and Mass Culture*, London, 1996

Bragg, Melvin, *Rich, The Life of Richard Burton*, London, 1988

Brookes, Ewart, *The Gates of Hell*, London, 1960

Burns, K.V. *Devonport built Warships*, Maritime Books, 1981

Campbell, Ian, *The Kola Run*, London, 1958

Clarke, David, *Location-Cornwall,* Bossiney, 1990

Cohn, Art, editor, *Michael Todd's 'Around the World in Eighty Days',* New York, 1956

Davies, W. H., *The Autobiography of a Super-Tramp,* New York, 1917

Dors, Diana, *Dors by Diana,* London, 1981

Dunn, Kate, editor, *Always and Always; Wartime letters of Hugh and Margaret Williams*, London, 1995

Fishgall, Gary, *Against Type, The Biography of Burt Lancaster,* New York, 1995

Flemming, Kate, *Celia Johnson,* London, 1991

Fontaine, Joan, *No Bed of Roses*, New York, 1978

Friedrich, Otto, *City of Nets*, London, 1986

Gardiner, Juliet, *Wartime Britain 1939-1945*, London, 2004

Guinness, Alec, *Blessings in Disguise*, London, 1985

Guthrie, Tyrone, *A Life in the Theatre*, London, 1959

Hall, Ivan, *Christmas In Archangel*, USA, 2009

Halliwell, Leslie, *Halliwell's Filmgoers Companion*, 6th edition, London, 1977

Harrison, Rex, *Rex, An Autobiography*, London, 1974

Higham, Charles, *Charles Laughton*, London, 1976

Hoskin, Jim, *Boskenna and the Paynters*, Penzance, 1999

John, Augustus, *Chiaroscuro, Fragments of Autobiography*, London, 1954

Kashner, S., Macnair, J., *The Bad and the Beautiful*, London, 2002

Kemp J. C. *The Birmingham Repertory Theatre*, London, 1948

Kemp, Paul, *Convoy!*, London, 1993

Knight, Laura, *Oil Paint and Grease Paint*, London, 1936

Kulik, Karol, *Alexander Korda, The Man who could Work Miracles*, London, 1975

Luke, Michael, *David Tennant and the Gargoyle Years*, London, 1981

Lund, P. and Ludlam, H., *Out Sweeps*, London, 1978

Macnab, Geoffrey, *Searching for Stars, Rethinking the British Cinema*, London, 2000

Mallalieu, J.P.W., *Very Ordinary Seaman*, London, 1944

Manvell, Roger, Editor, *The Penguin Film Review 3*, London, 1947

Manvell, Roger, Editor, *The Penguin Film Review 6*, London, 1948

Manvell, Roger, *Film*, London, 1944

Marshall, Michael, *Top Hats and Tails, The Story of Jack Buchanan*, London, 1978

McCallum, John, *Life with Googie*, London, 1979

Ministry of Information, *His Majesty's Minesweepers*, HMSO, 1943

Mitchell, Susie, *Recollections of Lamorna*, Headland, Penzance, 1977

Moorehead, Alan, *Gallipoli,* London, 1956

Morley, Robert, and Stokes, Sewell, *Robert Morley, "Responsible Gentleman"*, London, 1966

Morley, Sheridan, *Tales from the Hollywood Raj,* New York, 1983

Morley, Sheridan, *David Niven, The Other Side of the Moon,* London, 1985

Neagle, Anna, *'There's Always Tomorrow'*, London, 1974

Niven, David, *The Moon's a Balloon, London*, 1971

Niven, David, *Bring on the Empty Horses,* London, 1975

Noble, Peter, *Ivor Novello,* London, 1951

Norman, Barry, *The Hollywood Greats,* London, 1979

O'Hara, M., Nicoletti, John, *'Tis Herself,* London, 2004

Parker, John, *Who's Who in the Theatre, 10th edition,* London, 1947

Perry George, *The Great British Picture Show*, London, 1974

Pinter, Harold, *Old Times*, London, 1971

Prysor, Glyn, *Citizen Sailors*, London, 2011

Quinlan, David, *Quinlan's Film Star*s, London, 1981

Ryall, Tom, *Alfred Hitchcock and the British Cinema*, London, 1986

Schessler, Ken, *This is Hollywood,* USA, 1978

Schickel, Richard, *Walt Disney*, London, 1968

Server, Lee, *Robert Mitchum, Baby I don't Care,* New York, 2001

Shepherd, Donald, with Slater, R,. and Grayson, D,. *Duke. The life and Times of John Wayne*, London, 1986

Smith, P. C., *Convoy PQ18, Arctic Victory*, London, 1975

Sweet, Matthew, *The West End Front*, London, 2011

Thorn, R. S., *Star Doctor*, London, 1984

Tynan, Kathleen, *The Life of Kenneth Tynan*, London, 1988

Waley, H. D., Spencer, D, A., *The Cinema Today*, London, 1949

Wilcox, Herbert, *Twenty-five Thousand Sunsets*, London, 1967

Winn, Godfrey, *'PQ 17, A Story of a Ship*, London, 1947

Index

Printed in Great Britain
by Amazon

60664841R10231